D0075472

DAILY LIFE OF

NATIVE AMERICANS FROM POST-COLUMBIAN THROUGH NINETEENTH-CENTURY AMERICA

The Greenwood Press "Daily Life Through History" Series

The Age of Charlemagne
John J. Butt

The Age of Sail
Dorothy Denneen Volo and James M. Volo

The American Revolution
Dorothy Denneen Volo and James M. Volo

The Ancient Egyptians
Bob Brier and Hoyt Hobbs

The Ancient Greeks
Robert Garland

Ancient Mesopotamia
Karen Rhea Nemet-Nejat

The Ancient Romans
David Matz

The Aztecs: People of the Sun and Earth
Davíd Carrasco with Scott Sessions

The Byzantine Empire
Marcus Rautman

Chaucer's England
Jeffrey L. Singman and Will McLean

Civil War America
Dorothy Denneen Volo and James M. Volo

Colonial New England
Claudia Durst Johnson

Early Modern Japan
Louis G. Perez

The Early American Republic, 1790–1820: Creating a New Nation
David S. Heidler and Jeanne T. Heidler

18th-Century England
Kirstin Olsen

Elizabethan England
Jeffrey L. Singman

The Holocaust
Eve Nussbaum Soumerai and Carol D. Schulz

The Inca Empire
Michael A. Malpass

The Industrial United States, 1870–1900
Julie Husband and Jim O'Loughlin

Jews in the Middle Ages
Norman Roth

Maya Civilization
Robert J. Sharer

Medieval Europe
Jeffrey L. Singman

The Medieval Islamic World
James E. Lindsay

The Mongol Empire
George Lane

Native Americans in the Twentieth Century
Donald Fixico

Nature and the Environment in Twentieth-Century American Life
Brain Black

The Nineteenth Century American Frontier
Mary Ellen Jones

The Nubians
Robert S. Bianchi

The Old Colonial Frontier
James M. Volo and Dorothy Denneen Volo

Renaissance Italy
Elizabeth S. Cohen and Thomas V. Cohen

The Roman City: Rome, Pompeii, and Ostia
Gregory S. Aldrete

Science and Technology in Colonial America
William E. Burns

Science and Technology in the Nineteenth-Century America
Todd Timmons

The Soviet Union
Katherine B. Eaton

The Spanish Inquisition
James M. Anderson

Traditional China: The Tang Dynasty
Charles Benn

The United States, 1920–1939: Decades of Promise and Pain
David E. Kyvig

The United States, 1940–1959: Shifting Worlds
Eugenia Kaledin

The United States, 1960–1990: Decades of Discord
Myron A. Marty

Victorian England
Sally Mitchell

The Vikings
Kirsten Wolf

World War I
Neil M. Heyman

DAILY LIFE OF

NATIVE AMERICANS FROM POST-COLUMBIAN THROUGH NINETEENTH-CENTURY AMERICA

ALICE NASH AND CHRISTOPH STROBEL

The Greenwood Press "Daily Life Through History" Series

GREENWOOD PRESS
Westport, Connecticut • London

Library of Congress Cataloging-in-Publication Data

Nash, Alice.
   Daily life of Native Americans from post-Columbian
through nineteenth-century America / Alice Nash and Christoph Strobel.
      p.   cm.—(The Greenwood Press "Daily life through history" series)
   Includes bibliographical references and index.
   ISBN 0–313–33515–X
   1. Indians of North America—History—Juvenile literature. 2. Indians of North
America—Social life and customs—Juvenile literature. I. Strobel, Christoph.
   II. Title. III. Series.
E77.4.N36 2006
973.04′97—dc22   2006007009

British Library Cataloguing in Publication Data is available.

Library of Congress Catalog Card Number: 2006007009
ISBN: 0–313–33515–X
ISSN: 1080–4749

First published in 2006

Greenwood Press, 88 Post Road West, Westport, CT 06881
An imprint of Greenwood Publishing Group, Inc.
www.greenwood.com

Printed in the United States of America

The paper used in this book complies with the
Permanent Paper Standard issued by the National
Information Standards Organization (Z39.48–1984).

10   9   8   7   6   5   4   3   2   1

CONTENTS

Introduction   vii

Chronology   xxv

THE EASTERN WOODLANDS

1.	Daily Life among the Algonkians	3
2.	Daily Life in the Iroquois Confederacy	31
3.	Daily Life in the Colonial Northeast	55
4.	Daily Life in the Ohio Valley and the Great Lakes	81
5.	Daily Life in the Southeast	105

THE TRANS-MISSISSIPPI WEST

6.	Daily Life in the Southwest	139
7.	Daily Life in California and the Great Basin	169
8.	Daily Life in the Pacific Northwest	189
9.	Daily Life on the Great Plains	213

10.   The Survival of the "Disappearing Indian"   231

Bibliography   255

Index   263

INTRODUCTION

When Sarah Colwell, our editor, first asked us to write a one-volume reference work on daily life in Native North America, spanning the years from Columbus's first voyage in 1492 to the end of the nineteenth century, we thought, "It can't be done!" We imagined readers would pick up the book, looking for details about how to make arrowheads or build sweat lodges, and put it down in dismay when they found that it also included information about "Indians" using new technologies such as guns, copper pots, printing presses, stoves, and framed houses in their daily lives. Popular stereotypes have taught us that "real" Indians live only in the past. Then we thought, this is exactly why such a book is needed. We believe that readers are genuinely interested in learning about the daily life of Native Americans and will find it more rather than less interesting to think about how "daily life" changed over 400 years.

Most Americans can recognize a Plains Indian warrior in Hollywood movies when he rides a horse and wears a flowing war bonnet. It is harder to recognize the warrior in a child such as nine-year-old Luther Standing Bear (Brulé Sioux), sitting on a train, headed east toward a new type of battleground: the Carlisle Indian Industrial School in Carlisle, Pennsylvania. There, and in other schools like it in the late nineteenth century, Native American boys and girls as young as eight years old endured a program of forced assimilation that one educator described as "killing the Indian to save the man."[1] By the late nineteenth century, a man wearing "traditional" buckskin and a feather headdress was probably making a statement about his Indian identity or posing for a non-Native audience.

In real life, individuals and communities navigated a difficult and often painful series of choices between holding on to the core values, practices, and languages that made them a distinct people versus the demands of a dominant society that asked them to "kill" the Indian within so that they, too, might fulfill the American dream of a better life than what they had on the reservation.

All of this happened in a historical context that is as important as the details of daily life. After all, Native people did not simply wake up one day and decide to live on reservations. We argue that the common denominator of daily life for the many peoples of Native America during the four centuries after Columbus's historic voyage was change, despite the fact that people valued their Native lifeways and traditions and made heroic efforts to hold onto them. This often required a willingness to accept change in order to survive. Some traditions went underground, away from public view by non-Natives. Certain activities of daily life such as hunting, fishing, and basket-making gained a heightened significance as markers of Indian or tribal identity in a colonial world. Other practices expanded in response to new elements, as when people in the Northeast started to use glass beads to decorate clothing in patterns they had once made either with paint or with dyed porcupine quills, or when people living around the borders of the Great Plains incorporated an imported animal into their culture to such a degree that the horse is now thought of as a quintessential feature of Plains Indian life. By looking at daily life in Native America across four centuries of change, one can see a remarkable continuity of spirit, culture, and tribal identities. Not everything about precontact life was perfect. Not everything that happened postcontact was bad.

TALKING ABOUT NATIVE AMERICANS

In taking up the challenge of this book, we have had to make several key decisions. Given the variety and diversity of Native North America, and the enormous changes that took place over four centuries, we have been forced to simplify and focus on just a few groups in each of the main culture areas of the continental United States. When Columbus "discovered" the Americas in 1492, there were, by some estimates, over 500 nations spread across the area that became the United States of America. These nations spoke different languages and had very different cultures and histories. They lived in different ecological niches, which influenced their way of life. They encountered different groups of Europeans (English, Spanish, Dutch, French, Russian, and others) at different moments in world history. Some made treaties with European nations before the United States came into existence. Others held onto their independence until after the U.S. Civil War, when the U.S. reservation system ushered in a new configuration for daily life. In this book, we aim to strike a balance between clarity and precision in talking about indigenous peoples across time and space. There is no "right" way to organize such a discussion, so we have chosen the way that seems best suited for our purposes.

Languages

Language is a logical way to classify people because one can assume that people from the same language family literally have common ancestors. That is, their languages developed from a common language spoken generations before. The problem, for purposes of this book, is that people from the same language family may live in very different regions of North America (see Table 1). An extreme example would be the Yurok of northern California. Their language is classified as part of the Algic or Algonkian language family. Other Algonkian languages are spoken in a region that spans the U.S./Canadian border in the eastern parts of the continent. Along the Atlantic coast, Algonkian language families are found in a range from the northern parts of Quebec to as far south as the Carolinas. These languages are subclassified as Eastern Algonkian languages. Central Algonkian languages may be found in Ontario, around the Great Lakes, and as far west as Montana and Wyoming. The Yurok of northern California have a different way of life than their eastern relatives, but their language testifies to the connection.

A study of Native North America organized by language family would help students living in different parts of the United States today to think about indigenous peoples in a way that crosses state and regional borders. It would also highlight the diversity of peoples and cultures subsumed under the broad but problematic term, "Indian." In 1929, the linguist Edward Sapir wrote:

Few people realize that within the confines of the United States there is spoken today a far greater variety of languages . . . than in the whole of Europe. We may go further. We may say, quite literally and safely, that in the state of California alone there are greater and more numerous linguistic extremes than can be illustrated in all the length and breadth of Europe.[2]

Language is a critical aspect of indigenous culture and history, but the level of detail needed to address the topic completely is beyond the scope of this book. Readers who become interested in a particular culture, however, are urged to include questions about language in their research.[3]

The task of using language families as an organizing concept is complicated by the fact that languages are spoken by people, and people do not always stay in one place. This is especially true for indigenous peoples, whose histories include migration and diaspora both before and after 1492. After 1492, and especially after the establishment of the United States of America in 1776, indigenous peoples experienced change at

Table 1. Language Families and Culture Areas

Language Family/Branch	People	Culture Area	Location Today
Eskimo-Aleut	Inuit, Yupik	Arctic	Alaska
Athabascan (Na-Dené)			
	Navajo	Southwest	Arizona, New Mexico, Utah
	Apache	Southwest	Arizona, New Mexico, Oklahoma
	Tlingit	Northwest	Alaska
	Haida	Northwest	British Columbia
Algic			
Algonkian	Cree, Innu	Northeast	Eastern Canada
	Menominee	Ohio Valley/ Great Lakes	Wisconsin
	Shawnee	Ohio Valley/ Great Lakes	Oklahoma, Ohio
	Potwatomi/ Potawatomi	Ohio Valley/ Great Lakes	Michigan, Oklahoma
	Ojibwa	Ohio Valley/ Great Lakes	Ontario, Wisconsin, Michigan, North Dakota
	Delaware	Northeast, Ohio Valley	Atlantic coast, Oklahoma, Kansas, Ontario, Wisconsin

Language/Group		Region	Location
	Penobscot, Abenaki, Maliseet-Passamaquoddy, Wampanoag, Mohegan-Pequot, Nipmuc	Northeast	New England
	Mi'kmaq	Northeast	New Brunswick, Nova Scotia
	Blackfeet	Great Plains	Montana
	Cheyenne	Great Plains	Wyoming
	Yurok	California	Northwest California
Muskogean	Choctaw, Chickasaw	Southeast	Oklahoma, Mississippi
	Creek, Seminole	Southeast	Florida, Oklahoma
	Natchez	Southeast	Southern Appalachia, Oklahoma
Macro-Siouan			
Siouan	Crow	Great Plains	Montana
	Hidatsa	Great Plains	North Dakota
	Winnebago	Ohio Valley/Great Lakes	Wisconsin, Nebraska
	Omaha	Great Plains	NebraskaNorth Dakokta, South Dakota
	Lakota	Great Plains	South Dakota
	Catawba	Southeast	South Carolina

(continued)

Table 1. Language Families and Culture Areas (Continued)

Language Family/Branch	People	Culture Area	Location Today
Iroquoian	Mohawk, Seneca, Onondaga, Oneida, Cayuga	Northeast	New York, other parts of the U.S., and Ontario
	Huron-Wendat	Northeast	Ontario, Quebec
	Wyandot	Ohio Valley / Great Lakes	Oklahoma, Michigan, Kansas
	Tuscarora	Southeast	North Carolina, New York
	Cherokee	Southeast	Oklahoma, southern Appalachia
Caddoan	Caddo	Southeast/ Great Plains	Oklahoma
	Wichita	Great Plains	Oklahoma
	Pawnee	Great Plains	Oklahoma
Hokan			
Yuman	Mojave	Great Basin	Arizona
	Pomo	California	California
	Chumash	California	California
Penutian			
Maidu	Maidu	California	Northern California
Wintun	Wintu	California	Northern California

Language Family	Tribe	Region	State
Miwock	Miwok	California	California
Klamath-Modoc	Klamath, Modoc	California, Great Basin, Plateau	Oregon
Sahaptian	Nez Perce'	Plateau	Idaho
Zuni	Zuni	Southwest	New Mexico
Aztec-Tanoan Kiowa-Tanoan	Tewa	Southwest	New Mexico
	Kiowa	Great Plains	Oklahoma
Uto-Aztecan	Comanche	Great Plains	Oklahoma
	Hopi	Southwest	Arizona
	Pima, Papago	Southwest	Arizona
Salishan	Quinault	Pacific Northwest	Washington
	Coeur d'Alene	Plateau	Idaho
Wakashan	Makah	Pacific Northwest	Washington

Information compiled from William C. Sturtevant, Gen. Ed., *Handbook of North American Indians*. 20 vols. Washington, DC: Smithsonian Institution, 1978-.

an accelerated rate due to war, disease, and forced removals. A map of language families as they existed in 1500 would look quite different from the same map in 1600, 1700, 1800, or 1900. Precise definitions of language families, including which languages belong to which group, continue to change as linguists collect new data and deepen their understanding of indigenous languages and the histories of the people who speak or spoke them. The classification in Table 1 reflects the current consensus on language families.

Culture Areas

Another way to classify indigenous peoples is by culture area, that is, by ecological and geographic region. This is the concept that we have used in this book. The underlying assumption is that people who live in similar environments will share certain sociocultural characteristics that distinguish them from people who live in other regions. The resources available to them shaped their daily lives and material culture. These similarities are enhanced by the fact that people interact with their neighbors through trade, diplomacy, intermarriage, and war, and therefore are likely to share at least some cultural understandings. The Smithsonian *Handbook of North American Indians* defines the major culture areas in the United States as Subarctic, Pacific Northwest, California, Plateau, Plains, Northeast, and Southeast.[4] This is further illustrated in the Map of Culture Areas in North America.

To give just two examples, consider the Northeast and the Great Plains culture areas. The Northeast culture area is an ecosystem characterized by great forests of birch, pine, oak, and other hardwood trees. A dense network of rivers and streams provided a natural highway system, along which people traveled and traded. When we think of Northeastern material culture, we think of birch bark, deerskins, beaver, and canoes. In contrast, the Great Plains is an area where large herds of buffalo roamed the grassy landscape. Prior to about 1600, most people in this region lived along the major rivers. The famous "horse culture" associated with the Great Plains in Hollywood movies did not flourish until after the introduction of horses by the Spanish. The huge, flowing war bonnets that chiefs wore while riding across the plains would be impractical for warriors from the Northeast, who traveled mostly by canoe or on foot through the woods.

Culture areas are most useful when describing people who live in a contiguous geographic area within a defined period of time. The chapters in this book are organized by culture areas as they existed about 1600, but readers are urged to remember that people and tribal nations experienced tremendous change over time, including forced removal to other parts of the continent, without losing their identities. By 1900, relatively few Native peoples lived in the homelands occupied

TRIBAL LANDS AT TIME OF CONTACT

Map of culture areas in North America. Culture areas classify indigenous peoples by region, on the assumption that people who live in a common environment develop similar ways of life. But environment is not destiny. Each culture area contains people from different language families. From "Tribal Lands at Time of Contact," from *Encyclopedia of North American Indians,* edited by Frederick E. Hoxie. Copyright © 1996 by Houghton Mifflin Company. Reprinted by permission of Houghton Mifflin Company. All rights reserved.

by their ancestors, although some individuals and even families have survived in place, right up to this day. In some cases people chose to move for personal reasons. In others, they were pushed out by war, catastrophic illness, or U.S. government policy. Native peoples have lived in North America for at least 11,000 years; thus, they have a long history of social development and historical change. After 1492, the rate of change quickened, and the extent of those changes was dramatic and profound.

Names and Political Correctness

There is no easy answer to the problem of terminology when writing about indigenous peoples. "Indian," of course, is a name given in error by Columbus, who thought he had discovered India. What is striking is that the name has retained its power over five centuries. Today, there are good arguments for and against the continuing use of the term. For all their differences, indigenous peoples are united by the fact that they were sovereign nations before the creation of the United States. They are united by a common experience of colonization, and by the fact that the settler society views them as "Indians." Recognizing these commonalities gives indigenous peoples a base from which to organize for political and economic change. Any serious attempt to eradicate the word would wreak havoc on the complex body of legislation and treaty law created to regulate "Indian Affairs" between the U.S. federal government and Indian nations. Regionally, some communities are comfortable with the word *Indian*, especially in the Northeast, while others are not. Note that one of the most activist groups, the American Indian Movement, incorporates the word into their organizational name.

"Native American" is not a better solution. In fact, it only masks the problem. It may seem like a nicer term, but the fundamental problems remain unchanged. It does little good to make schoolchildren say "Native American" if they are still learning about "Indians" in ways that perpetuate deep-rooted stereotypes.

Indigenous peoples are not a homogeneous group and never were. Technically, anyone born in this country is a native. The word "America" is not indigenous; it comes from the name of an Italian explorer, Amerigo Vespucci. However, terms derived from indigenous languages, or terms that reflect indigenous worldviews, are also problematic. For example, one might say "Turtle Islander" or "the people of Turtle Island" instead of "Native American." This reflects *an* indigenous perspective, because the Iroquois believe that they live in a world created on the back of a turtle, but it would not be appropriate for all indigenous groups, because each group has its own belief about its origins and the origin of this continent. No single word can do the trick. In this book we use "Native American" interchangeably with other terms such as "indigenous," "Native," and "Amerindian." The latter is a compromise between imperfect choices. It has been used in the anthropological literature since about 1900 as "Amerind" or "Amerindian," and has become increasingly common since the 1970s as writers grapple with the problem of terminology. We use the word "Indian" when we want to highlight the ways in which indigenous people are viewed as a group by the dominant society. When possible, however, we use specific terms for tribal nations and communities.

Political Ties and Kinship

Names based on political ties and kinship offer the most precise, and most complex, way to speak about Native North Americans—precise, because this is how most people understand their own lives; complex, because definitions of political and kin ties are fluid and change over time. For example, the people who are commonly known as the Iroquois in U.S. history books call themselves the *Haudenosaunee* (Ho-dee-no-sho-nee), or the People of the Longhouse. The name "Iroquois" comes from an Algonkian word, "Irinakhoiw," which translates as "real adders" or snakes. It is a derisive term used by their enemies, popularized because the French picked up the term and enshrined it in their maps and documents. It was further popularized by the English, then the Americans. Today, Haudenosaunee people often refer to themselves collectively as Iroquois, although just as often they introduce themselves by nation and clan.

The Haudenosaunee are sometimes called "The Five Nations," because the original confederation of Iroquois nations that formed in the mid-fifteenth century included five peoples: the Mohawk, Cayuga, Onondaga, Oneida, and Seneca Nations. After the 1720s, it is proper to call them "The Six Nations," because they were joined by the Tuscarora from the south. The political distinctions become even more complex over time, as some Haudenosaunee held onto their original lands, others moved to safer locations, and everyone found themselves living on one side or the other of a new geopolitical border between the United States and Canada that cut across Haudenosaunee land. In this book we introduce the terms preferred by Native nations today but offer the more commonly known terms as well, to aid readers.

Most of the popular terms used to identify indigenous peoples today are names given to them by others, including, too often, their enemies. When European explorers first came to North America, they generally learned how to communicate with one group and then asked, "Who lives over there?" These names were recorded in documents and on maps and survive to this day. They are doubly offensive when the original name, in the enemy's language, is insulting. Most Native peoples have names for themselves that translate as "The People." It may seem confusing or too "politically correct" to learn a new set of names for indigenous peoples, but no one likes to be known by the name given to them by their enemies instead of their real name.

The best solution is to be specific, to call people by their own names whenever possible. Better still is to ask people what they want to be called, remembering that individual people will have different preferences. When a general term is needed, our solution is to use a variety of terms, acknowledging their limitations and not giving precedence to any of them. We use the terms Native American, Native, American Indian, and indigenous interchangeably.

STEREOTYPES AND MISINFORMATION

One of the biggest obstacles to learning about Native peoples is that most of what we know comes from inaccurate information. As Modoc scholar Michael Dorris notes, "For most people, the myth has become real and a preferred substitute for ethnographic reality." He reminds us that romantic images of "The Indian" were created for the benefit of European and later American audiences and adds, "It is little wonder, then, that many non-Indians literally would not know a real Native American if they fell over one, for they have been prepared for a well-defined, carefully honed legend."[5]

One common misperception, as noted above, is the idea that Plains Indian culture as depicted in Hollywood movies, with brave warriors on horses wearing buckskin and feathered bonnets, is the only standard for how "real" Indians look and act. This image is so strong that even today, some Native peoples from other groups wear war bonnets and other Plains regalia to make sure that they are recognized as Indians by the dominant society. Other common misperceptions include the idea that all Native peoples were nomadic, that all Native peoples were hunters, or that Native peoples disappeared and died out at some distant time in the past. These concepts will be examined as we talk about daily life for Native Americans over 400 years of history.

Some stereotypes have obvious negative connotations, and it is easy to see why they should be abandoned. Most non-Native people today understand that indigenous peoples were not simply "bloodthirsty savages" who lived to kill "the white man." Other stereotypes, however, are subtler. They seem harmless, even flattering, like the idea that Native American warriors were stoics who showed no emotion, or that all Native societies were matriarchies. Like many stereotypes about Native peoples, these myths have an element of truth. Face to face with an enemy, or in highly charged situations such as treaty negotiations, men exhibited great self-control so as not to give anything away. Among family and friends, however, there was much joking, laughter, and warmth.

The question of matriarchy is more complex, because people today use *matriarchy* to mean different things. It is true that the system of gender relations in indigenous societies was quite different from the system of patrilineal, patriarchal households brought over by European colonizers. Many (but not all) Native societies were and are *matrilineal.* That means that family ties are inherited through the mother's family, or lineage, rather than through the father's line, as in a patrilineal society. (Note that these words come from Latin root: *matri-* meaning mother, *patri-* meaning father, and *-lineal,* which refers to the family line.) But Native women did not have the same kind of power over men that men, in a patrilineal, patriarchal society, have over women. They did not need it, because power was organized in a different way. Among the Haudenosaunee, the classic example of a matrilineal clan-based society, no one could tell anyone else what to do, although there were ways for people to express their approval or disapproval. Haudenosaunee clan mothers had the power to

"The End of the Trail," by James Earle Fraser (1876–1953). This sculpture was created for the 1915 Panama-Pacific International Exposition in San Francisco, an event that celebrated U.S. expansion through the Panama Canal and beyond. Fraser depicted this imaginary Indian warrior as the last of a dying race. From James Fraser, "End of the Trail" (1915), plaster, 18' high, Fraser Studio Coll., 0191: Box 2, Folder 17, National Cowboy and Western Heritage Museum, Oklahoma City, OK.

choose the chiefs, and to remove them from office if they failed to do a good job, but they did not, themselves, become chiefs.

One way in which this stereotype is harmful is that it allows non-Native people to project their own needs and interests onto Native people, often under the guise of "helping" them. For examples, some feminist scholars and activists make assumptions about matriarchal societies and project their own issues onto Native women, who have been noticeably absent from the mainstream feminist movement of the twentieth century. Romanticized visions of Native American matriarchies are put forward to inspire non-Native women to become more empowered, yet when real Native women speak up and raise their objections or concerns, they are ignored and sometimes defined as troublesome. This comes from anecdotal evidence as well as direct observation. Another problem is that fantasies about a matriarchal past mask the reality of gender inequality in the present. Native peoples adapted patriarchal and patrilineal ways as they struggled to survive in a colonial world. One of the major areas of daily life affected by colonization lies in the realm of family and gender relations.

Another harmful stereotype is the image of Native Americans as a dying or vanishing race. The "vanishing Indian" first appears in the late seventeenth century after King Philip's War broke out in southern New England in 1675. In the aftermath of the war, New England writers began to speak of indigenous peoples in the past tense, as vanquished, "gone to Canada," or as remnants of a proud people. The stereotype took on new power in the late nineteenth century as the United States extended its control across the continent. In New England, local histories and newspapers included stories describing people such as Molly Ockett of Bethel, Maine, as "The Last of Their Race," even when it was known that they had family nearby.[6] Popular images such as James Earle Fraser's statue, "The End of the Trail," brought the "the vanishing Indian" into the twentieth century. First created as an 18-inch high plaster cast for the 1915 Panama-Pacific International Exposition in San Francisco, and awarded the Gold Medal for sculpture at the exposition, the statue depicts a weary and defeated Plains Indian warrior riding an equally weary horse. Images such as this reassured Americans that they could take up their Manifest Destiny in the continental United States without guilt because indigenous peoples would soon disappear.

In contrast, the photograph titled "Geronimo behind the Wheel" (1904), challenges and disrupts this idea. Geronimo (c. 1829–1909), also known as Goyathlay, was the Apache father, husband, visionary leader, and warrior who led the Apache resistance to U.S. and Mexican domination in the late nineteenth century.[7] He lives on in American popular culture as a heroic figure but with little or no attention paid to the context in which he earned his reputation. Indeed, as Jimmie Durham has pointed out, Goyathlay's popular name is most often invoked today when children and soldiers shout "Geronimo!" as they launch themselves into a swimming pool or

"Geronimo behind the Wheel" (1904). Far from being a defeated warrior at the end of his trail, Geronimo stares into the future, dressed in his best and confident behind the wheel. This photograph was taken by Walter Ferguson in 1904 when Geronimo was a prisoner of war at Fort Sill, Oklahoma. From National Archives and Records Administration (75-IC-1).

into battle. This photo shows Goyathlay a few years before his death, when he was a prisoner of war at Fort Sill, in Oklahoma. The photograph was taken at a ranch near Ponca City, Oklahoma, where Goyathlay was granted special permission to attend a meeting of the National Editorial Association. During these years, Goyathlay exploited the American public's desire to see him as a safe, romantic figure by charging money for photographs. There were no opportunities for independent subsistence at Fort Sill, and Native Americans needed cash to take care of themselves and their families just like everyone else.

Even in photographs, but especially in this one, Goyathlay asserts the reality of his personhood. Durham says, "In every image, he looks through the camera at the viewer, seriously, intently, with a specific message. Geronimo uses the photograph to 'get at' those people who imagine themselves as the 'audience' of his struggles. He seems to be trying to see us. He is demanding to be seen, on his own terms." The car, the top hat, and the three-piece suit, like the weapons he was photographed with during his early years, are part of his campaign. He is not defeated. Instead, he faces the future, clean and well-dressed, behind the wheel of a new-fangled contraption that symbolized the heights of modernity at the time.[8]

COMMONALITIES

For all the differences among Native groups, there are certain experiences that run through their histories. Indigenous societies shared, and still share, the experience of colonization. Yet, despite centuries of oppression, the disruption and displacement of Native nations, and the assault on Native religion and culture, indigenous peoples have not been defeated by these processes. Native Americans, American Indians, still live on this continent, and view themselves as members of their indigenous communities. They still live their lives imbued with the practices, values, and beliefs that connect them to their forebears.

Here are some principles to keep in mind as you read this book.

Native societies were not homogeneous. That means that even within a particular group, people had different opinions and concerns. Like all human societies, some people won the admiration and respect of the community, while others were considered troublemakers. These differences become even more important in the period after 1492 when Native peoples disagreed on how to respond to the European invaders.

Native societies and cultures were not static. One persistent stereotype about Native peoples is that they belong to timeless, unchanging cultures. Like all human societies, Native cultures were adaptable and resilient. They were very different in 1600 from what they were like in 1400 or 1800. People incorporated new inventions and materials. They moved to new environments and learned new ways, as when horses made it possible for people to move out onto the Great Plains.

The rate of change increased dramatically after 1492. The structure of this book attempts to keep change front and center as we talk about daily life for the diverse peoples of "Native America." In some cases the changes reflect choice, as when the Cherokees decided that their best chance of survival lay in learning to live in wooden houses and to send their children to schools run by missionaries. In some cases the changes are the result of outside pressures, as when the U.S. government forcefully removed the Cherokees and others from their homes in the Southeast and sent them out west to Oklahoma on a death march known as the "Trail of Tears." There, families had to adapt to live in a completely different environment, far removed from the familiar places described in their sacred stories about creation, living among unfamiliar Native peoples.

We start by devoting three chapters to the peoples of the Northeast Woodlands culture area. Chapters 1 and 2 give a detailed discussion of the culture, worldview, and social/political organization of the Algonkian and Iroquoian peoples, respectively, in the early contact period, that is, the long period of time that preceded the founding of Plymouth Colony by the English in 1620. Chapter 3 lays out the enormous changes that reshaped their lives in the following decades of epidemic disease, massive immigration from Europe (which historian Francis Jennings characterizes as an invasion), and missionary efforts to convert Native peoples to Christianity. Scholarly work on the Northeast has exploded since the 1980s, especially our understanding of how Native peoples survived after King Philip's War and through the "dark ages" of the nineteenth century, but little of this work has been integrated into mainstream reference texts.[9] This expanded focus on the Northeast is not meant to suggest that this region and its people are or were more important than the people of other culture areas. Rather, it introduces readers to the new consensus among scholars of Amerindian history. Although Chapters 4 through 9 give less detail on the specific changes that took place in other regions, the types of changes that took place in the Northeast have equivalents across North America. The bibliography points the way for readers interested in pursuing further research.

NOTES

1. "Kill the Indian to save the man" was the guiding philosophy of Richard Pratt, founder of Carlisle Indian Industrial School in Carlisle, Pennsylvania. For a first-person account of this experience see Luther Standing Bear, *My People the Sioux* (Boston: Houghton Mifflin, 1928).

2. Quoted in Frederick E. Hoxie, ed., *Encyclopedia of North American Indians: Native American History, Culture, and Life from Paleo-Indians to the Present* (New York: Houghton Mifflin Company, 1996), pp. 329–30.

3. See, for example, Lyle Campbell and Marianne Mithun, eds., *The Languages of Native America* (Austin: University of Texas Press, 1979).

4. William C. Sturtevant, general ed., *Handbook of North American Indians*, 20 vols. Washington, DC: Smithsonian Institution (1978).

5. Michael Dorris, "Indians on the Shelf," in *American Indians and the Problem of History*, ed. Calvin Martin (New York: Oxford University Press, 1987), 99.

6. Bunny McBride and Harald Prins, "Walking the Medicine Line: Molly Ockett, a Pigwacket Doctor," in *Northeastern Indian Lives, 1632–1816*, ed. Robert S. Grumet (Amherst: University of Massachusetts Press, 1996), 321–47.

7. James Riding In, "Geronimo (Goyathlay)," in Hoxie, 220–23.

8. Jimmie Durham, "Geronimo!" in *Partial Recall: With Essays on Photographs of Native North Americans*, ed. Lucy R. Lippard (New York: The New Press, 1992), 54–58; quotation from page 56.

9. Colin G. Calloway, ed., *After King Philip's War: Presence and Persistence in Indian New England* (Hanover, NH: University Press of New England, 1997).

CHRONOLOGY

c. 3500–1500 B.C.	Early agriculture in the Southwest.
c. 3000 B.C.	Construction of mound complex at Watson Brake, Louisiana.
c. 800–100 B.C.	Adena Culture.
c. 100 B.C.–300 A.D.	Hopewellian mound and earthwork construction flourishes in the Ohio Valley.
c. 100–1400	Hohokam culture thrives in the Southwest.
c. 700–1550	Mississippian chiefdoms dominate the Southeast.
c. 900–1300	Anasazi culture at its peak in the Southwest. Construction of Anasazi centers at Chaco Canyon and Mesa Verde.
c. 1200	Cahokia, a Mound Builder city close to the Mississippi River across the river from present day St. Louis, Missouri, is at the peak of its power.
c. 1300	Drought and attacks by competitors lead to an abandonment of Anasazi towns.
c.1400–1550	Mohawk, Oneida, Onondaga, Cayuga, and Seneca peoples unite to form the Iroquois League, also known as the Five Nations, sometime in the sixteenth century.

1492	Christopher Columbus sails west in search of a new route to Asia and finds a "New World."
1492–present	Numerous waves of epidemics introduced by non-Natives—for example small pox, measles, typhus, cholera, mumps, whooping cough, chicken pox, and yellow fever—lead to the death of millions of Indian men, women, and children all over the Western Hemisphere.
1497	Venetian navigator John Cabot and his son Sebastian, commissioned by Henry VII to discover a new trade route to Asia, reach the east coast of North America.
1503	Native groups at Newfoundland establish trade relations with European whalers and fishermen.
1507	Proposal that the "New World" be called "America" after the Florentine explorer Amerigo Vespucci, who made voyages to South America for Spain (1499–1500) and for Portugal (1501–1502).
1513	Juan Ponce de León claims Florida for Spain.
1518–1521	Hernán Cortés captures the city of Tenochtitlán, ruled by Montezuma, and conquers the Aztec Empire in Mexico.
1519–1522	Spanish fleet commanded by Portuguese navigator Ferdinand Magellan completes the first circumnavigation of the globe.
1521	Juan Ponce de León tries unsuccessfully to colonize Florida.
1523–1524	Giovanni da Verrazzano, Florentine navigator in the service of Francis I, explores the coast of North America from Cape Fear to Cape Breton.
1531–1550	New Spain expands to the north from Mexico, extending its conquests up the Pacific Coast.
1533	Spanish conquer Inca empire in Peru.
1534	Jacques Cartier explores the Gulf of Saint Lawrence on his first voyage to North America. 　　Ignatius Loyola founds the Society of Jesus, known as the Jesuit order.
1535–1536	Cartier sails up the Saint Lawrence River to Montreal and winters at Quebec.

1539–1543	Hernando de Soto and his army stage an invasion in southeastern North America that reaches from Florida to the Mississippi River. In their search for gold, the Spanish face consolidated resistance from several mound-building chiefdoms.
1540–1542	Francisco Vásquez de Coronado intrudes into the Southwest in search of gold; he meets Zuni people of New Mexico and reaches the Grand Canyon. His party includes Esteban, a Moorish or African man. Again Spanish efforts at empire-building face native resistance from the local Pueblo peoples.
1541–1542	Cartier and Jean-François de la Rocque de Roberval try to establish a settlement at Quebec.
1542–1543	First European exploration of California coast north of Baja by Juan Rodriguez Cabrillo's expedition.
1564	France establishes Fort Caroline on the Saint John's River in Florida.
1565–1574	Spain establishes presidios and posts in an effort to colonize the area north of the Florida peninsula.
1565	Pedro Menéndez de Avilés founds Saint Augustine in Florida.
1566	First Jesuit missionaries arrive in Florida.
1572	Powhatan, a Pamunkey leader, unites two dozen Algonkian-speaking tribes in the Chesapeake region to form the Powhatan Confederacy.
1579	Francis Drake drops anchor off the California coast and becomes the first European to encounter the native people of California.
1584–1586	Sir Walter Raleigh establishes a colony on Roanoke Island, off the coast of present-day North Carolina; abandoned 11 months later.
1587	Recolonization of Roanoke Island; it disappeared by 1590.
1598–1599	Acoma Pueblos defy Spanish authority in New Mexico. Spanish take Acoma and establish a colony in New Mexico.
1602	Bartholomew Gosnold explores the Atlantic Coast from southern Maine to Narragansett Bay; small pox breaks out among his Indian trading partners.

1603	Samuel de Champlain founds a French settlement in Acadia.
1607	Massasoit becomes chief of the Wampanoag. Founding of the Jamestown colony in Virginia, led by Captain John Smith; first permanent English settlement on the American mainland.
1608	Samuel de Champlain establishes a settlement at Quebec on the site of Stadacona, a recently deserted Iroquois village.
1609–1613	Champlain explores fur-trade routes, traveling the Canadian interior as far as Georgian Bay with Algonquins and Hurons as guides.
1609	Henry Hudson explores the Hudson River as far north as present-day Albany. Champlain accompanies a Huron-Algonquin war party against the Mohawks.
1610	Spanish establish the town of Santa Fe, New Mexico.
1614	Pocahontas, daughter of the Indian chief Powhatan, marries the English colonist John Rolfe at Jamestown. Dutch establish trading post near modern Albany, New York.
1620	Puritan Separatists (the Pilgrims) establish a colony at Plymouth on land that had been cleared by earlier Wampanoag inhabitants and abandoned after a small pox epidemic that swept the northeast from 1616–1619.
1621	The Pokanoket Indians of eastern Massachusetts sign a treaty that establishes an alliance with the Puritan colony.
1622	Opechancanough, Powhatan's brother and successor, leads the Powhatan Confederacy against the English in Virginia.
1625	Jesuits arrive in Quebec.
1630–1642	The "Great Migration"; about 20,000 Puritan settlers from England arrive in the Massachusetts Bay Colony.
1632–1674	The *Jesuit Relations* give annual reports of missionary efforts in New France.

1635	English colonists start to settle lands along the Connecticut River.
1636–1637	The Pequot War. Conflict with English colonists in Connecticut leads to the virtual destruction of local Pequot inhabitants.
1642–1643	Kieft's War. The Dutch wage war against the Indians of the lower Hudson Valley.
1643	Roger Williams's book on southern New England Indian languages, *A Key into the Language of America,* is published in London.
1644	Renewed war by the Powhatan Confederacy against the English.
1646–1665	The Iroquois launch devastating raids against neighboring tribes such as the Algonquins, Hurons, Nipissings, and Neutrals; refugees from these groups move east to Quebec or inland to the Great Lakes region.
1646–1675	Missionary John Eliot active among New England Indians.
1654	A canoe flotilla of Ottawa and Wyandot Indians, settling at Green Bay on Lake Michigan, arrive in Montreal to sell their furs.
1655	The Peach War. Some Manhattan women are killed while picking peaches in Governor Peter Stuyvesant's yard; Indians retaliate by attacking New Amsterdam.
1658–1664	Hostilities with Esopus Indians end with the cession of the Esopus Valley to the Dutch.
1661	Massasoit, chief of the Wampanoag and an ally of the Puritans, dies.
1663	John Eliot's translation of the Bible in the Massachusett language is published in Cambridge, Massachusetts.
1665	Caleb Cheeshateaumuck is first North American Indian to earn a degree at Harvard.
1666	French soldiers invade Iroquoia.
1667	The Five Iroquois Nations accept French terms for peace.

1673	Trader and explorer Louis Jolliet, accompanied by Jesuit missionary Jacques Marquette, follows the Mississippi River to the mouth of the Arkansas River.
1675–1676	King Philip's War. Indians of southern New England led by Metacomet (King Philip), a Pokanoket Indian, unite to drive out the English. Surviving Indians are killed or enslaved.
1675	Four Pueblo Indians in New Mexico are hanged, and others are whipped and enslaved for practicing sorcery and killing seven Franciscans.
1676	Mohawk converts to Catholicism move north to Caughnawaga in Canada. Bacon's Rebellion. Unhappy with Virginia Governor William Berkeley's restraint, frontiersmen led by Nathaniel Bacon attack a group of Susquahannocks and then march against Jamestown.
1677	The Covenant Chain, a system of alliances between the English colonies and the Five Nations Iroquois, is established at Albany.
c. 1680–1750s	Native peoples of the Great Plains acquire horses.
1680	Death of Kateri Tekakwitha, "The Lily of the Mohawks," a Catholic convert and the first Native American to be proposed for sainthood. (She was beatified in 1980.) The Spanish are driven from New Mexico by an uprising of the Pueblo Indians.
1682	René-Robert Cavelier de La Salle descends the Mississippi River to the Gulf of Mexico and claims the entire river valley for Louis XIV; he names the territory Louisiana. Franco-Iroquois wars; Anglo-American attack on Quebec.
1684	Anglo-French conflict in Hudson Bay; Franco-Iroquois hostilities recommence.
1689–1697	War of the League of Augsburg, known as King William's War in the colonies, brings French and English colonies with their respective Indian allies into conflict.
1692–1698	Spain reconquers New Mexico.

1701	Franco-Iroquois peace treaty; the Five Nations agree to remain neutral in future Anglo-French conflicts. The Society for the Propagation of the Gospel in Foreign Parts is established by the Anglicans to convert Indians and Africans.
1702–1713	The War of Spanish Succession (known as Queen Anne's War in the colonies) again brings conflict to French and English colonists and their respective Indian allies.
1703–1704	British and Indian allies attack and destroy several Spanish missions in Florida.
1711	Tuscarora War. Colonists in North and South Carolina join with the Yamasees to defeat the Tuscaroras. Tuscarora survivors migrate north and join the Iroquois nations. Moor's Charity School founded in Lebanon, Connecticut by the Reverend Eleazar Wheelock to educate Indian children; moved to Hanover, New Hampshire and renamed Dartmouth College in 1770.
1715–1728	Yamassee War. In response to abuses by the English, Yamassees attack South Carolina and are defeated by a coalition of English and Cherokee forces.
1720–1735	French–Fox Indian wars in the western Great Lakes region.
1722–1727	Dummer's War. Abenakis try to push back the line of English settlement in northern New England.
1722	After repeated attacks the Tuscaroras leave the Carolinas under the protection of the Iroquois Confederacy. They become the sixth nation of the heretofore "Five Nations."
1729	Destruction of the remaining Natchez towns and villages by the French, thereby destroying the probably last operative Missippian chiefdom and mound-building civilization.
1733	James Oglethorpe founds Georgia as refuge for English debtors.
1737	"Walking Purchase." Delaware Indians agree to sell Pennsylvania as much land as a man can walk in a day and half, which turns out to be 64 miles—the entire Lehigh Valley.

1738	Major smallpox epidemic hits Cherokee. An estimated 50 percent of the population is believed to have died.
1741	Russians begin trade with indigenous peoples on the Alaskan coast.
1744–1748	King George's War.
1754	Start of the Seven Year's War, also known as the French and Indian War. Virginia sends militia under Colonel George Washington to challenge French expansion in the Ohio Valley; Washington surrenders after being trapped by the French.
	The Blackfeet Indians of the northwestern Great Plains establish trade relations with the Hudson Bay Company.
1759–1761	Conflict between British colonists and Cherokees.
1759	Samson Occum, a Mohegan man educated in New England, becomes a fully ordained Presbyterian minister.
	British forces capture Quebec.
1760	French forces capitulate at Montreal, surrendering Canada and its dependencies.
1763	As European nations end the Seven Years' War with the Treaty of Paris, colonists and Native Americans challenge European authority.
	Britain issues the Royal Proclamation of 1763, forbidding colonists to settle west of the Appalachian Mountains.
	The Paxton Boys, asserting their claim to the Pennsylvania frontier, massacre 22 Susquehannocks and chase the survivors when they flee to Philadelphia for protection.
	Ottawa chief Pontiac, orator and war leader, leads an alliance of Indians in the Ohio Valley inspired by spiritual leaders such as Neolin, the Delaware Prophet, in an effort to drive out the white man.
	Treaty of Paris. Spain cedes Florida to Great Britain; France cedes Louisiana to Spain and cedes Acadia, Canada and Cape Breton to Great Britain.
1768	Treaty of Fort Stanwix: The Iroquois cede lands south of the Ohio River to the British—land also claimed by the Cherokee and the Shawnee.

1769	Spanish Franciscans open first mission at San Diego, California. This is the first of several missions founded in the region.
1774	Lord Dunmore's War forces Shawnee Indian into a peace that facilitates the British settlement of Kentucky.
1775–1783	American Revolution.
1776–1778	British establish trade relations with the Indians of the Northwest Coast.
1776	American Declaration of Independence.
1777	Bowing to military force, the Cherokee Indians cede lands to North and South Carolina.
1778	First United States–Native American treaty signed by the Delaware Indians and American officials.
1779–1783	Outbreak of smallpox epidemic in North America.
1779	American troops under General John Sullivan's leadership bring destruction to Iroquoia.
1782	Gnadenhutten Massacre.
1783	Treaty of Versailles. Great Britain recognizes independence of United States of America.
1787	Northwest Ordinance, a document that becomes the basis for colonizing Native lands north of the Ohio River, the region today known as the Midwest, promises to treat Indians with "the utmost good faith."
1790	Indian Trade and Intercourse Act. Ohio and Great Lakes Indians defeat General Josiah Harmar and his troops.
1791–1793	Native Americans on the Northwest Pacific coast trade with George Vancouver.
1791	Ohio and Great Lakes Indians defeat General Arthur St. Clair and his troops.
1794	Ohio and Great Lakes Native peoples defeated by American forces under the leadership of General Anthony Wayne at a place called Fallen Timbers.
1795	Treaty of Greenville; Ohio Indians suffer major land losses and the Midwest is opened up to American settlement.

1799	The Seneca prophet Handsome Lake begins to teach his Longhouse Religion. The Russian-American Company is chartered and given a monopoly to conduct trade in Alaska.
1802	Tlingits capture and destroy the Russian town of New Archangel (Sitka) on Baranof Island.
1803	Louisiana Purchase; France sells Louisiana to the United States.
1804–1806	Lewis and Clark explore the American West for the United States government.
1804	Tenskwatawa, the Shawnee prophet, receives his vision from the Master of Life. Along with his half brother Tecumseh, he becomes an advocate against alcoholism, condemns the loss of native lands and trade, and leads a pan-Indian resistance movement.
1805	Tlingit Indians destroy the Russian settlement at Yakutat.
1812–1815	War of 1812.
1812–1841	The Russian-American Company maintains a base at Fort Ross, in northern California.
1813–1814	Red Stick War. Muskogee independence fighters, led by prophets, attempt to resist American expansion. They are defeated by the U.S. military and Cherokee and other Muskogee Indians at the Battle of Horseshoe Bend in Alabama on March 27, 1814.
1817–1818	First Seminole War.
1817	New England missionaries establish a school for Cherokee youth.
1818	California authorities report that 64,000 Native Americans have been baptized by missionaries, though 41,000 of them have died.
1820s–1840s	Numerous Eastern Woodland Indian nations, including the Ottawas, Miamies, Shawnees, Seminoles, Muskogee, Choctaw, and Cherokees, are removed from their homelands and moved to Oklahoma, Kansas, and Iowa.
1821	Sequoyah completes Cherokee alphabet.

1823	The last California mission is established at Sonoma.
1824	Chumash Indians revolt against the Spanish in California.
1827	Cherokee Constitution.
1830	Indian Removal Act.
1832	Black Hawk War.
1835–1842	Second Seminole War.
1836	Muskogee Removal.
1837	Smallpox epidemic hits the northern plains.
1838	Trail of Tears.
1846	The United States annexes California.
1848–1849	California Gold Rush—massive decline in native population.
1848	The Treaty of Guadelupe Hidalgo cedes Alta California, Arizona, and New Mexico to the United States.
1851	Treaty of Fort Laramie: United States government attempts to establish tribal borders among the Native American populations of the Great Plains. Cherokee Female Seminary opens.
1855	Yakima Indians of the Pacific Northwest resist white colonization.
1860s–1930s	The United States government declares many native spiritual and cultural practices illegal. This period also witnesses the creation of Indian boarding schools. Native children are taken from their parents and sent to these institutions.
1861–1865	The Civil War.
1862	"Great Sioux Uprising:" The Dakota Indians resist white settlement expansion in Minnesota. Congress passes Homestead and Transcontinental Railroad Act. Both pieces of legislation spur American settlement of the West.
1864	Sand Creek Massacre. "Long Walk" of the Navajo: Navajos sent into exile from their homelands.

1866–1867	Red Cloud's War: The Lakotas and their allies are successful in forcing the United States government to close down a line of military forts reaching from Fort Laramie in Wyoming through parts of Montana.
1867	Treaty of Medicine Lodge. The United States acquires Alaska from Russia.

1868	The Seventh Cavalry defeats the Cheyenne in Oklahoma at the Battle of Washita.
	    Creation of Navajo reservation.
	    Second Treaty of Fort Laramie.

1869	Creation of Board of Indian Commissioners.
	    The Seneca Ely Parker is the first Native American to head the Bureau of Indian Affairs.
	    Completion of transcontinental railroad.

1871	The United States government abolishes the treaty system after having ratified over 367 treaties in previous decades.
1872–1873	Modoc War in California and Oregon.
1874–1875	War on the southern plains. Several of the Native war leaders are arrested and sent to prison at Fort Marion, Florida.
1876	Lakota and Cheyenne Indians defeat General Custer and the Seventh Cavalry at a place called Greasy Grass at the Battle of Little Big Horn. Part of "The Great Sioux War" of 1876–1877.
1877	Nez Percé War.
1879	Establishment of Carlisle Indian School.
1880s	The Great Plains buffalo and wild horse populations are on the brink of extinction.
1881	Surrender of Sitting Bull.
1883	*Ex Parte Crow Dog.*
1885	Major Crimes Act.
1886	End of Jicarilla Apache resistance led by Geronimo.
1887	General Land Allotment Act becomes federal law. Two-thirds of native-owned land is lost to white settlement.

1889	Wovoka, a Paiute Indian, receives a vision that inspires the Ghost Dance religion, which spreads rapidly among several native communities all over the Great Plains.
1890	Significant parts of Indian Territory are turned into Oklahoma Territory. Assassination of Sitting Bull. Wounded Knee massacre in South Dakota. The United States's Native American population reaches its lowest point at below 250,000.
1897	More than 6,000 Native Americans assemble at the Rosebud reservations for a six-day-long Fourth of July celebration. This patriotic cover enables the Lakota and their guests to celebrate several traditional ceremonies and rituals.
1898	Curtis Act. United States annexes Hawaii.

THE EASTERN
WOODLANDS

1

DAILY LIFE AMONG THE ALGONKIANS

When the English colonists known as the Pilgrims made landfall in 1620, they stepped off the *Mayflower* and into a world that was new, both for the English and for the Algonkian peoples who already lived there. This was not the first moment of contact between Europeans and indigenous people in the northeastern parts of North America. In fact, there had been steady if intermittent contact with Europeans for over a hundred years, since at least the late sixteenth century. Hundreds of European vessels had made the long Atlantic crossing on a regular basis since at least 1500. Explorers came in search of fame and fortune, hoping to find the fabled "Northwest Passage" to India. Fishermen came to fish for cod off the Grand Banks of Newfoundland. The fur trade started as a sideline, with fishermen and explorers bartering their goods for furs, but it soon became a major enterprise in its own right.

We do not know all the ways in which these early contacts affected the daily life of indigenous peoples, but some of the effects are clear. We know that the arrival of Europeans in what had formerly been a peripheral part of the indigenous trade networks of North America shifted the balance of power in the region. Now people living near the Atlantic coastal areas frequented by European ships had first access to the desirable goods carried on these ships. The new emphasis on trapping beaver, an individualistic activity that yields relatively small pelts and little meat, changed the patterns of seasonal life. Previously beaver was only one part of the annual round of subsistence. Hunting for larger game such as moose, caribou, and deer was a communal activity that yielded large quantities of meat that could be preserved for leaner times, along with skins, hooves, and sinew that were the raw materials of houses, clothing, and tools. Over time, as some Native people spent more time trapping pelts than hunting game, they became dependent on trade with the Europeans for basic food and material needs. The most important changes prior to 1620, however, came from disease. Frenchman Nicholas Denys wrote, in 1672:

The hunting by the Indians in old times was easy for them. They killed animals only in proportion as they had need of them. When they were tired of eating one sort, they killed some of another. If they did not wish longer to eat meat, they caught some fish. They never made an accumulation of skins of Moose, Beaver, Otter, or others, but only so far as they needed them for personal use.[1]

Europeans who visited this region in the early 1600s sometimes talked to older Native people about what life was like when they were young. Membertou, a Mi'kmaq sagamore (chief) at Port Royal, in Nova Scotia, was reputed to be over 100 years when he met French explorer Samuel de Champlain in 1603. He told Champlain that, in his youth, the Indians were "as thickly planted as the hairs on his head," but now their numbers were thinned.[2] The Mi'kmaq, whose homeland spans an area that includes parts of Maine as well as the Canadian provinces of Nova Scotia and New Brunswick, were among the first peoples in the Northeast to have regular contact with Europeans. They experienced devasting epidemics in the sixteenth century as European diseases such as small pox and measles swept through a population that had no prior exposure to them and therefore no resistance.

As the rate of European contact increased after 1600, so too did the occurence of epidemics.[3] In 1620, when the Pilgrims landed at the place they named Plymouth, they found empty *witus*, or houses, and cornfields overgrown with weeds. These marked the site of Patuxet, a Wampanoag village. The village was abandoned because a great sickness afflicted the people of Patuxet, and in the brief span of years between 1617 and 1619 about 90 percent of the people died. By some estimates, as much as 75 percent of the indigenous people of New England died from epidemic disease between 1500 and 1620. Thus, it was as much of a new world for them as it was for the Europeans.

This chapter presents the early contact period history of the Algonkian peoples of the Northeast. This grouping includes the Wampanoag, Narragansett, Mohegan, Pequot, Schagticoke, Shinnecock, Nipmuc, Norwottock, Agawam, Sokoki, Cowassuck, Abenaki, Penobscot, Passamaquoddy, Maliseet, and Mi'kmaq peoples. Their territories range from Long Island Sound on the south to the Hudson River valley on the west, the St. Lawrence River to the north, and the Atlantic Ocean to the east. It includes people now living on the Canadian side of the current U.S./Canadian border because, for a long time, that border had little meaning. The languages spoken by people in this group are part of the larger Algonkian language family, meaning that they share a common origin and therefore are more or less distantly related, although they do not think of themselves as "one people." Their histories include intertribal warfare as well as trade and alliance among neighboring groups. In terms of daily life, however, they shared much in common, dictated in part by the fact that they shared a similar worldview and lived in the Eastern Woodlands culture area.

THE CREATION AND SHAPING OF THE WORLD

Algonkian stories about the creation and shaping of the world inhabited by human beings vary greatly in detail but share a common core of key elements. The world is created by a supreme being, commonly referred to as the Great Spirit, Creator, or Manitou (an Algonkian word that means "spirit"). The term "Great Spirit" places the Creator at the upper end of a continuum in which many beings have a spirit, and some spirits are stronger than others. Once the world is created, other culture heros take center stage as they shape the world into its present form through wisdom, foolishness, or happenstance. Specific details of the stories explain why animals have their particular characteristics and how people should behave toward each other. Algonkian stories also explain the shaping of places such as the Aquinnah cliffs on Martha's Vineyard, which are a sacred place for the Wampanoag. Stories say that Moshup, the Wampanoag culture hero, could eat an entire whale at one sitting. He used to walk into the ocean, pick up a whale, and fling it against the cliffs to kill it before broiling it for dinner. It is said that the unusual markings on the cliffs come from the blood of these whales. However, Moshup, like other Algonkian culture heros, is also credited with teaching the people how to live in the world with respect.

In Penobscot stories, Gluskabe, the culture hero, opens his eyes on a world that already exists in familiar form, with heaven, earth, land and sea, fishes, animals, birds, even day and night. Stories about Gluskabe's adventures speak of his ability to transform himself and the world around him. Gluskabe makes mistakes, sometimes humorous and sometimes serious, but in the end he learns to use his powers wisely, reined in by his ever-patient grandmother Woodchuck. Gluskabe, like Moshup, eventually learns enough to pass on to others.[4]

In Western Abenaki stories Tabaldak, the Owner, creates all living beings except Odziozo, the one who shaped himself from earth that has been touched by Tabaldak. Tabaldak creates a man and a woman from stone but is displeased with the result, so he destroys them. Then he creates a man and a woman from living wood. They become the ancestors of the people. Odziozo, also known as the Transformer, reshapes the earth to create familiar features of the Champlain Valley. Stories about Tabaldak and Odziozo teach the names and qualities of things, and the rituals needed to keep the balance of power among all living things.[5]

The stories that we know about Algonkian creation are only a small part of what existed before the arrival of Europeans. Fannie Hardy Eckstorm, a folklorist and historian who wrote about the Penobscot and Passamaquoddy in the twentieth century, mourned the loss of oral tradition by commenting that these later versions were comparable to telling the story of Cinderella as, "Oh, it's about a girl who wanted to go to a dance when she should have been at home washing dishes; and she lost one of her shoes."[6] The essence of the story is there, but many details were lost during the dark years of epidemics, warfare, and diaspora after 1620, and through the efforts of Christian missionaries to stamp out what they viewed as pagan or heathen beliefs. It is a testament to the tenacity and creative adaptation of indigenous peoples that so much cultural knowledge has survived. One area of cultural continuity and strength for Algonkian peoples in the Northeast is their enduring connection to the land.

SUBSISTENCE AND SEASONAL CYCLES

Daily life in the eastern woodlands was shaped by the seasons of the year, each bringing its own special tasks, pleasures, and hardships. In the northern parts, where the climate was too cold for farming, people's

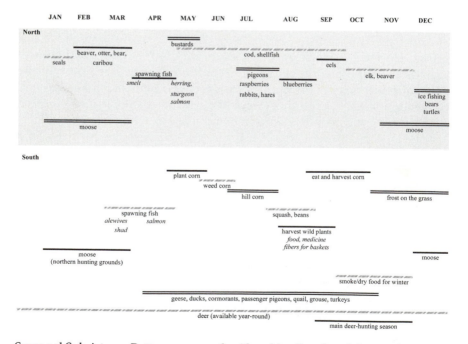

Seasonal Subsistence Patterns among the Algonkian Peoples of the Northeast. Information complied from Reuben Gold Thwaties, Jesuit Relations and Allied Documents, vol. 3:79-83; Peter Thomas, In the Maelstrom of Change, 5–6.

lives revolved around hunting and fishing. Elsewhere, the seasonal cycles revolved around horticulture, that is, the regular cultivation of corn and other crops. In both places, men and women made gender-defined contributions to the survival and well-being of their families. That is, certain tasks were generally done by men while others were more often done by women. Native peoples thought of the turn of the seasons in terms of food and ceremony.

The daily life of horticultural Algonkians during the early contact period is exemplified by the seasonal   **Horticulturalists** cycle of the Agawams and Norwottucks of the middle Connecticut River valley. We know much about their lives because an English fur trader named John Pynchon made notes in the 1630s.[7] According to Pynchon, the Agawams and Norwottucks marked the beginning of the year in late spring, after the earth and waters thawed, when they cleared their fields and planted corn. This heavy labor required everyone to help. Englishman Roger Williams, commenting on the Narragansett to the south, wrote:

When a field is to be broken up [hoed], they have a very loving sociable speedy way to dispatch it: All the neighbours men and Women forty, fifty, a hundred &c, joyne and come in to help freely.[8]

The first moon (or month) began in mid-April, known as the time for setting Indian corn. The second moon, which they called *msonesque nimock kesos,* was the time for women to weed the corn. (*Kesos* means moon.) In Native North America, horticulture was women's work. The third moon, corresponding to late June and early July, was *tow wa kesos:* the time to hill the corn. Women used hoes to push a few inches of dirt up around the base of each plant. Hilling helps corn stalks to grow straight and tall. At this time beans were also planted in each hill. The hoes were made from long sticks with a freshwater shell or shaped bone at the end.

Women and children continued to weed corn through the summer. They planted other crops such as kidney beans, gourds, pumpkins, squash, and Jerusalem artichokes. They gathered other plants and plant products such as nuts, berries, roots, and medicinal herbs. However, corn was the staple, and people's lives revolved around the rhythm of growing corn. Algonkians in the middle Connecticut River valley also cultivated tobacco. They smoked tobacco for pleasure and as part of their ceremonies, believing that the smoke rising up would carry their prayers to the Creator. But growing tobacco was men's work. Tobacco fed the spirit, which was important, but daily life revolved around the practical matter of feeding the body.

During fourth moon, or *matterl la naw kesos,* squashes ripened and Indian corn began to be edible. Late summer was also a time for gathering herbs and processing the ash splints and sweetgrass needed for baskets.

By the fifth moon of late August, there was an abundance of ripened corn. The sixth moon, *pas qui taqunk kezos,* or late September, was the time to harvest the bulk of the corn crop, although, as the names of the months suggest, people had been eating corn for several weeks. This was also a time to finish preparations for winter, by drying berries and gathering nuts for the cold months ahead.

The seventh moon of late October marked the end of the corn-growing season, characterized by white frost on the grass and ground. Pynchon tells us that the eighth moon was called *quinnikesos,* but he did not record its meaning. The ninth moon, *pap sap quoho,* included the date on which they marked the midpoint of the winter season, on January 6. The tenth moon began in late January, a time when the sun did not yet have the strength to thaw the waters and the earth. By late February and early March, the ice on the river began to disappear. The twelfth month, *namoss-ack kessos,* marked the time of catching fish, when the fish began to spawn. Shad, alewives, eels, and salmon traveled north, up the Connecticut River, in the spring, and down again in autumn. People gathered at the places where natural waterfalls forced the fish to congregate. Some fish were caught with nets and weirs. Others were caught by torchlight with spears. These were times when people from different villages might gather together, working hard to dry and preserve the fish for storage but also taking advantage of the occasion for socializing. It was a happy time, as people worked hard, ate well, and enjoyed gatherings, dances, storytelling, and courtship.

The Algonkians of southern New England had a rich and varied diet in addition to the horticultural products grown by women. From April to October, birds were plentiful, including geese, ducks, cormorants, passenger pigeons, quail, grouse, and turkeys. The men also hunted deer, which were available all year round in this area, although the primary hunting time was in the fall. The men observed the deer throughout the spring and summer, noting their habits and favorite drinking places, so they would know where to find them when hunting during the late fall and early winter moons. They sometimes headed further north in search of moose, a large game animal whose heavy skin provided excellent waterproof boots and clothing. In the promotional literature written by Englishmen during the early seventeenth century, there is an uneasy tension in the descriptions of how easily the Algonkians could obtain food throughout the year. On the one hand, this was an important selling point for promotional literature: prospective colonists were wooed with stories about how easily they could not only survive but prosper in the colonies. On the other hand, Native men were described as lazy, their wives as overworked "squaw drudges," because they did not follow traditional European work and gender roles.[9] The truth, as often happens, lies somewhere in between. It took hard work, careful planning, and much knowledge for Native people to benefit from seasonal cycles. Yet when everything went well, Native people enjoyed greater plenty and variety in their daily diet than the average French or British householder could ever dream of.

Further north, the growing season was too short to cultivate corn. Some Algonkian peoples, including the Passamaquoddy, Maliseet and Mi'kmaq, lived mainly by hunting and gathering, although they traded meat for corn with their neighbors to the south. Their language, culture, and worldview were similar to those of the Algonkian peoples of southern New England, but the climate and ecology of the lands on which they lived affected their daily lives in specific ways. One can see the difference between their seasonal cycle and that of the horticulturalists, thanks to descriptive data recorded by Father Pierre Biard, a Jesuit missionary who lived among the Mi'kmaq about 1610. The Mi'kmaq lived near the Atlantic coast north of the St. John River. Their diet included more fish and shellfish than groups living further inland. Biard noted the Mi'kmaq months in terms of their European equivalents, so he started his list with January.[10]

Hunter-Gatherers

For the Mi'kmaq, January was the time of seal hunting. Seal meat tasted something like veal, according to Biard. The Mi'kmaq also rendered the fat and used it as a "sauce" throughout the year, storing it in moose bladders. Boots and clothing made from sealskin were beautiful, warm, and waterproof. From February to mid-March, the men hunted and trapped for beaver, otters, moose, bears, and caribou. They were most successful in these activities when the snow lay deep on the ground, because they traveled lightly over the crusty top of the snow on snowshoes, while the heavier game floundered. In dry winters, or if it rained, they fared less well.

In mid-March the rivers thawed and, as in the warmer climates to the south, the fish began working their way upstream to spawn. Biard wrote, "Anyone who has not seen it could scarcely believe it. You cannot put your hand into the water, without encountering them."[11] The Mi'kmaq enjoyed smelt, herring, sturgeons, salmon, and eels. By the end of April, birds started to arrive, building nests and laying eggs near the coast. From May to mid-September the Mi'kmaq gathered shellfish and had no fear of starvation due to the large numbers of cod and other fish. Fishing, of course, meant that people also had to work at drying and preserving the fish, sometimes smoking it over a fire or drying it on platforms in the sun.

Late summer brought raspberries and blueberries, and a new wave of birds such as wild pigeons who came to eat them. This time of year was characterized by much feasting and gathering as people dried food for the winter and celebrated before splitting up into smaller groups for the winter. By mid-September, many groups withdrew from the coast, moving inland.

Late fall and the winter months were a time for hunting and storytelling. The English travel writer John Josselyn noted that people hunted moose in fairly large groups that consisted of both men and women, often husbands and wives but also including brothers and sisters. Both sexes were needed because, while hunting large game was "men's work," it required the labor of both men and women to process the results of a successful hunt. Men chased down the moose, running lightly over the top of the snow on snowshoes, while women set up the winter hunting camp. When the hunters returned to the camp with news of their success, the women went out to cut up and process the meat and hides. Deer might be carried on a pole by two men, but a moose had to be cut up for traveling. Part of the meat would be eaten on the spot, with great feasting and celebration. The rest had to be dried, frozen, or smoked. Hides also needed processing. Once removed from the carcass, they had to be scraped and cleaned, then smoked. To be useful for clothing or the outside of a wigwam, the moose hide also had to be tanned, a smelly, labor-intensive process.

Winter was a great time for storytelling. Some stories were told specifically to keep the children amused, although such stories always carried a moral or taught a lesson. Older men and women, or those too sick for hunting, stayed behind in the village to care for the children while their parents were away hunting. Other stories related family or tribal histories, lessons in how to behave, or humorous incidents. Certain stories were only to be told in winter, when the other-than-human beings tended to be quiet or asleep, so that it was safe to talk about them.

Overall, whether Algonkian peoples lived in areas where they could practice farming or not, their daily lives were dominated by the seasonal cycle of subsistance. Everyone had to work together for the group to survive, especially during the hard months of winter. In a world where people had to provide all of the necessities of life for themselves, relationships mattered more than money. Algonkian peoples viewed the world through the lens of kinship. Family relationships could be extended to allies and friends, but strangers were likely to be enemies. Daily life was shaped by a circle of relationships that expanded from the extended family to the family band to the village and larger political units.

THE STRUCTURES OF DAILY LIFE

Family and interpersonal relations shaped the daily life of Algonkian peoples from birth to death. Children were born into a world of relationships that included human kin but also other-than-human beings such as animals, the wind, plants, and even some stones. The latter concept is perhaps the most unfamiliar, and misunderstood, of Algonkian cultural characteristics, yet it is crucial for understanding the Algonkian way of life.

Algonkian peoples believed that all living beings have a spirit. Human beings coexist in the world with other-than- **Protocol** human Persons who are different from human beings, but still Persons. They are not gods, or deities, or evil spirits, although the English and French men who wrote about Algonkian peoples in the early seventeenth century interpreted them as such. Like all Persons, they liked to be treated with respect. The consequences of not treating others with respect could be serious, even violent. Thus, a core feature of daily life in this period was protocol, the spoken and unspoken rules for how to treat others. This does not mean that everyone always behaved. All human societies have people who fall along a continuum of behavior that is defined as good and bad, with the majority somewhere in the middle.[12]

Protocol defined the behavior of daily life on every level. Before cutting down a tree, one had to ask the tree's permission. Successful hunters had to have good aim and a knowledge of where to find deer or other game animals, but they also had to have a strong enough spirit to convince the game, through ritual offerings and invocations that are sometimes interpreted as prayers, to give itself up to the hunter for the survival of his people. Algonkian people left offerings of tobacco near dangerous places such as rapids and falls to appease any spirits that might harm them if angered.

Relationships within families, in villages, and in intertribal relations were all mediated, or disrupted, by protocol. People needed each other to survive, but living in close proximity to others, even (and sometimes especially) our own families, can lead to tension and conflict. Algonkian peoples structured their daily lives in ways that minimized the possibility of conflict but also provided acceptable outlets for strong emotions. This included a preference for individual autonomy combined with a sense of responsibility to the group. It also included a careful division of work and other cultural activities by age and sex, which minimized arguments over who was supposed to do what.

An important characteristic of Algonkian culture during this period is that nobody had the right to tell anyone else what to do. One might make suggestions, and a respected person could have great influence, but when people disagreed they were more likely to go their own way than to argue. This applies to parent-child relationships as much as intertribal relations. In Algonkian folklore, children are heroes as often as adults. Children were raised to view their parents and older kin with respect, to listen to their wisdom, and to learn from them. Moral lessons were often conveyed through stories.

Algonkian children grew up in households that we would think of as extended families. A household might **Households** consist of a senior man and his wife, one or two sons with their wives and children, and sometimes other siblings, and cousins. Households were slightly larger in the north than in the southern parts, with an average of five people per adult male among the hunter-gatherers and four people per adult male among the horticulturalists. Some men had more than one wife, especially if they were prominent leaders. It was not uncommon for a man to marry two sisters, which was viewed as a good option because the women already knew how to get along with each other. Male leaders had more than one wife because they needed the labor performed by women, who prepared the food and made the clothing and other items that their husbands gave away.

People lived in different types of houses, depending on the season and climate. In the northern parts, where birch trees grew to enormous sizes, people stitched together large sheets of bark to use as a covering on their wigwams. A wigwam is a conical dwelling made by joining 10 to 12 poles at the top, then covering it with sheets of bark. Wigwams could be small enough to hold just a few people. They could also be made large enough to sleep 15 to 18 people. Properly made, a wigwam provided a warm and comfortable home for the winter. It had a fire pit in the center to provide warmth and an opening at the top to allow smoke to escape. The edges were areas for storage and sleeping. Contrary to what early European visitors perceived, the wigwam was more than just a smoky, "savage" place. The interior space was sharply defined, with the place of honor designated as the space opposite the door. Men and women sat on different sides. It was considered insulting to leave a guest standing outside or even sitting just inside the door.

In southern New England, beyond the ecological range of the giant birch trees, people covered their houses with woven mats or with other types of bark. The mats were made by women, woven from rushes and other waterproof plant fibers that effectively kept out both rain and freezing winds. Indeed, William Wood noted that "they be warmer than our *English* houses."[13] These dwellings were rounded rather than conical and are known as *witus*. People slept on platforms constructed around the edges inside the *witu*, and the spaces underneath made excellent storage areas. They could also hang things from the poles overhead, especially medicinal plants and food.

Algonkian peoples also built larger structures or longhouses with a rectangular shape and two entrances. These might be used to shelter multiple families. They were also used for council meetings, dances, and other large public gatherings.

Family Bands   The basic unit of Algonkian social structure was the family band, a fluid unit that changed with the life cycles of its members. Multiple bands living together formed villages that were loosely governed by a council made up of male representatives from each family band. Under pressure from epidemics, warfare, or European settlement, Algonkian people could disperse into the woods as nuclear families or unite into larger political alliances such as the Wampanoag Confederacy in southern New England and the Wabanaki

Confederacy to the north. The people of southern New England were living in large villages with established cornfields by the time the English arrived in the early seventeenth century, but family bands continued to be an important factor in local and intertribal politics.

Algonkian peoples had a variety of ways in which they organized their domestic and family life. Some groups traced lineage by matrilineal descent, meaning that a person's family ties were determined by the mother's line. This was expecially common among horticultural groups, where the corn produced by women ensured that everyone would eat year-round. Other groups traced lineage by patrilineal descent, meaning that a person's family ties were determined by the father and his family. This was common among the hunter-gatherers. For the latter, leadership was still determined by personal power; that is, a leader who lost the ability to bring success in war or hunting would also lose his or her followers. In southern New England, a core of important families emerged by 1600 who are sometimes called "royal families," because the English liked to refer to their leaders as kings and queens, princes and princesses. However, Algonkian leaders never had the kind of authority held by European monarchs to tell others what to do.

Family and domestic life were also organized around a gendered division of labor. It would be a mistake, however, to look for evidence of women's status or inferiority in the specific tasks they performed. If we consider the larger context of work to be done, it becomes clear that the labor of both men and women was equally important, and the labor of one could not be completed without the labor of the other.

Gendered Division of Labor

In general, men were responsible for hunting and trapping, providing meat, furs, and leather hides. Women processed all of this. They helped to butcher meat in addition to drying and preserving it. They bore the primary responsibility for cooking. They scraped hides, tanned leather, and prepared furs so that they could be worn or traded. Men cut down the poles for wigwams and *witus* and cut out the bark sheets used to cover them, but women wove the mats and stitched the pieces of bark together. Both men and women helped with decoration. Birchbark wigwams in particular might be painted with designs. Women made clothing out of leather hides and decorated them with paint, shell beads, and porcupine quills. In contrast to European gender roles, however, it was not unusual for men to sometimes do women's work and vice versa, as needed. Roger Williams noted in 1643 that, among the Narragansett,

sometimes the man himselfe, (either out of love to his Wife, or care for his Children, or being an old man) will help the Woman which (by the custome of the Countrey) they are not bound to [do].[14]

Age and Life Cycle

Age was another important category of social organization. In childhood, boys and girls were given considerable freedom to play under the watchful eye of parents and relatives, but these pastimes helped prepare them for the tasks they would be expected to perform as adults. Girls might be given dolls made from corn husks or leather. Boys might be given child-sized bow-and-arrow sets. Both would have enjoyed summer activities such as swimming and gathering shellfish. Both might have been called on to chase away the crows and other birds hoping to feast on the family cornfields. Parents taught their children by example, through the work of everyday life.

As they grew up, young men and women expanded their range of activities. Young men gained the admiration and respect of others when they demonstrated unusual skill in hunting, fishing, diplomacy, or war. They were expected to be more impulsive and hot-headed than the older men, and it was not unusual for them to initiate raiding parties against the advice of their elders. Algonkian stories frequently center on the consequences of such raids. Young men had to prove themselves to be good providers if they hoped to marry well. Likewise, young women gained prestige and status from their ability to perform women's tasks.

Married couples, or men and women in the prime of life, consitute another age cohort. They bore a greater responsibility for the daily well-being of the family or larger group. Women in particular were defined by the daily rhythm of work, which included cooking and child care. Men also worked hard but on a different timetable. Much of their work took place away from the village, when they went out hunting or on war parties. This is one reason why the English viewed Algonkian men as lazy and described their women as "slaves" and "drudges." For the English, farming was men's work. Hunting and fishing were viewed as leisure activites for the nobility.

As men and women grew older, they often gained added prestige and respect. Women in particular moved into new arenas of political and social life as they left their child-bearing years behind. Instead of being devalued, they were honored for the children they had borne and the wisdom they had gained over the years. The senior woman in a household held great influence over the patterns of daily life, assigning tasks and settling disputes. Older women had a greater role in political councils than younger women. An "Old Woman" or "Old Man" often has a critical role in Algonkian folklore and oral tradition, because their spirits get stronger with time and experience, and this more than compensates for the physical changes associated with age. Grandparents held an important place in Algonkian families, telling stories and passing on oral tradition to the youngest children while the parents were busy with other tasks.

Algonkian peoples had strict moral codes that differed in
some important ways from the values brought over by the   **Marriage**
Protestants and Catholics of Europe. The biggest difference
was that there was no moral stigma attached to the dissolution of a marriage, although every community had customary ways of trying to help
couples to address their problems before this point. Great efforts were
made to ensure that young people made good choices, and parents and
elders were often involved in the selection of marriage partners. Intertribal
gatherings were an opportunity for political councils and trade, but they
were also an opportunity for young people from different villages to meet
each other. Another way for young people to meet was through travel;
young men sometimes went off on journeys, either alone or with a cousin
or other friend, and married women from other places.

Given the importance of kin ties among the Algonkian peoples, marriages
were serious business because they united families as well as individuals.
However, there was no value attached to the concept of forcing people to
stay married who were unhappy with each other. Imagine what it would
be like to live in a wigwam during the winter months with an unhappy
married couple who were constantly bickering. It would be uncomfortable
for everyone. Thus, while Algonkian peoples valued marriage and took
it seriously, unhappily married couples could part without social stigma,
especially if there were no children.

This was possible in part because of the gendered division of labor,
which gave both men and women equal access to the materials of daily
life. If a woman wanted to leave her husband, she could turn to her
brothers or other male relatives for meat. If man had no wife, he could
ask his sisters and other female relatives for help. Of course, this still
meant that people had to be careful about protocol and treating each other
with respect. People who were known as moochers or selfish ones might
wear out their welcome. Algonkian storytellers can make an audience
roar with laughter when they tell stories about people who show up just
when supper is ready but are never around to help with the preparaton or
clean-up. The ideal was for people to get along with each other, but the
texture of daily life came from the fact that this ideal was not always possible or easy to achieve.

SOCIAL AND POLITICAL LIFE

Early European explorers viewed the indigenous peoples of the
Americas as savages, people who lived without law, government, or
religion—at least, by European standards. This negative view does not
hold up to scrutiny. A systematic study of these early accounts, written
by the same men who described Native peoples as "savage," makes it
clear that indigenous peoples had a consistent worldview and social
organization, albeit one that sometimes differed from European ways. To

understand how leadership and political power functioned in Algonkian society, it is important to consider certain aspects of Algonkian society that were unfamiliar to these early explorers.

Spirit Power and Prestige

In Algonkian worldview, all animate beings have a spirit, but some spirits are more powerful than others.[15] Spirit power could be displayed through success in hunting or warfare (for men) or through skills such as tanning hides, preparing feasts, or preserving the fire (for women), as well as through clothing and adornment, through knowledge (especially foreknowledge or clairvoyance), or simply by a quiet manner that indicated power held in restraint. People with unusually strong spirits were feared as well as admired because spirit power could not always be controlled. It could be used voluntarily, through ritual or an act of will, or involuntarily, through unrestrained emotion. It could be lost as well as gained. The ability to demonstrate strength of spirit, for both men and women, was essential for prestige. People with only a small measure of spirit power had to rely on others for food, for social stability, and for protection from supernatural forces.

Reciprocity

Sharing and reciprocity were important cultural values. People shared by giving gifts, feeding others, and exchanging goods. Roger Williams wrote, "It is a strange truth, that a man shall generally finde more free entertainment and refreshing amongst these Barbarians, then amongst thousands that call themselves Christians."[16] People were expected to share meat and other food with family but also with travelers and strangers. Enemies, however, were outside the circle of social obligation. In stories, those who are greedy or refuse to share food always come to a bad end. Shared resources helped everyone to survive during hard times.

The ideal of reciprocity shaped early Algonkian encounters with the fur trade. European traders entered into trading relationships with the expectation of making a profit. Native peoples viewed these transactions as an exchange of gifts, an expression of protocol whereby people showed respect for each other.[17]

Leadership

The first prerequisite for a leader was to be able to care for his or her people. Success in hunting, war, and in the timing of seasonal movements (for example, to be at the right place on the river when the spawning runs began) all depended on spirit power. A successful leader attracted other men who gave part of the meat and skins from their hunting for redistribution to the community. A male leader's power and prestige allowed him to marry well and take additional wives, who enhanced his status by preparing feasts, processing skins, preserving food, and making clothing, all of which could be given away as gifts, and by bearing children, who would extend his sphere of influence through their own marriages.[18] Female leaders also benefitted from their marriage arrangements, but the available evidence does not tell us how they achieved the benefits that male leaders derived from the work performed by their wives.

Leaders were supposed to exemplify all of the above qualities. They fed others before feeding themselves. They attracted followers by making good decisions. They consistently demonstrated that their spirit power was strong by leading successful war or hunting parties, healing, or other activities that contributed to the well-being of the group. They inspired respect but could not demand obedience. People followed them as long as they continued to be good leaders. One of the great changes brought by colonization, as we shall see in Chapter 3, was that colonial laws and policies worked to keep people who did not live up to this standard in positions of power.

Note that there are not one but two Algonkian words adopted into the English language as synonyms for chief: *sachem,* used in southern New England, and *sagamore,* more commonly used among the northern hunter-gatherers. Both words are derived from the same root, *sa:kima:wa,* or leader.[19] English writers sometimes referred to Algonkian leaders as kings, princes, or chiefs, but the persistence of *sachem* and *sagamore* as loan words suggests that their power and prerogatives were recognizably distinct from European norms. It would be more accurate to say that a sachem or sagamore was first among equals. Pierre Biard wrote of the Mi'kmaq: "They have Sagamores, that is, leaders in war; but their authority is most precarious, if, indeed, that may be called authority to which obedience is in no wise obligatory. The Indians follow them through the persuasion of example or of custom, or of ties of kindred and alliance; sometimes even through a certain authority of power, no doubt."[20]

Land Native people did not own land in the way Europeans did, but they had a strong sense of territorial boundaries. Algonkian peoples also viewed their relationship with the land as reciprocal. Hunter-gatherers to the north recognized territorial boundaries, but certain resources such as bountiful fishing places might be shared by more than one group.

In southern New England leaders were associated with *sachemships,* or specific territories inhabited by the sachem and his or her followers.[21] Algonkian peoples in the coastal areas had a formal structure for determining leadership, dominated by certain families that the English recognized as similar to the royal families of Europe. Here again, however, leaders who could not demonstrate the ability to care for others lost status. The rules for choosing leaders were flexible enough that, if one leader needed to be deposed, another could be agreed upon without resorting to the artificial system of primogeniture (inheritance by the eldest son) practiced by the English.

Female leaders were sometimes referred to as queens, as when Christopher Levett met a women he called "the reputed Queene" of Quacke near present-day Portland, Maine.[22] However, Algonkian women could be leaders in their own right, not just as the wives of a king. English documents from southern New England refer to such women as *sunksquaws* or *squaw sachems*.[23] In the seventeenth century, English writers routinely used the word "squaw" as a synonym for "Indian woman." It was not pejorative and had no other meaning, although today the word in English is pejorative and should not be used.[24] "Squaw" comes from the Algonkian language. It is technically a suffix, *skw, that means "woman" or "wife."[25]

It should also be noted that leadership was often dispersed within Algonkian communities. One person might be recognized for abilities in war, another for leadership in civil or religious matters. Leaders were guided by discussions with other people in the community through formal council. Larger tribal confederations such as existed among the Mi'kmaq and the Wampanoag met together in Grand Councils, presided over by someone recognized as the Grand Sachem or Sagamore. Such a person had to be widely respected. While the Algonkians did not have the formal political organization of the Iroquois Confederacy, which will be discussed in Chapter 2, they had an efficient system that allowed groups to operate autonomously in times of peace but still come together for unified action when faced with an external threat. Intertribal ties became increasingly important after 1600 as Native people faced the common threat of European colonization.

RELIGION AND CEREMONIAL LIFE

As noted above, the Algonkian worldview recognized the existence of many animate beings in the world, each with its own spirit, including humans and animals but also plants, stars, the sun, the wind, and some stones. They did not worship these other-than-human beings as gods. Rather, they entered into relationships with them, as with any other person. These relationships were mediated by socially established protocols that defined respectful behavior. Europeans, however, frequently misinterpreted this through a cultural lens that turned powerful spirits into devils and other-than-human Persons into a pantheon of heathen gods.

Music and Dance   Rituals involving dance and drumming were perhaps the most visible expression of Algonkian religion and ceremonial life. Drumming had a particular role in communicating with other-than-human spirits. Both men and women used resonant pieces of wood or hand drums to accompany singing or dancing. They also made rattles from animal horns or turtle shells. Flutes were made from reeds or carved pieces of wood. Sparse documentary evidence for this early period indicates that flutes were more often used by young men as part of their courtship of a young woman than in religious ceremonies or for public celebrations.

European explorers witnessed Indian dances along the Atlantic coast from the sixteenth century on. In 1534 Jacques Cartier, anchored near Chaleur Bay (New Brunswick), recorded the approach of seven canoes of Mi'kmaq, who danced and showed "many signs of joy, and of their desire to be friends." On another occasion, Cartier and his men went ashore to trade. He noted that some of the Mi'kmaq women stayed on the opposite shore where they danced and sang, "standing in the water up to their knees."[26] Although Cartier's account is not especially descriptive of the physical movements involved, his report of similar greetings on other occasions establishes that singing and dancing were an important part of the ceremony involved in meeting or leaving strangers. Samuel de Champlain made similar observations some 70 years after Cartier as he traveled from southern Maine to Cape Cod.[27]

Roger Williams reported that the Narragansett people of southern New England held feasts or dances of distinct types. He distinguished first of all between public and private events, then between ceremonies and celebrations. Ceremonies, he wrote, took place on occasions of "sicknesse, or Drouth, or Warre, or Famine"; celebrations took place during times of "caulme of Peace, Health, Plenty, Prosperity."[28] Of the celebrations, Williams particularly noted the winter dances, saying that "they run mad once a yeare in their kind of Christmas feasting."[29] Daniel Gookin described harvest time "dancings, and feastings, and revellings" that could last up to a week at a time. In these, the men danced singly and in the course of their turn gave away all of their possessions, "according to [their] fancy and affection." Gookin equated these giveaways with profligacy and cautioned that "much impiety is committed at such times."[30]

Ceremonies seemed stranger than celebrations to the English, especially when conducted by *powows*, or Indian **Healing** shamans. "Shaman" has become a generic word in the late twentieth century that subsumes the diversity of spiritual and healing powers recognized among different ethnic groups across time and space.[31] *Powow* is even more problematic, having changed from a word used by a specific group to refer to a particular type of healer, what John Josselyn called a physician or "Indian priest," to a present-day term (more commonly spelled "powwow") for pan-Indian events that feature dance, music, and crafts. Among seventeenth-century Massachusett speakers, *powow* referred specifically to one who had the power to heal or harm through spiritual means. Edward Winslow wrote, "The Powah is eager and free in speech; fierce in countenance; and joineth many antic and laborious gestures with the same, over the party diseased." Quite different abilities were attributed to *pineses*, warriors whose spirit power could make them invulnerable in battle if they only had time to prepare. Winslow also mentioned a third type of spirit power that was so rare and secret he could not determine its name.[32]

Powows and their healing ceremonies attracted particular notice from English writers. John Josselyn observed that powows placed a sick person on the ground and danced "in an Antick manner round about him, beating their naked breasts with a strong hand, and making hideous faces, sometimes calling upon the Devil for his help."[33] Indeed, Roger Williams claimed that powows cured only with the help of the Devil and that Indians knew nothing about herbal medicine.[34] It may be that curing ceremonies, being highly visible and audible, received more attention than the quiet administration of herbal medicines and poultices.[35]

Outbreaks of European disease posed a serious challenge to Native healers. The coastal areas from Portland, Maine to Cape Cod were hit particularly hard from 1617 to 1619, when 60 to 90 percent of the people in some villages died virtually overnight. Another epidemic hit the Connecticut River Valley in 1635.[36] These villages became sites of horror, with people dying so fast that their bodies could not be buried. When the Pilgrims came to the Wampanoag village of Patuxet in 1620, they found cornfields planted and growing but nobody there to tend them because an epidemic had struck the year before. The Pilgrims gave thanks to their God for this clear evidence of his plan for their survival and renamed the village Plymouth, after the port they had left behind. Some Algonkian peoples turned to the Christian God, believing that their own ceremonies and healing practices had failed. Others listened politely to Christian missionaries but continued in their own beliefs.

THE INTRODUCTION OF EUROPEAN TRADE GOODS

Prior to the development of the fur trade with Europeans, Algonkian peoples had to make everything they used and needed for daily life. They made their clothes from animal hides. Their tools were made from stone and bone. Their building materials for houses, utensils, and canoes consisted of wood, bark, plant fibers, skins, and stone. Yet they lived comfortable lives and believed in making things that were beautiful as well as useful.

The new objects acquired by trade did not, however, change Algonkian society just by their presence. People did not fall down in amazement the first time they saw a steel knife or a copper kettle, nor did they abandon their bows and arrows, skins, and wigwams for guns, cloth, or houses. More important, they did not see their traditional ways as inferior to those of the Europeans. The most popular trade goods in the early contact period were those that fit into preexisting lifeways, and even these were not always used according to European norms. Steel knives were useful tools and weapons, and in many circumstances a notable improvement over bone or stone tools. However, they did not replace the crooked knife, a tool made from a beaver incisor that had both practical and ceremonial uses. They did not replace the stone scrapers that women used to prepare

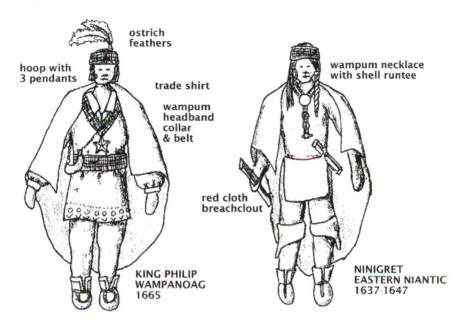

ostrich feathers

hoop with 3 pendants

trade shirt

wampum headband collar & belt

wampum necklace with shell runtee

red cloth breachclout

KING PHILIP
WAMPANOAG
1665

NINIGRET
EASTERN NIANTIC
1637-1647

Men's clothing styles, seventeenth century. Algonkian people selectively incorporated European trade goods into their daily lives. Based on written documents, archaeological evidence and a few rare portraits, it is possible to reconstruct seventeenth-century clothing. Native people used new materials such as cloth in familiar patterns. Certain goods such as ostrich feathers or fancy red cloth coats became status items. From Tara Prindle/nativetech.org.

hides, because steel knives ripped the skin. Knifes might also be worn around the neck, not just for adornment or as a handy weapon but as a declaration of the wearer's spirit power, which gave him access to the strangers and their goods.

Copper kettles and iron pots had an obvious advantage over stone or hollow-stump kettles, which could not be transported. Prior to this, Algonkian people made drinking and cooking vessels shaped out of bark, sealed with plant fibers or pitch, and often decorated with intricate designs, as well as vessels carved from wood. Some sources say that large immovable cooking vessels were also carved from tree stumps or large stones. Women had to boil water or make soups and stews through a labor-intensive process of heating stones and dropping them into the vessel until the contents were sufficiently heated. The copper and iron kettles introduced through the fur trade were more portable and more durable than their indigenous counterparts, although bark containers in particular continued to be made and used for generations. These kettles were especially useful for making maple sugar, which required a long period of boiling down maple sap.[37] Copper kettles were even useful after they were worn out because they could be cut up to make arrowheads, amulets, or rolled copper beads.[38]

Guns made an impressive noise, but in the early contact period they were valued more as high-status objects than for any practical use. Early trade guns were clumsy, and useless without powder and shot, which could only be obtained from Europeans. Guns needed to be repaired by a blacksmith, and in the early contact period these were few and far between. Wabanaki people who had contact with guns soon learned their strengths and limitations. In 1607, Englishman Humphrey Gilbert reported that during one skirmish along the Gulf of Maine, a warrior managed to climb aboard the English ship and seize the firebrand that was needed to light the fuse on their matchlock guns. Without fire, the guns were useless. The warrior threw the firebrand overboard and followed it into the water to make his escape.[39] Long-barrelled rifles looked good but proved to be impractical in the woods, where they were likely to get caught on branches, and because they were less efficient in battle than a bow and arrow, which could be fired quickly and accurately.

One item related to warfare that was never replaced was the war club, sometimes called a head-knocker by the English. These clubs were carved from a single piece of wood with a burl or knot at one end. The burl was carved into a smooth rounded shape, like a ball. The handle might be decorated with carving or inlaid with wampum or other beads. War clubs were used in battle to strike people on the head, and a skillful blow could be fatal. Like the war club, bows and arrows could be made as needed, instead of having to deal with a trader. It was many years before guns became practical and therefore more desirable than indigenous weapons.

Other objects were never replaced by trade goods. Indeed, they were copied by Europeans and are familiar objects even today, at least, for anyone who spends time on outdoor activities. These items include snowshoes, moccasins, and canoes.

Not all trade goods were utilitarian. Every schoolchild has heard that the island of Manhattan was purchased by the Dutch for $24 in beads. This story is sometimes told to point out that Indians were ignorant of "civilized" practices such as commercial exchange, and at other times it is used to argue that Europeans cheated indigenous people out of their land. The truth, as often happens, is somewhere in between. It is true that the Dutch paid for the land with what seemed to them like inexpensive trinkets. However, glass beads were valued on multiple levels by Algonkian peoples. They were familiar analogues to the beads made by indigenous peoples from shells, stone, and bone.

High-quality glass beads were made for the fur trade in various sizes, shapes, and colors. The smallest beads were used for decorating clothing and other objects made from leather, such as moccasins, pouches, and headbands. Indigenous decorative techniques included painting on leather and embroidery with dyed deer or moose hair as well as dyed and flattened porcupine quills. All of these techniques persisted after contact, but Native artisans quickly embraced the use of glass beads to develop intricate patterns and techniques. Larger beads were worn as jewelry, or used to decorate personal possessions. Glass beads embodied qualities seen in nature, such as the clear shimmer of water or the reflection of sunlight on mica. They were made from colors seen in nature but not reproducible from natural dyes. Patterns and symbols used in personal adornment often embodied spirit power, thereby enhancing the status and prestige of those who wore them.

Another type of bead was never replaced by glass, but its manufacture was transformed by the introduction of metal tools. Wampum beads were small, cylindrical beads made from shell in two basic colors: purple or dark blue, and white. Purple wampum was made from the quahog, a type of

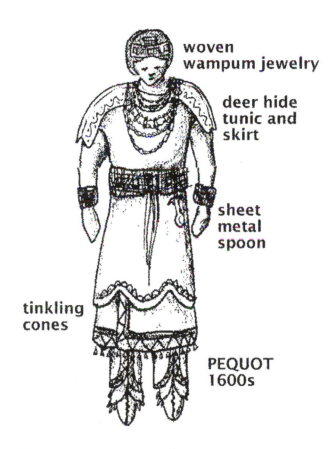

Pequot woman, seventeenth century. Like Native men, Native women incorporated European goods such as glass beads and metal ornaments in traditional ways. From Tara Prindle/nativetech.org.

shellfish found only in the Long Island Sound. White wampum was made from freshwater shells. They were used for adornment, but their primary value came from their ritual use by the Iroquois nations to the west, which will be discussed in greater detail in Chapter 2. The Narragansetts and other Algonkians living near Long Island Sound became wealthy from their increased ability to control the production of wampum. Algonkians living in other areas had to acquire it by trade or tribute.

Over time, trade goods were integrated into Algonkian ways of life. People became accustomed to kettles, steel axes, and even guns. Men and women incorporated items of European clothing into their wardrobe, including cotton shirts, knit stockings, and beaver hats. Algonkian peoples did not "lose" their culture after coming into contact with Europeans. Rather, they adapted selective elements of European material life in distinctively Indian ways. Cloth became a popular item, especially in deep shades of red and blue, but it was mostly used to make familiar garments such as leggings, breechclouts, and capes that could also be made from tanned hides. King Philip, or Metacomet, an important Wampanoag sachem, sometimes wore an exotic, imported ostrich feather that surely marked him as special in a world where most of his peers wore turkey or eagle feathers. As wampum became more plentiful, people increasingly adorned themselves with strings of beads and woven wampum jewelry. Metal cones proved to be a popular addition to women's clothing for special occasions because they made a tinkling sound when attached to a skirt, although this would be impractical for everyday wear.

Certain items acquired a high status value, especially the red cloth trade coats that the English reserved for important allies. A man or woman wearing a high-status trade item immediately demonstrated to all that they had great spirit power, as people who were able to interface with European strangers and receive tokens of respect. It was this aspect of the fur trade that had the biggest impact on Algonkian lifeways. To acquire trade goods, leaders had to engage in relationships with the Europeans who brought them. These transactions, in the long run, led directly to the displacement of Algonkian peoples from their homelands.

STRANGERS IN THEIR OWN LAND

From the beginning, European fur traders needed a place from which to operate. They needed good harbors and deep rivers for their ships and some assurance of safety when they brought their longboats to shore. They needed to build dwellings, and a place to store both the furs they hoped to receive and the goods to be given in exchange. They needed food. They needed a location that would be attractive for Native traders and convenient for themselves. This means that from the beginning, they chose places that were also desirable places for Native people.

To achieve all this, the English had to negotiate an understanding with the indigenous inhabitants. They were too few in number to successfully occupy prime locations by force, and in any case that would be counter-productive for trade. During the first few decades of English colonization in Algonkian territories, the safety of English colonists depended on the good will of their Indian neighbors, which meant personal relationships.

After 1620, with the founding of Plymouth Colony, and especially after 1630 when the Great Migration began, that is, the period when increasing numbers of English men and women immigrated to New England with their families, the English were mainly concerned with establishing homes and communities in the New World. In the southern half of New England, English colonists came in family groups that had little tolerance for individualism or nonconformity. Indeed, single men and women were required to live with families. Colonies and towns were established in short order. At first glance the records left by these early settlers make the world seem entirely English, as people cleared land and planted fields, quarreled over fences that failed to keep pigs out of a neighbor's corn, built churches, and generally tried to create a new England in America. A closer look reveals the continuing presence of Native peoples and communities as people traded corn, baskets, venison, and berries for bread, metal goods, trade cloth, and beads. Further, the English were well aware of the inter-tribal conflicts going on around them. At Springfield, on the Connecticut River, and along the Gulf of Maine, especially on the Kennebec River, the English established trading posts and fishing villages.

Welcome to the Neighborhood

Algonkian peoples were willing and sometimes eager to have trading posts nearby, with convenient access for their own families. They wanted to establish good relations with the English, understanding, from their own traditions of protocol and how to manage strangers, that it was better to have them as allies than as enemies. As in all communities there were people who were curious about the newcomers. They wanted to learn the language and ways of the newcomers, not necessarily because they saw them as better than their own ways but because they were different. There were also some Algonkian peoples who wanted nothing whatsoever to do with them, either out of simple disinterest or because they saw them as a danger. Then there were the majority of folk who enjoyed having some of these new goods, who came out of curiosity once or twice, but who were not particularly enamored of them in any way. It also may be that certain people were designated to be the primary contacts with the English, in the tradition of people who were able to transcend boundaries: intermediaries and go-betweens.

"Indian Deeds"

In New England history, the term "Indian deeds" has a specific meaning. It refers to documents that record land transactions, mostly from the seventeenth century, in which English men acquired lands inhabited by the Native inhabitants.

These deeds are actually "English deeds" in that they follow the legal practice of English colonists; however, they are commonly referred to as "Indian deeds" to indicate that these are the first step in the chain of ownership that gave English colonists legal title—in English law—to the land. These documents offer unusual insight into the world of Algonkian peoples in the early contact period because they were, for the most part, negotiated by real people who knew each other face-to-face. People and places are referred to by their Indian names. Special clauses tell us that Native people accepted some conditions and rejected others. There are a fair number of these documents from two regions in particular for the seventeenth century: the Gulf of Maine and the Connecticut River Valley. The earliest deeds were negotiated by fur traders such as John Pynchon in Springfield who established personal relationships with local leaders.

English concepts of property allowed land to be surveyed and mapped on paper, so that a defined "estate" could be bought, sold, or handed down from one generation to the next. In contrast, Algonkian concepts of land ownership were simultaneously fixed and fluid. People "owned" what they used. Thus, hunting territories generally belonged to men; horticultural land belonged to the women who worked them. Exact boundaries shifted over the lifetime of an individual, so that the territory of a man's youth might not be the same as the territory of his old age. Family cycles mattered, as did circumstances of warfare, diaspora, or periods of great stability. The nature and degree of control over territory probably changed somewhat in the late sixteenth century as the Little Ice Age disrupted horticultural patterns, so that people who once grew their own corn now had to trade for it, and the expansion of the fur trade made certain places more desirable than others.

Deeds tell us that during the early contact period, Algonkian peoples viewed land ownership as both communal and individual. That is, land was owned collectively by the tribe, but some individuals were acknowledged as having the right to dispose of particular tracts, mostly acting as spokespersons on behalf of their kin. The English could not just pay someone to sign a fake deed. They needed to identify the person with legitimate authority to make an agreement on behalf of himself or herself and any others who might contest the deed. This is why deeds often include multiple grantors, either naming other local sachems and sagamores or naming several members of one family. More important, deeds tell us that Algonkian peoples had an understanding of boundaries, of what territory was theirs and what was not. In places where a deed included two or more adjacent territories, or even if the land abutted someone else's territory, the English learned to obtain the consent of the neighboring sachems and sagamores, just to keep everything tidy. The latter either gave their consent in the body of the deed or signed as witnesses, demonstrating that they witnessed and approved the transaction.

In some cases Algonkian leaders signed deeds for lands that were already depopulated. In essence, they gained strong neighbors, allies, and trading partners in exchange for land that they no longer needed because so many of their own people had died. These deeds often include usufruct rights or even ongoing payment of tribute by the English, such as the payment of a bottle of rum or a cloth coat each year. The English may have interpreted the latter as an extended payment, but it is likely that Algonkian leaders understood this as tribute, an ongoing recognition that this was their land.

Native people sometimes offered land to induce Europeans to settle nearby. In 1615, Dohannida, one of the five sagamores from Pemaquid who had been taken to England by George Weymouth in 1605, encouraged his friend John Smith to settle at nearby Monhegan Island. He hoped that Smith and his men would aid them against the Tarrantines, or Mi'kmaq, to balance the influence of the French who, as Dohannida said, lived among the Mi'kmaq as one nation.[40]

While not all Indians may have liked the idea of having Englishmen nearby, the stipulations in deeds indicate that, given a chance to negotiate, Native people sought to frame the transactions in reciprocal terms. In 1636, Cuttonis, the "owner" of lands at Agawam (Springfield, Massachusetts), together with his mother, Kewenusk, and others, sold land on both sides of the Connecticut River to William Pynchon, who had a truckhouse there, reserving for themselves the right to plant corn in their own fields, to hunt and to fish, and to gather nuts. In exchange they received wampum, coats, hoes, hatchets, and knives—all in all, a positive, reciprocal transaction. Cuttonis and his people continued to live in the area, but their situation changed as the English population increased. In 1661, Cuttonis and five other men—Coo, Mattaquallant, Menis, Wallny, and Tagnalloush—mortgaged their remaining land at Agawam to Samuel Marshfield in exchange for goods already received. They promised to pay the debt with interest by the following summer in wampum, corn, or pelts. But their strategy failed when they could not produce the necessary goods on time. Marshfield took possession of their land.[41]

Overall, most of the trading was done by a few individuals or families. Unfortunately, the people who had the most to gain from the fur trade were leaders or leading families who used trade goods to enhance their own prestige, either by giving them away as gifts, using them to facilitate relations with others, or using them for a time before passing them on.[42] This is not to say that leaders simply sold out their own people; it enhanced everyone's sense of stability in the community to have visible leaders who could display their power effectively, at least in the short term. Certainly the fur trade depended in part on the good will of the women who processed the skins and pelts, a skilled, labor-intensive process. Unwilling workers would probably produce skins like the ones sold to John Pynchon by a man named Chockapeasnet, which Pynchon described as "the worst old Beaver I had."[43] But when the number of fur-bearing animals declined and warfare disrupted seasonal cycles so that hunters could no longer count on bringing in pelts, men who were enmeshed in the fur trade sold land to continue the relationships. Selling land further disrupted native economies, as English colonists cleared the land and brought in livestock, which altered the ecology of those areas.

By the 1660s the beaver trade had pretty much dried up in northern New England. English merchants began to systematically entrap Indians rather than beavers. That is, they gave out goods on credit, to be paid for at the end of the hunting season. Sometimes they asked for a mortgage to guarantee the debt. When the debts could not be paid, these creditors used English law to take the land as payment. They never "purchased" the land at all. Algonkian peoples who lived closest to the English soon became entangled by English laws. Behaviors newly defined as "criminal" caused some people to be arrested and thrown in jail, while others were fined. Whether the debts were incurred by trading on credit or through fines imposed by the English courts, they led to the same result. Leaders who had previously reserved land for themselves and their families were now forced to mortgage or sell it to pay the debt.[44]

As the beaver population declined, the English population increased. And, in a vicious cycle, wherever the colonists went, they changed the land. Cutting down trees changed patterns of precipitation, which in turn affected both plant and animal life.[45] English farmers introduced new crops such as wheat and barley, which depleted the soil and competed with indigenous plants. English pigs got into Indian cornfields and destroyed crops. The colonists dammed waterways for their mills, disrupting the ecosystems that had once supported beaver. Wherever they went, the forest receded, medicine plants became harder to find, and wildlife sought new places for foraging and mating. These changes were gradual, but by the 1660s the consequences were becoming clear. Hunters had to travel further for deer. Trappers had to travel further for beaver. Women had less land on which to plant their cornfields. Warfare and epidemics had long-term disruptive effects beyond the immediate traumas they engendered, because people had less time and less stability for labor-intensive activities and regular crop cultivation. Native people came to rely on trade goods, not because they were superior, but rather because they were convenient and available in a changing world.

NOTES

1. Nicholas Denys (1672) quoted in James Axtell, ed., *The Indian Peoples of Eastern America: A Documentary History of the Sexes* (New York: Oxford University Press, 1981), 114.

2. Reuben Gold Thwaites, *The Jesuit Relations and Allied Documents: Travels and Explorations of the Jesuit Missionaries in New France, 1610–1791*, 73 vols. (Cleveland, OH: Burrows Brothers, 1896–1901), 1:177.

3. The literature on epidemics and pre-Columbian mortality rates is vast. Two classic works to start with are Alfred W. Crosby, *The Columbian Exchange: Biological and Cultural Consequences of 1492* (Westport, CT: Greenwood Press, 1972) and Henry F. Dobyns, *Their Numbers Become Thinned* (Knoxville: University of Tennessee Press, 1983).

4. Joseph Nicolar, *The Life and Traditions of the Red Man* (Bangor, ME: C. H. Glass & Co., 1893), 7–10, 14, 84–85.

5. Gordon M. Day, "The Western Abenaki Transformer," *Journal of the Folklore Institute* 13 (1976): 77–84.

6. Fannie Hardy Eckstorm, *Old John Neptune and Other Maine Indian Shamans* (Portland, ME: The Southworth-Anthoensen Press, 1945), 27.

7. The following discussion of seasonal subsistence in the Connecticut River Valley is drawn from Peter A. Thomas, *In the Maelstrom of Change: The Indian Trade and Cultural Process in the Middle Connecticut River Valley, 1635–1665* (New York: Garland, 1990), 96–107.

8. Roger Williams, *A Key into the Language of America*, ed. John J. Teunissen and Evelyn J. Hinz (Detroit: Wayne State University Press, 1973), 98–100.

9. David D. Smits, "The 'Squaw Drudge': A Prime Index of Savagism," *Ethnohistory* 29 (1982): 281–306.

10. The following description is taken from Biard's account of his travels, published in Thwaites, 3: 77–83.

11. Thwaites, 3: 79–81.

12. The discussion in this section is drawn from Chapter 1 of Alice Nash, *Spirit, Power and Protocol* (Amherst: University of Massachusetts Press), forthcoming.

13. William Wood (1634), quoted in Axtell, p. 119.

14. Williams, 98–100.

15. On the importance of spirit power, see Elisabeth Tooker, "Introduction" to *Native North American Spirituality of the Eastern Woodlands: Sacred Myths, Dreams, Visions, Speeches, Healing Formulas, Rituals and Ceremonies*, ed. Elisabeth Tooker (New York: Paulist Press, 1979), 13–30; Wilson D. Wallis and Ruth Sawtell Wallis, *The Micmac Indians of Eastern Canada* (Minneapolis: University of Minnesota Press, 1955), 142–46; Ruth Holmes Whitehead, *Stories from the Six Worlds: Micmac Legends* (Halifax, Nova Scotia: Nimbus Publishing Ltd., 1988), especially her introductory essay, "Introduction: The World of The People," 1–21.

16. Quoted in Kathleen J. Bragdon, *Native Peoples of Southern New England, 1500–1650* (Norman: University of Oklahoma Press, 1996), p. 131.

17. Bragdon, 131–34.

18. Biard, in Thwaites, 2: 73–79; 3: 87, 93.

19. Bragdon, 249 n.3.

20. Biard, in Thwaites, 2: 73.

21. Bragdon, 140–55.

22. James Phinney Baxter, ed., *Christopher Levett, of York: The Pioneer Colonist in Casco Bay* (Portland, ME: The Gorges Society, 1893), 104–5.

23. Ann Marie Plane, "Putting a Face on Colonization: Factionalism and Gender Politics in the Life History of Awashunkes, the 'Squaw Sachem' of Saconet," in *Northeastern Indian Lives, 1632–1816*, ed., Robert S. Grumet (Amherst, MA: University of Massachusetts Press, 1996), 140–65.

24. Marge Bruchac, "Reclaiming the Word 'Squaw' in the Name of the Ancestors" (1999), online at www.nativeweb.org/pages/legal/squaw.html.

25. Note that the asterisk in *skw is used by linguists to indicate that this is a suffix, that is, a part of a word that must be preceded by something else.

26. Ramsay Cook, ed., *The Voyages of Jacques Cartier,* trans. H. P. Biggar (Toronto: University of Toronto Press, 1993), 20, 22.

27. H. P. Biggar, ed., *The Works of Samuel de Champlain,* 6 vols. (Toronto: The Champlain Society, 1936), 1: 293, 296, 323, 325, 335, 336, 338, 344, 349, 350.

28. Williams, 191.

29. Williams, 192.

30. Daniel Gookin, "Historical Collections of the Indians in New England (1674)," *Massachusetts Historical Society Collections,* 1st ser., 1 (1792): 141–227.

31. The classic anthropological study is Mircea Eliade, *Shamanism: Archaic Techniques of Ecstasy,* trans. Willard R. Trask (Princeton, NJ: Princeton University Press, 1964).

32. Edward Winslow, *Good News from New England* [1624], in *Story of the Pilgrim Fathers,* ed. Edward Arber (Boston: Houghton, Mifflin, and Co., 1897), 583–86.

33. Paul J. Lindholdt, ed., *John Josselyn, Colonial Traveler: A Critical Edition of "Two Voyages to New-England"* (Hanover, NH: University Press of New England, 1988), 93–95.

34. Williams, 245.

35. For oral traditions about herbal medicine see William S. Simmons, *Spirit of the New England Tribes: Indian History and Folklore, 1620–1984* (Hanover, NH: University Press of New England, 1986), 100–105.

36. Thomas, 165.

37. Gordon M. Day, "Western Abenaki," in *Northeast,* ed. Bruce Trigger, vol. 15 of *Handbook of North American Indians* (20 vols.), gen. ed. William C. Sturtevant (Washington, DC: Smithsonian Institution Press, 1978), 153.

38. Calvin Martin, "The Four Lives of a Micmac Copper Pot," *Ethnohistory* 22, 2 (1975): 111–33; and Laurier Turgeon, "The Tale of the Kettle: Odyssey of an Intercultural Object," *Ethnohistory* 44, 1 (1997): 1–29.

39. William Strachey, "The historie of trauaile into Virginia Britania (1607)," pp. 397–415 in *The English New England Voyages, 1602–1608,* ed., David B. Quinn and Alison M. Quinn (London: The Hakluyt Society, 1983), 411.

40. John Smith, "A Description of New England" [1616], *Collections of the Massachusetts Historical Society,* 3rd ser., 5 (1836): 117, 130–31.

41. Harry Andrew Wright, ed., *Indian Deeds of Hampden County* (Springfield, MA: [n.p.], 1905), 11–12, 46–47.

42. Thomas, 321.

43. Carl Bridenbaugh and Juliette Tomlinson, eds., *The Pynchon Papers,* Vol. 2, *Selections from the Account Book of John Pynchon, 1651–1697* (Boston: The Colonial Society of Massachusetts, 1985), 129.

44. See Jean M. O'Brien, *Dispossession by Degrees: Indian Land and Identity in Natick, Massachusetts, 1650–1790* (Cambridge: Cambridge University Press, 1997), 171–81.

45. William Cronon, *Changes in the Land: Indians, Colonists, and the Ecology of New England* (New York: Hill and Wang, 1983), 122–26.

2

DAILY LIFE IN THE IROQUOIS CONFEDERACY

West of the Hudson River, the longhouses and cornfields of the Iroquois Confederacy spread out across the region encompassed by present-day New York State. The Iroquois continue to live in New York State today, with additional communities in Quebec and Ontario. They call themselves the *Haudenosaunee,* or People of the Longhouse. From a Haudenosaunee perspective, the geopolitical border between the United States and Canada is a recent invention.

Like the Algonkian peoples of New England, the Iroquois live in the Eastern Woodlands culture area. Thus, they share certain cultural characteristics, including similar seasonal subsistence patterns, the use of moccasins and snowshoes, and the belief that they live in an animate world. Where Algonkian peoples talked about *manitou,* or Spirit, the Iroquois speak of *orenda.* However, there are important differences in their history and culture. First, the Iroquois did not experience the same degree of mortality during the early contact period as the Algonkians who lived along the Atlantic coast. Being further inland, they had time to watch how the English, Dutch, and French newcomers treated Native peoples to the east. Second, the Iroquois organized both their domestic and political life around a strict matrilineal clan system in which lineage is traced through the mother instead of through the father, as in European society. Third, the flexible structure of the Iroquois Confederacy enabled the Iroquois to identify and respond to challenges on multiple levels: as individuals, as families, as clans, as villages, as nations, and as a unified confederation of nations. This unity made the Iroquois desirable as allies and fearsome as enemies.

There were five member nations in the Confederacy during the early contact period. From east to west they are the Mohawks, the Oneidas, the Onondagas, the Cayugas, and the Senecas. During the early eighteenth century they were joined by a sixth nation, the Tuscaroras, who migrated north from North Carolina during a period of turmoil and change. This is why the terms "Five Nations" and "Six Nations" appear in the literature. They refer to the Iroquois Confederacy at different moments in its history.

Books about the Iroquois often focus on their military strength, but the Haudenosaunee see their greatest strength as spiritual. This strength comes from their culture. The Haudenosaunee share a common view of how they are supposed to relate to each other and the world around them, as laid out in their creation story. They share a common ritual known as the Condolence, which is the legacy of a great leader known as Deganawidah, or the Peacemaker, who articulated the spiritual and political foundation of the Iroquois Confederacy. They also share a highly structured system of matrilineal family clans. These core systems were in place long before 1600, and they continue to this day.

IN THE BEGINNING

Haudenosaunee stories about the creation of the world as we know it do not begin with a void, as in Genesis, or a world made from nothing by an omniscient God. This is characteristic of indigenous beliefs across North America. While each culture group has their own story about creation, the stories generally begin with people and a world already in existence, somewhere other than here, although the people may not be human-beings-just-like-us. This has an immediate if subtle effect on the texture of daily life because there is no concept of human existence on Earth that takes place in a defined period of time, with a clear beginning and ending. The popular (but incorrect) idea that Native peoples have no concept of linear time stems from this difference. Through the passage of daily life, they understood that one day follows the next in a linear order. However, their concept of vast scales of time tended to be circular, or conceived of as timeless, rather than linear. This seemed strange to the European Christians who came with specific ideas about a world that began with Genesis and would end with Revelation.

The story of Sky Woman and how the world was created on the back of a turtle has been passed down from time immemorial through oral tradition. As with most sacred stories, this story was told in a ritual context that kept it relatively unchanged from one generation to the next. Oral tradition is not like a game of "telephone," where one person repeats something to another and after several tellings it is changed almost beyond recognition. When important stories are told in a formal, public setting, storytellers must be sure to get all of the key elements right or the listeners will complain, because they also know the story. On the other hand, oral tradition is not the same as a printed text. The person telling the story has some flexibility to consider the nature of the occasion, who is in the audience, or how to keep the story fresh. Over time, distinctive variations appeared in different communities, and even within particular clans. This is why there are slightly different versions of the Iroquois creation story in print. The story told here is drawn from several printed versions but mainly from the story told by John Buck (Onondaga) to the Tuscarora scholar and ethnologist J.N.B. Hewitt in 1899.[1]

Above the visible sky is a place called Sky World that is like and yet unlike the world we know. In this world there grew a marvelous tree that grew fruit to feed the people of Sky World and blossoms that filled the air with a fragrance not unlike our tobacco. The tree stood near the village of a great chief known as He-Holds-the-Earth. Far from this place there lived a young girl with her mother. Her father had died, although death was a rare occurrence in Sky World, but he continued to talk to his daughter and watch over her. One day the father told his daughter that she must go to the village of He-Holds-the-Earth. He instructed her not to speak with anyone until she arrived at the village, when she should tell He-Holds-the-Earth that she would be his bride. Her mother made her corn bread for the journey, and the young girl set off.

After several adventures, she arrived at the village of He-Holds-the-Earth. On hearing her announcement, he gave her several tasks to perform, such as making mush from a string of white corn. She succeeded. He accepted the corn bread she had brought and agreed to marry her. She stayed with him for two nights. During this time they slept apart from each other, with only the soles of their feet touching. On the third day he gave her a basket of dried meat to take home to her family as his gift. He also instructed her to tell her people to take the roofs off of their homes. When she arrived home, everyone followed this instruction. That night, it rained corn into their lodges.

Soon after, the young girl returned to the village of He-Holds-the-Earth to live as his wife. However, she became pregnant even before they were married, just from his breath. He-Holds-the-Earth did not believe her. He became jealous, and then ill. One day he had a powerful dream. He called everyone together and asked them to guess what it was. All of the people tried to guess, including Deer, Spotted Fawn, Bear, Beaver, Wind, Daylight, Night, Star, Spring Water, Corn, Bean, Squash, Sunflower, Red Meteor, Turtle, Otter, Wolf, and Duck. Finally Aurora Borealis, the fire dragon, guessed his dream.

In the dream, He-Holds-the-Earth saw that the great tree must be pulled up by the roots for him to get well. This was done, and the people laid him down near the hole. Some say that Sky Woman looked down through the hole and lost her balance. Others say that her husband pushed her. Some say that she grabbed seeds and plants in her hand as she tried to stop herself from falling. Others say that she was given supplies to carry with her, including corn, dried meat, a mortar and pestle, a small pot, a bone, and some wood. In any event, she fell. The chief, her husband, regained his health and replanted the great tree.

The woman, who is now known as Sky Woman, fell for a long time. She fell through darkness, with only water below her. As she fell, the creatures who lived down below saw her coming. They gathered together and held a council in which they agreed that they would try to help. The Loons flew up and caught her gently in their wings to break her fall. They set her down on the back of a Turtle. The others dove deep into the water in an effort to bring up dirt from the bottom. Many died in the attempt. Finally Muskrat dove deeper than anyone else and brought up a handful of mud that they placed on Turtle's back. This was the beginning of the world as we know it. This is why the Haudenosaunee call this world Turtle Island, or the World on the Turtle's Back.

Soon after this, Sky Woman gave birth to a daughter who grew faster than people grow today. One day Sky Woman noticed that her daughter was pregnant with twins. Their father was the West Wind. The twins argued even inside their mother's womb. One child wanted to be born in the normal way. The other was in a hurry and burst out through his mother's armpit, which killed her. Sky Woman buried her daughter and raised the twin boys. The grave soon became covered with good plants: corn, beans, squash, tobacco, and wild potatoes. These became the principal food of the people who came after. Some say the plants grew from the body of Sky Woman's daughter. Others say that they were gifts from the West Wind to his sons.

Together, the twins shaped the world we know today. In English, their names are often given as "Good Twin" and "Evil Twin," but good and evil as opposing forces are an unfamiliar concept to Haudenosaunee culture. Haudenosaunee people know the one born in the usual way as *Tharonhiawagon*, which means "Upholder of Heaven" or "Sky Grasper." He is also known as the right-handed twin, and by the name of Sapling. *Tawiskaron* is the one who burst from his mother's side. He is also known as Flint, the left-handed twin, and sometimes as Old Warty, in contrast to the smooth sapling Tharonhiawagon. Like the right and the left hand, or like night and day, each provided a balance to the other. For example, Tharonhiawagon made rivers that ran in two directions and were very straight. Tawiskaron put in rocks, twists, and a one-way flow. Tharonhiawagon made the animals give themselves to human beings as food. Tawiskaron locked most of them up and made others who were dangerous to human beings. The world has everything we need to live, but we must work for it and pay attention to the world around us.

Tharonhiawagon is the one who created human beings out of clay. He shaped them, both men and women, and set them down to dry. Some versions of this story say that he baked them. Some were cooked too little; these became the white man. Some were cooked too much; these became the black man. Others were just right, and these became the Haudenosaunee. In any case, he spoke to them, and at his word, they lived. Tharonhiawagon divided the people into three clans: Wolf, Bear, and Turtle. He taught them how to grow corn, to hunt and fish, and to perform ceremonies. He taught them to burn tobacco, because the smoke is pleasing to the people of Sky World. He also taught them how to live as a people, treating each other with respect.

The brothers struggled against each other through many adventures too long to record here. Sometimes they competed through games, such as gambling with fruit pits and playing lacrosse. At other times they simply fought, each trying to overcome the other through skill, strength, and cunning. In the end, Tharonhiawagon won. Tawiskaron died, but he didn't die, like Sky Woman's father so long before. Tharonhiawagon buried his brother in a cave where his spirit lives to this day, surrounded by other beings that could do great harm if they were set free, such as the poison beaver, the poison otter, and snakes. Tawiskaron's voice can still be heard in the world.

When Tharonhiawagon came home without his brother, Sky Woman flew into a rage. She loved both of her grandsons. Sky Woman threw Tharonhiawagon's belongings out of their home and berated him for killing his brother. Tharonhiawagon became angry in turn and claimed that she had always favored Tawiskaron over him. In his anger, Tharonhiawagon grabbed Sky Woman and cut off her head and threw it into the sky. We can see it there at night, in the face of the moon. Eventually Tharonhiawagon left the earth and journeyed to Sky World, following the path we know as the Milky Way. He lives there still.

DAILY LIFE IN THE EARLY CONTACT PERIOD

One important difference between Haudenosaunee and Euro-American society is how human beings understood their relationship to the world around them, including plants, animals, and the land itself. In Genesis 3:26, God gives man "dominion over the fish of the sea, and over the fowl of the air, and over the cattle, and over all the earth, and over every creeping thing that creepeth upon the earth." In the Iroquois story of creation, human beings are not the point of creation. They are created by Tharonhiawagon to live on Turtle Island but given instructions on how to coexist with others. They live surrounded by other beings who are not gods to be worshipped, in the European sense, but rather powerful animate beings who have lives and purposes of their own. This includes the inhabitants of Sky World but also animals, trees, and even rocks, who must all be treated with respect. The world is a balance between opposing forces, but neither force is all good or all bad. Life is supposed to be good but not too easy.

As the story of Sky Woman and her family suggests, family and gender roles among the Haudenosaunee did not follow the pattern of European society in the early contact period. Sky Woman was a strong and capable woman. She journeyed alone to find a husband and won him by successfully performing certain tasks. This is quite the opposite of European stories where the prince must win the princess. Indeed, Sky Woman makes many journeys, back and forth to her home village, and later down to the world below. While He-Holds-the Earth is given credit for having a spirit so powerful that Sky Woman became pregnant without intercourse, one could also read this story as one that emphasizes women's power to create life over the man's role as progenitor. It makes sense, then, that the Haudenosaunee traced their lines of descent through the female line.

Matrilineal Clans   The basic unit of Haudenosaunee society was the clan. A clan is a group of people who are related by virtue of their descent from a single person, or clan ancestor. Children always belonged to their mother's clan. Because people in the same clan were related, they could not marry each other. Husbands went to live in the longhouse of their wife's family, although they still belonged to the clan into which they had been born and continued to play a role there. One consequence of this matrilineal system was that fathers and uncles had very different positions in Iroquois and Euro-American families. Among the Iroquois, maternal uncles, that is, the mother's brothers, played a more influential role in a child's life than the biological father. The key decision makers in the clan were women.[2]

Three clans are represented in all of the Five Nations: Turtle, Wolf, and Bear clans. Note that these are the three original clans created by Tharonhiawagon The two easternmost Haudenosaunee nations (Mohawk and Oneida) have only these three clans. The other nations (Onondaga, Cayuga, and Seneca) have additional clans, including Snipe, Heron, Beaver, Deer, Eel, and Stone. It is said that the Stone Clan originated from English captives taken in war who were adopted into Haudenosaunee families. Since they were born to another people, they did not have clans. The Stone Clan became the clan of these adopted Haudenosaunee.

Each of the Five Nations had more than one village. Each village had one or more longhouses for each clan. When travelers came to a strange village, they looked for a longhouse with their clan symbol over the door. Mohawks traveling far from home could arrive hungry, tired, and thirsty, and be assured of a welcome by other members of their clan, even though these relatives might be Seneca, Cayuga, Onondaga, or Oneida. In a world where people depended on each other to survive, kin ties were better than gold.

The interlocking system of family, household, clan, village, nation, and confederacy made the Haudenosaunee people strong. They could call on others for support in times of trouble, whether trouble came in the form of famine or war. They could function independently when things were going well, or when circumstances made it necessary for people to go their own way in order to survive. Yet their identity as Haudenosaunee, or people of the longhouse, allowed them to embrace diversity while living under one roof, metaphorically speaking. We see this especially in the period after Europeans arrived, when the Haudenosaunee were forced to make choices between, first, the Dutch, the French, and the British; then, during the American Revolution, between the British and Americans, and later, during the War of 1812, between the United States and Canada. Haudenosaunee people today live on both sides of the U.S./Canadian border, yet they continue to see themselves as sovereign nations united by their common concerns as members of the Iroquois Confederacy.

The Longhouse

The longhouse was both an actual dwelling and a metaphor for the Iroquois Confederacy. The average longhouse was about 25 feet wide. The length depended on the number of families living there. Each longhouse had three to five fire pits. The fires were aligned down the center axis of the longhouse, with one family unit on either side. These family units might be nuclear families, that is, a married couple and their young children, with an average of five or six people per family unit. The living space might also be occupied by an older couple, with their grown children and grandchildren living in other fire spaces.[3]

People slept on raised platforms around the edges of the longhouse, with their feet to the fire. These platforms were covered with woven mats and soft pelts. For a pillow, people placed a block of wood, a stone, or a bundle of personal belongings under their heads.

The longhouse is an apt metaphor for the political organization of the Iroquois Confederacy. The original Five Iroquois Nations imagined itself as a longhouse or family stretching across the area of present-day New York State. Each nation had its own fire. The Seneca were the keepers of the western door of the longhouse. The Mohawk were the keepers of the eastern door, and the Onondaga played a key role as the keepers of the central fire. Iroquois people regularly met at Onondaga for important Confederacy business.

The typical early contact period village contained 30 to 150 longhouses, surrounded by a wooden palisade. Villages were always built near good sources of drinking water. Iroquois cornfields could support a village settlement of up to 1,500 people.

Subsistence

The Iroquois were horticulturalists. They used the technique known as slash-and-burn agriculture to lay out vast fields next to their villages. They did not aim for the perfectly clear fields created by Europeans, with their plows and draft animals. Rather, they used controlled burning to clear the land of trees and brush, then planted their crops between the stumps.

Women were the farmers, planting and tending the staple crops of corn, beans, and squash. Overall, villages and cornfields were women's domain. Their labor provided food, and they were the ones who controlled its distribution. Corn could be eaten fresh, or dried and stored for the winter months. When there was a surplus, and there often was, it could be traded with those who lived further north.

Men's domain lay outside the village, in the woods where they fished or hunted and in the paths that they traveled for war, trade, or diplomacy. In the early contact period, hunters could find deer, bears, and other animals within a day's journey of their villages. Over time, as certain places were overhunted and others became inhospitable to game animals due to either European settlement or the ecological changes wrought by clearing land, Iroquois hunters had to go farther and farther away. They hunted south into Pennsylvania, north into the Champlain and St. Lawrence valleys, and into Ontario. Some people speculate that men enjoyed hunting and warfare in part because it took them out of the village and into their own domain.

Men hunted with bows and arrows and, once the fur trade began, with guns. They also used snares and dead-fall traps for deer, small mammals, and birds such as the partridge and turkey, as well as migratory birds such as geese, ducks, and passenger pigeons.

After the harvest, hunting parties left the village for an extended period. Both men and women went out. Children and old people stayed behind. As with the Algonkians described in Chapter 1, men and women performed different tasks. Women minded the camp while the men went out hunting. They butchered and dried the meat, and prepared meals in camp.

The seasonal cycle of Iroquois life was divided into 13 moons, or months. Both subsistence activities and ceremonial life followed the seasonal cycle. The cold months of January and February could be a hungry time for those who had not managed to lay in a good supply of food. Even those who had stored plenty of food, however, were glad when the time came to leave the village and head out into the maple groves where everyone helped to collect maple sap from the trees. The sap could be boiled to make maple syrup, a nice sweetening for otherwise bland dishes such as cornmeal mush, and boiled some more to make sugar.

In spring came the passenger pigeons, millions of them, so many that they could be caught with nets. Everyone moved to the fishing places when the fish began to spawn. The men built weirs out of stone that directed the fish into places where they could easily be speared or herded into basket traps. The women worked at processing the fish but also used this time to gather spring greens and other plants. Then, when the white oak leaves had grown to the size of a squirrel's foot, it was time to move back to the village and plant corn. Men helped with the heavy work of clearing the fields, but the rest of the work belonged to the women, who prepared and planted the corn.

June brought the berry moon. Berries were an important part of the Iroquois diet. Strawberries, the first fruit to ripen, were especially important. Blueberries, blackberries, huckleberries, and raspberries each had their season. People enjoyed them fresh, but berries were also dried by spreading them on bark trays that were left out in the sun. These could be carried on long journeys and eaten plain, or baked into bread throughout the winter. This is also the time when it is easy to peel bark off of trees. Men used this season to build or repair houses and stockades, to make elm bark into utensils, and to build canoes.

The corn ripened by late summer. After the harvest, the Iroquois held husking bees, working together to husk the ears of corn and prepare them for winter storage in corn barns, which were large holes dug in the ground, lined and covered over to keep the corn dry and safe.

The Haudenosaunee people also harvested tobacco, which apparently grew with little or no effort on their part. The leaves were gathered and strung up to dry. Tobacco was smoked for both ceremonial and social purposes. The Haudenosaunee remembered that its aroma was pleasing to the people of Sky World.

When the leaves began to turn red, families separated from their villages and communal longhouses and went into the woods to hunt deer. Some men continued to hunt until the snows were deep on the ground, returning when they saw that the Pleiades reached the zenith of their journey across the sky at dusk.

There were no set times for meals. People ate when they were hungry, and travelers were fed on arrival. There was a strong communal ethic about sharing food.

While cornfields supported village life, intensive cultivation took its toll on the land. About twice in each generation, the Iroquois moved their villages to places with fresh soil and a new supply of local firewood. These changes were gradual rather than abrupt. A "New Town" sprung up as the "Old Town" started to decline, with residents moving from one place to the other. This causes some confusion in the historical record, at least, for non-Iroquoian people. When a village, such as Kahnawake, moved, was it the same village or not, if the people who lived there stayed more or less the same?

Although the European colonist thought of trees primarily as a source of heat and building supplies for houses and **Material Life** ships, the Iroquois, like other Eastern Woodland peoples, brought wood technology to a high art. They used the bark of elm trees much as people to the east used birch-bark: to cover their longhouses and canoes, and to make vessels for cooking and storage. They traded with the Hurons to the north for basswood and slippery elm. The Iroquois made rope from the outer bark of the basswood and the inner bark, or bast, of the slippery elm. They knew how to bend and shape wood to make curved longhouse frames, snowshoes, toboggans, basket rims and handles, and lacrosse sticks.

Women processed fibers from nettles, milkweed, and Indian hemp to make tough cords that were then braided into burden straps, prisoner ties, and rope. A burden strap passed across the forehead and attached to a heavy pack-basket or other load that was carried on a person's back. The strap helped to distribute the weight, easing the strain on the shoulders. Women wove baskets but the materials they used, primarily ash and maple splints, were prepared by men. Iroquois women also used corn husks to make slippers that were cool and lightweight for summer.

Like their Algonkian neighbors, the Haudenosaunee wore clothing made from tanned hides, primarily deerskin, and warm furs for cold weather. They wore leather moccasins decorated with porcupine quills and painted designs. Both men and women adorned themselves with tattoos so that anthropologist William Fenton characterizes the Mohawks in particular as "walking galleries of the tattooist's art."[4] Tattoos ranging from geometric designs to clan symbols were created by pricking the design onto the skin with a sharp bone tool, then rubbing it with charcoal. Both men and women wore earrings, necklaces, and other ornaments made from shells, copper, bone, and carved stone.

Religion and Ceremonial Life Many elements of Haudenosaunee religious and ceremonial life have their origins in the story of Sky Woman and the creation of the world on Turtle's back. These rituals form the core of daily life in the early contact period and for later generations. Most involve long speeches and recitations of oral tradition, along with plenty of food, dancing, and fun.

Seasonal Festivals

The Iroquois ceremonial calendar followed the seasonal pattern of subsistence. The year was divided into lunar months, with four seasons. The high point of the ceremonial cycle was the great midwinter festival, at the winter solstice in late December, the shortest day of the year. This festival took place when the men returned from their fall hunting with loads of smoked and dried meat, on the first new moon after their return. This was a time of great spiritual importance. The Iroquois believed that dreams carried important messages from the spirit world, as in the creation story when He-Holds-the-Earth became ill and asked the people of Sky World to guess his dream, so that it might be fulfilled and he might get well. The midwinter festival was the time when people shared new dreams and fulfilled the ceremonial obligations they had undertaken during the previous year. They also cleaned their homes and visited their neighbors.

The green corn festival was held in late summer, when the corn, beans, and squash ripened. Women celebrated their communal labor in the fields and gave thanks for a good crop. The strawberry festival in mid-June celebrated the first berries to ripen. To ensure a good harvest, men performed a thunder ritual to ask the sun to refrain from scorching the earth, and to bring the thunder with its nurturing rain. Men danced the war dance in honor of the sun, considered the patron of war and addressed with terms of great respect as their elder brother. They also played the hoop and pole game, using the poles like spears to catch the rolling sun.

Medicine and Healing

The Iroquois believed that physical illness could be caused by a variety of factors. Healers were skilled in binding wounds, setting broken bones, and using herbs to treat coughs, fevers, and other common complaints. When sickness was caused by supernatural means, other remedies were required. Ritual healers used techniques that included singing and drumming, to counteract bad spirits, and blowing or sucking to remove the cause of the illness. Sometimes a cure required help from one of the medicine societies. Medicine societies often specialized in particular ceremonies or cures, so there might be more than one in each village. Some rituals required that the healers wear masks, or false faces, to enhance their power and invoke particular spirits. In the early contact period, Europeans called these healers conjurers, or jugglers.[5] These terms imply that the healers were at best tricking their patients, if not dealing with the devil himself. Today the popular term is *shaman,* but this generic term does not convey the specificity of each healer's abilities.

Lacrosse

All human societies have games and other forms of amusement. Lacrosse is one of the games played by the twins, Tharonhiawagon and Tawiskaron, in the creation story. The presence of the game in the creation story is a clue to its importance as a ritual practice. The basics of the game are simple. Players use special sticks shaped at one end with a shallow cup or net to hold the ball. They may not touch the ball with their hands. There is an art to keeping the stick in motion so that the ball will not fall out when the player is running with it. Players score points by hurling or carrying the ball past the opponent's goal. In the old days, the goals were said to be three miles apart. Young men might play lacrosse as a form of training for battle, or it might substitute for the battle itself. The best players were those who had strong minds and spirits as well as strong bodies. The game allowed both players and spectators considerable enjoyment as well as an opportunity to release powerful emotions, including aggression, that otherwise might be expressed in more disruptive ways.

In the particular ritual known as the mourning war, Haudenosaunee men, often at the urging of female relatives, conducted raids on enemy tribes for the express purpose of taking captives. Some of these captives were tortured and even killed as a way of purging grief for a deceased family member.

Mourning Wars

Others were adopted through a ritual of resuscitation or requickening, in which the deceased was brought back to life in the person of the adoptee. Long before Europeans arrived on the scene, the Iroquois practiced mourning wars against each other. From oral tradition, they remember this as a time of great inhumanity and destruction. The story of how this dark period came to an end is told in a series of linked traditions that describe the origins of the Condolence Ceremony and the Great Law of Peace, and how these principals became the basis of the Iroquois Confederacy. Ironically, the Iroquoian mourning war complex spun out of control once again in the seventeenth century as mortality rates from epidemic disease, warfare, and war-related famine brought death and destruction to Haudenosaunee communities, creating a harsh cycle of raid, retaliation, and more grief to assuage.[6] As will be discussed in Chapter 3, the Haudenosaunee continued to value peace among themselves, but turned their aggressions outward.

THE IROQUOIS CONFEDERACY

The Iroquois Confederacy, sometimes also called the League of the Iroquois, dates back to at least the mid-fifteenth century, even before Columbus began his search for a passage to China. This was a time when warfare was a way of life. The Haudenosaunee attacked not only their distant enemies, such as the Mahicans who lived along the Hudson River and the Mi'kmaq far to the east, but each other. This way of life could not be sustained, but it was hard to imagine another way of life.

Origins   Among the Onondaga, a man named Tadodaho came to be feared as an unusually cruel and ruthless chief. His evil, twisted nature was so strong that it even afflicted his body. His face was contorted, and he had snakes in his hair. Some people believed that Tadodaho had fearsome powers, because bad things happened to his enemies, worse than dying in battle. There were rumors that he might even be a cannibal, eating the flesh of those who opposed him. Under his ruthless leadership, the land and its people were in despair.

Only one person had the courage to oppose Tadodaho. His name was Hiawatha. He sent messages to other villages and invited all the Onondaga people to come to a great council of peace and friendship. His work was interrupted, however, by a terrible personal tragedy: his daughters died in an untimely fashion. Some people say that they were killed by Hiawatha's enemies, people who wanted his peace efforts to fail. Others say that they died from disease, or supernatural means. In any event, Hiawatha was overwhelmed with grief. He left the village and entered the forest. He traveled far, with grief clouding his mind. The Iroquois say that his mind became crooked with grief.

The Condolence   One day an idea penetrated the depths of Hiawatha's despair. He envisioned a ritual of condolence that would help his mind to become straight. He understood that people in extreme grief cannot heal themselves, so the ritual needed another person. The ritual involved strings of beads. At first, he strung short pieces of rush together, because that was all he had. Later he replaced the pieces of rush with shell beads, which became known as wampum. Hiawatha spoke to himself, saying,

This would I do if I found anyone burdened with grief even as I am. I would take these shell strings in my hand and console them. The strings would become words and lift away the darkness with which they are covered. Holding these in my hand, my words would be true.[7]

This is the origin of the Condolence, a ritual performed to this day in Iroquois communities. The ritual may be used for personal comfort, but it is also used in a larger context to straighten crooked minds, minds that have been distorted by grief, hatred, or other strong emotions. The Condolence was a required part of diplomatic negotiations and the installation of a new chief.

Renewed by this insight, but still not healed, Hiawatha turned his steps to the east and soon came to a Mohawk village. In this village, there lived a man named Deganawidah, who had come from the Huron country to the north. Deganawidah was also a man of peace; in fact, he is also known in Iroquois tradition as the Peacemaker. He welcomed Hiawatha. He understood the depths of his grief and heard Hiawatha's mournful plea. Deganawidah took up the three strings of beads brought by Hiawatha and spoke the words of the Condolence.

With the first string, he said: "When a person has suffered a great loss, the tears blind his eyes and he cannot see. With these words, I wipe away the tears so that you may see clearly." With the second string, he said: "When a person has suffered a great loss, grief clogs his ears so that he cannot hear. With these words, I remove the obstruction from your ears so that you may hear clearly." With the third string, he said: "When a person has suffered a great loss, grief fills his throat so that he cannot speak, and the sounds that he makes do not make sense. With these words, I clear your throat so that you may speak clearly."

Over time the Condolence developed more elaborate forms, and the ritual may include as many as 15 strings of wampum. However, these are the "three words" that form the heart of the ritual. Grief makes a person's mind crooked; it inhibits their ability to function. The Condolence acknowledges the power of grief and frees people to go back to living a straight life. It enabled Hiawatha and Deganawidah to join together in creating the Iroquois Confederacy.

Deganawidah, the Peacemaker, had a vision of peace that would end the constant state of warfare among the **The Great Law** Iroquoian peoples. Iroquoians believed that grief could only be resolved by vengeance. In the tradition known as the mourning war, Iroquoian warriors sought revenge when any of their people were killed in war. Moreover, people viewed warfare as a balm for the grief that came from any death, as from disease, accidents, or old age. Women urged their young men to go to war whenever death came to their villages. Violence begat violence, and it seemed impossible to end the cycle of retribution. Deganawidah believed it was possible. He left his own country because the people who had known him from childhood thought he was just strange. A prophet is never honored in his own land.

The first people to accept Deganawidah and his vision were the Mohawks. They liked the idea of peace, but achieving it would be difficult. Hiawatha's arrival and the message of the Condolence offered them hope. If people could ease their grief though the Condolence, they would not need to keep making war.

Structure and Function of the League

As Deganawidah's message spread to the other nations, other people accepted the Great Peace. This is the basis for the political organization known as the League of the Iroquois or the Iroquois Confederacy. The structure of the confederacy gave each village, and each of the five original nations, a high degree of autonomy for day-to-day life. In times of stress or danger, however, they came together to make decisions and to present a united front. The Confederacy was a decision-making body, not a government in the Euro-American sense.

Confederacy decisions were made in council by 50 chiefs from all of its member nations. Each of these 50 offices is named for the first man who held it. If the United States followed this practice, we would have "George Washingtons" rather than "Presidents," and each congressperson would run for office to win the honor of bearing the name of their political forebear. In the Iroquois Confederacy, the 50 chiefs were chosen or named by the clan mothers in their home community. This system is less arbitrary than it sounds. Who knows the men of a community better than the older women who have watched them grow up, who know what kind of men their fathers and grandfathers were?

Clan Mothers, Not Matriarchs

Haudenosaunee women are frequently touted as exemplars of female power, clan mothers who ruled in a matriarchal society. The problem with the word *matriarchy* is that it evokes an image of women dominating men, the mirror-image of extreme patriarchy, although patriarchy itself has many different forms. The consensus in the literature is that, although women display considerable amounts of political power in some cultures, a matriarchal society, in which women as a group hold power over men in the way that men as a group hold power over women in patriarchal societies, has never existed.[8] Iroquoian women had and continue to have considerable power, serving as faithkeepers or religious leaders and expressing their opinions in the political realm. Clan membership, the key organizational principal of Iroquois life, was determined by matrilineal descent, that is, children belonged to their mother's clan. The Iroquois were also matrilocal. Men went to live with the wife's family after marriage, so that women had the security of living among their own kin. But women did not serve as chiefs in league councils.

The reputation for political power among Iroquoian women comes from the fact that clan mothers had the authority to bestow on individual men the names associated with chiefly offices. In effect, women chose the chiefs. Women also had the power to take back the name, thereby deposing them. But clan mothers did not have the authority to tell these men what to do while they held office. In fact, although men were appointed by the clan, chiefs were expected to make decisions for the good of all the people rather than strictly in the interests of their own clan.[9]

Keeping a Clear Mind

In keeping with the traditional value of balance, exemplified in the creation story by the existence of twins who embodied very different values and actions, the Confederacy is divided into two parts, or moieties. The Elder Brothers are the Mohawk, the Onondaga, and the Seneca. The Younger Brothers are the Oneida and Cayuga. When any of the 50 chiefs died, the Confederacy came together for an extended ceremony of Requickening and Condolence to restore balance, spirit structure, and the structure of the Grand Council. The "clear-minded" moiety, that is, the ones who had not experienced the loss, condoled the other by formal recitations of the Deganawidah epic and the words of condolence. This ritual had to take place before a new chief could be installed. This ensured that the Grand Council and all its members could do their jobs with a clear mind.

The Condolence also became an intrinsic part of diplomatic rituals. Again, the goal is to make sure that all participants have a clear mind, unclouded by grief or other negative emotions, before they begin. Diplomatic councils and negotiations also included feasting, an exchange of gifts, the recitation of grievances or concerns, and time for people to think before responding. These rituals were so important to the Iroquois that Europeans quickly learned to respect and participate in them; otherwise nothing got done.

Warfare continued to be a major aspect of men's work for centuries after the founding of the Iroquois **War and Peace** Confederacy. This seems like a contradiction; therefore it needs to be considered more carefully. Like all human societies, the Iroquois developed ideologies that shaped, guided, and justified their actions. Thanks to the Great Law of Peace, the Iroquois stopped fighting among themselves and ended the bitter cycle of mourning wars by invoking the Condolence and paying restitution whenever people wronged each other. However, it did not exclude Iroquois conflicts with other tribes, people who had not accepted the Great Law. Through the mid-eighteenth century, Iroquois warriors traveled far from home to extend the influence of the Confederacy, by force or by diplomacy. From a psychological point of view, external wars gave the Iroquois an outlet for aggressions that were frowned upon inside the community. War had other benefits within this cultural system. Young men gained respect and prestige by demonstrating their bravery and skill in war. They played an important role by bringing back captives who might be adopted to replace deceased relatives or tortured to purge grief and increase the spirit power of the community.[10]

THE IMPACT OF COLONIZATION ON DAILY LIFE

The Five Nations of the Iroquois Confederacy acquired their first trade goods through intermediaries. Living inland, but accessible by major waterways, the Iroquois initially traded with other indigenous peoples who lived closer to the Atlantic coast where European fishermen and explorers dropped anchor in the early contact period.

Frenchman Jacques Cartier, who traveled down the St. Lawrence River in 1534, met and traded with a group of people known to us as the St. Lawrence Iroquoians, that is, people who spoke an Iroquoian language who lived along the St. Lawrence River. By the time that Samuel de Champlain traveled the same route in the early seventeenth century, these people had disappeared.[11] It seems that they were killed or driven off by diseases and by intertribal war with the Mi'kmaq to the southeast.

Trade and Intertribal War The Mohawks, as the easternmost people of the Confederacy, were the first to enter the fur trade. They traded on their own behalf and acted as middlemen for the other nations. They also made raids to acquire trade goods by force. For the Mohawks, the Adirondack region functioned as a beaver preserve though the mid-seventeenth century, when the beaver population became severely depleted. To keep up with the demands of the fur trade, they traveled further—into other peoples' territories—to trap beaver.[12]

The first documented encounter of the Iroquois with European firearms took place in 1609, at the southern end of Lake Champlain, close to where the Richilieu River began its journey north to the St. Lawrence. Samuel de Champlain, the French explorer for whom the lake was named, accompanied a combined party of Algonquin, Montagnais, and Huron warriors. At a critical moment, Champlain stepped forth with his metal suit of half-armor and a metal helmet, and fired his musket, which erupted with a shockingly loud noise. Two Mohawk chiefs were killed on the spot, and a third received a mortal wound. The Iroquois suffered a bitter defeat, with at least 5 men killed and another 12 taken captive.[13] As Champlain no doubt intended, this display strengthened the friendship and trade relations between the French and these indigenous allies. Champlain might not have been so pleased if he could have forseen the generations of warfare between the French and the Iroquois that followed his little demonstration.

In the following decades, Algonkian-speaking tribes from the north side of the St. Lawrence explored the possibility of peace with the Iroquois. The French did their best to disrupt the negotiations because they wanted the Algonquins, Montagnais, and Attikamekw to continue bringing their furs to French trading posts. If they made peace with the Iroquois, these furs might wind up in the hands of Dutch or English merchants. Indeed, Native traders preferred English trade cloth, especially the heavy woolen strouds, over French cloth. French traders had to resort to an underground trade with the merchants in New England or piracy to acquire the items demanded by their customers.

Further west but still on the north side of the St. Lawrence River, the Algonquins and the Attikamekw (Têtes-de-Boule) faced a more difficult situation. The most direct route to Montreal, the nearest French establishment, required trading parties to reach Montreal from the west. They had to portage around the dangerous stretch of the St. Lawrence River that came to be known as the Lachine Rapids, an ironic name given by the French who, on viewing them for the first time, realized that the St. Lawrence would not, after all, provide easy access to China (La Chine). The final miles to Montreal were the most dangerous because fur-laden

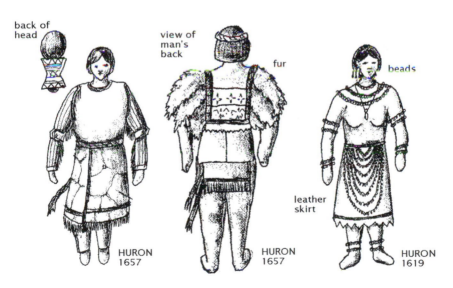

Wendat (Huron) clothing styles, mid-seventeenth century. Reflecting the colder climate to the north, the Huron wore heavier clothing made from deer and caribou hides, sometimes trimmed with fur. Glass beads became popular for jewelry and in embroidered trim. From Tara Prindle/nativetech.org.

canoes were frequently attacked by the Iroquois, especially the Mohawks and the Onondaga, who could take their booty and sell it either in Montreal or Albany.

The Wendat, the most powerful group living on the north side of the St. Lawrence and the people who posed the greatest challenge to Iroquois control of the fur trade, were, ironically, also Iroquoian, that is, people who spoke a related language and who shared a matrilineal clan-based way of organizing both politics and family life. The Wendat were given the nickname of Huron by the French because some of their men wore a distinctive headpiece that, to French eyes, looked like the tufted hair on a boar. In 1600 some 25,000 Wendat people lived in agricultural villages that spread across southwestern Ontario, around Georgian Bay and the lake known today as Lake Huron. Their political confederacy rivaled that of the Iroquois. In addition to what they could access through their own traditional hunting territories, the Wendat competed with the Iroquois for access to furs traded still further inland through the Great Lakes and beyond. The Wendat circumvented Iroquois efforts to control the trade because the Ottawa (Odawa) River provided access from Georgian Bay and points further west and enabled them to reach Montreal despite the best efforts of the Iroquois to prevent them. Unfortunately, this situation contributed to competition between the Iroquois and the Wendat, and the latter were virtually annihilated in a series of wars known as the Beaver Wars that culminated with the destruction of Huronia. Some of the Wendat survivors moved west, and today are known as the Wyandot. Another small group of survivors moved east, closer to their allies and trading partners, the French, establishing themselves near Quebec City.

Wampum in a Wartime Economy

The formation of the Iroquois Confederacy and adoption of the Condolence affected not just the Iroquois but also their neighbors, near and far, including the Wabanaki. Coming out of a crisis in which they had turned their aggressions against each other, the Iroquois worked hard to make peace among themselves. The Condolence was an important part of this effort. Over time, the freshwater shells used by Hiawatha were replaced by wampum, a combination of purple and white beads made from saltwater shells. *Wampum* comes from an eastern Algonkian word, *wampumpeag*. As the use of an imported word suggests, wampum beads were not indigenous to Confederacy territory. Whelk was the most common source for white beads. The purple-to-dark-blue beads that make wampum so distinctive are made from quahog shells. Quahog are only found on Long Island Sound and Narragansett Bay. The production of wampum was largely controlled by Algonkian-speaking peoples such as the Shinnecock on present-day Long Island, the Mohegans and Pequots along the coast of Connecticut, and the powerful Narragansett nation, who established a virtual factory production line for wampum and at different times in the seventeenth century expanded their military reach to receive tribute from other groups in the region.

On one level, the use of a foreign material suggests that the ideology of the Condolence might have been extended to their relations with non-Iroquoian peoples, certainly through trade and potentially through inter-marriage or alliance. Unfortunately, the expansion of the Confederacy and the growing importance of wampum coincided with the early contact period and the introduction of both European goods and European diseases. Wampum became an item of tribute demanded by the Iroquois from other nations, either to ward off a threatened attack or as a token of submission.

Wampum became one of the most valued commodities in the fur trade. Wampum was light, easy to carry, and it was always in demand among the Iroquois and their neighbors. English and Dutch merchants soon began to use wampum in place of cash, which was in short supply in the colonies. Indeed, wampum was recognized as an official form of currency by them for a 30-year period, ending in 1664.

The Native peoples of the middle Connecticut River Valley, including the Sokwaki, Pocumtuck, Nonotuck, Agawam, and others who traded with the English at Springfield in the 1640s and beyond, were not simply trading for red cloth coats or steel knives on their own behalf. They traded with English middlemen for wampum because they needed it to satisfy the Iroquois. Palisaded forts such as the one built by the Sokwakis at Fort Hill (Northfield, Massachusetts), were built for protection against the Mohawks, not the English, and indeed, the fort at Squakheag was destroyed by Mohawks in 1666. Native peoples from this region dispersed, joining other Native communities, as will be seen. It is deeply ironic that wampum, which originated from the need to condole people in mourning, became inextricably linked with decades of warfare.

Changes in Material Life

Over time, the Iroquois incorporated a wide variety of trade goods into their daily lives. Evert Wendell, a Dutch fur trader in Albany, kept a detailed account of his transactions with the Iroquois and other Native peoples from 1695 to 1726. Wendell made a separate page for each person with whom he did business, keeping track of their credits and payments over a period of years. His customers brought in furs to sell and purchased goods that included cloth, steel knives and axes, powder and shot, and ready-made clothing. Women were as likely as men to have accounts in their own name, although people often purchased items for family members. When Wendell was unsure of the name, or perhaps just in case a person changed their name, as sometimes happened to mark an important occasion, he included a vivid description that includes tattoos, hairstyles, missing body parts (some people were missing the tip of their nose, a common punishment), and kin ties. One customer by the name of Peckwanek was identified as "an English savage with red hair." This was probably an English captive who had been adopted by and incorporated into an Iroquois family.[14] One can imagine Native people coming into Wendell's trading post with family members, dropping their loads of fur and looking over the goods.

Archaeological evidence indicates that before 1620 the Five Nations mainly used trade goods as raw material for traditional crafts. Thus, new goods were being used in old ways. For example, brass kettles replaced ceramic pots. Iron axes replaced stone celts. Blankets, especially when made from the heavy woolen cloth known as duffels, or trade cloth, replaced skins. In other cases, trade goods were used in ways that were never intended by their makers. Brass pots were used for cooking, but they were also cut up and made into tools, arrowheads, beads, earrings, and other forms of jewelery. Fishing lures were also used for personal adornment.[15]

The availability of new materials and styles allowed for new forms of cultural expression, most visibly in the area of clothing and adornment. Note that some aspects of Iroquois life, such as the longhouse, were so closely integrated with other aspects of Iroquois social and political structures that they persisted well into the nineteenth century. Glass beads and metal tools such as awls and needles enabled people to embellish clothing in new ways, although women continued to use traditional methods such

Iroquois clothing, eighteenth and nineteenth century. Iroquoian clothing styles exemplify creative adaptation rather than culture loss. Metal cones, trade shirts made from linen or cotton, and silver brooches were combined in distinctively Native ways. From Tara Prindle/nativetech.org.

as porcupine quill embroidery. Another example of change may be seen in the carved hair combs made before and after the introduction of metal tools. Before, combs were made from deer antlers, with three to five thick teeth and decorated with geometric or abstract figures. Combs made in the seventeenth century are similar but more elaborate, with 25 or more thin teeth and intricately carved human or animal figures that sometimes had glass beads for eyes. Similar changes took place with other carved items such as pipes, ladles, and effigies. Metal tools allowed artisans to refine and elaborate their craft.

Metal cones, silver brooches, finger-woven garters and belts, and other trade goods were used for decoration on clothing, and high-status men in particular began to wear the fancy red and blue coats that English traders reserved for their friends. Iroquois men adopted European wear such as worsted stockings and cloaks but never developed a liking for breeches, which they regarded as "an encumbrance." Instead, they sometimes wore linen or cotton shirts and let the flaps hang in the front and back in place of a breechclout.[16] In the more remote parts of Iroquoia, cloth did not become common until the mid-eighteenth century. People who lived closer to European settlements, and especially those who lived in villages that were associated with Catholic or Protestant missions, had greater access to European goods.

Missionaries in Iroquoia

The Iroquois had some exposure to Christianity through their dealings with Dutch, French, and English officials and traders. However, the two biggest influences in the seventeenth century came from people living within their own communities. French Catholic missionaries went alone or in small groups to live in Iroquoian villages, where they produced few initial converts but left a wealth of information about Iroquois language and culture. The second influence came from other Native peoples who were captured in war and adopted into Iroquois communities, notably the Huron-Wendat, who had already converted to Christianity.

The Five Nations Iroquois had little direct experience with Christianity until the 1640s, and missionary efforts did not really increase until the 1660s. Issac Jogues was the first Jesuit missionary to actually live in Iroquoia. He was captured by the Mohawks in 1642 and demonstrated such courage and spiritual strength when tortured that he was adopted by the Wolf Clan at Ossernenon. There he cared for the sick, led people in prayer, and earned a reputation as a shaman, or person of great spirit power. In 1644 he escaped, with help from the Dutch. Jogues returned again in 1646 on a diplomatic mission and left a box of personal items behind to show that he intended to return. Unfortunately, while he was away the Mohawks were struck by a plague of worms that ruined their corn and a terrible sickness that killed many people. Some of the young men claimed that Jogues and the box he left behind were to blame. When he returned late in the year, he was executed, although some people protested.[17]

As part of a truce with New France made in 1653, the Seneca, Onondaga, and Mohawk invited missionaries to come to their communities. This was partly a gesture of goodwill toward the French. However, it was also meant to appease the growing number of Native Christian adoptees in their midst. The French had established missions near Quebec that attracted displaced local Algonquin and Montagnais peoples, who started to convert to Christianity by the 1630s. The Huron-Wendat had made an early alliance with the French, seeking allies against the Five Nations Confederacy, and many converted to Catholicism to demonstrate a new kind of brotherhood with the French and to stablize their own communities in a time of great disruption. The Iroquois launched a massive campaign against Huronia in 1649 that effectively brought an end to this period of Huron-Wendat history. Some of the survivors went west, where they became known as the Wyandot; several hundred others moved east, to the French Catholic mission of Lorette, near Quebec City. Others were adopted into Iroquois communities, where they formed their own Christian factions. In 1656 the French sent over 50 priest and lay brothers, with soldiers for protection, to establish Sainte-Marie de Gannentaha, a mission near Onondaga. Marie de l'Incarnation, the first superior of the Ursuline convent in Quebec, gave more credit to the adopted Native Christians than to the priests when people from the Confederacy started to convert.[18]

In the 1660s, a group of Iroquois went to live on the south shore of the St. Lawrence River, next to the recently established French village of La Prairie. They moved north to find greater stability in an unstable world. While they remained Iroquois, they now became allied to the French, which sometimes put them on opposite sides in battle with their relatives to the south. A group of predominantly Mohawk converts established another village, Kahnawake, in 1676. The Jesuits established the mission of Saint François Xavier du Sault at Kahnawake. By 1701 there were seven Catholic missions established along the St. Lawrence River. While most of these villages came to be associated with one major group, these were always places that attracted refugees from other areas.[19]

Factionalism   Political differences within and between the Iroquois Nations increased through the seventeenth century. In terms of intertribal politics, including matters of trade and war, the structure of the Confederacy allowed for considerable autonomy, and these differences were more or less on a continuum with pre-contact ways of making policy and resolving problems. The presence of Europeans produced new factions that shifted over time. In the early part of the seventeenth century, it seemed advantageous to ally with the Dutch and logical to define the French as enemies, since the French had allied themselves with the Algonquins, Montagnais, and Huron-Wendat enemies of Iroquoia. After New Netherlands became a British possession in 1674, the choices were less clear. The Iroquois hoped for, and made, alliances with colonial officials in New York and in the New England colonies. Distinct anglophile and francophile factions emerged; that is, some people thought it best to maintain a strong alliance with the English while others preferred to ally with New France. These factions also reflected religious differences, as many of the Iroquois allies of the French were Catholics by 1700.

LOOKING FORWARD

By the mid-eighteenth century, the Haudenosaunee had experienced enormous changes in their daily life, yet they remained a strong and independent people. They suffered massive depopulation from epidemic disease. They became increasingly dependent on European trade goods. They were caught in the middle of the imperial rivalry between the Dutch, French, and British, which sometimes worked to their advantage but more often against it. And they experienced a series of major wars that threatened their land and sovereignty. The structured yet flexible system of the Confederacy and the spiritual concepts articulated in the Great Law of Peace gave Haudenosaunee people a unified identity even as they made vastly different choices about where and how to live.

The Haudenosaunee survived thanks to an unusual set of advantages. First, they had a favorable geographic location. Haudenosaunee lands encompassed major trade routes and waterways that gave them access to both European markets and furs from farther inland. Second, their inland location gave them a measure of protection from European expansion and disease. They did not have to deal with the immediate invasion of their lands, as did the Algonkian peoples of New England to the east, where the English population that started from a handful of families in 1620 grew to about 40,000 people by 1645.[20] Third, their position in the middle of competing European powers also gave them a certain amount of room to maneuver, as they played one nation off the other, pursuing their own needs in strategic ways. Fourth, they continued to grow corn and other crops throughout this period, despite the destructiveness of almost constant warfare and the lure of trade. Women's work as horticulturalists gave the Iroquois an independent means of subsistence. Fifth, the cultural practice of adopting outsiders, and especially captives taken in war, allowed Haudenosaunee communities to recover from periods of high mortality. Spiritual and cultural practices made it possible to assimilate strangers so well that their descendants became Haudenosaunee, whatever their origins. This practice contributed to their ability to absorb cultural innovations without losing their identity as Haudenosaunee people. The sixth and related factor is the political structure of the Iroquois Confederacy itself, which endures to this day.

NOTES

1. Carol Cornelius, *Iroquois Corn in a Culture-Based Curriculum: A Framework for Respectfully Teaching About Cultures* (Albany: State University of New York Press, 1999), 79–82; see also Daniel K. Richter, *The Ordeal of the Longhouse: The Peoples of the Iroquois League in the Era of European Colonization* (Chapel Hill: University of North Carolina Press, 1992), 8–11.

2. Barbara Alice Mann, *Iroquoian Women: The Gantowisas* (New York: Peter Lang, 2000), offers a rich description and analysis of Iroquoian women's roles from creation to the present.

3. The following discussion of Iroquois culture and ritual draws mainly on William Fenton, "Northern Iroquoian Culture Patterns," in *Northeast,* ed. Bruce Trigger, 296-321, vol. 15 of the *Handbook of North American Indians,* gen. ed. William C. Sturtevant (Washington, DC: Smithsonian Institution, 1978).

4. Fenton, 303.

5. Barbara Graymont, *The Iroquois* (New York: Chelsea House, 1988), 40–41.

6. Richter, 30–74.

7. Paul A.W. Wallace, *The White Roots of Peace* (Philadelphia: University of Pennsylvania Press, 1946), 21.

8. Eleanor Burke Leacock, "Introduction" to Frederick Engels, *The Origin of the Family, Private Property and the State in Light of the Researches of Lewis H. Morgan* (New York: International Publishers, 1972), 35.

9. Elisabeth Tooker, "Women in Iroquois Society," in *Extending the Rafters: Interdisciplinary Approaches to Iroquoian Studies,* ed. Michael K. Foster, Jack Campisi, and Marianne Mithun (Albany: State University of New York Press, 1984), 109–23.

10. Graymont, 45–46.

11. Graymont, 46.

12. Fenton, 297.

13. Gray 7–57.

14. Dingman Versteeg, longhand notes and translations of an account book kept by Evert Wendell, "Trade with Indians, Albany 1695–1726." New York Historical Society.

15. Richter, 79–80.

16. Richter, 79–80.

17. Richter, 112–13.

18. Richter, 106–9.

19. Evan Haefeli and Kevin Sweeney, *Captors and Captives: The 1704 French and Indian Raid on Deerfield* (Amherst: University of Massachusetts Press, 2003), 55–59.

20. Alden T. Vaughan, ed., *The Puritan Tradition in America, 1620–1730,* rev. ed. (Hanover, NH: University Press of New England, 1972, 1997), 63.

3

DAILY LIFE IN THE COLONIAL NORTHEAST

The onset of permanent European settlement in the Northeast transformed the daily lives of both Algonkian and Iroquoian peoples. In some cases these changes happened virtually overnight, as when epidemic diseases swept through a village and killed up to 90 percent of the inhabitants. In other cases, Native people had years and sometimes generations of intermittent contact before the invasion began. Algonkian peoples who lived closest to the English got to know them first in traditional terms of alliance and friendship. Whether they liked the English or not, there were many reasons to establish friendly relations with them if possible. In the first two decades after 1620, when Native communities around Massachusetts Bay were still in shock from catastrophic disease, tens of thousands of English men, women, and children arrived from overseas. They cleared land, planted crops, and built houses and churches across the land. Algonkians continued to live in and around New England, but their lives were affected by the English presence, whether they sought to live peacefully as neighbors while accommodating English ways, or whether they tried to have minimal contact. The Iroquois were spared the worst effects of this massive immigration, or invasion, thanks to their inland location west of the Hudson River, but they also experienced enormous changes with the arrival of Europeans.

ORAL TRADITIONS ABOUT FIRST CONTACT

In 1634, Englishman William Wood heard an oral tradition about the first time Algonkian peoples in New England saw a European ship. He reported that

They tooke the first ship they saw for a walking Iland, the Mast to be a Tree, the Saile white Clouds and the discharging of Ordinance for Lightening and Thunder, which did much to trouble them, but this thunder being over, and this moving Iland stedied with an Anchor, they manned out their cannowes to goe and pick strawberries there.[1]

This story must have been at least a generation old by the time Wood heard it. It captures the moment when Algonkian peoples sought to understand something new through the lens of the familiar. English writers drew similar analogies when they described moose, which did not exist in England, as large horses with horns, or when they described ritual specialists who practiced medicine, healing, divination, and other arts deemed by the English to be "supernatural" as witches and sorcerors. Some readers have interpreted stories like this as evidence that Algonkian peoples were naive, perhaps awed by the arrival of Europeans. Knowing the skillfulness of Algonkian storytellers, who routinely turn the mundane events of everyday life into a sidesplitting commentary, it is also possible that the person who told this story to Wood intended to make him laugh.

Algonkian peoples knew something about Europeans from at least 1500, when Basque, French, and English fishing boats started coming to the banks of Newfoundland on a regular basis. Those who did not actually encounter Europeans for themselves no doubt heard stories about them. Archaeological evidence shows that European trade goods traveled further and faster than the Europeans themselves, thanks to indigenous trade networks. By 1603, English sailors reported with surprise that they met Wabanaki people along the coast of northern New England who were skilled in the use of shallops, a coastal fishing boat with a mast and sail, and wore European clothing. The Mi'kmaq "commander" of such a vessel spoke "divers Christian words" and wore "a Wastecoate of blacke worke, a paire of Breeches, cloth Stockings, Shoes, Hat and Band." He also drew a map of the coast that included the European fishing stages at Placentia in Newfoundland.[2] Some Native people spoke English or French before 1600 because they had been taken as captives or visitors to Europe, where they were exhibited as objects of curiosity or questioned for information that could be used to further colonial efforts.

Accounts of first contact are always shaped by hindsight. Mi'kmaq oral tradition tells a story similar to the one above about a floating island with tall trees on which bears crawled about—a comment on the hairiness of European men—but the story also remembers an event that probably happened closer to 1600 than 1500. The protagonist in this story went out to investigate and saw a strange type of canoe being lowered into the water—the long boat, used for exploring coastal areas and inland rivers where the water might be too shallow for a sea-going vessel. He saw that the bears were in fact men, who jumped into the canoes and paddled ashore. The story continues:

Among them was a man dressed in white,—a priest with his white stole on,—who came towards them making signs of friendship, raising his hand towards heaven, and addressing them in an earnest manner, but in a language which they could not understand.[3]

Whereas sailors brought trade goods and disease, missionaries brought Christianity, which had a different but equally significant impact on the daily life of Algonkian and Iroquoian peoples in the Northeast.

THE SEVENTEENTH CENTURY

Scholars still debate the exact ways in which the introduction of trade with Europeans affected indigenous peoples in North America, but one pattern is clear. There was an increase in the nature and scope of intertribal conflict from the late fifteenth century on that reflects increased competition to control both the movement of furs to Europeans and the distribution of European goods to Native consumers. Some of these intertribal wars were fought among people from the same language family. The Five Nations Iroquois virtually destroyed the Huron-Wendat confederacy in the early seventeenth century. Algonkian peoples fought each other on a smaller scale. More often intertribal wars were fought between the Algonkians and the Iroquois. The latter conflicts, collectively known as the Beaver Wars of the seventeenth century, reflect the expansion of the Iroquois Confederacy as a political and military power in the Eastern Woodlands.[4] The increase in intertribal war is reflected in a new village form, the palisaded village, in which Native peoples augmented their defenses by building wooden stockades around their dwellings.

A key point to make note of here is that intertribal wars originated in rivalries that predated the arrival of Europeans, although they were exacerbated by the fur trade. Early Native alliances with Europeans, such as the alliance made by the Wampanoag sachem Massasoit with the Pilgrims, reflect a larger strategy on the part of Native leaders. Massasoit, whose people had recently been decimated by epidemic disease, viewed the English as strong allies to help him resist encroachments by the Narragansetts to the south. It would be a mistake to view Native actions purely in relation to the English and other Europeans, although the English and French were quick to exploit Native rivalries for their own purposes.

Sidney Perley, the nineteenth-century historian of Salem, Massachusetts, commented that the seacoast areas were mostly abandoned when English planters arrived. Algonkian peoples who survived the epidemics, which killed up to 90 percent of the population in some places over a three-year period from 1617 to 1619, cared little about arguing over land with the English. According to Edward Johnson, who spent time on the

The Impact of Epidemic Disease

Merrimac River in the early 1630s and for a brief period was even licensed as a trader, the epidemics were preceded by a comet that both the English and the Algonkians interpreted as a portent of things to come, for good or ill. Soon after the comet was sighted,

> there befell a great mortality among them, the greatest that ever the memory of Father to Sonne tooke notice of. . . . Their Disease being a sore consumption, sweeping away whole Families, but chiefly yong Men and Children, the very seeds of increase. [T]heir Powwowes, which are their Doctors, working partly by Charmes, and partly by Medicine, were much amazed to see their Wigwams lie ful of dead Corpses, and that now neither Squantam nor Abbamocho could helpe, which are their good and bad God[,] and also their Powwows themselves were oft smitten with death's stroke[.] [H]owling and much lamentation was heard among the living, who being possest with great feare, oftimes left their dead unburied, their manner being such that they remove their habitations at death of any, this great mortality being an unwonted thing, feare them the more, because naturally the Country is very healthy etc.[5]

Johnson's account is infused with his conviction that God was clearing the way for the English, but his observations resonate with what we know from other sources.

Like the English, Native peoples believed in signs and portents. Well into the eighteenth century, Euro-American or Euro-Canadian officers complained that Native forces would disappear or find excuses to avoid fighting when the signs were unfavorable. Further, a disaster of this magnitude surely made people question their own spirit power and wonder what they were doing wrong. This helps to explain the relative ease with which the English were able to move into coastal areas and lay out their towns and farms with confidence, secure in their belief that the king of England had a right to distribute these lands. Except for isolated incidents of violence, usually triggered by specific acts, Native people either kept their distance or established peaceful relations with the English.

As noted in Chapter 1, Algonkian leaders made agreements on behalf of themselves and their people to let the English live in areas where the population had been drastically reduced in the wake of epidemics. They signed deeds that took their form from English legal tradition but incorporated conditions that must have been negotiated by the sachems and sagamores who signed them. Indian deeds from Maine and Massachusetts reserve specific rights for the signers, their kin, and sometimes for their descendants. These included the right to hunt, fish, gather plants and firewood, and plant corn.

The Pequot War (1637)   Like the Algonkians and the Iroquois, the English had their own traditions of warfare. The Pequots, whose territory lay within the borders of Connecticut colony, were the first group to experience the full meaning of this. Where Native Americans understood small-scale conflicts with

Englishmen through the lens of the raid and counter-raid that character-ized intertribal war, the English interpreted revenge killings and similar acts as treachery and a threat to the project of colonization. Where the Pequots viewed the English as newcomers who were, perhaps, wearing out their welcome, the English believed that they had a God-given right to inhabit the land, even if that meant clearing it of its original inhabitants.

On May 1, 1637, the General Court of Connecticut declared war on the Pequots, a powerful tribe perceived as a dangerous enemy by the English. The English convinced the Narragansetts, a neighboring tribe, to join them against their old enemies. The English and their Native allies attacked the stockaded Pequot fort on the Mystic River by surrounding it and then set-ting it on fire. Hundreds of Pequots burned to death inside the fort, most of them women and children. The surviving Pequots were killed, or rounded up and sold into slavery. The Narragansetts were as horrified by this new scale of killing as the other Native peoples, and the word spread quickly. It is significant that Native peoples did not mount any large-scale resistance to English colonization until 1675, a generation later.[6]

Ministers such as John Eliot came to believe that the only way for Native people to become truly Christian would be to change their way of life entirely, to fix them in English-style communities that came to be known as "praying towns," since that was the main activity that distin-guished the inhabitants from Native people in other places. Eliot wrote, "A place must be found . . . some what remote from the English, where they must have the word constantly taught, and government constantly exercised, means of good subsistence provided, incouragements for the industrious [and a] meanes of instructing them in Letters, Trades and Labours."[7] The place he chose was Natick, Massachusetts, formerly inhab-ited by Nipmucs and more recently promised to a group of Englishmen, who were persuaded to settle instead in the Connecticut River Valley to the west. Soon there were 14 praying towns in the Massachusetts Bay Colony, including Natick, Marlboro, Punkapog (Canton), Magunkaquog (Ashland), Hassanamesitt (Grafton), and Chabanakongkomun (Webster). By the mid-1600s, about 25 percent of the Native peoples of southeastern New England had converted to Christianity.[8]

English Praying Towns

Algonkian peoples lived in a wide variety of dwelling types after the English colonies were established. Some people continued to live in the rounded, mat-covered witus of southern New England and the conical, bark-covered wigwams from further north through the end of the nine-teenth century. Others built framed wooden houses in the English style. But the distinction between "English" versus "Algonkian" style should not be drawn too sharply. Most people incorporated elements from both ways of living according to their means and personal preference. Indeed, distinctively "Indian" ways were recognized by both Native and English communities.

This is evident in the way Algonkian peoples mixed old and new skills. For example, Sarah Hannit was the wife of Japhet Hannit, a Wampanoag convert who had become a preacher and missionary to other Native peoples in southern New England. Sarah Hannit was known for her skill at making bark mats of exceptional quality, which she embroidered with fibers taken from the inner bark of the walnut tree and dyed in several colors. She also knew how to care for her husband's linen clothing, when he wore English dress.[9] In more practical terms, Native peoples found ways to merge seasonal subsistence activities with the new cash economy. One minister reported that

they begin to grow industrious, and find something to sell at Market all the year long; all winter they sell Brooms, Staves, Elepots, Baskets, Turkies. In the Spring, Craneberries, Fish, Strawberries; in the Summer Hurtleberries, Grapes, Fish; in the Autumn they sell Craneberries, Fish, Venison, &c. and they find a good benefit by the Market, and grow more and more to make use thereof; besides sundry of them work with the English in Hay time, and Harvest.[10]

Literacy

In Massachusetts, minister John Eliot translated the Bible into Algonkian by 1663, published as *Mamusse Wunneetupanatamwe Up-Biblum God Naneeswe Nukkone Testament kah Wonk Wusku Testament.* The Protestant faith, and especially the Puritan sect, believed that God manifested his will directly through the Bible. Ministers could teach or facilitate understanding, but each person was expected to read well enough to access the Bible for him- or herself. This is why literacy rates for both men and women in this period tend to be higher among Protestants than any other religious group. "Praying Indians" were encouraged to read the Bible. Some also learned to write, both in English and in their own language.[11]

Eliot was assisted in his work by a Nipmuck man who became known as James Printer, because printing was his trade. James was one of the few Algonkian men who attended Harvard College in the seventeenth century and lived long enough to benefit from it. Most of the would-be scholars, selected for their promise and intellect, died almost immediately from diseases they contracted through their daily life in an unfamiliar and, for them, unhealthy environment. It is important to note that churches became one of the main forums in which Native people held onto their language and culture. Ministers such as Eliot worked hard to learn Native languages in the seventeenth century, and it was common for Indian languages to be spoken in church. By the eighteenth century, few ministers could "speak Indian," the idiomatic phrase used especially by elders in the Northeast today. Churches became spaces of resistance to colonial domination and centers of activity that maintained a distinct ethnic identity.

Literacy was also important for keeping legal records. Records were kept in English, in Indian, and in bilingual documents, depending on their context and use. For example, in Natick, the town scribe in the early eighteenth century was Captain Thomas Waban, the oldest son of John Eliot's first convert. Documents pertaining to Native interactions with non-Native people, such as property boundaries or the disposition of English cattle found on Natick lands, were written only in English. Internal matters such as fines for failing to attend the town meeting and some town election results were recorded only in Massachusett. Other matters required bilingual documentation, such as regulations about cutting trees for firewood. This suggests that while many Native people were bilingual, they saw the continued use of their own language as an important assertion of Indianness.[12]

Indian Courts and Gendered Crimes

Algonkian peoples had clear moral guidelines and customary laws that governed marriage in Native communities, but these forms of marriage were quite different from those of the English. When Native people agreed to live in English praying towns, they placed themselves under the jurisdiction of English law. Wampanoag conversion narratives (public declarations in which candidates for baptism had to convince the minister and congregation of their readiness) suggest that at least some converts accepted the idea that Native forms of marriage, household, and gender relations were "sinful." For example, Algonkian men, especially leaders, who were obliged to give gifts and feed anyone who was hungry, sometimes took more than one wife; gifts and food were women's realm. Under the new system of Christian morals, and English law, polygyny became "bigamy," a crime. While Algonkian people valued stable personal relationships, the process of divorce was uncomplicated for marriages that did not work out. Algonkian people valued personal restraint, but in a system where children were always cared for by their families, there was no condemnation for young people who experimented with sex. People who showed a lack of restraint were more likely to be teased or mocked than punished with whipping or fines, which were the usual penalties for people convicted of "fornication" under English law. In legal terms, these behaviors were criminalized.[13]

The Native leaders of praying towns, together with their missionaries, soon drafted laws designed to codify Christian practices and values. During the 1640s John Eliot helped his converts at Noonahetum (Concord, Massachusetts) to codify prohibitions against adultery, sodomy, fornication, polygyny, and wife-beating. In Natick, single men were required to set up their own individual wigwams, instead of living with their sisters or grandmothers, and women were fined for following the practice of menstrual seclusion. These laws were generally administered in a separate system of Indian courts by Indian magistrates and judges. Their authority was limited, however, subject to oversight by the English courts.

By the mid-seventeenth century, Native peoples had three formal venues through which to mediate their disputes: on a congregational level; in Indian courts; or in English courts. The evidence suggests that people also used informal strategies such as intervention by extended kin, the women of the community, or missionaries. In general, English courts handled cases where one party was English, cases that involved murder, or appeals from the Indian courts. Colonial officials showed little interest in interpersonal disputes between Native people. One factor may be that English magistrates and judges found it difficult to come to a decision about cases involving people who could only explain themselves through translators and, even then, based their arguments on unfamiliar values. Disputes between Native people were mostly heard in the Indian courts. Unfortunately for researchers, Indian courts kept minimal written records, except for brief notations that served as an aid to memory.

These multiple jurisdictions were shaped by both Native and English practices. During the early decades, non-Christians continued to be governed by sachems with justice meted out in accordance with local values, while residents of praying towns were subject to the authority of new leaders who were generally chosen from elite families but always subject to approval by English officials. After King Philip's War, the colonies extended civil control over even those communities that wished to remain apart.

English definitions of normative behavior affected both men and women, but certain laws affected Native women in particular ways because they applied only to women. One example of this is infanticide, that is, the murder of an infant. English women by custom gave birth in the presence of other women, including a midwife and female relatives and friends. Under English law, if a child was born dead and there were no witnesses, the legal presumption was infanticide: the woman must have given birth in secret in order to kill the child. In contrast, Algonkian women traditionally gave birth away from the main village. While there were often other women present, there was no particular stigma attached to giving birth alone. In 1683, a Wampanoag woman named Awashunkes was accused of helping her daughter, Betty, to commit infanticide. Both Awashunkes and Betty swore that the child had been born dead. In the end, Betty was prosecuted only for fornication (sex outside of legal marriage) and Awashunkes was acquitted of infanticide. However, the incident had political overtones because Awashunkes was a female sachem who ruled at Saconet, near present-day Little Compton, Rhode Island, in conjunction with her son, Peter. Awashunkes had fought against the English in 1675. Her leadership was controversial even among her own people as she first headed an anti-English faction, then allied openly with Metacomet (King Philip), and finally made peace with the English. As a female leader enmeshed in a new legal system, Awashunkes was vulnerable to charges that would not have been brought against a man.[14]

Despite the best efforts of missionaries and colonial officials to transform indigenous lifeways, however, Indian households in New England remained distinctive. Men, instead of becoming farmers and patriarchs, continued to find work away from home, whether it was hunting, trapping, or, later on, selling baskets or going to sea in the whaling industry. Women, instead of conforming to a more subordinate role, continued to be active and visible. Even the framed houses built by converts looked different—generally smaller than English houses with only one communal room, or at most two. Native peoples were willing to adopt English ways but they continued to be a people apart.[15]

By the 1670s, the English looked with some satisfaction at what they had wrought, but many Algonkian peoples had become **King Philip's War (1675–1678)** alarmed. The English took up too much space. They kept insisting that the Indians were subject to the British Crown, when they were a free people who had governed themselves from time immemorial. English colonists changed the land, they changed the people, and they came in ever-increasing numbers. Soon there would be no place left for the Indians. In 1675, the conflict commonly known as King Philip's War or Metacom's Rebellion erupted in southern New England and then spread north and east into Maine.[16] This conflict pitted the Algonkian peoples of New England against the English and, eventually, Algonkian peoples against each other, as some groups made the choice to ally themselves with the English in order to survive.

Metacom, or Metacomet, a Wampanoag sachem from Pokanoket, was the son of Massasoit, the powerful leader who befriended the Pilgrims. After Massasoit died, Metacomet's older brother Wamsutta became sachem. Wamsutta told the English that in his tradition, people took new names to mark important life passages. He asked them to give him an English name. Because Wamsutta and his brother Metacomet were leaders, with a dignified bearing, the English named then Alexander and Philip, respectively, after two brothers who were kings of ancient Macedonia.

The impact of war was disruptive and traumatic even for those who tried to remain neutral, as the men had no time for hunting and English soldiers destroyed food supplies by burning villages and cornfields whenever they could. Northern villages strained their already stretched resources to accommodate refugees from the south. By the spring of 1676, weary people from New England headed north in search of a safe haven. Jacques Vaultier, a missionary at the French Catholic mission of Sillery, near Quebec City, noted the arrival of a large group of Abenakis from Acadia who made their way north "after suffering during The winter from so unusual a famine that many of them died."[17]

The Aftermath of King Philip's War

During the war, Christian residents of Natick, Marlboro, and Punkapog (Canton) were exiled to Deer Isle in Boston Harbor. After the war, those identified most closely with Metacomet and his warriors were killed or sold into slavery in the West Indies. Others were forced to work as indentured servants in English homes. Many of the children placed in English households as indentured servants lost contact with their families, their culture, and their language. The colonies of Rhode Island, Connecticut, and Massachusetts sold the adult survivors into a life of enslavement in the West Indies. Children were kept as indentured servants in English homes. Over time, this system developed into "pauper apprenticeship," that is, the practice of placing poor or parentless children in English homes. They were supposed to be given food, shelter, and training for a defined period of time in exchange for their labor. Narragansett tribal historian Ella Wilcox Sekatau notes that in her people's oral tradition, this was just "another name for slavery."[18] The stereotyped image of Native peoples in New England as poor, degraded, or "vanishing" comes from this period.

By 1684 only four praying towns continued as officially recognized Indian communities in Massachusetts Bay: Natick, Punkapog, Wamesit (Lowell) and Chabanakongkomun. Despite the hardships, these communities stabilized for the time being, although that changed after about 1700 due to the onset of intercolonial wars and new economic conditions that forced many Native peoples to sell their land to pay debts. Still, Native people continued to live in or close to their original homelands in communities that received less attention than the praying towns. In June 1698, two English ministers, the Reverend Grindal Rawson of Mendon and the Reverend Samuel Danforth from Taunton, set forth to visit all of the Native communities that they could find in southeastern Massachusetts. To their surprise, they counted 32, some too small to be called villages, still within the bounds of Plymouth Colony and on the islands of Martha's Vineyard and Nantucket.[19]

Calumet and Covenant Chain   Even as New England officials worked to bring Algonkian peoples under the jurisdiction of English law and Christian morality, they recruited the Iroquois to join them in war. The Iroquois Confederacy held a prominent place in colonial politics because of their military strength, which made them desirable foes and formidable allies. They were also known for their skill in diplomacy, which they raised to a high art. English and French officials spent hours, days, and weeks at a time meeting the Iroquois on their own ground. Cadwallader Colden of Albany, who represented the British colonies at treaty negotiations with the Confederacy in the early eighteenth century, described the difficulties inherent in translating and transcribing these exchanges. He wrote:

[I]t will be a difficult Task to show the Wit, and Judgement, and Art, and Simplicity, and Ignorance of the several Parties, managing a Treaty, in other words than their own. As to my part, I thought myself uncapable of doing it, without depriving much of the Indian Genius, by my Contracting or Paraphrasing their Harrangues, and without committing often gross Mistakes. For, on these Occasions, a skillful Manager often talks Confusedly and Obscurely with design; which if an historian should endeavour to amend, the Reader would receive the History in a false Light.[20]

Colden reminds us that published records of treaty negotiations with the Five Nations Iroquois give us only a shadow of the oratorical skills of Iroquois spokesmen.

Important negotiations began with the Condolence, the ritual cleansing of negative emotions described in Chapter 2. The men sometimes smoked the long-stemmed pipe known as the calumet, or peace pipe. Tobacco soothed the spirit and carried their thoughts up to Sky World. Iroquois orators used strings of wampum and elaborately woven wampum belts to anchor their words and commemorate important agreements, and the French, English, and later Americans learned to give wampum belts in return to demonstrate their seriousness and good faith. It was better to have the Iroquois as allies than as enemies.

The calumet was an intertribal object and symbol of peace from the Northeastern Woodlands to the Great Plains that predated the arrival of Europeans. It is sometimes described as a "signature" or confirmation of agreements made about war, peace, alliance, or anything that required collaboration between men, because each party breathed the sanctified smoke into their lungs and sent it up to the sky. Each calumet had its own design and decoration that included carving, paint, feathers, or fur.[21]

The Covenant Chain is a network of alliances that linked the Iroquois Confederacy and their allies to the English, with New York as the designated intermediary for the British colonies. The metaphor is based on the metal chains given by the English as gifts, which are strong but made up of many parts. To maintain goodwill, the English had to observe Haudenosaunee protocol. The Covenant Chain endured for almost a century, until the American Revolution ended British authority in the region.[22]

Missionary activities had always been part of the French colonial agenda in New France. The mission of St. Joseph de Sillery was founded near Quebec in the 1630s as a reduction, a place where Algonquin and Montagnais converts to the Catholic faith were supposed to settle down and live like Christians. Early reports from the Jesuit missionaries sounded promising but, by the 1640s, the number of people being baptized at the mission was on the decline. Then, in the 1660s and 1670s, a new period of

Missions on the St. Lawrence River

mission history began in New France. A series of Native villages was settled in the St. Lawrence Valley in conjunction with Catholic missions. For
Native peoples, these villages offered a much-needed stability in a world
disrupted by war and diaspora. For the French, the new converts were also
much-needed allies and trading partners. Two of these have a particularly
strong connection to the English colonies: Kahnawake and Odanak.

Kahnawake

Kahnawake is the spelling used by the Mohawks today, but in older history books it is written as Caughnawaga. It means "at the rapids." During
the 1660s, a number of Iroquois moved to the northern reaches of their
homeland and established a new community on the south shore of the
St. Lawrence River near Montreal, not far from the Lachine Rapids. They went
partly for trade opportunities, since the new location put them in a key
location for dealing with French merchants in Montreal and the flotilla of
canoes that arrived from inland areas to the north and west with their loads
of beaver and other pelts each spring. For many, however, the move also represented a growing interest in learning more about the new religion taught
by the early Jesuit missionaries. The mixed population included adoptees
such as the Huron-Wendat, who had already converted to Catholicism.
The largest group at Kahnawake were Mohawks, and Mohawk language

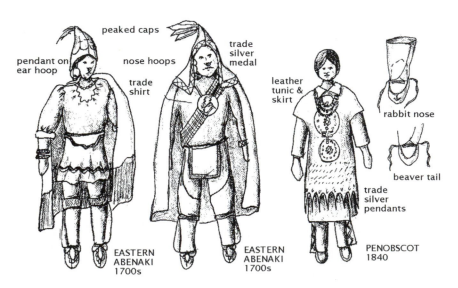

Algonkian clothing, eighteenth century. The conical pointed cap may have originated in birchbark. Eastern Abenaki people today still wear pointed caps made
from black cloth and decorated with ribbonwork or beaded embroidery as regalia.
From Tara Prindle/nativetech.org.

and culture quickly became dominant in this community. The Kahnawake Mohawks became known as staunch allies of the French. This created problems when the French went to war against other Iroquois nations, although Kahnawake Mohawk warriors had a way of falling sick or missing their shots when the time came for fighting their kin. They were more enthusiastic about fighting the English. Warriors from this community participated in raids against New York and New England during the four intercolonial wars that broke out between 1689 and 1763.[23]

In 1704 the Kahnawake Mohawks played a key role in the attack on Deerfield, Massachusetts, by a mixed group that included French, Mohawk, Abenaki, and Huron-Wendat forces. Over 100 English men, women, and children were taken captive and brought to New France. While Deerfield was only one of many towns attacked during these years, the "Deerfield Captives" received unusual publicity because one, the Reverend John Williams, was closely related to the prominent Mather family in Boston. Williams wrote an account of this ordeal, *The Redeemed Captive Returning to Zion*, that became a classic of American literature. The book records his struggle to woo his children back from their new Mohawk and Abenaki families, since they were immediately adopted, and his struggle to redeem them from the Catholic faith, since their new families were practicing Catholics.[24]

Odanak

Odanak is the Abenaki name of a village better known in U.S. history books as St. Francis. It means, simply, "at the village." Odanak was formally established in 1701, but the community has a longer history that brings together people from two different places. The area had long been part of the northern hunting grounds of Wabanaki people from the Connecticut River Valley, including Sokokis from present-day Northfield, Massachusetts, and the Champlain Valley. The new village also included an influx of people from the region known to the French as Acadia, which at that time encompassed parts of Maine as well as Nova Scotia and New Brunswick. The largest group came from the Kennebec River valley in Maine. This group had frequented the French Catholic mission at Sillery, near Quebec City, since the 1660s. In both cases they moved north to find greater stability, increasingly so after King Philip's War. As with the Iroquoian people at Kahnawake, the French welcomed Algonkians from New England as allies and converts to Catholicism. The Abenakis and Sokokis of Odanak are collectively known in older texts as the St. Francis Indians.[25]

Daily Life at the Catholic Missions

The richly detailed missives filed by Jesuit missionaries, known collectively as *The Jesuit Relations*, chronicle the successes, failures, and frustrations of the men who left their homes in France and traveled to a new world to spread the word of God to a people they perceived to be heathen and savage.[26] From these accounts, it is clear that part of the attraction of Catholicism was the new framework it offered for daily life, creating an island of stability in an increasingly unstable world. In other cases, and sometimes for the same people at other points in their lives, the Christian life had too many rules that ran counter to indigenous culture and worldview. The priests liked to present their victories as unqualified successes, but more often even the most devout converts maintained ties to their families and former way of life.

Missions were always established in places that were already frequented or inhabited by Native people. Physically, the "mission" might include a church or chapel, a dwelling for the priest, and possibly one or two additional structures or gardens. Socially a varying percentage of people in the village could be counted as part of the mission, but there were always people living in and around the village who explicitly distanced themselves from the missionaries and the regulations of the Christian life. This is why it is important to make a distinction between the name of a mission such as St. François de Sales and the name of the village, Odanak, or the mission of Sault St. Louis, which was located in the village of Kahnawake.

Both Algonkian and Iroquoian converts to Catholicism enjoyed the rituals and paraphernalia associated with this new faith. Catechumens, or people who were preparing for baptism, learned ritual movements such as kneeling and making the sign of the cross. Missionaries commented on how faithfully their neophytes attended daily Mass and then held prayer meetings in their wigwams and longhouses at night. Their devotion highlighted the laxity of the French population of New France. To become Christians, Native people learned to recite prayers and the Catechism—ritual intonations—and to sing elaborate European-style church music for the glory of God. They also enjoyed the custom of giving name-day feasts in honor of their patron saints, both within their own households or on a larger, more public scale.[27] All of these rituals paralleled aspects of their own culture.

French priests, and especially the Jesuits, worked hard to analyze and document Native languages, producing myriad grammars and dictionaries. They also translated prayers, catechisms, and other liturgical texts into Native languages as an aid to teaching. There is some evidence of people using written texts as mnemonic devices, linking a memorized recitation of the contents to the written or printed page. However, Catholic ritual suited people from an oral culture who were able to memorize and recite prayers even in Latin with great accuracy.

THE EIGHTEENTH CENTURY

Daily life for Algonkian and Iroquoian peoples in the eighteenth-century Northeast was marked by the need to sustain families and communities during long periods of warfare that took men away from home for long periods of time, and sometimes for good. In periods of peace, men had to travel further than ever before to find good hunting or other subsistence activities, including maritime occupations such as whaling. This left women with the work of day-to-day life, even as they were urged to become more ladylike by giving up "men's work" in farming. Some people chose to accommodate English ways. Others left their traditional homelands in search of a space and place where they could live free of colonial constraints. With hindsight, U.S. history books describe this period as a time of inevitable loss and defeat for Native peoples. A closer look reminds us of the creative energy and intellect that enabled them to survive a turbulent period of history with a strong sense of themselves as sovereign peoples with a distinct history and culture.

During much of the seventeenth century, the Haudenosaunee competed with the French for control of the inland fur trade. With a relatively **The Great Peace of 1701** small population and a strong commercial incentive to control the number of fur traders, the French issued licenses to selected men and sent them down the St. Lawrence River and into the *pays d'en haut,* the upper Great Lakes. There they had to establish good relations with the local people or risk an unpleasant death. The Haudenosaunee, by virtue of their geographic location across present-day New York State, maintained a strong position as middlemen between Dutch, French, and British traders in the east, and inland Native peoples who had access to the best pelts. Anyone passing down the St. Lawrence River to the Great Lakes had to deal with the Haudenosaunee eventually. The French tried to circumvent this by using the Ottawa River, which allowed them to travel west via a waterway north of the St. Lawrence. They also exploited the ongoing intertribal warfare between the Haudenosaunee and other Native groups whenever possible. For example, they offered support to people who otherwise might not have chosen to go to war. The French also launched direct attacks of their own.[28]

In August 1701, a remarkable event took place in Montreal. Louis-Hector de Callière, the Governor-General of New France, welcomed 1,300 representatives of 40 First Nations who came from as far away as the Great Lakes and southern Illinois to the west, James Bay to the north, and Acadia to the east. After several weeks of negotiation, feasting, and gift exchange, the participants signed a treaty of peace that effectively put an end to the long conflict between New France and the Iroquois Confederacy. The Haudenosaunee signed in part because they had learned from hard experience that they could not count on their English allies to keep their promises of support against the French. Haudenosaunee people were divided over what course to pursue. Some advocated policies that were pro-French or pro-British, while others thought it best for the Confederacy to be neutral. The Mohawks in particular faced a dilemma because the Catholic Mohawks in places such as Kahnawake had committed themselves to an alliance with the French, while other Mohawks to the south fought with the English colonies. In the end, the Mohawks of Kahnawake signed the treaty. Their English-allied brethren did not, an example of how the Confederacy did not enforce unanimity on its members.[29] The Iroquois Confederacy kept their pledge of neutrality in French-English confrontations through the end of the French regime in Canada, although some individuals and factions chose sides.

The "French and Indian" Wars   Four intercolonial wars took place in the period from 1689 to 1760. These wars were fought by French and English forces together with their Native allies. Each began with a war in Europe that was translated across the Atlantic to the New World. The intercolonial wars were: King Williams's War, 1689–1697 (the War of the League of Augsburg in Europe); Queen Anne's War, 1702–1713 (the War of the Spanish Succession), King George's War, 1744–1748 (the War of the Austrian Succession), and the so-called "French and Indian War," 1756–1763 (the Seven Years' War). This created confusion for the Native allies of the French and British because the wars ended in North America when the mother countries made peace, rather than in response to the war's progress here. Francis Parkman, the prolific historian of the nineteenth century, portrayed the French-allied nations as pawns of the French, but even a cursory view of the documents with a less jaundiced eye makes it clear that both French and English officials spent considerable time worrying about how to maintain the allegiance of Native peoples.

Captives and Captive-Taking   Both Iroquoian and Algonkian peoples took captives in war. As noted in Chapter 2, the Iroquois took captives in the particular context of the *mourning war.* When someone in the community died, Iroquois women urged their men to bring home a captive to take that person's place. The rationale was that extreme grief created an imbalance, and captives offered two different ways to ease grief. They might be tortured, which allowed relatives, especially the women, who did not generally go to war, to vent their rage and grief on the body of an enemy. They might also be adopted in place of the deceased in a ceremony knows as "requickening" because it brought the loved one back to the living. Algonkian peoples also took captives in war, but they were more likely to be taken as available and used as needed. They were not taken expressly for adoption, although good candidates might be adopted. Unmarried women and children made the best adoptees, since they had less trouble learning the language and found it easier to form bonds with their new families.

One of the best-known accounts is that of Mary Jemison, who was born to a British family in Pennsylvania but raised as a Seneca woman.[30] Jemison was 15 years old in 1758 when her home in western Pennsylvania was attacked by a French and Shawnee war party. The captives were taken first to Fort Duquesne, then a French fort, today the city of Pittsburgh. Two Seneca women claimed Jemison and brought her back to their town at the mouth of the She-nan-je River, some eighty canoe miles from the fort. Her new sisters called her "Dickewamis," meaning "a pretty girl, a handsome girl, or a pleasant, good thing."[31] Many years later, when she was about 80 years old, Jemison dictated the story of her adventures to James Seaver, who wrote them down. She had spent over 60 years among the Iroquois.

The Senecas held to the ways of their ancestors. During the 15 years or so that Dickewamis spent with them prior to the commencement of the American Revolution in 1776, they enjoyed a period of peace when the only acts of war that she witnessed took place during rituals and feasts, in which the chiefs and warriors demonstrated their skills for a cheering audience. Each season brought its proper tasks and ceremonies. The women planted and tended their crops. Children were born and raised; young couples were married; the clan mothers kept each household running. Dickewamis might have taken it for granted, but Mary Jemison thought it important to tell James Seaver, her amanuensis, that the Seneca in peacetime were the happiest of people. They prized honesty, chastity, and fidelity. They moderated their passions, keeping the principle of balance in all things. She found them "candid and honorable in the expression of their sentiments, on every subject of importance."

Dickewamis married twice among the Seneca. Her first husband died young. She had six children by her second husband. The village was destroyed by American soldiers during the American Revolution, and Jemison and her family fled further west. Several years after the war ended, when the first Americans moved to the area west of Utica, New York, near the Genesee River, they found blue-eyed Mary Jemison living with her Seneca husband and family. They called her "The White Woman of the Genesee."

When James Seaver met her in 1823, he commented on her dress, a mixture of clothing styles that he found incongruous:

Her dress at the time I saw her, was made and worn after, the Indian fashion, and consisted of a shirt, short gown, petticoat, stockings, moccasins, a blanket and a bonnet. The shirt was of cotton and made at the top, as I was informed, like a man's without collar or sleeves—was open before and extended down about midway of the hips.—The petticoat was a piece of broadcloth with the list at the top and bottom and the ends sewed together. This was tied on by a string that was passed over it and around the waist, in such a manner as to let the bottom of the petticoat down half way between the knee and ankle and leave one-fourth of a yard at the top to be turned down over the string—the bottom of the shift coming a little below, and on the outside of the top of the fold so as to leave the list and two or three inches of the cloth uncovered. The stockings, were of blue broadcloth, tied, or pinned on, which reached from the knees, into the mouth of the moccasins.—Around her toes only she had some rags, and over these her buckskin moccasins. Her gown was of undressed flannel, colored brown. It was made in old yankee style, with long sleeves, covered the top of the hips, and was tied before in two places with strings of deer skin. Over all this, she wore an Indian blanket. On her head she wore a piece of old brown woollen cloth made somewhat like a sun bonnet.[32]

At this time Jemison and her family lived in a timbered house, about 20 by 28 feet, with two fireplaces plus "a shingled roof, and a framed stoop." She also had a framed barn, larger than the house at 26 by 36 feet, to house her cattle and horses. Jemison had become quite the property owner, and she rented out her other houses. Yet for all these trappings of Euro-American life, Jemison was still Dickewamis, a Seneca woman. Seaver noted, "Her habits, are those of the Indians—she sleeps on skins without a bedstead, sits upon the floor or on a bench, and holds her victuals on her lap, or in her hands."[33]

Revolutionary Choices During the American Revolution, the Iroquois Confederacy as a whole thought it best to remain neutral, and the Grand Council issued a declaration of neutrality. In traditional Iroquois fashion, however, people and communities were free to make their own choices. In some cases, factions split along religious lines. For example, many of the Mohawks still living in the Mohawk Valley (New York State) belonged to the Church of England. They sided with the British. In contrast, the Oneida to the west were also Protestant, but they followed the Puritanism of their influential missionary, Samuel Kirkland. They sided with the Americans.[34]

Advocates of neutrality were hard-pressed to make their case even without internal factionalism as British and American forces fought their battles across Iroquois lands. When some Iroquois warriors decided to fight with the British, American forces feared that Iroquoia would become a source of warriors and supplies for the British. American soldiers invaded Iroquois lands, burning crops and houses and scattering the people. After the war, many of the same soldiers who participated in these actions successfully petitioned for these lands and established prosperous farms and businesses for themselves. Overall, the American Revolution and its aftermath were a disaster for the Haudenosaunee. This was true for groups that fought on the side of the Americans, such as the Oneida and Tuscarora, as well as those that fought mostly for the British. When the British surrendered in 1783, they made no provision for their Native allies. The United States assumed that Native people living on lands ceded by Britain automatically forfeited the land and became subject to U.S. law.[35]

The Code of Handsome Lake Handsome Lake (Seneca) was born at Conawagus River on the Genesee River in 1735.[36] He lived through the years when his people were forced to leave their lands and relocate to Buffalo Creek (present-day Buffalo, New York), and the Tonawanda, Allegheny, and Cattaraugus Reserves. The Seneca remember this as a time of great despair, when they were hated by

"Handsome Lake Preaching." Handsome Lake, a late eighteenth-century Seneca prophet, stands in the longhouse holding a string of wampum and preaching to his followers. The wampum signifies that the words he is speaking are true. The sketch was made in 1905 by Seneca artist Jesse Cornplanter. From New York State Library (SC 12845-29).

their American neighbors, cheated out of their lands, and unable to support themselves in traditional ways, so that they lived in great poverty. Handsome Lake was one who turned to alcohol to ease the pain and almost drank himself to death. Then, in 1799, he fell into a coma-like state in which he had a vision from the Creator, known today as the Gaiwiio, "The Good Message."

The Code of Handsome Lake is a set of directions or instructions to help the Haudenosaunee people hold onto their traditional values while adapting to a modern world. There are 130 parts or sections to the Gaiwiio, which is recited each year during a three-day ceremony held in the fall by those who follow the Code. Not everyone does; the Code of Handsome Lake incorporates elements of Christianity and Euro-American culture, so that some say it is too Christian, preferring to follow a Longhouse tradition free of Christian elements, while others think it retains too much of the old ways. However, there is no doubt that the Code of Handsome Lake played, and continues to play, an important role in guiding Haudenosaunee people in preserving the core of identify and sovereignty in a colonial world.

The 130 sections of the code may be grouped into six broad areas. The first is ceremonial renewal. The Code specifies that certain rituals and ceremonies must be maintained by the Haudenosaunee, although people could make accommodations such as using domesticated cows and pigs for feastings instead of hunting game. Overall it emphasizes the importance of ceremonial life. A second part of the Code governs the rituals and practices associated with planting and harvesting the Three Sisters—corn, beans, and squash. The next two parts of the Code define acceptable and unacceptable behavior. On the prohibition side, the Code forbids alcohol, witchcraft (the use of spirit power or medicine to harm others), gambling, fiddle music (a type of music often associated with drinking places at the time), and other behaviors deemed to be harmful, such as spreading or listening to gossip, lying, or boasting. On the other hand, the Code urges people to attend ceremonies with a thankful heart, to raise a good family of people who treat each other well, to be generous and offer food to strangers, and to send at least two children from each community to Euro-American schools so that they could learn the ways of the dominant society.

The fifth part of the Code speaks of two paths, and Handsome Lake's journey on the Sky Road, or Milky Way, to Sky World. This part is recited on the third day. Handsome Lake said that, in his vision, the messengers sent to guide him showed him two paths. One was wide and crowded with many people, leading to the house of the Punisher. The other path was narrow and lead to the Creator's land. Handsome Lake also reported an encounter with Jesus, who said, "They slew me because of their independence and unbelief." Jesus instructed Handsome Lake to tell his people that they would be lost if they followed the way of the white man. This is the part of the Code that creates the most controversy. Is it too Christian or not Christian enough?

The sixth element of the Code is a recitation of people, places, and events that the Iroquois should remember. It includes historical events from the past as well as predictions for the future. The Code of Handsome Lake is what anthropologists call a "revitalization movement." This is when people reach back into the past to bring new life to old traditions. The Code of Handsome Lake keeps the best of the old ways and rejects the worst of the new. It asserts the uniqueness of Haudenosaunee language, history, and culture while offering practical guidelines for living in the modern world as Haudenosaunee people.

EMIGRATION AND SURVIVAL

In the aftermath of the American Revolution, both Algonkian and Iroquoian communities faced a new world—again. In New England, Algonkian peoples went about their business in established towns that were predominantly inhabited by Native peoples, such as Mashpee, on

Cape Cod, Old Town (Indian Island) in Maine, as well as on lands that were formally set apart as reservation land. Others continued to move through the land in ways that echoed their traditional seasonal rounds. In 1861, John Milton Earle was charged with writing a report on the number and living conditions of Native peoples in Massachusetts for the Massachusetts Governor and Council. He found it a difficult task:

Situate as most of them are, near the seaboard, in the immediate vicinity of our fishing and commercial ports, the temptation to a race naturally inclined to a roving and unsettled life, are too great to be resisted, and nearly all of the males, first or last, engage in seafaring as an occupation. Thus, the men are drawn away from home, and are often absent for years at a time, frequently without their friends knowing where they are. The women, left behind, seek employment wherever it can be had, usually in the neighboring towns and cities. . . . After thus leaving home, they frequently remove from place to place, keeping up no correspondance or communication with those who have left; till at last their place of residence ceases to be known by their friends, and all trace of them is lost.[37]

Others moved their families and communities to new locations, looking toward the future.

While conversion to Christianity is usually viewed as evidence of assimilation to Euro-American ways, a vision- **Brothertown** ary Mohegan leader named Samson Occum formed a new, self-governing community of Native peoples based on Christian principles but as far away from the English as possible. Occum was born at Mohegan in 1723 and became a Christian during the Great Awakening of the 1730s. With his mother's encouragement, he enrolled in a private Christian school run by Eleazar Wheelock in Connecticut, where he studied Greek, Latin, and Hebrew, among other subjects. Occum became a minister and spent his life working in Native communities such as Natick, Massachusetts, and Montauk, on Long Island. However, his talent and achievements did not prevent him from experiencing discrimination. He became bitter when the Society for the Propagation of the Gospel in London would only pay him half the salary that they gave to English missionaries in New England, despite the fact that he soon had a wife and 10 children to support. The biggest betrayal came from Wheelock, his former teacher. Occum made three trips to Oneida communities in New York to recruit students for Wheelock's school and spent two years on a speaking tour of Britain where he gave more than 300 sermons to raise money for Wheelock's school. He raised over 12,000 pounds. Then, in 1773, Wheelock decided to stop recruiting Native students and used the money to found what became Dartmouth College.

This is the context in which Occum decided to found a community that he called Eeayam Quittoowauconnuk, or Brothertown, in 1774. Occum turned to his friends at Oneida and negotiated for a tract of land on their territory, where he was joined by Pequot and Mohegan followers. The community was briefly interrupted during the American Revolution, when people took refuge at the Christian community of Mahicans at Stockbridge, Massachusetts.[38]

Wisconsin The Christian Oneida who had fought for the Americans played an important role in helping other communities to survive. They had already given part of their land for Samson Occum to establish the Brothertown community. After the Revolution they accepted Protestant refugees from Stockbridge who had served in the American army but returned home to find that their land titles were not recognized by the new federal government.

Unfortunately the Oneida soon felt the hardships of dispossession. In the 1784 Treaty of Fort Stanwix, the Continental Congress promised to protect Oneida and Tuscarora lands in exchange for their military help in the Revolutionary War. Unfortunately these promises were not honored by New York State, and the federal government did not enforce them. Pressed from all sides, some Oneida remained but a large group decided to move west. They chose Wisconsin Territory because their minister, Eleazer Williams, negotiated an agreement with the Menominee to allow the Oneidas to settle on their lands around Green Bay in 1822. In exchange, the Oneida agreed to pay the Menominee $3,000 over three years. Note that Williams was of Mohawk and English descent, being a grandson of Eunice Williams who had been captured from Deerfield, Massachusetts in 1704 and raised at Kahnawake.[39]

As for the other nations living at Oneida, they had to move as well. The Stockbridge people moved first to Indiana and then to Wisconsin, where they were joined by Munsee Delaware people. The Stockbridge-Munsee moved to a reservation in Wisconsin in 1856. The Brothertown Indians also purchased land in Wisconsin and moved there in the 1830s.[40]

Six Nations Reserve at Grand River During the mid-seventeenth century, two important figures emerged as leaders among the Mohawk. Joseph Brant, also known as Thayendanegea, was a Mohawk war chief. His sister, Molly Brant, was a clan mother in her own right with additional influence as the wife of Sir William Johnson, the Superintendent of Indian Affairs for New York. After the end of the American Revolution, Joseph Brant negotiated an agreement with the British that allowed the Mohawks and other members of the Six Nations Iroquois Confederacy to acquire new lands on the Grand River in Ontario, Canada after 1784. At Grand River, Brant lived like an aristocrat. He ate from fine china and drank from crystal goblets while being waited on by an African servant in livery, thoroughly at home with these aspects of British culture. In 1797 he signed a treaty with New York State that ceded eight million acres of Mohawk land. This created hard feelings among those Mohawks who still lived in New York. They complained that Brant did not have the authority to do this because he was only a war chief and not a Confederacy chief.

By 1803, the New York and Canadian Iroquois decided to go their separate ways. People from Six Nations Reserve were excluded from Confederacy meetings held at Onondaga . Brant disowned them and established their own Council at Grand River. In subsequent years, this arrangement offered certain benefits. The Grand Council at Onondaga took the lead in Confederacy negotiations with the United States, while Grand River took the lead in comparable negotiations with Canada.[41]

CONCLUSION

Faced with unpleasant options, Algonkian and Iroquoian peoples made choices that faced the future rather than the past, fighting for their homelands when possible but withdrawing when that seemed to be the best way to secure the safety of their families. During the seventeenth and eighteenth centuries they tried a number of different strategies to pursue their own interests. Three things they consistently set their course by were the well-being of their relatives, access to traditional places, and sovereignty. Other than major catastrophes such as epidemic disease, which could not be predicted or outwitted, the biggest obstacles faced by both Algonkians and Iroquoians in the Northeast—the rapids they had to pass and the rocks they tried to avoid—all came from relationships with other people. The English were encroaching as neighbors and destructive as enemies. The French offered relative safety in mission towns but only on condition that their "domiciled Indians," as they called them, agreed to live as Catholics and fight in the French interest. Intertribal rivalries led some Native peoples to work against each other in the seventeenth century, but it soon became clear that, to the Europeans, they were all "Indians."

NOTES

1. William Wood (1634), quoted on page 73 of George R. Hamell, "Strawberries, Floating Islands, and Rabbit Captains: Mythical Realities and European Contact in the Northeast during the Sixteenth and Seventeenth Centuries," *Revue d'études canadiennes / Journal of Canadian Studies* 21/4 (Winter 1986–1987): 72–94.

2. Gabriel Archer, "The Relation of Captaine Gosnols Voyage to the North part of Virginia, begunne the sixe and twentieth of March [1602]," in *The English New England Voyages, 1602–1608*, ed. David B. Quinn and Alison M. Quinn, Hakluyt Society Publications, 2nd ser., no. 161 (London: The Hakluyt Society, 1983), 117.

3. Silas Tertius Rand, *Legends of the Micmacs*, Wellesley Philological Publications (London: Longmans, Green, and Co., 1894), 225–27.

4. For a good summary of the literature on the Beaver Wars, see William A. Starna and José António Brandão, "From the Mohawk-Mahican War to the Beaver Wars: Questioning the Pattern," *Ethnohistory* 51:4 (Fall 2004): 725–50.

5. J. Franklin Jameson, ed., *Johnson's Wonder-Working Providence, 1628–1651* (New York: Barnes and Noble, 1967).

6. John Underhill, *Nevvs from America; or, A New and Experimentall Discoverie of New England; Containing, A Trve Relation of Their Warlike Proceedings These Two Years Last Past, with a Figure of the Indian Fort, or Palozado . . . .* (London: Printed by J.D. for Peter Cole, 1638; repr. New York: Da Capo Press, 1971).

7. Quoted in Jean M. O'Brien, *Dispossession by Degrees: Indian Land and Identity in Natick, Massachusetts, 1650–1790* (New York: Cambridge University Press, 1997), 28.

8. Harold W. Van Lonkhuyzen, "A Reappraisal of the Praying Indians: Acculturation, Conversion and Identity at Natick, Massachusetts, 1646–1730," *The New England Quarterly* 63:3 (1990): 396–428.

9. Ann Marie Plane, *Colonial Intimacies: Indian Marriage in Early New England* (Ithaca, NY: Cornell University Press, 2000), 105–6.

10. Thomas Shepard, quoted in O'Brien, 44–45.

11. For an extraordinary collection of manuscript documents written by Native people in their own language including wills, land deeds, and marginal notes from personal bibles, see volume 1 of Ives Goddard and Kathleen J. Bragdon, *Native Writings in Massachusett* (Philadelphia: American Philosophical Society, 1988), 2 vols.

12. O'Brien, 94–97.

13. Plane, 64. The following discussion also draws on Plane.

14. Ann Marie Plane, "Putting a Face on Colonization: Factionalism and Gender Politics in the Life History of Awashunkes, the 'Squaw Sachem' of Saconet," in *Northeastern Indian Lives, 1632–1816* ed. Robert S. Grumet (Amherst: University of Massachusetts Press, 1996), 150–53.

15. Plane, *Colonial Intimacies*, 67–95.

16. Although the war ended in southern New England with the death of Metacomet in 1676, the violence continued on the Eastern Frontier until 1678. See Frank T. Siebert, "The First Maine Indian War: Incident at Machias (1676)," *Proceedings of the 14th Algonquian Conference* (1976): 137–56; Emerson W. Baker and John G. Reid, *The New England Knight: Sir William Phips, 1651–1695* (Toronto: University of Toronto Press, 1998), 135.

17. Reuben Gold Thwaites, ed., *The Jesuit Relations and Allied Documents: Travels and Explorations of the Jesuit Missionaries in New France, 1610–1791*, 71 vols. (Cleveland: Burrows Brothers, 1896–1901), 60: 233.

18. Ruth Wallis Herndon and Ella Wilcox Sekatau, "Colonizing the Children: Indian Youngsters in Servitude in Early Rhode Island," in *Reinterpreting New England Indians and the Colonial Experience,* ed. Colin G. Calloway and Neal Salisbury (Boston: Colonial Society of Massachusetts, 2003), 137–61.

19. Laura E. Conkey, Ethel Boissevain, and Ives Goddard, "Indians of Southern New England and Long Island: The Late Period," in *Northeast*, ed. Bruce Trigger, vol. 15 of *Handbook of North American Indians*, gen. ed. William C. Sturtevant (Washington, DC: Smithsonian Institution Press, 1978), 177–89.

20. Cadwallader Colden, *The History of the Five Indian Nations, Depending on the Province of New-York in America* (Ithaca, NY: Cornell University Press, 1986 [1886]), vi–vii.

21. Frederick E. Hoxie, ed., *Encyclopedia of North American Indians: Native American History, Culture, and Life from Paleo-Indians to the Present.* (New York: Houghton Mifflin Company, 1996), 98.

22. Colin G. Calloway, *First Peoples: A Documentary Survey of American Indian History,* 2nd ed. (Boston: Bedford/St. Martin's, 2004), 145–47.

23. Evan Haefeli and Kevin Sweeney, *Captors and Captives: The 1704 French and Indian Raid on Deerfield* (Amherst: University of Massachusetts Press, 2003), 55–77.

24. John Williams, *The Redeemed Captive Returning to Zion* (Cambridge: Applewood Books, 1987).

25. Haefeli and Sweeney, 73–77.

26. See Thwaites, *The Jesuit Relations,* 71 vols.

27. Thwaites 63: 33–35; 67: 89–91.

28. Daniel K. Richter, *The Ordeal of the Longhouse: The Peoples of the Iroquois League in the Era of European Colonization* (Chapel Hill: University of North Carolina Press, 1992).

29. Gilles Havard, *The Great Peace of Montreal of 1701: French-Native Diplomacy in the Seventeenth Century,* trans. Phyllis Aronoff and Howard Scott (Montreal: McGill-Queen's University Press, 2001); Pocumtuck Valley Memorial Association, *Raid on Deerfield: The Many Stories of 1704,* online history resource at www.1704. deerfield.history.museum.

30. This discussion is based on Mary Jemison's narrative, published as James E. Seaver, *A Narrative of the Life of Mrs. Mary Jemison,* with an introduction by June Namias (Norman: University of Oklahoma Press, 1992).

31. Seaver, 76.

32. Seaver, 56–57.

33. Seaver, 58.

34. Hoxie, 301.

35. Alice B. Kehoe, *North American Indians: A Comprehensive Account,* 3rd ed. (Upper Saddle River, NJ: Prentice Hall, 2006), 242–44.

36. This section is based on Carol Cornelius, *Iroquois Corn in a Culture-Based Curriculum: A Framework for Respectfully Teaching about Cultures* (Albany: State University of New York Press, 1999), 83–90.

37. John Milton Earle, quoted in O'Brien, 210.

38. Hoxie, 434–36. Note that Mohegans and Mahicans are related groups.

39. Hoxie, 441–42.

40. Hoxie, 611.

41. Hoxie, 302; Kehoe, 244.

4

Daily Life in the Ohio Valley and the Great Lakes

For much of its human history the Ohio Valley and the Great Lakes region have been places in transition and flux. The climate in the northern mid-American section is shaped by harsh and long winters, especially as one moves further north. These areas are blessed with a growing seasons and average rainfall conducive to agriculture, with moderately mild springs and fall, and warm and often humid summers. In both the Ohio Valley and in the Great Lakes, the landscape is dominated by woodlands of impressive hardwood forests as well as significant areas of open grasslands and prairies. The two regions are also home to many waterways—lakes, rivers, and streams.

The landscape and climate shaped the daily life of the first peoples of the Ohio Valley and the Great Lakes through the centuries. Trees provided abundant fuel, raw material to build shelter, boats for river transportation, and tools to make life easier. The animals of the forest, the fish in the rivers and Great Lakes, and the birds of the air provided a reliable sources of food. The woods also contained an abundance of plant foods, such as roots, berries, and nuts, that could be gathered for immediate consumption or dried for later eating. By 1492, many people of the Ohio Valley and the Great Lakes had been farming for generations. The women cultivated corn, squash, beans, pumpkins, sunflowers, and other plants as the main staple of their diets.

As with other Amerindian peoples in different regions, Native American lifeways in the Ohio Valley and the Great Lakes were changed and at times severely disrupted by European colonization. The American Revolution, like no other single event, dramatically changed the daily life of Native peoples in the two areas. In U.S. history, the American Revolution is celebrated as the moment when people of European descent declared their political independence from Great Britain. The Revolution had a different meaning and outcome for Native Americans. This is true for all indigenous peoples along the eastern seaboard and ultimately across the continent, but it had a particular effect in the Ohio Valley and the Great Lakes because this was a key arena of the war and the early decades of American expansion. The victory by the Americans initiated a new period of struggle in the effort to maintain sovereignty and autonomy for indigenous peoples confronted by colonization. Their revolution lasted in many ways until the end of the War of 1812, when the last Native American effort at militant resistance to American expansion in the region was defeated by the Americans.

THE MOUND BUILDERS

For the two millennia before Columbus "discovered" the Americas, the Ohio as well as the Mississippi River valleys were sites of American Indian exchange networks by peoples whom we know mostly through the archaeological record, such as the Adena (c.a. 500 B.C.–100 B.C.), the Hopewell (c.a. 200 B.C.–400 A.D.) and the Mississippians (c.a. 700 A.D.–1500 A.D.). These complex and diverse ancient civilizations are often lumped together as Mound Builders, named after the earthen monuments that they built all over the Eastern Woodlands but predominantly west of the Appalachian Mountain chain. Archaeological evidence in the form of highly developed artifacts from mound burial sites and other earthworks suggests that powerful ruling elites existed among the Mound Builders, and that they had complex ceremonial and religious organizations. Unfortunately in the last 200 years, because of various forms of development, such as the expansion of American farming, the building of towns, cities, suburbs, and highways, which have accompanied the history of white settlement, much of the archaeological record has been destroyed. This, in part, explains why we still have so many unanswered questions about the Mound Builders' history, and why so much of our knowledge about them, especially about their daily life, remains unclear.

The ancient mound sites built by Native Americans are phenomenal architectural masterpieces. The earliest construction of earthworks dates as far back as about 4000 B.C. The earthworks often consisted of intricate geometric designs, such as squares, circles, octagons, rectangles, and hexagons, which were built either standing alone or in groups. Smaller mound sites encompassed up to 10 acres, while the larger ones enclosed hundreds of acres. The earthworks in Newark, Ohio, for example, display a relatively well-preserved octagon and a 1,200-foot-wide circle. Other mound structures include effigy mounds

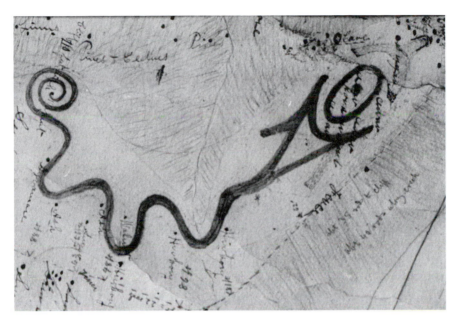

Plan of the Serpent Mound. Seen from above, the Serpent Mound, near Cincinnati, Ohio, is one of many earthworks in the shape of an animal in the Ohio and Mississippi River Valleys. It stretches some 800 feet in length, or 1,300 feet if measured in a straight line. From Peabody Museum, Harvard University, Photo 2004.24.6051.1.

that appeared in the form of snakes, birds, and bear paws, as well as other animal shapes and forms. They were particularly common in the upper Great Lakes region. Perhaps the most famous survivor of these mounds is the Serpent Mound, which can be found in modern Adams County, Ohio. It has been heavily eroded since 1846 but it is still an impressive sight, reaching about 800 feet in length (1,300 feet if the mound could be measured in a straight line) and about 4 feet high and 20 feet wide. At the time of its creation, the effigy mound stood 5 feet high and 30 feet wide.

For the ancient Native American peoples of the Mississippi and the Ohio River valleys, the mounds played a central role as places of sacred architecture. Some earthworks functioned as burial sites, such as the dome-shaped burial mounds of the Adena of the Ohio River valley. Native Americans used other structures as sacred and ritual spaces, as with the Serpent Mound. The hilltop enclosure at Fort Ancient in Warren County, Ohio, which encompasses about 100 acres surrounded by an embankment with numerous openings varying in height from 4 to 23 feet, probably served as a combination of both—a place for burial but also a space used for rituals and ceremonials.

The construction of mound complexes and entire mound sites played a central part in the daily lives of the ancient Indian peoples of the Ohio Valley and the Great Lakes. At a time in history that predated the use of caterpillar tractors, excavators, and trucks, the construction of elaborate sites required the efforts of large communities whose members carried thousands of tons of earth in baskets. Furthermore, such projects required considerable amounts of time and sophisticated architectural planning. This commitment by early Native peoples in the region seems to suggests that the mounds played an extremely important role in the spiritual and ceremonial life and view of the world of the region's Indian populations.

The Mound Builders participated in a vast exchange network that included much of the eastern section of the North American continent. Ancient Native American groups like the Adena and Hopewell produced artworks out of materials that they acquired from trade with faraway places. They obtained, for example, mica from North Carolina and Arkansas, obsidian from the Yellowstone region in western Wyoming, and copper from the northern Great Lakes. Ancient societies also used shark and alligator teeth as well as conch shells in their artwork. The waterways of the Eastern Woodlands, such as the Ohio, the Missouri, and the Mississippi Rivers, and their tributaries, were used as the major avenues of transportation for the exchange networks of the Mound Builders.

Evidence of these connections as well as the Mound Builders' artistry can be found in burial sites all over the Eastern Woodlands. They are represented by the effigy pipes made of stone in human or animal form, animal or human effigy cut-outs of copper or mica, marine shell gorgets, human shaped statues, engraved stone tablets, copper plates, and various ceramic figures and pottery.

Mound Builders, especially during the Mississippian period (ca. 700 A.D.–ca. 1500 A.D.), also built urban centers. Cahokia (a site occupied between about 700 A.D. and 1250 A.D.) in Collinsville, Illinois (close to St. Louis, Missouri) is arguably the most famous and largest precontact city north of Mexico. The core of the settlement, an area of more than 200 acres, was surrounded by a wooden palisade. The city also was made up of hundreds of mounds, several of which are assumed to have reached over 100 feet in size. These earthworks, it is believed, served as the bases for the houses of the elite and as public buildings. The largest one, Monks Mound, was the focal point of the urban center. Despite hundreds of years of erosion, Monks Mound today measures 100 feet in height, over 1,000 feet in length, and 790 feet in width. The city also had plazas, a wooden post monument, and residential districts. Estimates of Cahokia's population vary widely from about 10,000 to 50,000 at its peak. It was a grand city, comparable in size to any of the major European urban settlements at the time. Cahokia's citizens procured food for its large population by raising crops such as corn, squash, pumpkins, and beans, and supplementing their diet by hunting and fishing.[1]

By the time Europeans began to colonize the Western Hemisphere in the late fifteenth and early sixteenth century, the Mississippian Mound Building centers of the Eastern Woodlands were in rapid decline—a demise that remains somewhat of a puzzle today. Much of the scholarship stresses the impact of disease as a major factor in their decline. Scholars argue that alien pathogens led to mortality rates in Native communities from a low estimate of 50 percent and, with sustained contact over several decades, running as high as 90 percent. Long-distance trade connected the aboriginal population of the Ohio Valley with the Gulf Coast, a region ravaged by diseases introduced by Spanish conquistadors and shipwreck survivors in the sixteenth century. This contact could easily have led to the spread of deadly epidemics along the inland waterways of North America. Thus, waves of epidemics in the Ohio Valley could have caused dramatic depopulation and changes in the social landscape.[2] Other scholars have, however, also pointed out that there is convincing evidence that the Mound Building cultures of the Ohio and the upper and middle Mississippi River valleys were already in decline before 1500, as the region underwent a broader pattern of population redistribution and decline.[3]

FORT ANCIENT PEOPLES

The lifeways of the Mound Builders influenced the daily lives of generations of Native Americans in the Ohio Valley and the Great Lakes region, even after these once-powerful and culturally productive civilizations began to decline. Archaeologists who study the early Native peoples of the Ohio Valley often refer to the groups that lived in the region from about 1000 A.D. to the late seventeenth century as Fort Ancient peoples. We do not know what they called themselves.

Even more than for their forebears, the Fort Ancient way of life was dominated by maize (corn) horticulture. Due to this reliance on corn production, their settlements were usually found in fertile bottomlands beside waterways. Periodic flooding kept these areas productive for agriculture. Like their ancestors, Fort Ancient people also grew sunflowers, squash, and tobacco, and gathered nuts, fruits, berries, and medicinal herbs, with most of the planting and gathering work done by women. Their subsistence economy was supplemented by meats procured by male hunters who brought in deer, turkey, elk, bear, and in some areas also bison.

Fort Ancient villages were built and organized around a central plaza, which was the center for ceremonial activity. The settlement's inhabitants lived in single-family dwellings. These houses often had storage pits for corn. Fort Ancient villagers also continued to bury the remains of some of their loved ones in mounds, while others were buried in graves near their houses or on the edge of the plaza. They also gave gifts to the dead.

Archaeological evidence from grave sites shows that pipes, tools, and ornaments were left with the deceased.

For reasons that are still unclear, many of the Fort Ancient sites in the Upper Ohio Valley were abandoned by the seventeenth century. Most scholars believe that the inhabitants of the region were probably forced out by the intertribal impact of colonial expansion and warfare taking place far away to the south and east. As noted in Chapters 1 and 2, the arrival of Europeans and their goods, along with the increase in death rates from epidemics and war, had a ripple effect that spread across the inland continent long before Europeans themselves arrived in any great numbers. This turned much of the Upper Ohio Valley into an area of low population density as the indigenous inhabitants were uprooted.[4]

NATIVE MIGRANTS: THE AMERINDIAN RESETTLEMENT OF THE OHIO VALLEY

A gradual resettling of the Ohio Valley began during the years between 1720 and the 1750s, as Native migrants from various groups set out to begin a new life in the region. Many of these groups sought refuge from Euro-American encroachment and related pressures. For instance, an increasing number of Delaware and Shawnee from the Susquehanna and Delaware River regions to the east moved their towns to the Upper Ohio Valley. The Delaware, an Algonkian-speaking people, largely centered their settlements on the Allegheny, the Beaver, and the Muskingum Rivers. The Shawnee, another nation of Algonkian speakers, may have been one of the groups originally driven out of the Ohio Valley region by the Haudenosaunee, also known as the Iroquois, during the seventeenth century. The Shawnees settled for the most part around the Scioto, and the Miami and Mad Rivers, where they were also joined by some Shawnee migrants who came from the south. At roughly the same time, other Amerindian nations moved their towns and villages from the Great Lakes region to the Ohio country, to place themselves in a more advantageous position between French and British trade. The Miamis, for example, came back to their homelands on the southern tip of Lake Michigan after having been forced by the Haudenosaunee to a temporary exile around present-day Green Bay, Wisconsin during the so-called Beaver Wars of the seventeenth century. The Miamis now rebuilt their town in parts of what eventually became the states of Indiana and Ohio. By the mid-eighteenth century, the rich hunting grounds of the Upper Ohio Valley also began to lure some members of the Six Nations Iroquois—mostly the Seneca—to move west. These Haudenosaunee people came to be known as the Mingos. Members of a group that the English called Wyandots, remnants of the Huron-Wendat nation dispersed by the Haudenosaunee during the Beaver Wars, migrated to the Detroit and Sandusky River area from southwestern Ontario.[5]

Their new haven offered rich hunting grounds and fertile lands for farming at a safe distance—at least for a time—from Euro-American society. The relocation to a new region enabled Native migrants to revitalize their societies by maintaining their way of life, which they were increasingly unable to do in the areas closer to the coast. The westward move by Native people such as the Delaware or Shawnee, who were fleeing the pressures of colonial expansion and intertribal competition on the eastern seaboard, was more than just a flight from hardship. It was a movement *to* a place that offered things that they needed to survive as a people, both physically and culturally. They did not stop being Delaware or Shawnee, just as people from England could not sever themselves from their British roots simply by relocating to North America. Rather, they adapted to a changing world through a series of active, positive choices.

Factionalism among Amerindian societies and confederacies was an integral part of the political and social organization of daily life in the Ohio Valley and the Great Lakes.

Social Organization, Leadership, and Religion

The Shawnees, for example, had five major divisions, the Chillicothe, Mequashake, Piqua, Wakatomica, and Kispoko. The Delaware organized into three major groups called Turtle, Wolf, and Turkey. The political structures of confederacies, which generally drew support from a wide range of Amerindian societies and groups, were also flexible and fluid organizations. Their members often pursued different goals. At particular moments of crisis, Amerindian confederacies moved toward a unified resistance by building powerful coalitions, as did the people of the Great Lakes and Ohio River valley under the leadership of the Ottawa chief Pontiac, who resisted British efforts at colonization in 1763. At all times, however, confederacies faced immense internal divisions and strains. The traditional style of flexible leadership, which allowed people to make their own choices, offered little precedent for keeping people together when they disagreed over major issues, such as whether to side with the British, the French, or the increasingly independent colonists. Thus it becomes more useful to focus on towns and villages as the key units of social and political organization rather than categories such as tribe, ethnicity, or political confederacy.

Many of the Ohio and Great Lakes Amerindian communities had a dual system of leadership, with separate civil and war chiefs. Both were members of the village council and represented their group's interests in the councils of confederacies and tribes. Traditionally the civil chiefs' leadership authority was largely ceremonial and depended on consensus in their groups. Yet increasing colonial encroachment and contacts with colonial officials led to a larger centralization of Amerindian leaders' power. War chiefs, in contrast, obtained their social standing by demonstrating proficiency in battle and ideally only assumed power in times of war. But as Anglo-American expansion led to increasing warfare, war chiefs like the Miami leader, Little Turtle, or the Shawnee leader, Tecumseh, began to play an increasingly powerful role in Ohio and Great Lakes Amerindian societies. Still, even powerful chiefs hardly possessed absolute power, and rather owed their popularity to their leadership skills.

Religion and culture were also important determining factors in the life of indigenous peoples in the Ohio Valley and the Great Lakes region. Amerindians in the region believed that evil spirits and witchcraft were the cause of many diseases. They also believed in the existence of a supreme deity often referred to as the "Master of Life" or the "Great Spirit." This powerful god could generally only be addressed and contacted indirectly through sacrifices to spirits of lesser power, which the

Sketch of Pontiac, an Ottawa chief who united Native peoples from the Great Lakes and Ohio Valley in an effort to drive the British out of their homeland. From Ohio Historical Society (SC208).

Delaware, for example, called "Manitous," and to which they could also establish contact through visions. Furthermore, Natives in the Ohio Valley and the Great Lakes believed that the soul of a person would continue to exist after death, and that they remained in the vicinity of the villages for some time, where they had to be appeased through sacrifices, before they went to an afterlife.[6]

Most Ohio Valley and Great Lakes Amerindian **Farming and Hunting** societies depended on agriculture and hunting as a means of subsistence. Food production was based on a division of labor by sex—women farmed and gathered food, and men provided meat through hunting. As in other parts of the Eastern Woodlands, Native American women farmed corn (maize), beans, pumpkins, squash, and sweet potatoes. They worked the rich soil of the river valleys and prolonged the fertility of their fields by burning brush and trees before starting a new field and also burning the stubble at the end of harvest time. When a field's productivity declined, the women planted their crops in a new location.[7] To many Anglo-American observers, the emphasis in Native agriculture on female labor appeared alien and frequently led to contemptuous remarks about the poor conditions under which Amerindian women suffered.

Yet, European observers generally failed to draw a complete picture of Native American agriculture in the eighteenth century, and the power that women held in their societies. To ease the labor of farming, women frequently worked the fields communally, receiving assistance from the children and at times from the men. Women also had considerable control in starting and ending relationships with their male companions. Moreover, since Amerindian women in the Ohio Valley and the Great Lakes were the main agricultural producers and gatherers of plants, they were also the main distributors of food—a position that gave women a greater authority and respect in their own households than many of their contemporaries in Euro-American society enjoyed.[8]

Though Eastern Woodland peoples were farmers, other subsistence activities such as hunting, trapping, and fishing played a central role in their societies as well. These activities were largely the domain of Native American men. The Amerindian peoples of the Great Lakes and the Ohio Valley recognized the achievements of skillful hunters and warriors. Success in hunting and war was a means to demonstrate one's manhood to the community, and Native men took pride in their ability to protect and provide for their extended families. Throughout the summer, while the women tended the fields, the men supplemented the family diet with fish and meat. They also frequently joined raids on enemy groups. After the fall harvest, families and smaller groups all but abandoned their villages as they left for winter hunting camps. Here the men hunted deer, turkey, and bears and trapped fur-bearing animals such as beaver, while the women maintained the camps and tended the furs and animal skins.[9]

The Fur Trade
The trans-Atlantic trade in animal skins and pelts played a central role in the daily lives of the Amerindian peoples of the Ohio Valley and the Great Lakes in the eighteenth and early nineteenth century. Native Americans in the region played an active role in this European-dominated market system. Moreover, being situated between the French, who tried to assert control over the Ohio and Mississippi River valleys from their position north and east of the Great Lakes, and the British, who were eager to expand their control to the west, Native Americans in the Great Lakes and the Ohio Valley at times found themselves in a position to turn French-British rivalries to their benefit. Frequently the Anglo-French competition aided Natives in maintaining control over their lands and in getting better terms of trade during the first half of the eighteenth century.

The dangers and drawbacks of being tied into an international trade system emerged for the Native peoples in the Great Lakes and the Ohio Valley over time and to a degree that varied across time and space. Throughout the eighteenth and early nineteenth century, the expansion of trade in the region led to a decline in the population of game animals. Native Americans in the Ohio Valley and the Great Lakes region supplied beaver pelts and deerskins to the trans-Atlantic commercial system. With the growing Amerindian population in the region that participated in trade relations, a strain was put on the local deer and beaver populations as groups such as the Shawnee and Miami increased their participation in the commercial market, now hunting deer, beaver, and other animals for the trade value of their skins rather than simply for meat. Trade goods became an increasingly important part of daily life, especially during times of war when the normal rhythms of hunting and horticulture were disrupted.

The involvement in the deerskin and fur trade led to changes in the social norms and organization of Amerindian communities in the Ohio Valley and the Great Lakes region. "Hunting for the market," writes historian Eric Hinderaker, gradually undermined "some of the ruling hunting assumptions of earlier hunting practices, which emphasized the sacred qualities of animals and the importance of reciprocity and the propitiation of spirits." For many Amerindians, hunting transformed increasingly from a means of subsistence to an activity driven by market incentives. At the height of the commercial relationship, a skillful hunter might kill anywhere from 50 to 150 deer during a single hunting season. Most of the meat procured during these massive hunting excursions was wasted.[10]

Canoes
With the abundance of waterways and lakes, Native Americans made wide use of canoes as means of transportation and travel in the Great Lakes and the Ohio Valley—just as they did throughout the Eastern Woodlands. The construction of a canoe was a complex and labor-intensive process. Canoes consisted of a framework of saplings that were covered with bark, generally birch or elm. The bark

pieces used as coverings were stitched together with strings made out of root. The casing was then put over the frame and was sealed with tar or pitch. Canoes were light and Native Americans often portaged the boats from one lake or river system to another. Thus, the waterways functioned in many ways as the highways for the Native peoples in the region.

Trade with Europeans introduced alcohol into the daily lives of Ohio and Great Lakes Amerindians. After its introduction alcohol and alcoholism became more and more of a problem for Native societies. A folktale among the Menominee of the Great Lakes region in modern Wisconsin, who were involved in the fur trade with the French, describes the effect alcohol had on the individuals that first tried the drug during an early encounter with Europeans. The Menominee, suspicious that the white traders might attempt to poison them, gave the alcohol to "four useless old men." **Alcohol**

The men drank the liquid, and although they had previously been very silent and gloomy, they now began to talk and grow amused. Their speech flowed more and more freely, while the remainder of the Indians said, "See now it is beginning to take effect!" Presently the four old men arose, and while walking about seemed very dizzy, when the Indians said, "See now they are surely dying!" Presently the men dropped down and became unconscious; then the Indians said to one another, "Now they are dead; see what we escaped by not drinking the liquid!" There were sullen looks directed toward the strangers, and murmurings of destroying them for the supposed treachery were heard.

Before things came to a dangerous pass, however, the four old men got up, rubbed their eyes, and approached their kindred saying, "The liquor is good, and we have felt very happy; you must try it too." Notwithstanding the rest of the tribe were afraid to drink it then.[11]

Alcohol consumption had a harmful impact in Native communities in the Ohio Valley and Great Lakes region, especially as advancing American colonization threw the indigenous peoples of the region into a cultural crisis by the late eighteenth and early nineteenth century. Major land losses, poverty, and cultural and social dislocation led to crisis in many Native towns and villages. These developments disrupted the patterns of daily life. White officials wanted to exploit the weaknesses within Native communities. They intended to completely transform Amerindian societies. President Thomas Jefferson, for example, wrote in a frequently quoted letter to Indiana's territorial governor William Henry Harrison in February 1803.

The decrease of game rendering their subsistence by hunting insufficient, we wish to draw them to agriculture, to spinning and weaving. The latter branches they take up with readiness, because they fall to the women, who gain by quitting the labours of the field [for] these which are exercised within doors. When they withdraw themselves to the culture of a small piece of land, they will perceive how useless to them are their extensive forests, and will be willing to pare them off from time to time in exchange for necessaries for their farms & families. . . . In this way our settlements will in time either incorporate [Native Americans] with us as citizens of the United States or remove [them] beyond the Mississippi.[12]

The pressures on Amerindian lands and their traditional way of life reinforced the consumption of liquor and alcoholism among Native American communities on the Ohio and Great Lakes frontier. Federal and territorial governments, as well as most white settlers, offered little help. Indeed, they eagerly sought ways to obtain more Native land, taking advantage of the fact that many Native Americans used alcohol as a means to temporarily escape their harsh social circumstances and new realities.

Moravian missionaries among a Delaware community on the White River near present-day Muncie, Indiana, closely observed the disruptive role that alcohol played among Native Americans in the region.

It is simply indescribable how the Indians cling to this terrible whisky drinking. When strong drink is brought into their towns, they will not stop until all is gone, even if there is a hundred gallons to begin with. They give the shirt from their back for the last drop. When one comes into one of their towns at the time of such carousals, most of them are naked and practicing every imaginable abomination. A drunken spree like this seldom passes without some of them losing their lives. There were a good many examples of this kind this summer.[13]

The Moravian missionaries wrote on a different occasion in their diary.

We heard that the Schawanoses [Shawnees] had murdered, in pitiful fashion, in their town, an Indian of their own nation, while drinking whisky. First they chopped three holes in his head with their tomahawk or Indian hatchet, and as he did not fall dead at once, one of them jumped on him with a knife and ran it into his body, while another cut his stomach open. . . . Thus also lately a Delaware Indian murdered a Schawano woman. A drunken bout never takes place among the heathen without one or the other losing his life or being at least terribly maltreated. Many of them drink themselves to death, of which we have seen and heard pitiful cases since we are here. The guzzling of whisky among these heathen is so dreadful that no one can imagine it. One hundred or more gallons of whisky are brought to such an Indian town by the heathen, and then they do not stop drinking till there is not a drop left.[14]

Such ghastly and violent incidents were not uncommon, and were frequently reported on the frontier. Furthermore, alcohol was becoming increasingly a part of daily life in Native communities. At a time of massive social and cultural dislocation, alcohol was even, according to historian Andrew Cayton, incorporated as "part of the rituals and ceremonies central to the daily lives of the Miami, Shawnee, and Delaware."[15]

Native American material culture in the Ohio Valley and the Great Lakes changed dramatically due to trade and the growing influence of European colonialism. Amerindians in the region incorporated European **Changes in Material Culture** guns, kettle, fabrics, and other material items into their daily life. Such developments, however, varied from group to group and over time.

The Menominee in the Great Lakes region in the eighteenth century, for example, were encouraged by the French to buy commodities on credit, to be paid back in the future with fur. The adoption of European material culture, and the close relations with the French, strengthened the Menominees' position in comparison to their neighbors. But it also led to significant changes in the Menominees' way of life. As a result, they spent significantly less time farming their gardens and fields of wild rice, and instead spent more time trapping for fur.

The Delaware in the Tuscarawas and Muskingum River valley, in what is today eastern Ohio, who lived in relatively close proximity to white settlement by the second half of the eighteenth century, integrated more European material culture into their daily life, and at a more rapid rate than many of their neighbors. In the 1770s, the Delaware were also joined by a group of Amerindians who had been converted by the Moravian Church, and who had been invited to establish mission towns in the area.

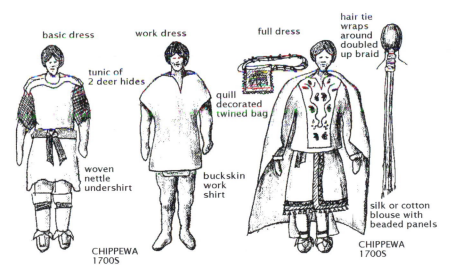

Chippewa/Ojibwa women's clothing in the eighteenth century. Like their Algonkian relatives in the Northeast, the Chippewa (also known as Ojibwe) incorporated new materials such as cloth and trade beads into their daily lives. The elaborate clothing on the right includes silk, fancy beadwork, and metal cones which hang loosely and make a pleasant noise when the wearer moves. From Tara Prindle/nativetech.org.

The Moravian presence, along with other influences, led to significant changes in the Delaware way of life. Many of them adopted pigs, chicken, and cattle, which were previously not a part of indigenous Eastern Woodland ways of farming. By the second half of the eighteenth century, a growing number of Delaware, like numerous other Amerindians in the region, also adopted European-style housing that could be seen standing alongside the traditional wigwams.[16]

Adoption of Outsiders As with other Eastern Woodland Amerindian peoples, Native Americans in the Great Lakes and the Ohio Valley were open to the adoption of outsiders into their societies. While many Euro-American captives taken in war eagerly sought to return to their homes, a considerable number remained in Native communities. Most of the colonists who were adopted by Native peoples and who chose to stay with them were women and children. Eastern Woodland Amerindians used the adoption of war captives to replace the deaths of loved ones in their societies. By the second half of the eighteenth century, a considerable number of Euro-Americans taken in war lived in Amerindian towns in the region and helped to reshape the patterns of daily life in their newly adopted towns and villages. Adoptees often functioned as culture brokers who familiarized their communities with European languages, technology, customs, cultures, and tools. They joined their Native peers on hunts, labored around the house and in the fields, carried weapons in war, and some "white Indians" even took important leadership positions in their new communities.

Captives who refused to go home generated reams of frustrated writing by colonial officials who decried the existence of "white savages," describing them as depraved and culturally inferior. The phenomenon also suggests that the Amerindian way of life was attractive to numerous colonists. Benjamin Franklin, a founding father and famous figure in eighteenth century Euro-American society, observed, for example:

When an Indian Child has been brought up among us, taught our language and habituated to our Customs, yet if he goes to see his relations and make one Indian Ramble with them, there is no perswading him ever to return. [But] when white persons of either sex have been taken prisoners young by the Indians, and lived a while among them, tho' ransomed by their Friends, and treated with all imaginable tenderness to prevail with them to stay among the English, yet in a Short time they become disgusted with our manner of life, and the care and pains that are necessary to support it, and take the first good Opportunity of escaping again into the Woods, from whence there is no reclaiming them.[17]

Another eighteenth century writer, Hector de Crevecoeur, put it more bluntly. He noted that, "[T]housands of Europeans are Indians . . . and we have no examples of even one of those Aborigines having from choice become Europeans."[18]

As the territorial encroachments of Euro-
Americans became increasingly felt, a growing
number of indigenous peoples in the eighteenth
and nineteenth century Ohio Valley and the
**Amerindian Prophets
and Militant Resistance**

Great Lakes came to embrace cultural values and lifeways that they
imagined to be traditional. Native American prophets became the main
advocates of such strategies, and their followers used their leaders' messages in their efforts to resist colonial expansion.

The Delaware prophet Neolin, whose "nativist" and anti-European
preaching supported the uprising of an alliance of Great Lakes and Ohio
Valley peoples against the British in 1763, passed on a strong message in
support of militant resistance and rejection of Euro-American culture that
he believed was given to him by the Master of Life:

I am the Master of Life, whom thou desirest to know and to whom thou wouldst
speak. Listen well to what I am going to say to thee and thy red brethren. I am He
who made heaven and earth, the trees, lakes, rivers, all men, and all that thou seest,
and all that thou hast seen on earth. Because [I have done this and because] I love
you, you must do what I say and [leave undone] what I hate. I do not like that you
drink until you lose your reason, as you do; or that you fight with each other. . . .
This land, where you live, I have made for you and not for others. How comes it
that you suffer the whites on your lands? Can't you do without them? I know that
those whom you call the children of your Great Father supply your wants, but if
you were not bad, as you are, you would well do without them. You might live
wholly as you did before you knew them. Before those whom you call your brothers came on your lands, did you not live by bow and arrow? You had no need of
gun nor powder, nor the rest of their things, and nevertheless you caught animals
to live and clothe yourselves with their skins, but when I saw that you went to
the bad, I called back the animals into the depths of the woods, so that you had
need of your brothers to have your wants supplied and cover you. You have only
to become good and do what I want, and I shall send back to you the animals to
live on. I do not forbid you, for all that, to suffer amongst you the children of your
father. I love them, they know me and pray to me, and I give them their necessities and all that they bring to you, but as regards those who have come to trouble
your country, drive them out, make war to them! I love them not, they know me
not, they are my enemies and the enemies of your brothers! Send them back to the
country which I made for them! There let them remain.[19]

The popularity of the anticolonial resistance movement led by Pontiac
and Neolin was also spurred by British policy. The British, who defeated
the French in 1760 and had pushed them out of much of North America,
now also significantly changed their policies toward the Amerindians.
They decided to stop giving Native peoples diplomatic gifts and supplies,
which had been at the center of Indian/white relations since the days of
first contact. This unilateral change in political protocol, combined with
the fear of increasing encroachments by the land-hungry, who continued to push the western borders of British settlement, and inflamed by

Neolin's preaching, led many of the Amerindians of the Ohio Valley and the Great Lakes to strike against the British. Although their resistance effort failed in pushing the British out of the region, it contributed to the willingness of the British government to pass the Proclamation of 1763, which forbade colonists—at least for a limited time—to settle west of the Appalachian Mountains.[20]

Neolin was, however, not the only prophet active in the region. The Moravian missionaries John Heckewelder and David Zeisberger, who were working in several mission towns in the Muskingum and Tuscarawas River valley around the time of the American Revolution, wrote about several Native American prophets that were active in their immediate vicinity. Like Neolin, most prophets attributed the loss of power among their societies to the presence of Euro-Americans and their goods, especially alcohol. By trying to separate themselves from the whites, and by revitalizing their old lifeways, Native prophets believed that Native communities could maintain their land, resources, and sovereignty.[21]

THE OHIO AND GREAT LAKES INDIANS' REVOLUTION

The American Revolution had a significant impact on the daily life of the Native peoples of the Ohio Valley and the Great Lakes. It marked not only the commencement of a war of independence for white Americans, but also for Native Americans whose way of life faced increasing white encroachments. Unlike the American Revolution, which lasted from 1775–1783, the Indians' Revolution in the Ohio Valley and the Great Lakes region lasted to the mid-1790s. It was only at that point that the Native people of the region were decisively defeated by the Americans. The militant resistance by Tecumseh and Tenskwatawa in the early nineteenth century can be seen as part of the Indians' Revolution, as this struggle was a part of an ongoing attempt by Native Americans in the region to maintain their sovereignty and autonomy.[22]

Whose Side Are You On? The outbreak of the American Revolution required hard decisions on the part of the Ohio Valley and Great Lakes Indians. Some, remembering the high casualties that they had suffered in earlier wars involving Indian and European nations, argued that it was best to stay out of the conflict altogether. Due to increasing pressures on their territory, though, most Native Americans in the region eventually became involved in the fighting. A majority assisted the British because they posed less of a threat to their territory than did the Americans. Others, however, sought closer ties with the United States in hopes of preserving their homeland. Still others, to avoid white encroachments and the pressures of the Revolutionary War, moved further west.

Those Native groups who wanted at least partial accommodation with the United States saw this strategy as a means to get territorial guarantees that would stop colonial advances onto their land without bloodshed. They were encouraged in this belief by several assurances and statements made by American officials. In addition, some Native groups, including factions of the Delaware and the Mequashake Shawnee, opted for closer diplomatic contacts with the United States, since they lived in the vicinity of American settlements in the eastern and southern parts of what is today the state of Ohio. People who wanted to stay on or near their homelands and familiar places had to get along with their new American neighbors.

Most Amerindians who lived north of the Ohio River, however, saw little use in seeking an understanding with the Americans. They sided with the British. These groups had little faith that American settlers, who crossed the Ohio River in ever increasing numbers, would respect the boundaries of their lands. They also did not believe that United States officials would adhere to the treaties they had made. Oppositional leaders complained of the many mistreatments they had received at the hands of whites. Thus, for more and more Amerindian communities in the region, militant resistance was seen as the only viable way to maintain their independence and to stop the advance of white colonization.

Other Native Americans who wanted to avoid being caught up in the revolutionary struggle revived old migratory patterns by choosing to move westward to areas that had not been affected by warfare. As the fighting in the region intensified by 1779 and 1780, for example, a growing stream of Shawnee left the volatile region, moving further south in the Ohio Valley. In the years after the revolution, some 1,200 Shawnees moved to Missouri.

Even after the British sued for peace with the Americans in January 1783, the Amerindian **Treaties and Massacres** peoples of the Ohio and Great Lakes region continued their resistance against American expansion. Native peoples in the region were especially outraged by the claims that the United States now owned their lands. The Americans maintained that the British had ceded the territory north of the Ohio River through the Treaty of Paris. In contrast, the Natives argued that Britain could not give up their homelands, since they never had been conquered by either Britain or the United States. In their attempts to restrain American expansion, many of the Native peoples in the Ohio Valley and the Great Lakes tried to show a united front. The Indian confederacy that emerged from these efforts was supported by a wide array of Indian nations, such as the Miamis, Wyandots, Kickapoos, Delawares, Shawnees, Weas, and Piankeshaws. On occasion this confederacy also got help from groups like the Ottawas, Ojibwas, Potawatomis, and from some Iroquois. The Ohio Confederacy, as it is often called, argued that the territory north of the Ohio River was communally held by all Native Americans who lived on it, and that it could only be sold with the permission of all tribes. Moreover, the Indian alliance believed in the territorial separation of Anglo-American lands and Indian country at the Ohio River.[23]

As in other parts of North America, warfare had a tremendously disruptive effect on the daily life of Native Americans. Native families had to constantly worry about surprise attacks and their security. American troops went on numerous campaigns to destroy Indian towns and villages, as well as crops—attempting to strike terror into Indian country. American troops killed not only the warriors, but also, on occasion, women, children, and the elderly. In the Fall of 1779, for example, the American Allegheny campaign of 600 soldiers was scheduled to attack at harvest time. The American soldiers blazed a 400-mile long path of devastation through the Native territory on the north side of the Ohio River. Late in the summer of 1780 and again in 1782, another force of 1,000 men marched against the Shawnee towns and villages. Such acts of war left behind death and destruction and created worries among Native families about how they would subsist in the future.

While violence was committed on all sides, several massacres committed by American militiamen among Ohio and Great Lakes Indians during this period stand out as atrocities that were condemned even at the time. One of the worst massacres in the region took place in 1782. A group of over 90 Christian Indians who advocated pacifism were slaughtered at their village of Gnaddenhuetten, the site of a Moravian mission, on the Tuscarawas river in what is today eastern Ohio. The Moravian Indians had never participated in the fighting. They were taken captive by the militiamen, who falsely accused them of siding with the British. After a night of praying and singing hymns the Christian converts—including a majority of women and children—were killed, one after another, with a cooper's mallet. The hatred embodied in this act by the person swinging the mallet when a bullet would do gives some indication of the level of frontier violence. The American militiamen then set the houses on fire, perhaps hoping to hide the evidence of their victims within.[24]

In the summer of 1786, American militiamen committed another especially brutal massacre. This time about 900 militiamen from Kentucky led an attack on Mequakshaketown on the Mad River. Moluntha, the leader at Mequakshaketown, had been a declared friend of the Americans and had signed a treaty with the United States. The last thing they expected after that was violence. Moluntha and his people were caught by surprise. Soldiers shot several fleeing Indians, burned their town, and destroyed their crops. Moluntha, who had chosen the path of peace through negotiation with the Americans, was murdered while holding on to an American flag and a copy of the treaty that he had signed with the United States.[25]

Massacres and acts of war exacerbated patterns of revenge, hate, violence, and war, which came increasingly to shape Native American daily life in the second half of the eighteenth century in the Ohio Valley and the Great Lakes. American raids led to Amerindian counter-raids. Isolated

frontier farms and settlements became favorite targets. There was also
an upsurge in the ritualized torture of white prisoners as more and more
Native fighters came to believe that Euro-Americans in general did not
deserve the mercy of the Indians, because they had shown no mercy
to them. The Moravian missionary David Zeisberger observed that the
Delaware and the Shawnee in particular were keen on prosecuting those
militiamen who had participated in the brutal killings at Gnadenhuetten.
"As soon as it is known that any prisoner had part in that affair," the missionary wrote, "he is forthwith bound, tortured, and burnt."[26]

The Indians' Revolution in the Ohio Valley and the Great Lakes came
to an end by the mid-1790s. Throughout the 1780s, the Ohio confederacy
had attempted to negotiate for a peaceful solution with the United States.
But as the Americans were unwilling to give up their territorial demands
north of the Ohio River, and the Indians would not give up their lands,
the situation deteriorated. The federal government ordered several campaigns against the Amerindians during the first half of the 1790s.

The first two of the three military expeditions were embarrassing
failures for the United States. The first campaign, in the fall of 1790,
sent 1,500 soldiers under the command of Colonel Josiah Harmar out to
destroy some abandoned Indian villages and towns. Eventually, however,
the American troops were led into an ambush. The Americans suffered
over 200 casualties and withdrew. A year later, a renewed effort was led
by Arthur St. Clair. After the U.S. forces had moved onto Indian lands,
their poorly secured camp was attacked by surprise by a much smaller
force of Indian fighters. At this battle, with over 600 dead or missing and
almost 300 wounded soldiers, the United States experienced its biggest
defeat yet at the hands of a Native American force.

Although Native Americans in the Ohio Valley and the Great Lakes
region could win battles, however, they did not win the war. They lacked
numbers, weapons, and safe havens for their women and children in
times of war. The final American military campaign led to a decisive
defeat of the Native American forces. It drastically changed power relations in the region, and altered the patterns of daily life of the Native
peoples who lived north of the Ohio river. In 1794 General Anthony
Wayne led a well-trained army of 3,000 men north of the Ohio river. They
defeated the Indians at a place called Fallen Timbers in what is today
northwestern Ohio.

The Indians' military defeat was followed by the treaty of Greenville of
1795, imposed on the Indians by the United States. This treaty dramatically altered the Indians way of life in the region. The treaty forced Native
peoples to cede substantial territories in Ohio and Indiana. It also spurred
the movement of American settlers north of the Ohio River, straining
existing land resources. Increasing Euro-American settlement led the
federal government to purchase more land through several other treaties.
The Treaty of Greenville of 1795 ended Indian militant resistance north

of the Ohio River for over a decade, until the new confederacy under the leadership of Tecumseh tried once again to resist the patterns of American colonization. This, however, was to be the final effort at militant resistance in the region.[27]

The Indians' Revolution Continues

After Neolin, another man who became famous as a prophet in the Great Lakes and Ohio Valley region was Tenskwatawa, also known as "the Shawnee Prophet," who was active in the early nineteenth century. Along with his half brother Tecumseh, the famous Shawnee war chief, who took on much of the political leadership, Tenskwatawa advocated territorial separation of Amerindians and white Americans as well as militant resistance against U.S. expansion. As with previous revitalization movements, the Shawnee Prophet and his followers thought that a separation of the Native and the American world would restore their old patterns of daily life. It would bring the "Master of Life" to "overturn the land," which Indians "alone shall inhabit."[28] Once, when Governor Lewis Cass of Michigan demanded that Native Americans should adopt Euro-American ways of agriculture, meaning that men should do the farming instead of women, Tenskwatawa told him that Native peoples could not "live like you whites." Tenskwatawa believed that Indians should adhere to their traditional ways. Men should be hunters and fighters, and women should raise corn. He also told Cass that, "[Y]ou [too] would think it hard to be compelled to live as we do." The prophet emphasized again and again that "we cannot live as you do. . . . We wish to live as our fathers have lived before us."[29]

Like Neolin and Pontiac, Tenskwatawa and Tecumseh worked hard at building a unified coalition of various Indian communities. Historians often refer to such alliances as pan-Indian because they united Native peoples from different tribes and villages. Tecumseh also complained about American efforts to take over indigenous lands by creating disunity among Native American nations. He said,

The Great Spirit said he gave his great island to his red children. He placed the whites on the other side of the big water, they were not contented with their own, but came to take ours from us. They have driven us from the sea to the lakes, we can go no farther. They have taken upon themselves to say this tract belongs to the Miamis, this to the Delawares & so on. but the Great Spirit intended it as the common property of all the Tribes, nor can it be sold without the consent of all.[30]

Thus, Tecumseh became a strong advocate for unity among Ohio Valley and Great Lakes Indians.

On another occasion, Tecumseh said,

Brothers—We all belong to one family; we are all children of the Great Spirit. . . . We are friends; we must assist each other to bear our burdens. The blood of many of our fathers and brothers has run like water on the ground, to satisfy the avarice of the white men. We, ourselves, are threatened with a great evil; nothing will pacify them but the destruction of the red men.

Making a broad appeal to all of his "brothers," an expression of commonality that makes his use of the term "Indian" mean something powerful and positive, Tecumseh reminded all Indians that "We must be united."[31]

American officials did everything they could to crush the pan-Indian alliance. In 1811, American troops attacked the pan-Indian coalition in a surprise assault. This became known as the Battle of Tippecanoe. The alliance forged by the brothers, Tecumseh and Tenskwatawa, suffered but was not decisively defeated. Not surprisingly, during the War of 1812, Tecumseh and his supporters sided with the British against the Americans. The war ended in a disaster for the militant Indians. who were defeated by the United States. Tecumseh was killed at the Battle of Thames, north of Lake Erie, while attempting to fight back an American offensive on Canada. Tenskwatawa moved into Canadian exile for several decades but would infamously help the United States with the removal of the Shawnee from Ohio in the 1830s.

The militant resistance of Tecumseh was not the only strategy that shaped Native daily life and indigenous responses to American expansion in the Ohio Valley and the Great Lakes. Other **"Government Chiefs and Accommodation."** Native Americans, after having experienced several decisive defeats, took heed when they saw the Euro-American population grow from 5,000 people in 1796 to 230,000 in 1810 while Amerindian populations declined sharply, counting their numbers only in the tens of thousands.[32] Many decided that accommodation and negotiation with the Americans would be more fruitful than war to guarantee the survival of their communities. These leaders, such as Little Turtle (Miami), Tarhe (Wyandot), and Black Hoof (Shawnee) are often called "government chiefs" because they sought to cooperate with the U.S. government. Yet, it is important to point out that these leaders pursued strategies of partial accommodation in an effort to maintain their communities' cultural and political autonomy and independence. They also hoped that an adoption of "the white man's road" would help their people to improve their deteriorating social and economic situations.

Federal Indian policy seemed to encourage Native Americans who sought accommodation with the United States. President Thomas Jefferson (1801–1809) proclaimed a commitment to the "civilization policy," already advocated in the 1780s and 1790s by Secretary of War Henry Knox. Jefferson maintained that "humanity enjoins" the United States "to teach" Native people Euro-American ways of "agriculture and the domestic arts." Like many other Americans, Jefferson believed that the "civilization policy" would bring Indians "to that industry which would enable them to maintain their place in existence and prepare them in time for that state of society which to bodily comfort adds the improvement of the mind and morals."

Several Native leaders accepted the federal government's suggestion and followed the road of "civilization." In their labors to transform their communities, some chiefs in the region sought out the assistance of missionaries. The Quaker William Kirk, for example, assisted the Indians of the Shawnee town of Wapakoneta on the Auglaize River in northwestern Ohio in their efforts to clear land, to set up orchards, to grow vegetables, to build more log cabins, and to erect fences. With Kirk's help, the Wapakoneta Shawnee also obtained farm implements, two yokes of oxen, cattle, and hogs. On April 10, 1809, the Shawnee leaders of this community thanked President James Madison, for sending "our friends, the Quakers, to help us, and we find that they are good people and concerned for our welfare and have done a great deal for us in instructing our young men in a good way on how to use the tools we see in the hands of our white brothers." Yet the federal government soon undermined the Wapakoneta Shawnee's and Kirk's progress, by discharging the Quaker missionary late in 1808. Shawnee leaders protested, but federal officials maintained that Kirk's efforts with the Shawnees were too expensive.

Government chiefs, like indigenous prophets, also worried about alcoholism in Native societies. They saw the sale of alcohol as a threat to the social fabric of their communities. For instance, the Miami chief Little Turtle believed that "[t]his liquor that they introduce into our country is more to be feared than the gun or the tomahawk; there are more of us dead since the Treaty of Greenville, than we lost by the years of the war before." Thus, Indian leaders lobbied the federal government and missionaries to declare the trade of alcohol illegal and to enforce the law. Although a federal law that forbade the sale of alcohol had been passed in 1802, the sale of bootleg liquor continued. Yet, the authorities were either unable or unwilling to enforce the laws, and white and Indian traders alike would continue to make a profit by selling alcohol.

Beyond the lofty rhetoric of "civilization," United States officials often failed to deliver plows, guns, hoes, or horses, or to provide the services of blacksmiths, which they had agreed to furnish to the indigenous peoples in the Ohio Valley and the Great Lakes as part of their annuities, guaranteed to the Natives by treaties. Indian leaders also repeatedly complained about the poor quality, as well as damaged and belated goods. Furthermore, federal, state, and territorial leaders continued to obtain even more Native American land through a series of treaties. Many Native leaders who lived north of the Ohio River found it hard for their communities to subsist on their ever-shrinking land base, especially with the insufficient annuities provided by the U.S. government, and they gave in to government pressures to sell ever more of their land. Thus, the vicious spiral of land loss and poverty continued and Native daily life in the region was shaped increasingly by loss of land and poverty.[33]

Despite these tough economic and social conditions, as well as the lack of federal support, Native Americans in the Ohio Valley and the Great Lakes attempted to maintain their autonomy and to keep their cultures intact as much as they could, by attempting to adhere to as many of their ceremonial and cultural traditions as they deemed possible. Ultimately, however, Native efforts at accommodation would not save them from the federal government's efforts to move them west of the Mississippi River. Thus, most Ohio Valley and Great Lakes Indians, along with many other Native peoples of the Eastern Woodlands, faced forced relocation from their homelands to areas to the west. By the 1820s and especially the 1830s, Indian removal had become the policy increasingly pursued by the federal government. The impact of removal on the daily lives of Native Americans is a theme that we will explore in some more detail in the next chapter.

NOTES

1. For an introduction to the Mound Builders see for example George Milner, *The Moundbuilders: Ancient Peoples of Eastern North America* (New York: Thames & Hudson, 2004); Lynda Norene Shaffer, *Native Americans before 1492: The Moundbuilding Centers of the Eastern Woodlands* (Armonk, NY: M. E. Sharpe, 1992); David Penney, *North American Indian Art* (New York: Thames & Hudson, 2004), chapter 2.

2. Shaffer, 86–92.

3. Neal Salisbury, "The Indians' Old World: Native Americans and the Coming of Europeans," *William and Mary Quarterly* (July, 1996), 435–58; Daniel Richter, *Facing East from Indian Country: A Native History of Early America* (Cambridge, MA: Harvard University Press, 2001), 2–7.

4. James O'Donnell, *Ohio's First Peoples* (Athens: Ohio University Press, 2004), 23–28.

5. Michael McConnell, *A Country Between: The Upper Ohio Valley and Its Peoples, 1724–1774* (Lincoln: University of Nebraska Press, 1992), 5–20.

6. This discussion of social organization, leadership, and religion is based on David Zeisberger, "History of Northern American Indians," ed. Archer Butler and William Nathaniel Schwarze, *Ohio Archaeological and Historical Publications,* Vol. 19 (Columbus, OH: F. J. Heer, 1910.

7. On the subsistence of the Shawnee see James Howard, *Shawnee!: The Ceremonialism of a Native American Indian Tribe and its Cultural Background* (Athens: Ohio University Press, 1981), 43; on the Delaware see Herbert Kraft, *The Lenape: Archaeology, History and Ethnography* (Newark: New Jersey Historical Society, 1986), 138–58.

8. Susan Sleeper Smith, *Indian Women and French Men: Rethinking Cultural Encounter in the Western Great Lakes* (Amherst: University of Massachusetts Press, 2001).

9. On hunting and warfare see John Heckewelder, *History, Manners, and Customs of the Indian Nations* (Philadelphia: Historical Society of Philadelphia, 1881), 89–90, 163–69.

10. Eric Hinderaker, *Elusive Empire: Constructing Colonialism in the Ohio Valley, 1673-1800* (New York: Cambridge University Press, 1997), 67; for a general discussion see chapter 1 and 2; Christoph Strobel. *Contested Grounds: The Transformation of the American Upper Ohio Valley and the South African Eastern Cape, 1770–1850* (Ph.D. Dissertation: University of Massachusetts Amherst, 2005).

11. Menominee folk tale in Peter Nabokov, ed., *Native American Testimony: A Chronicle of Indian-White Relations from Prophecy to the Present, 1492–1992,* revised edition (New York: Penguin, 1992), 37.

12. Andrew Cayton, *Frontier Indiana* (Bloomington: Indiana University Press, 1996), 201–2.

13. Lawrence Henry Gipson, ed., *The Moravian Indian Mission on White River* (Indianapolis: Indiana Historical Bureau, 1938), 484.

14. Gipson, 164–65.

15. Cayton, 204.

16. Zeisberger, 17–18, 45–46, 86; Strobel.

17. Benjamin Franklin quoted in James Axtell, *The European and the Indian: Essays in the Ethnohistory of Colonial North America* (New York: Oxford University Press, 1981), 172.

18. Hector de Crevecoeur, quoted in Axtell, 172.

19. "The Master of Life Speaks to the Wolf," in *World,* 138.

20. Gregory Dowd, *War under Heaven: Pontiac, the Indian Nations, and the British Empire* (Baltimore, MD: Johns Hopkins University Press, 2002).

21. Strobel.

22. For an important study of how the American Revolution affected specific Amerindian communities, see Colin G. Calloway, *The American Revolution in Indian Country: Crisis and Diversity in Native American Communities* (New York: Cambridge University Press, 1995).

23. Strobel.

24. See for example Richard White, *The Middle Ground: Indians, Empires, and Republics in the Great Lakes Region, 1650–1815,* New York: Cambridge University Press, 1991, 390–91.

25. Strobel, 77.

26. David Zeisberger, *Diary,* 1: 133.

27. Strobel, 85–89.

28. Speech of the Trout, May 24, 1807, in *ASPIA,* 1: 798.

29. Quoted in John Sugden, *Blue Jacket: The Warrior of the Shawnees* (Lincoln: University of Nebraska Press, 2000), 238.

30. Harrison to Eustis, August 6, 1810, 1: 456–59.

31. "We Must Be United," in *Native American Testimony,* 96.

32. Helen Hornbeck Tanner, ed., *Atlas of Great Lakes Indian History* (Norman: University of Oklahoma Press, 1987), 66, 96, 101.

33. This section is based on Strobel, quote on page 90; see also 92–93, 168–77.

5

DAILY LIFE IN THE SOUTHEAST

The Native peoples of what is today the southeastern United States, like their neighbors to the north, are classified as Eastern Woodland Indians. Their ways of life were shaped by the sylvan landscape they inhabited, although, given the region's geographic location, the weather was warmer than in those areas further north. The climate was shaped by regular precipitation, generally milder winters, falls, and springs, and hot and humid summers. As was the case for Native peoples to the north, Native communities in the Southeast, including major groups such as the Cherokee, the Creek (more commonly known today as the Muskogee), the Choctaws, and the Chickasaw, utilized and took advantage of their natural resources. Their ways of subsistence were based on farming, hunting, fishing, and the gathering of foods. Native peoples in the region utilized the waterways for travel and transportation.

The experience of European and American colonization in the Southeast altered the patterns of daily life of Native Americans tremendously. It led Native Americans in the region to suffer increasing territorial losses, and to incorporate Euro-American goods and culture into their ways of life. In the 1830s, however, the Amerindians of the Southeast, like their neighbors to the north, faced their strongest challenge yet—forced removal from their homelands. The United States's removal policy was a fearsome and powerful colonial process that reshaped the lives of Native communities east of the Mississippi. The largest southeastern nations, including the Cherokee, Creeks, Choctaws, Chickasaw, and the Seminoles, were forcefully relocated to a place referred to as "Indian Territory" (later known as Oklahoma) west of the Mississippi River. Here they had to pick up the pieces of their lives, only to face new challenges from Euro-American settler and business interests in the late nineteenth century. The people who managed to avoid removal and stay in their original homelands faced different challenges as they struggled to survive without drawing undue attention to themselves from the dominant society.

EARLY CONTACT IN THE SOUTHEAST

By the time of European contact, the Mound Building Mississippian chiefdoms dominated much of the Southeast. Just as in the Ohio Valley and the Great Lakes, the lifeways of these ancient peoples had some influence on the patterns of daily life of the southeastern Amerindian communities that emerged after the decline of the Mississippian towns, such as the Creeks and the Cherokees. The weakening of Mississippian communities in the Southeast was brought on, in part at least, by Spanish efforts at conquest and colonization in the region during the sixteenth century.

The larger southeastern Mound Builder towns were settled by as many as 2,000 to 3,000 people. The more sizeable Mississippian communities, such as the one at the Ocmulgee site near Macon, Georgia, were built around central earth mounds that were "shaped," according to historian Michael Green, "like pyramids with the top cut off." Furthermore, and judging from evidence in burial sites in the form of grave offerings, there existed strict social stratification in Mississippian societies in the Southeast. The ruling class in each town managed both ceremonial and political affairs. Power was centralized with a ruler or chief who is believed to have held absolute authority over his people. Chiefdoms could vary in size ranging from several towns and villages to political entities that spanned several areas. For instance, at its peak of power before the mid-fourteenth century, the Coosa chiefdom dominated an area that reached from northeastern Tennessee to northwest Georgia, and to central Alabama.

De Soto and the Decline of the Mississippian Chiefdoms

Although there is some evidence that suggests that the Mississippian chiefdoms of the Southeast were in decline before Spanish attempts at colonization in the sixteenth century, many of the Mound Building societies were still a force to be reckoned with. Hernando de Soto, a Spanish explorer, crossed the region with a fighting force of over 700 men in search of silver and gold. He hoped to find treasures such as those his countrymen had been able to take, through conquest, from the Aztecs in Mexico and the Incas in Peru. De Soto quickly alienated the local communities he encountered by commandeering food, by taking people to be used as slaves, and by capturing Native leaders as hostages.

De Soto did not find the riches he was looking for. Instead, he faced almost immediate resistance to his demands and actions. The opposition to the Spanish came at a high price for the Mississippian peoples. During one attack by the Spanish on a Mississippian chiefdom, for example, de Soto's men killed more than 3,000 people. The Spanish, with their horses and protective armor, had less than 150 casualties. Eventually, however, the Native peoples of the Southeast forced the Spanish to retreat. Thus, the Mound Builders achieved what the Incas and Aztecs had not been able to do. They successfully threw back a Spanish invasion attempt.

The Spanish entrada had a devastating impact on Native Americans. Spanish colonists introduced several epidemics, which killed huge numbers of Native people. As in other parts of the Americas, disease disrupted established ways of life as the populations of entire villages were wiped out or decimated. These demographic catastrophes, which led to population losses of anywhere from 50 to 90 percent, either disabled or weakened Native communities to the point where tremendous social, political, and cultural disruption ensued. Few of the Mississippian chiefdoms survived the impact of disease. Scholars believe the survivors, as individuals or as remnants of much larger communities, were then forced to reorganize their societies into smaller villages, towns, and loosely organized confederations, which eventually led to the creation of nations such as the Creek and Cherokee Nations. Perhaps as a result of these traumas, mound building activities came to an end in many parts of the Southeast.[1]

Languages Many of the Native peoples of the Southeast spoke and speak languages that were part of the Muskogean language family. This includes the Creek of Alabama and Georgia, the Choctaw and Chickasaw of Mississippi, and smaller groups such as the Koasati of Alabama or the Apalachee of northwestern Florida. Scholars believe that many of the mound building Mississippian towns in the Southeast spoke Muskogean languages. Other Native nations in the Southeast, like members of the Powhatan Confederacy, spoke Algonkian languages. The Cherokee, who lived in parts of the Carolinas, Georgia, and Tennessee, as well as the Tuscarora of North Carolina, spoke languages related to the Iroquoian language family. Other languages spoken by Native peoples, such as Yuchi, are called "language isolates," meaning that they are apparently unrelated to known Amerindian language families. Two other language groups represented in the Southeast are the Caddo and Siouan language families. Moreover, and as in other parts of the Americas, many Native languages were lost before any attempts were made to document them.[2]

Daily Life among the Coastal Peoples of the Carolinas and Virginia Not all Amerindians in the Southeast were the descendants of Mound Builders. In some coastal regions east of the Appalachian mountains, Native peoples and communities organized their social and cultural lives in ways that were more fluid than the highly structured systems that characterized Mound

Builder cultures. The chiefs in the Southeastern Woodland societies of the Carolina Piedmont, groups that would later form the Catawba Nation, were not as powerful as the paramount leaders of Mississippian societies. The villages of Piedmont peoples, like many of the other coastal groups, were much smaller than Mississippian town and cities.

The small size of the coastal communities reinforced the need to make decisions by building political consensus. This enabled villagers to air their views independently in council meetings. Thus, Native leaders in smaller village settings had no power to rule by force, but rather had to guide by example and persuasion. It could thus often take a long time for a community to make a collective decision.

The chiefs among the Piedmont peoples represented their people's political and diplomatic interests to the outside world. They also performed tasks of importance to their community's spiritual life. Chiefs, along with religious leaders or healers, were in charge of leading ceremonies and rituals for mourning and healing, as well as for religious and military purposes.

The healers functioned both as religious leaders and as curers. This knowledge was passed down to the spiritualist from a predecessor, by whom he had been trained as a young man. Healers were expert ethnobotanists. They knew the healing powers of specific plants, barks, roots, and berries. In colonial times, Amerindian healers often baffled Euro-American doctors with their skills. In addition, Native peoples believed that their healers had the power to establish contacts with the world of spirits through rituals and prayers. This power was associated with healing because it was widely believed that spirits had the power to cause or prevent illness, injury, and death.[3] Successful healers knew the right protocol for appeasing or banishing the spirits that caused problems.

Coastal groups such as the Powhatan Confederacy, which included numerous Algonkian groups in the tidewater region of what is today the state of Virginia, and the Native communities of the Piedmont, lived predominantly in villages. Piedmont settlements consisted of 5 to 15 houses, whereas the Powhatan generally lived in communities of about 20 houses. Both groups built their dwellings with a framework of bent and tied-up saplings. The houses of the Catawba in the Piedmont region were generally dome-shaped. They housed at least 10 people. The outer walls were covered with bark strips and the roofs were reinforced by mats made out of cattail grass. Piedmont villages were surrounded by a palisade and built around an open center in the middle of the settlement. The center plaza was also the place were the community built its council house. This building was much larger than the regular dwellings. The square council house was large enough to seat every member of the community. It was used for council meetings as well as to welcome visitors.[4]

Powhatan buildings, on the other hand, were larger than those of the Piedmont peoples. They were the homes of extended families. The buildings had arched roofs and were shaped like a tunnel with an entrance on each one of the narrow sides of the building. The roofs and walls of Powhatan dwellings were made out of marsh plants, woven together as mats, which could be removed to let in fresh air. This made it easier for the Powhatans to regulate temperature, light, and smokiness in their homes, especially compared to those dwellings inhabited by the peoples of the Piedmont region. The most important communal and spiritual place for the Powhatan was their temple. Though it was built in much the same fashion as the regular houses, it was generally bigger and usually stood a little distance from the settlement. In several cases, temples were built on top of a hill overlooking the community. Although we know little about precontact and early Powhatan religion, the architectural features and size of the temple tell us that this was a place of tremendous spiritual and ritual importance to the community.[5]

As among other Woodland Amerindians, coastal peoples such as the Powhatans based their daily subsistence on agriculture, hunting, fishing, and gathering. Women gathered foods such as roots, plants, and a wide variety of berries and nuts, and they farmed small plots of land. Here they grew corn, squash, beans, gourds, and in separate fields, attesting to its ritual and ceremonial importance, tobacco. Children frequently helped women with their agricultural labors and, along with the elderly, also protected and guarded the fields from scavenging animals and birds.

Native women fulfilled other important roles in the daily lives of their communities. They processed animal skins—tanning them, and sewing them together to make clothing, pouches, and bags. Women were expert basket weavers using such materials as reeds and hemp. They made pots out of clay and crushed quartz, which they used to cook. Furthermore, women were in charge of tending the fire.

Men also contributed to their community's subsistence. They hunted for deer, raccoons, squirrels, wild turkeys, and rabbits. They mostly pursued animals with bow and arrow, and especially in the summer, when single or small groups of hunters were active, they used deerskins as camouflage. During winter hunting season, however, groups among the Powhatan Confederacy would create large hunting parties. They worked together to drive herds of deer out of their hideaways in the underbrush using noise, fire, and dog. Sometimes they drove their prey into rivers or lakes where the animals could be killed by hunters in boats. Native hunters also used traps to capture animals.

Fishing and the collecting of mussels and oysters took on special importance as a way to procure food for Amerindian groups who lived near the Atlantic coast and inland rivers. Native men fished either by using dugout canoes or by wading in the water. They used long nets, fishing lines, and spears, and on occasion even a bow and an arrow with a line

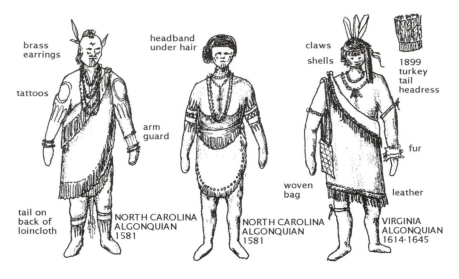

Southeastern Algonkian clothing, seventeenth century. Southeastern Algonkians used turkey feathers, shell beads, tattoos, and leather fringe for personal display. Note the personal bag made from plant fibers with the technique known as finger weaving. From Tara Prindle/nativetech.org.

attached to it, so that in case of a successful shot, the hunter would be able to easily retrieve the fish.[6]

Daily Life among the Creek and Cherokee

Patterns of subsistence and social organization among Creek and Cherokee communities were similar to those of many Eastern Woodland groups. Women farmed and gathered foods while men hunted and fished. The Creeks and Cherokees lived in villages or towns. The political and social organization of their communities was less rigid that of the Mound Builders. Like the coastal groups of the Piedmont and the Chesapeake regions, the Creeks and Cherokees governed themselves through a political ideology based on the ideal of consensus. In contrast to the principles of democratic government, where the majority wins and the losers must accept the decision, consensus politics requires people to keep talking until they come to an agreement. Sometimes that means that people agreed to go along with everyone else, for the good of all. At other times it meant that people separated and went their own ways.

Creek towns were built around the square ground, a rectangular and open space used for ceremonial and political purposes. The square was encircled by small buildings with open fronts facing toward the square, in which community leaders, elders, and chiefs would sit to hold counsel. At the center of the Creek town was also a game field as well as a council house, which was a cone-shaped building that stood up to 30 feet tall and measured somewhere between 30 and 60 feet in diameter. The council house included the Creeks' ceremonial fire and served as an alternative meeting place if bad weather did not allow for meetings to occur on the square ground.[7]

Many southeastern peoples were matrilineal societies. Girls learned necessary skills from, and looked to, their mothers as persons of respect, while the same role in a matrilineal society was not played by a boy's father, but rather by his mother's brothers, who took on much of the responsibility of raising a male child to become a man. The emphasis on tracing one's ancestry through the line of the mother also meant that couples in matrilineal societies would move in with the family of the wife, after the marriage, rather than with that of the husband.

Games played a central role in the daily life of Native Americans in the Southeast. Every town had a ball-game field. But games functioned not only as an athletic competition, but also as summertime entertainment for the entire community.

The Choctaw Game of Ishtaboli

The game of *ishtaboli* among the Choctaws was a stick game related to lacrosse (played by Native groups such as the Iroquois and the Cherokee) except that it was played with two sticks instead of one. Ishtaboli attracted crowds of spectators, many of whom made bets on the team they favored. Older men functioned as the judges or referees of the game. A good deal of planning went into the activity. Three or four months before the game, two "champions," who functioned as the captains of their team, alternately chose members of the tribe to play on their side. Ceremonial dances with chants and drums that involved athletes and spectators occurred all night before the game. George Catlin, a nineteenth century American traveler who wrote a book called *Notes on the Manners, Customs, and Conditions of the North American Amerindians,* described a game of ishtaboli after a visit to the Choctaws in 1834.

In the morning at the appointed hour, the game commenced with the judges throwing up the ball and firing a gun. An instant struggle ensued between players, as some six or seven hundred men mutually endeavored to catch the ball in their sticks and throw it into their opponent's goal. Hundreds ran together and leapt toward each other's heads, and darted between their adversaries legs, tripping and throwing and foiling each other in every possible manner.

As we can see, ishtaboli was a high-contact sport that prepared young Native men for battle. But the exhilaration, fun, and excitement of the game described by Catlin, who "almost dropped from" his "horse's back with irresistible laughter at the succession of droll tricks and kicks and scuffles which ensue in the almost superhuman struggles for the ball," was certainly an experience shared by many of the spectators and players. Thus, games like ishtaboli offered people a chance for collective entertainment and was a social activity that also provided an outlet for strong emotions. Reports suggest that the spectators as well as the participants experienced a heightened sense of community during these games.[8]

Green Corn Ceremony   Ceremonies and celebrations, even more than games, were highlights of the social calendars of the Native peoples of the Southeast. The Green Corn Ceremony, which lasted several days, was celebrated late in the summer when the corn was becoming ripe enough to be eaten. It played an especially important role among agricultural societies in the region. In preparation for the ceremony, public buildings and places were cleaned and repaired. The ceremony also included fasting and the use of plant infusions in an effort to cleanse the body from old foods. Men drank great quantities of "black drink," a purgative tea made from holly twigs and leaves. This ceremonial drink was also used on other occasions that required ritual purging. Another important part of the ritual was the extinction of all fires. Spiritual leaders kindled a new fire to symbolize a new beginning. This fire was then used to reignite other fires in the community. Then came the time for celebration, with dancing and feasts.

For the Native peoples of the Southeast the Green Corn Ceremony symbolized the beginning of a new year, the renewal of the community, and a time of cleansing. Charles Hudson, an expert on southeastern Amerindians, observes that the ceremony provided and provides an opportunity to Native people to "try to straighten out their affairs and make resolutions to be better people in the coming year." It was and is a time of forgiveness, to seek reconciliation in the community, and to remind people who were lax about fulfilling their social roles that they needed to do a better job.[9]

EUROPEAN COLONIZATION IN THE SOUTHEAST

European colonization dramatically altered daily life for Native Americans in the Southeast. The Timucuans, of what is today the state of Florida, were the first Native peoples in the region to encounter permanent European settlements. By the second half of the sixteenth century, Spanish colonists established a strong military presence at St. Augustine, on the Atlantic coast on the northeastern part of the Florida peninsula. This became the place from which other mission stations in the region were established. By the early seventeenth century, Franciscan missionaries, with the support of Spanish troops, succeeded in establishing several missions in the northern parts of Florida and along the Atlantic Coast, then others in present-day South Carolina and Georgia. Spanish officials believed that the missions would play a vital role in protecting their empire's interest in the region against encroachment from other European nations. Missionaries exploited Timucuan labor to grow wheat and other foods to feed the Spanish military garrisons in the area. Native workers were also used by the Spanish to build fortifications—often dangerous and life-threatening labor. On top of all this, the Spanish unwittingly brought epidemic diseases that had a devastating impact on the indigenous population. Spanish colonization disrupted traditional Timucuan lifeways, economies, and political sovereignty, and missionary efforts to Christianize the Amerindians furthered the process.

Colonial rivalries between the Spanish and the English played out in a series of events in the region, but the most massive blow fell on the Timucuans. In 1703–1704, English troops, accompanied by Amerindian allies, destroyed the Spanish missions in the Southeast. During this campaign, thousands of Timucuan and Apalachee people were captured, marched off, and sold into slavery by the English. The few survivors left their territory in northern Florida and moved closer to the Spanish towns of St. Augustine and St. Marks, seeking greater security and stability. Splinter groups of the Creek Nation (Muskogee) settled on these vacated lands in nothern Florida and became known as the Seminole. They adopted runaway African slaves into their communities. This drew the anger of English plantation owners in the southern British colonies.[10]

The people of the Powhatan Confederacy, whose territory encompassed the area of Chesapeake Bay, were the first Native North Americans to witness the establishment of a permanent English settlement on their land, at Jamestown, in 1607. In the early months, the Powhatans supplied the colony at Jamestown with food in exchange for copper and other metals, indicating that the Amerindians were eager to establish peaceful relations with the English. In a speech in 1609, the Powhatan leader asked John Smith, the leader of the English colony: "What can you get by warre . . . ?" Thus Virginia's Native settlers seemed eager to maintain friendly relations with the English, especially in the realm of trade. Powhatan believed that poor relationships with the newcomers could threaten Native patterns of daily life, and that ultimately friendship and peaceful exchange would be more beneficial to both his people and the English.

Think you I am so simple, not to know it is better to eate good meate, lye well, and sleep quietly with my women and children, laugh and be merry with you, have copper, hatchets, or what I want being your friend: then be forced to flie from all, to lie cold in the woods, feed upon Acornes, rootes, and such trash, and be so hunted by you, that I can neither rest, eate nor sleepe; but my tyred men must watch, and if a twig but breake, every one cryeth there commeth Captaine Smith: then must I fly I know not whither: and thus with miserable feare, end my miserable life, leaving my pleasures to such youths as you, which through your rash unadvisednesse may quikly as miserably end, for want of that, you never know where to finde. Let this therefore assure you of our loves, and every yeare our friendly trade shall furnish you with Corne; and now also, if you would come in friendly manner to see us, not thus with your guns and swords as to invade your foes.[11]

Increasingly, however, the presence of the English, as well as that of other European colonial powers along the Atlantic seaboard, was seen by a growing number of coastal Native American peoples as a threat to their sovereignty, their land, and their way of life. In 1609, when English colonists from Jamestown took the Powhatans' corn by force, Powhatan warriors responded immediately. Sporadic warfare continued between the Powhatans and the colonists until 1614. English pressures on Powhatan lands resulted again in hostilities in the 1620s and 1640s. Peace factions found it difficult to argue their position when English actions constantly infuriated the younger men.

These dynamics played out across the region in response to French colonization as well. Stung Serpent, a high-ranking noble among the Natchez of southern Mississippi, questioned the value of the contacts, exchanges, and interactions that his people had with French colonists. He articulated his concerns in a 1723 speech:

Why did the French come into our country? We did not go to seek them. They asked land of us, because their country was too little for all the men that were in it. We told them they might take land where they pleased, there was enough for them and for us; that it was good the same sun should enlighten us both, and that we should walk as friends, in the same path, and that we would give them our provisions, assist them to build, and to labor in their fields. . . . Before they came, did we not live better than we do, seeing we deprive ourselves of a part of our corn, our game, and fish, to give a part to them? In what respect, then, had we occasion for them? Was it for their guns? The bows and arrows, which we used, were sufficient to us to live well. Was it for their white, blue, and red blankets? We can do well enough with buffalo skins which are warmer; our women wrought feather blankets for the winter, and mulberry mantles for the summer.[12]

Stung Serpent's speech lit the spark that had been smoldering for some time. In the ensuing conflict, the French virtually exterminated the Natchez, thereby destroying the last surviving chiefdom of Mound Builders. The few fortunate Natchez survivors were left with little choice but to join the ranks of their northern neighbors, the Chickasaw, who also resisted the encroachments of the French on their homelands.

Warfare and the Trade in Slaves and Deerskins   For Native American communities that lived on the inland peripheries of the various European settlements in the Southeast, the degree of change and adaptation required during much of the seventeenth and eighteenth century was less dramatic, less cataclysmic, than it was for the coastal groups, who suffered the first impacts of European conquest and subjugation. Nevertheless, the colonial encounter had significant impact on the lifeways of Amerindian peoples in the Southeastern interior. There, indigenous peoples altered their trading practices and sought close commercial relations with the Europeans. They also began to incorporate European material goods and domestic animals into their daily lives. Due to the cross-cultural contacts, Native Americans began to use iron axes, kettles, and European clothing instead of similar items made from stone, clay, or animal skins. They began to ride horses and raised European livestock such as cows, pigs, and chickens, which affected the gendered division of labor.

In this "New World," the Southeastern tribes expanded traditional practices of captive-taking in war to join in the Atlantic slave trade, at the instigation of their English neighbors.[13] The insatiable appetite among Europeans for workers for their Caribbean plantations was partly satisfied by the use of Native Americans as slaves. European traders bought Amerindian war captives, traditionally taken by warriors during the intertribal conflicts in the Southeast, and then sold them as slaves to plantation owners in the colonies all over the Western Hemisphere. This new market increasingly provided an incentive for southeastern Amerindian warriors to attack their enemies with the goal of acquiring captives. This new context supplemented traditional motives for intertribal war and coexisted with them in varying degrees across time and space. The risk of frequent warfare, and the danger of either being killed or sold off as a slave, became a part of daily life in the region as thousands of Native Americans were abducted from their homelands.

Native Americans in the Southeast also participated in the international deerskin trade. Like the sale of captives, this was a profitable transaction. It enabled Amerindians to purchase Euro-American goods, including alcohol. Charlestown, Carolina's major trade center, exported about 54,000 deerskins during its early years. This number reached its peak in 1707 at 121,355 hides.[14] Through much of the eighteenth century, Native hunters sold hundreds of thousands of deerskins a year to European traders, putting considerable strain on the local deer population. Instead of leading to greater stability, however, the long-term effect of the market in deerskins undermined Native economies and increased intertribal conflict. As war and diaspora pushed more and more Native peoples into competition for the same hunting territories, a greater number of hunters competed for a declining number of deer and other game animals.

Imperial competition among the English, Spanish, and French reinforced the patterns of conflict in the Southeast. Native peoples participated in several European wars, often choosing allies who would help them to fight against long-time enemies. This exacerbated traditional rivalries in the region—rivalries that predated the arrival of Europeans and continued to play out in ways that are obscured by a narrow focus on "Indian-White" relations, as though Native people only acted in response to Euro-American triggers.

An appeal by the Chickasaw, who lived in what is today northern Mississippi, to the English governor of South Carolina provides a glimpse of the disruption of daily life created by constant warfare, the frustrations it caused in local communities, and the growing military and economic dependence on European allies that southeastern Amerindians felt by the mid-eighteenth century.

This is to let you know we are daily cut oft by our Enemies the French and their Indians who seems to be resolved to drive us from this Land. Therefore we beg of you, our best Friends, to send back our People that are living in other Nations in order to enable us to keep our Lands from the French and their Indians. We hope you will think on us in our Poverty as we have not had the Liberty of Hunting these 3 Years but have had enough to do to defend our Lands and prevent our Women and Children from being Slaves to the French. Our Traders that come here are not willing to trust us Gun Powder and Bullets to hunt and defend ourselves from our Enemies, neither are we able to buy from them. Many of our Women are without Flaps and many of our young Men without Guns which renders them uncapable of making any Defence against such a powerful Enemy. We are thankful to you for your last Presents without which it would not have been possible for us to keep Possession of this Land. . . . We hope you will still take Pity on us and give us a Supply of Powder and Bullets and Guns &c. to enable us to outlive our Enemies and revive a dying Friend. We have had no less than four Armies against us this Winter and have lost 20 of our Warriours and many of our Wives and Children carried off alive, our Town set on Fire in the Night and burnt down, many of our Houses &c. destroyed our Blanketts &c. We were out a hunting at the Time where we was all attacked by the Back Enemy at our Hunting Camp where we lost several of our Warriours, Women and Children so that we were obliged to leave our Hunting Camps and return to our Nation.[15]

Continuous warfare throughout the Southeast, spurred on by Euro-American colonization and imperial rivalries, as well as by the deer and slave trade, led to a significant weakening of the Amerindian population. These developments made Native communities in the region especially vulnerable to outside threats. Whereas in earlier years, the Amerindian peoples in the southeastern interior had been able to keep European powers at bay, by the second half of the eighteenth century, they increasingly had lost their ability to do so.

NATIVE AMERICANS OF THE SOUTHEAST AND "CIVILIZATION"

By the time of the American Revolution, many Native American communities in the Southeast faced a bleak and desperate situation. European colonization had brought war, land loss, poverty, and social, political, economic, and cultural disintegration. To counteract these developments and to revitalize their societies, many Native Americans hoped that if they could at least partially adopt the way of life and culture of Anglo-Americans, their survival on their own homelands would be guaranteed. Such efforts at what nineteenth-century Euro-Americans called the adoption of "civilization" dramatically transformed Native American daily life in the Southeast.

Cherokee Daily Life and "Civilization"

In the late eighteenth and early nineteenth century, the U.S. federal government, urged on by Euro-American men and women who believed themselves to be acting in the best interests of Native Americans, initiated a "civilization program," to aid and encourage Native peoples to transform their communities and give up their old ways. The word "civilization" is often defined in ways that exclude indigenous societies and relegate them to the realm of "savage" or "barbaric" people who are somehow on a lower scale of social evolution. One implication of this is that the people defined as "civilized" are entitled, even obligated, to decide what is in the best interest of people who are not, just as adults get to decide what is in the best interest of children. The troubling aspects of this way of talking about indigenous people become clear when we consider the example of the Cherokee.

Officials of the early republic, such as Thomas Jefferson, wanted Native Americans to either change their "savage" ways, or move west of the Mississippi, where they would ostensibly be free to roam to their hearts' content, and be even "protected" from civilization. There was little or no consideration given to the fact that other Native peoples already lived on those western lands. As part of the civilization program, U.S. administrators expected Native Americans to adopt Anglo-American ways of farming, with the inherent challenge to traditional gender roles that played out all across North America. Euro-Americans wanted Native men to abandon their hunting practices and take up farming. This switch, officials believed, would free up Native "hunting grounds" to be acquired for settlement by non-Native citizens of the new nation.[16] They ignored that fact that for Native peoples, farming was women's work. Both men and women objected, and most resisted the change as long as possible.

Missionaries became major allies in the work of bringing "civilization" and Christianity to the Amerindians east of the Mississippi. Native nations such as the Cherokee insisted that they could adopt Euro-American lifeways such as living in wood houses, educating their children to read and write, and other accoutrements of "civilization" without becoming Christian. Euro-Americans disagreed. Government officials and missionaries asserted that they served as "friends and fathers" to Native Americans. They set out to bring both Christianity and schools to indigenous communities. They also wanted to "inculcate" Amerindians with "habits of industry and sobriety, and instruct them to live a quiet and peaceable life in all godliness and honesty."[17] Most missionaries and officials labored under the assumption that their Christian, Euro-American culture was superior to that of the Amerindians, and that they were doing them a favor to help them adapt to the realities of "modern" life. They argued that Natives had to assimilate to Euro-American political, social, economic, and cultural standards.[18] This meant a total overhaul of Native American patterns of daily life.

Still, it is important to emphasize that the transformations that happened among southeastern tribes could not have taken place unless Native people were willing, or believed that it was necessary, to embrace change. Among the Cherokee, for example, parents voluntarily sent their children off to missionary boarding schools because they believed that their progeny would acquire useful skills there. This was certainly true. In boarding schools Native children learned to read and write in English, but they also studied geography and math. The Cherokee never asked to live in a colonial world, but faced with the challenge of doing so, they set out to succeed on their own terms.

Boarding schools and missionary education, however, undermined and challenged the very fabric of Cherokee society in ways that could not always be foreseen. Students were taught that the Amerindian way of life was inferior to that of Euro-American people. Some of the children internalized those lessons, especially those who went home only infrequently. Students were educated in Christian morals that included behaviors that were quite alien to precontact Cherokee morality, such as attending church services, prayer sessions, and Bible study. Many students embraced, at least partially, the values taught to them by their teachers. A letter by Sally Reece, a young Cherokee student, provides a Native perspective not only on how "civilization" had changed the fabric of Cherokee life, but also how missionary teachings influenced the way of thinking of many of their students. She wrote,

First I will tell you about the Cherokees. I think they improve. . . . They come to meeting on Sabbath days. They wear clothes which they made themselves. Some though rude, have shoes and stockings. They keep horses, cows, sheep, and swine. Some have oxen. They cultivate fields. They have yet a great many bad customs but I hope all these things will soon be done away. They have thought more about the Saviour lately. I hope this nation will soon become civilized and enlightened.[19]

Boarding schools also challenged the established gender dynamics of southeastern Amerindian societies. Boys, not girls, worked the fields in missionary schools. Girls were trained in the domestic arts such as cooking, cleaning, sewing, and ironing. The missionaries believed that this was the only appropriate division of labor for male and female children. Imagine the conflicts that arose when these students returned to their families and communities.

The assault on indigenous systems of morality eventually had an impact on the adults as well, either because they had been students in missionary schools during their youth, or because they were influenced by their children. For instance, by the nineteenth century, males in the Southeast increasingly either labored next to the women or did all of the agricultural work by themselves. Cherokee social norms also began to emphasize that a woman's proper place was in the home.[20]

Literacy flourished among the Cherokee during the first half of the nineteenth century, boosted by the invention of an alphabet for writing the Cherokee language, which was invented by a Cherokee man named Sequoyah. The alphabet was actually a syllabary. It consisted of 86 symbols that stood for syllables in Cherokee. The system was relatively simple to learn. It enabled the Cherokee to read and write in their own language. This is a good example of how the Cherokee people adopted Euro-American standards of "civilization" on their own terms. If literacy was a requirement for civilized society, they were willing to become literate—in their own language, using a writing system of their own invention. In 1828, the Cherokee Nation, which also owned a printing press, began the production of a bilingual newspaper in Cherokee and English called the *Cherokee Phoenix*. The paper printed news, matters of public and private interests, editorials, and religious materials. The *Cherokee Phoenix* was sold to Cherokees but also found readers among Euro-Americans in America and even in Europe.[21]

The name itself reminds us that many of the Cherokee children who were educated in Euro-American schools gained a good knowledge of the classics of Western European literature. The phoenix is a magical creature from Greek mythology that rises from the dead and bursts into flame with a new life, a potent symbol of resurrection and rebirth. This

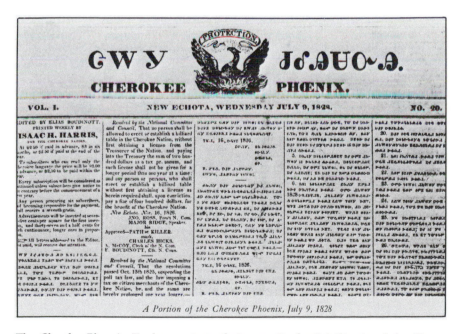

A Portion of the Cherokee Phoenix, July 9, 1828

The *Cherokee Phoenix*. To demonstrate their capacity for "civilization," the Cherokee not only became literate in English but also developed a system for reading and writing Cherokee.

was the vision held by many Cherokees at this time: that they could give up some of their old ways in order to find a new life as a Cherokee people in a changing world.

The Cherokee response to the external pressure on them to become "civilized" also included a brilliant move that ultimately worked against them, as it generated a powerful backlash from their American neighbors. In 1826, the Cherokee Nation codified their laws into a written legal system that mirrored the written laws of the United States. They created a Cherokee Nation police force to enforce those laws within the bounds of their sovereign territory. That year, John Ridge, a member of an important Cherokee family, wrote a letter to his friend, Albert Gallatin, the Secretary of the Treasury during Thomas Jefferson's presidency, in which he outlined the laws that he considered most important to his people.

1. Law to regulate our Citizens agreeable to the Intercourse laws of the U. States for the purpose of securing peace on the frontiers.
2. A law prohibiting the introduction of Intoxicating liquors by the whites.
3. Regulating intermarriages with the whites, making it necessary for a white man to obtain license & be married by a Gospel minister or some authorized person.
4. Against Renting land and introducing white people without special written permission of the Legislative Council. Penalty: Expulsion of the white people so introduced as intruders, a fine of $500 on the aggressor and one hundred stripes on the naked back.
5. Giving indefeasible title to Lands improved—houses &c.—to the Citizens with power to sell or transfer them among each other, but not to Citizens of the adjoining States.
6. Regulating Taxes and defining the duties of collectors.
7. Law, prohibiting the sale of any more Lands to the United States except it be done by the concurrences of the Nat. Committee & Council; Penalty: disgrace & death to the offender.
8. A law to protect the orphan & widow to the father's [and] husband's property after death.
9. Regulating the Salary of the two head chiefs, District & circuit Judges, the pay of the members of the Legislative Council and their clerks during active service and officers of the Nation generally.
10. Regulating the Judicial Courts of the Nation, defining their Powers.
11. Against stealing.
12. Against murder.
13. Defining the Powers.[22]

As demonstrated by these concerns, the new Cherokee laws especially aimed to maintain the nation's land base and its political autonomy. But the legal system also reflected some of the social changes that had occurred in Cherokee society due to "civilization." For example, law eight, which codified that a dead husband's wife and children should inherit the deceased's property, broke with older Cherokee customs. Traditional Cherokee law would have given a dead man's inheritance to his sister and her children, in accordance with the matrilineal system that used to exist among the Cherokee.

The reforms in the Cherokee legal system culminated with the 1827 passage of their Constitution, which was influenced by the Constitution of the United States. The legislative branch of the Cherokee Nation, called the General Council, was divided into two bodies elected by voting members of the tribe. The chamber equivalent to the U.S. House of Representatives was the National Council. The National Committee was equivalent to the U.S. Senate. Beyond its various legislative tasks such as passing budgets and laws, the General Council also elected the executive branch of the Nation, which consisted of the Principal Chief, his deputy, and a treasurer. Note that, in an effort to demonstrate their "civilized" condition, Cherokee men excluded Cherokee women from the franchise. They also denied voting rights to the African slaves owned by a small number of wealthy Cherokee men, who used slave labor to increase the profits on their plantations.

The Cherokees, like other Native Americans in the Southeast, believed that they would be able to stay on their homelands and maintain their autonomy and sovereignty if they demonstrated that they were as "civilized" as their American neighbors. They accepted missionary schools for their children, adopted Anglo-American forms of agriculture, which included plantation slavery, they developed an alphabet and became literate in their own language, and they adopted a national Constitution that mirrored the U.S. Constitution yet reflected Cherokee values, for the most part. Faced with new challenges and increasing pressures in a colonial world, the Cherokees transformed the "civilization" program of the United States into a self-directed strategy for survival and cultural revitalization.[23]

The Effects of Removal on Daily Life   The Indian Removal Act of 1830 ushered in yet another major disruption in Native American daily life in the Southeast, when the federal government mandated that Native peoples should be moved west. The relocation of Native peoples was a larger trend that occurred all through the lands lying between the Appalachian Mountains and the Mississippi River. In the end, and despite Amerindian resistance, only a few Natives managed to remain in their homelands in the Southeast.

The idea of moving Native peoples off of their lands in the east and removing them to the West emerged in the early nineteenth century. Many officials believed that the relocation of Native peoples would protect them from settler pressures, encroachment, and violence. At the same time, land was a commodity of vital importance to the development of the early U.S. economy, which was largely based on agricultural production. Whatever the intentions of those who claimed to be helping the Indians, most such efforts led to another round of land loss for indigenous peoples. The discourse of "civilization" worked against Native peoples here because hunting, fishing, and small-scale horticulture were viewed as inefficient uses of the land. Many Euro-Americans believed that their ways of using the land were more efficient, more civilized, than Native ways of using the land. For some, this justified their right to take possession of the land. Some Euro-Americans criticized the government's "civilization policy" because of its harmful effect on indigenous peoples, but the loudest complaints came from those who thought that it had failed in the effort to "civilize" them.

On the other hand, most Native Americans believed that they had already ceded more land than they could afford, and that they needed all of their remaining territory to guarantee the survival of their communities for at least the next seven generations. Their leaders, when pressured by the federal and state government to give up more land, mostly tried to evade the issue, or refused to negotiate further cessions. They insisted that, as sovereign nations, they would only sell their land if they as a community decided that it suited their collective interests. Moreover, Native peoples east of the Mississippi looked at "civilization policy" differently than Anglo-Americans. They adopted into their daily lives only those parts of the federal program that they viewed as benefiting and strengthening their communities and ignored the aspects that they considered harmful. Thus, Native communities held firm in the belief that they were sovereign nations with cultural traditions that were worth preserving.

External challenges to the Native American societies in the Southeast became increasingly insurmountable as the states and the federal government stretched and flexed their muscles in the first decades of the nineteenth century. The state of Georgia, for example, had long viewed the Cherokee as a impediment to their own expansion. The acquisition of Cherokee lands would allow cotton farmers in Georgia to expand their holdings. Then, in the late 1820s, Euro-American prospectors discovered gold in the Cherokee hills. Miners rushed onto Cherokee land to stake a claim. This spurred the state of Georgia to declare that it held jurisdiction over Cherokee territory. The Cherokees objected. They pointed out that they were a sovereign nation in their own right, one that predated the creation of the state or even the colony of Georgia. They deliberately used language meant to remind their American neighbors that states such as Georgia and the federal government of the United States had only recently acquired their sovereign status. The Cherokee Nation underscored its own status as a much older sovereign nation. With their written Constitution, they demonstrated their willingness and ability to meet the Euro-American definition of a "civilized" nation. Ironically, their strategy backfired. Instead of making Americans think of the Cherokees as good neighbors, their claim to status as a civilized, sovereign nation inflamed public sentiment in states such as Georgia, which had managed to convince themselves that the Cherokee and other "savage" nations would soon die out or disappear beneath the inevitable weight of "progress." Instead of pulling their people out, Georgia sent its militia out to protect the Euro-American miners and squatters living on Cherokee lands. Cherokee protests against these acts were largely ignored.

Georgia's sentiments were echoed in other parts of the early republic. Andrew Jackson was elected president of the United States in 1828 on a surge of expansionist fervor that included support for the policy of Indian removal. Jackson rejected the notion that Native American communities were sovereign nations and made this issue central to his presidential campaign. This helped him to gain many votes in the western states. Early in his administration, Jackson introduced the Indian Removal Act, which was passed by Congress in 1830. Though Jackson knew quite well that Native peoples such as the Cherokee and Creek were farmers and not "wandering hunters," he still asked in his State of the Union Address of 1830:

What good man would prefer a country covered with forests and ranged by a few thousand savages to our extensive republic studded with cities, towns and prosperous farms, embellished with all the improvements that art can devise or industry execute, occupied by more than 12 million happy people and filled with all the blessings of civilization, liberty and religion.[24]

President Jackson also argued that the forced relocation of Native Americans would be a benevolent act. He maintained that on western lands, which the United States acquired from France through the Louisiana Purchase of 1803, Amerindians would be secure from Euro-American violence and encroachments. There they would be able to pursue "civilization" in peace.

In the decade that followed the Indian Removal Act of 1830, U.S. officials pressured Native nations in the Southeast such as the Choctaw, Chickasaw, and Creek to sign treaties of removal. This process highlights the ironies and inconsistencies of the relationship between the United States and the sovereign Indian nations that exist within its borders. On the one hand, states such as Georgia refused to recognize Indian nations as legitimate governments with legitimate territorial claims. On the other hand, Congress saw the need to negotiate treaties in order to legitimate the process by which they removed the people and claimed the land. This contradiction generated frustration, anger, and sometimes an internalized self-hatred amongst the Native Americans that became a part of their daily lives.

The Choctaws who lived on land within the borders of the state of Mississippi were the first of the major southern tribes to face the long journey to a place then called Indian Territory, that is, present-day

Oklahoma. Small children, babies, and old people along with everyone else were forced to leave their homes in the winter of 1831. A total of about 6,000 Choctaw travelers faced harsh weather and rugged conditions without the help of the supplies, tents, wagons, provisions, and weapons that they had been promised by the federal government. Things were so bad that even many of the soldiers sent to escort them to their new homes suffered and died from cold and hunger. By some estimates, one-third of the people who set forth from their eastern homes died along the way. One of the Choctaw chiefs described their passage as "a trail of tears and death." This phrase was picked up by Eastern newspapers for their horrified public, and the phrase, "the trail of tears," has been associated with Indian Removal ever since.

Meanwhile, American settlers, too impatient to wait for the relocation of the Creeks, moved onto their lands early in the 1830s. The Creeks lobbied hard against the presence of Euro-American squatters and against removal. Yet their efforts to remain on their Alabama homelands, or to remove Euro-American squatters from Creek territory, were unsuccessful. After several years of harassment, Jackson ordered their deportation in 1836. The conditions of Creek removal were horrifying. One observer from Arkansas described the following scene late in 1836.

Thousands of them are entirely destitute of shoes or cover of any kind for their feet; many of them are almost naked, and but few of them [have] anything more on their persons than a light dress calculated only for the summer, or for a warm climate. In this destitute condition, they are wading in cold mud, or are hurried on over the frozen ground, as the case may be. Many of them have in this way had their feet frost-bitten; and being unable to travel, fall in the rear of the main party, and in this way are left on the road to await the ability or convenience of the contractors to assist them. Many of them, not being able to endure this unexampled state of human suffering, die, and are thrown by the side of the road, and are covered over only with brush, etc—where they remain until they are devoured by the wolves.

It is now past the middle of December, and the winter, though cold, is by no means at its worst stage, and when the extreme of winter does fall upon these most miserable creatures, in their present suffering and desperate condition, the destruction of human life will be most deplorable.[25]

Other Creeks were taken south to New Orleans and then loaded onto steamboats heading north on the Mississippi River to Arkansas, where they were then expected to travel by foot to Indian Territory. The boats used for these missions were substandard, and the contractors paid little regard to safety and the needs of their passengers. One boat, with 600 Creeks, and operated by a drunken crew, got into an accident and sank. Over 300 Creek people died in the incident and many of the survivors were badly burned by the steam that escaped from the ship's boilers.

Removal was as deadly and traumatic for the Creeks as it was for the Choctaws. Although it is difficult to estimate how many people died during the forced relocation, we know that prior to removal a census produced by the Bureau of Indian Affairs counted over 25,000 Creeks. In 1857, 25 years later, a similar census taken in Oklahoma counted only 14,888. This constituted a population decline of about 40 percent.[26]

Other Native Americans resisted removal as well. In 1836, the U.S. army's effort to forcefully relocate the Seminole from their homes in the swamps of Florida led to a violent confrontation. The Seminoles were seen as a thorn in the side of the Americans, because, much to the anger of many southern plantation owners, they had adopted and incorporated runaway African American slaves into their society. The U.S. war against the Seminoles lasted for six years and cost the lives of hundreds of people and some 20 million dollars, an enormous amount of money at that time. Even so, the United States did not win an unequivocal victory. The war ended in 1842 when about 3,000 Seminoles finally agreed to move west, hoping for a more stable existence. The United States government called off the campaign, and about 1,000 Seminoles remained in Florida.

The Cherokee also resisted removal. Like other Native peoples in the South, they resolved to stay on their own land. The Cherokee believed that they had successfully embraced the "civilization program" initiated by the U.S. government, thereby countering the argument that as "savages" they would be happier out west or that they were an impediment to progress. With the assistance of sympathetic missionaries and politicians, they took their case to the U.S. Supreme Court. There they argued that the state of Georgia's legal and territorial infringements violated Cherokee sovereignty. In the famous 1832 Supreme Court case, *Worcester v. Georgia*, Chief Justice John Marshall decided in the majority decision that the actions by Georgia were "repugnant" and violated the U.S. Constitution.

President Jackson, on the other hand, ignored the Supreme Court ruling, and vowed not to enforce it. Georgia, encouraged by the federal government's position, continued to promote Euro-American settlement on Cherokee land. Thus, realizing that they would obtain no official support, some Cherokee, under the leadership of Major Ridge, John Ridge, and Elias Boudinot, decided that resistance had become futile. This small minority group signed a removal treaty with the U.S. government in December of 1835, called the Treaty of New Echota. With the signature of this document, the so-called "Treaty Party," which included only a few hundred members, ceded the Cherokee homelands in exchange for five million dollars and agreed to move west. In many ways their vision was consistent with the effort to be recognized as a civilized people by mainstream American society, charting a future for their children that would combine Cherokee and Euro-American ways. However, the decision of a small but prosperous minority to sign the 1835 Treaty and accept payment on behalf of the entire nation gave the United States a legal basis to justify the forced removal of everyone else. All three leaders of the treaty party—Major Ridge, John Ridge, and Elias Boudinot—were killed by unidentified assailants in 1839.

A clear majority of the Cherokee people maintained a steady opposition to Removal and rejected the treaty—especially since they had been kept out of the negotiations. The leader of the anti-Removal majority, known as the National Party, was John Ross. Ross protested that the Treaty of New Echota was not binding on the Cherokee Nation because it had been "signed by unauthorized individuals." He argued that it would "never be regarded by the Cherokee nation as a Treaty. The delegation appointed by the people to make a Treaty, have protested that instrument 'as deceptive to the world and a fraud upon the Cherokee people.'"[27] In a unified stance of resistance, about 15,000 Cherokee people—almost the entire nation—signed a petition to protest the removal treaty. Still, the U.S. Senate ratified the document, giving the Cherokee two years to leave their homelands in the east.

Not surprisingly, those Cherokee who had signed the petition against Removal made no effort to comply with this order. They were caught off-guard and unprepared when federal troops entered their lands in 1838. The military rounded up the Cherokee and placed them in stockades to limit the possibility of resistance. Evan Jones, an American missionary and a close confidant of Cherokee leader John Ross, described the following inhumane scenes that the Cherokee had to endure during this process.

The Cherokees are nearly all prisoners. They have been dragged from their houses, and encamped at the forts and military posts, all over the nation. In Georgia, especially, multitudes were allowed no time to take any thing with them, except the clothes they had on. Well-furnished houses were left a prey to plunderers, who, like hungry wolves, follow in the train of the captors. These wretches rifle the houses, and strip the helpless, unoffending owners of all they have on earth. Females, who have been habituated to comforts and comparative affluence are driven on foot before the bayonets of brutal men. Their feelings are mortified by vulgar and profane vociferations. It is a painful sight. The property of many has been taken, and sold before their eyes for almost nothing—the sellers and buyers, in many cases, being combined to cheat the poor Indians. These things are done at the instant of arrest and consternation; the soldiers standing by, with their arms in hand, impatient to go on with their work, could give little time to transact business. The poor captive, in a state of distressing agitation, his weeping wife almost frantic with terror, surrounded by a group of crying terrified children, without a friend to speak a consoling word, is in a poor condition to make a good disposition of his property and is in most cases stripped of the whole at one blow. Many of the Cherokees, who, a few days ago, were in comfortable circumstances, are now victims of abject poverty. Some, who have been allowed to return home, under passport, to inquire after their property, have found their cattle, horses, swine, farming-tools and house furniture all gone. And this is not a description of extreme cases. It is altogether a faint representation of the work which has been perpetuated on the unoffending, unarmed and unresisting Cherokees.[28]

A description by a Cherokee child provides a glimpse of the trauma and stress that this event caused for Native children and their families. She recalled:

When the soldiers came to our house my father wanted to fight, but my mother told him that the soldiers would kill him if he did and we surrendered without a fight. They drove us out of our house to join other prisoners in a stockade.

The child also described the suffering caused when Native families were forced to travel hundreds of miles from their homelands in the Southeast to the unfamiliar place called "Indian territory," as if it was where they belonged:

My father had a wagon pulled by two spans of oxen to haul us in. Eight of my brothers and sisters and two or three widow women and children rode with us. My brother Dick who was a good deal older than I was walked along with a long whip which he popped over the back of the Oxen and drove them all the way. My father and mother walked all the way also. The people got so tired of eating salt pork on the journey that my father would walk through the woods as we traveled, hunting for turkeys and deer which he brought into camp to feed us. Camp was usually made at some place where water was to be had and when we stopped and prepared to cook our food other emigrants who had been driven from their homes without opportunity to secure cooking utensils came to our camp to use our pots and kettles. There was much sickness among the emigrants and a great many children died of whooping cough.[29]

Starting in 1838, more than 13,000 Cherokees were forced by the U.S. government to march west. Because of poor supplies, inhumane treatment, and traveling in the dead of winter, an estimated 2,000 to 4,000 Cherokee died along the way. It was truly a Trail of Tears.

LIFE IN A NEW HOMELAND: THE "FIVE CIVILIZED TRIBES" IN THE WEST

Removal meant a total readjustment in the daily life of those Native Americans who had to endure it. For one, displaced Native peoples encountered a different physical environment in their new and unfamiliar surroundings. Present-day Oklahoma is one of the most diverse regions in the continental United States, with 10 different ecoregions including prairies, cypress swamps, hardwood forests, and the rugged foothills of the Rocky Mountains. It took time for people to learn how to live in these new lands, away from the sacred landscape associated with their stories of creation, away from the places where the bones of their ancestors lay buried. Moreover, many people had lost significant amounts of property and farm lands. They had to start their lives over from scratch.

Adapting to a new life west of the Mississippi was not easy. In many communities, it generated tensions almost immediately. For instance, among the Cherokee in what is today northeastern Oklahoma there existed three distinct factions resulting from historical developments in previous decades. There was already bad blood between the Treaty Party and the National Party over the Treaty of New Echota of 1835. Many members of the National Party, which had opposed the Removal, regarded anyone associated with the Treaty Party as a traitor who had sold out Cherokee interests to the United States. The Treaty Party was blamed, at least in part, for the loss of Cherokee homelands and for the removal. The Cherokee's ability to build political consensus was further complicated by a third faction—the Old Settler Party. The Old Settlers were Cherokees who had preferred to seek new homes in the west rather than trying to accommodate to Euro-American ways. They took advantage of early U.S. government efforts to solve the Cherokee problem by offering people incentives to move west. The Old Settlers moved first to Arkansas in the early nineteenth century. There they were pressured to leave and move to Oklahoma in the late 1820s. Understandably, the relatively small Old Settler Party had some concerns about the major influx of other Cherokee people. The assassination of John and Major Ridge as well as Elias Boudinot in the summer of 1839 only led to an escalation of the situation. Though some Cherokee leaders attempted to curtail violence by drafting a constitution on September 6, 1839, a civil war broke out that haunted the Cherokee Nation until the second half of the 1840s.[30] Thus, at a time when Cherokee life had already been disrupted by Removal, the Nation suffered from additional warfare, rivalry, and a cycle of retribution and personal vengeance that brought new terror to families and communities. Such bloodshed further complicated the Cherokees' transition as they tried to make the best of their new homelands in the West.

Tension erupted again among the western Cherokee during the American Civil War. Though most Cherokees wanted to remain neutral in the conflict, some Cherokees decided to fight with the South, especially those who owned slaves, while others fought on the side of the Union. The conflict brought renewed violence into the daily lives of Native Americans.

These Native American pioneers in the West fought hard to survive in their new homelands, trying to make the best out of a bad deal. They build new homes and started new farms, eagerly attempting to replicate as many of the patterns of daily life from the East as they could. Native Americans in Indian Territory were also keen on maintaining their independence, as well as their religious and political structures, to the best of their abilities.

As in the East, many members of the "Five Civilized Tribes" in the West, as the Cherokee, Creek, Chickasaw, Choctaw, and Seminoles are sometimes collectively called, continued to be influenced by Anglo-American culture.

Anglo-American education and schools for their children remained an important component in their daily life. There were public school systems with numerous small schools, many of which were run by missionary organizations. But Native communities also tried to push for more advanced education whenever possible. In 1851, for instance, the Cherokee Nation opened a seminary (high school) for men, and, more astonishingly for the mid-nineteenth century, another for women. The Cherokee Female Seminary emulated Mount Holyoke Female Seminary, the first all-female school in the United States for higher learning. The founding of a school for young Native women set a milestone in the history of women's education in this country.

Commercial farming also persisted among the Five Civilized Tribes. Large landholders sold their corn, cotton, and other crops to nearby markets. The profits they made were largely spent on consumer goods. Entrepreneurial Native American businessmen developed new ventures with significant nonagricultural assets. The products that large Native landholders and businessmen consumed, their economic aspirations, and their way of life, were in numerous ways reminiscent of that of many Euro-American southern farmers and entrepreneurs. An observation by an American officer, Colonel Ethan Allen Hitchcock, who inspected Indian Territory for the government, provides a glimpse at these similarities, and the moderate luxuries enjoyed by upper-class Native Americans during these years:

Lewis Ross the merchant is wealthy and lives in considerable style. His house is of the cottage character, clapboarded and painted, his floor carpeted, his furniture elegant, cane bottomed chairs, of high finish, two superior mahogany Boston rocking chairs, mahogany ladies work table with drawers, a very superior Chickering piano on which his unmarried daughter, a young lady of about 17 or 18, just in from school at Rawway New Jersey, plays some waltzes, and sings some songs.[31]

Furthermore, like their Euro-American counterparts in the South, many of the wealthier Native farmers in Indian Territory continued to own slaves. In 1860, for example, Cherokee plantation owners and farmers possessed an estimated 4,000 slaves. The Cherokee population in the West of about 20,000 people maintained about 102,000 acres under cultivation. It is estimated that the members of the Cherokee Nation owned about 20,000 horses and mules, 240,000 head of cattle, and 15,000 hogs. Their renaissance, like the phoenix that they took as the symbol of their Cherokee language newspaper, testifies to the strong spirit of the Cherokee and their determination to survive, despite many obstacles.

It is important to point out, though, that not everyone among the Five Civilized Tribes in Indian Territory lived in big houses or mansions. There certainly existed class divisions in these societies. It is true that some Native farmers and entrepreneurs did extremely well in profitable businesses such as salt production and cattle ranching. Some people had managed to sell their properties in the East at a good price and therefore had start-up capital for their business ventures in the West. Still, most Native Americans in Indian Territory did not have such advantages and lived a more modest life. Many had only a couple of acres of land and resided in small cabins and houses, often consisting of only one room, and eked out a modest living.

Like other Native American communities in the American West, the Five Civilized Tribes would face severe trials toward the end of the nineteenth century, including a new wave of land losses. The coming of the railroad, land speculators, and a new influx of Euro-American settlers challenged the patterns of daily life to which Native Americans in Indian Territory had grown accustomed in the decades after Removal. The land allotment policy of the federal government, which aimed to privatize reservation lands, and the Curtis Act of 1898, which ended Native American land tenure, threatened Native sovereignty and the continued existence of their communities in the region. The survival of the Five Civilized Tribes was further undermined when the former Indian Territory, which was supposed to be theirs in perpetuity, became the state of Oklahoma. Yet despite such challenges the Native peoples of the region, along with their cultures and values, did not disappear, as many Euro-Americans during the late nineteenth century might have hoped.[32]

ESCAPEES OF REMOVAL: THE EASTERN CHEROKEE

Standard accounts of Indian Removal that emphasize the forced march of the Trail of Tears contribute to the same discourse of disappearance seen in the Northeast when people said that all the Indians had died out or moved away, leaving the land conveniently available for Euro-American claims. In reality, some Native Americans in the Southeast managed to avoid removal. Parts of the Choctaw Nation of Mississippi, the Seminoles of Florida, and many Cherokee people continued, and continue, to live in their preremoval homelands despite the forceful relocation of their kin. There they continued their daily lives and maintained their Native communities and identities throughout the nineteenth and twentieth century, into the present day. This section focuses on the experiences of a group that has come to be known as the Eastern Band of Cherokee, about 1,000 people who evaded the Trail of Tears in the 1830s. This group remained in their remote homelands in the mountains of western North Carolina.

The community of Cherokees who settled along the Oconaluftee River in North Carolina had in many ways severed its ties with the main Cherokee Nation even before the Removal era. Unlike mainstream Cherokee society, they took a strong stand against the accommodationist program of their kin. They continued their traditional way of subsistence based on Amerindian ways of agriculture, hunting, and fishing, although they also raised cash by selling livestock, ginseng, and other medicinal herbs to Euro-American traders. Further, they maintained their traditional forms of government, religion, and culture. They rejected mission schools, Christianity, and the republican constitutional forms of government adopted by their Cherokee relatives in Georgia and Tennessee.

Through astute maneuvering, the community on the Oconaluftee River escaped removal. They were aided in this by a Euro-American adoptee named William Holland Thomas, who was an orphan when he was adopted by Yonaguska, the leader of the Cherokee band in western North Carolina. As an adult, Thomas became a trader, his background and his command of English and Cherokee making him well equipped for this role. Alert to the rumors of removal, Thomas helped the Oconaluftee community to consolidate their territorial base by buying up available tracts of land around their homelands. He also lobbied in Washington, D.C. and before the North Carolina state legislature, making the case that the North Carolina Cherokee should not be removed. The Oconaluftee community argued that the removal treaty of 1835 was not legally binding on them. They maintained that they had become citizens of North Carolina and, therefore, were no longer part of the Cherokee Nation. This argument was tacitly accepted by North Carolina and the federal government.

However, their situation on the Oconaluftee River remained precarious throughout the removal period. Tensions rose after a traditionalist leader named Tsali and his followers killed two American soldiers and wounded another when the military tried to force them off their land. Tsali and his band fled to the mountains. Federal officials demanded that the murderers be turned in for punishment. The Oconaluftee Cherokee were faced with a difficult decision. If they turned Tsali and his followers over to the United States for punishment, they gave up one of their own but also eroded their own sovereignty by acknowledging that the United States had the right to judge them. On the other hand, if they refused, the U.S. army would be unrelenting in their search for the men. In the end, they chose a third way. They decided to execute the men themselves, demonstrating the strength of their own forms of justice and satisfying the military's demand for retribution. Cherokee oral histories suggest that Tsali surrendered himself voluntarily to Euchella, the son of Yonaguska. Tsali is remembered today as a hero and a martyr who gave himself up to prevent further bloodshed and to enable at least some of his people to remain on their homelands. As a result, Euchella and the Oconaluftee community avoided removal. During this time, the Cherokees in North Carolina were joined by other Cherokee peoples from Tennessee and Georgia who sought refuge among them.

The newly created Eastern Band of Cherokees, consisting of the Oconaluftees, Euchella's band, and refugees from other places, united disparate peoples largely on the basis of their desire to stay on their own homelands in the east. As a group, they tended to be people who thought that their own Cherokee ways were civilized enough. The Eastern Band of Cherokee also came to eulogize Tsali as a folk hero whose noble self-sacrifice had enabled them to remain on their ancestral lands.

Throughout the nineteenth century, the Eastern Band of Cherokee faced continual challenges to their survival. The U.S. government, for example, periodically attempted to convince them to move west to join up with the Cherokee Nation in Oklahoma. The Civil War brought new trials and tribulations to the Eastern Band's way of life. During the war, more than 200 Eastern Cherokee men signed up to fight for the South. They were recruited by William Holland Thomas, who was an ardent supporter of the Confederacy. While a small percentage of elite Cherokee men owned slaves in the early nineteenth century, most of the slaveholding Cherokee were now living west of the Mississippi. The Eastern Band Cherokee men who fought for the Confederacy enlisted due to the personal loyalty that they felt toward Thomas, rather than in defense of slavery. This became clear when a group of 20 to 30 Cherokee soldiers who had been taken prisoner by Union forces switched sides and joined the Union army after hearing the abolitionist point of view. The Eastern Band, like the Cherokee Nation out west, eventually split over the question. The hostility between the Confederate and Union factions among the Eastern Cherokee continued even after the war was over.

The period of Reconstruction after the Civil War brought major transformations and new threats to the daily life of the Eastern Band of Cherokee. William Holland Thomas, who had helped to save their lands in an earlier time, now became a source of potential land loss. Thomas had invested heavily in the Confederacy and accumulated debts that he was now unable to pay. His creditors claimed the right to take Cherokee lands that had been placed in Thomas's name in payment of his debts. The strategy that once protected them had now become a liability. In this case, the story has a happy ending, as the federal government stepped in on the side of the Cherokees in the courts and helped them to regain much of their property.

The men of the Eastern Band of Cherokees began to participate in the state and federal political system after 1870 when the Fifteenth Amendment to the U.S. Constitution gave all adult men the right to vote regardless of "race, color, or previous condition of servitude." The voting rights of Cherokee men largely followed the status accorded to people of African descent, who lost many rights as discriminatory Jim Crow laws became entrenched in North Carolina and all over the South in the late nineteenth century.

This did not mean that the Cherokees had given up their view of themselves as a sovereign people, or forgotten their traditional ways. But they were no longer a people living outside the bounds of "settled" society. To survive, they began to make choices similar to those they had scorned in their Cherokee kin who pursued accommodationist strategies in the early nineteenth century. In 1868 the Eastern Band of Cherokees drafted a constitution of their own that provided for the election of a chief and council. The federal government recognized them as a distinct tribal entity, separate from the Cherokee Nation in Oklahoma. The boundaries of the Eastern Cherokee Reservation, also known as the Qualla Boundary, were surveyed and established by 1870, establishing their claim in federal as well as Cherokee eyes. However, these interactions with the federal government as well as outside pressures brought significant social and cultural changes to the Cherokees living in North Carolina.

To further protect themselves in relation to American laws, Cherokee leaders applied for a corporate charter from the state of North Carolina, which was granted to them in 1889. This provided the community with significant legal protection from outside threats. They developed a timber industry that brought in much-needed cash. Unfortunately, it led to serious deforestation of their lands. The corporate charter also functioned as a base for the group's political government from the late nineteenth century on.

The Eastern Band of Cherokee faced new challenges in the area of education in the late nineteenth century. In 1892, the federal government took control of the Cherokee school system, which at the time consisted of several day schools located in various Cherokee settlements and one boarding school, which had been opened up by Quaker missionaries in the 1880s. In keeping with federal education policies that promoted assimilation, the teachers did their best to stamp out Cherokee culture, language, and tradition as part of their curriculum. In this, they followed the example set by educator and former army officer Richard Henry Pratt, founder of Carlisle Indian Industrial School in Pennsylvania, whose motto was "Kill the Indian to save the man."[33] This created much pain and confusion for children as well as for their parents, many of whom continued to value the old ways.

In an effort to provide links between their past and their future, and despite many challenges, the Eastern Band of Cherokee were eager to maintain as many of their cultural beliefs and practices as their situation allowed. Traditional culture and community values remained a strong part in their daily lives. The Cherokee in North Carolina continued to use their time-honored medicines and hunting charms, told their stories and myths, and maintained their oral traditions.

Although the Cherokee had abolished their village councils as the established form of government, community cohesion was reinforced by the so-called *gadugi*, or work cohort. The members of a *gadugi* collectively worked the land of their affiliates. If a coworker became sick or otherwise unable to do his part, his land would be taken care of by other members of the *gadugi*. This provided an important social safety net for people in the community. According to one anthropologist the *gadugi* aided "the social survival of the Cherokee town, carrying on the economic functions of the town long after its political functions were lost." Work companies also worked for outsiders as a way to raise cash for their members. According to historian Theda Perdue, the "gadugi embodied the communal values of traditional Cherokee culture and applied them to the modern world." Thus, while the Eastern Band of the Cherokee would continue to face numerous threats to their nation's survival in the years to come, the ability to balance cultural continuity while adapting to the harsh realities of their political circumstances in the nineteenth century prepared them well for an often uncertain future in the twentieth century.[34]

NOTES

1. Michael D. Green, *The Creeks* (New York: Chelsea House Publishers, 1990), 14–20.

2. Alice B. Kehoe, *North American Indians: A Comprehensive Account,* 2nd ed. (Upper Saddle River, NJ: Prentice Hall, 1992), 178.

3. James H. Merrell, *The Catawbas* (New York: Chelsea House Publishers, 1989), 30–32.

4. Merrell, 27–28, 30.

5. Christian F. Feest, *The Powhatan Tribes* (New York: Chelsea House Publishers, 1990), 21–23, 30–31.

6. Feest, 22–25, 27.

7. Green, 22–23.

8. Jesse O. McKee, *The Choctaw* (New York: Chelsea House Publishers, 1989), 54–57.

9. Charles Hudson, *The Southeastern Indians* (Knoxville: University of Tennessee Press, 1976), 365–75; Kehoe, 184–85.

10. Frederick E. Hoxie and Peter Iverson, eds., *Indians in American History*, 2nd ed. (Wheeling, Ill.: Harland Davidson, 1998).

11. Powhatan, "Speech to Captain John Smith," quoted in Colin G. Calloway, ed., *The World Turned Upside Down: Indian Voices from Early America* (Boston: Bedford, 1994), 38–39.

12. Antoine le Page du Pratz, "Reply of the Stung Serpent," quoted in Calloway, 91.

13. Historian James H. Merrell was the first to use this phrase, "the Indians' New World," to describe the experiences of Native Americans after 1492. See James H. Merrell, *The Indians' New World: Catawbas and their Neighbors from European Contact through the Era of Removal* (Chapel Hill: University of North Carolina Press, 1989).

14. Kehoe, 189.

15. Chickasaw Headmen, "Speech to the Governor of South Carolina" quoted   in Calloway, 129–32.

16. See for example Anthony F.C. Wallace, *Jefferson and the Indians: The Tragic Fate of the First Americans* (Cambridge, MA: Harvard University Press, 1999).

17. David Zeisberger, Benjamin Mortimer, and John Heckewelder to Arthur St. Clair, Oct. 28, 1798, in *St. Clair Papers,* 2: 433–434.

18. See for example Robert Berkhofer Jr., *Salvation and the Savage: An Analysis of Protestant Missions and American Indian Response* (Lexington: University of Kentucky Press, 1965); Henry Bowden, *American Indians and Christian Missions: Studies in Cultural Conflict* (Chicago: University of Chicago Press, 1981), see especially 163–78; George Tinker, *Missionary Conquest: The Gospel and Native American Cultural Genocide* (Minneapolis, MN: Fortress Press, 1993).

19. Sally Reece to Daniel Campbell, July 25, 1828, quoted in *The Cherokee Removal: A Brief History with Documents,* ed. Theda Perdue and Michael D. Green (Boston: Bedford Books, 1995), 48.

20. Theda Perdue, *The Cherokee* (New York: Chelsea House, 1989), 41–42.

21. Perdue, 43–44.

22. John Ridge to Albert Gallatin, Feb. 27, 1826, in Perdue and Green, 39.

23. Perdue, 45–47.

24. Quoted in Calloway, 211.

25. Quoted in Green, 81–82.

26. Green, 83.

27. John Ross, "Letter," in Perdue and Green, 155.

28. Evan Jones, "Letters," in Perdue and Green, 172.

29. Rebecca Neugin, "Recollections of Removal," in Perdue and Green, 179.

30. Perdue, 62–63.

31. Theda Perdue, *Slavery and the Evolution of Cherokee Society, 1540–1866* (Knoxville: University of Tennessee Press, 1979).

32. The discussion of the "Five Civilized Tribes" of the West benefited from Perdue, *The Cherokee*, chapter 5; and Green, chapter 6.

33. Frederick E. Hoxie, ed., *Encyclopedia of North American Indians: Native American History, Culture, and Life from Paleo-Indians to the Present* (Boston: Houghton Mifflin Company, 1996), 78.

34. The discussion of the Eastern Band of Cherokee is based on Perdue, *The Cherokee*, chapter 6.

THE TRANS-MISSISSIPPI WEST

6

DAILY LIFE IN THE SOUTHWEST

The Southwest is a region with an extremely diverse ecology and climate, encompassing the modern states of Arizona and New Mexico, southern Utah, and Colorado, as well as western Texas and southeastern California. Groups such as the Pueblos, the Pima, and the Yuma have long established ancestral roots in this region. Other Native nations, such as the Navajo and the Apache, are fairly recent immigrants, having arrived in the Southwest sometime before 1500 A.D.

The landscape is one of stark contrasts, including magnificent high mesas and deep canyons, dry lands or actual deserts with little plant life, pine forests, meadows, and mountains covered with snow. Despite the harshness of its climate, which is characterized by the extremes of droughts and floods, sandstorms and blizzards, Native communities flourished in the Southwest and pursued various ways of life that were well suited to particular ecosystems. In the flood plains of desert areas, Native Americans farmed by taking advantage of seasonal floods to water and fertilize their fields. Other Amerindian peoples in the region made use of irrigation to increase their agricultural production. Whether they practiced horticulture or not, seasonal subsistence activities such as gathering, hunting, and fishing played an important role in their daily lives.

As in other parts of North America, the coming of Europeans dramatically altered the patterns of daily life among the Native Americans of the Southwest. The arrival of Spanish missionaries, conquistadors, and horses in the sixteenth century initiated dramatic changes that continued across the centuries as Mexico and the United States contested each other's claims to southwestern lands well into the nineteenth century. Throughout, Native Americans in the region accommodated or resisted the newcomers according to what they thought would be best for themselves and their future generations. The four centuries between 1492 and 1900 brought enormous challenges to the indigenous peoples of the Southwest.

PEOPLE OF THE PUEBLOS

When Spanish explorers first arrived in the Southwest, they encountered Native Americans who lived in multistory stone or adobe dwellings clustered together like apartment houses in an urban area. The Spanish word for village is "pueblo." This term is used today as the general name for both the people and their communities. Though we refer to all of the Native Americans discussed in this section as Pueblo Indians, it is important to note that the term encompasses people from four different language groups—Tanoan, Keresan, Zuni and Uto-Aztecan—each with their own distinctive cultures and histories. Nonetheless, they share similar

Pueblo dwellings, about 1880. What appear to be windows are in fact doors, reached by ladders. This style of dwelling dates back at least a thousand years. These were the largest multiple-household dwellings, or apartment buildings, in North America until after 1900. From Denver Public Library, Western History Collection.

cultural patterns, including a sedentary lifestyle centered on town or village life in houses made with similar design and building techniques, farming, and rich ceremonial cycles that often were, and are, kept hidden from outsiders.

Long before Columbus arrived in the Western Hemisphere, indigenous peoples in the Southwest lived in cities built out **The Anasazi** of stone. These ancient civilizations built towns on the tops of mesas, which are flat-topped elevations rising off the desert so starkly that the sides of the mesa are almost vertical. They also constructed significant urban settlements, such as Mesa Verde in southwestern Colorado, a fortified cliff city that consisted of over 200 multilevel one-room structures. The architects and builders of Mesa Verde, whose city-building culture blossomed in the Four Corners area of Arizona, Colorado, New Mexico, and Utah, especially from 1100 to 1300 A.D., are called the Anasazi. The name comes from a Navajo term meaning "the Ancient People." The Anasazi cultivated corn, beans, and squash for subsistence and planted cotton from which they wove blankets and clothing. They stored rain and flood water in reservoirs and ditches to have a ready supply in drier times. Moreover, they traded with their neighbors for goods such as turquoise, sea shells, birds, jewelry, minerals, and garments.

By the thirteenth century, however, Anasazi culture was in decline. This development was probably caused by a series of long droughts that led to crop failures and soil erosion. It is likely that tensions rose as people began to compete for a shrinking base of farm land, leading to an increase in warfare in the region. Many scholars assume that such tensions led to a dispersal of the Anasazi and that these groups joined up with other pueblo dwellers, such as the Hopi of Arizona and the Pueblo communities on the Rio Grande River. The mystery of what happened to the Anasazi, who left such remarkable evidence of their daily lives, continues to fascinate all who learn about them.

Pueblo stories about the beginning of the world as we know it have been passed down from one genera- **Emergence and** tion to the next through oral tradition and ritual. While **Migration** many people in Pueblo communities know these stories, certain people are trained to recite them as oral tradition in their original languages. The stories are actualized in ceremonies and ritual dramas that are sometimes open to the general public but more often performed within strict limits of privacy. Some of these stories have been written down and translated into English, but these versions are always problematic because the Pueblos, like other indigenous peoples in North America, have strict rules that limit storytelling to certain times of year. There are also restrictions on teaching sacred information to outsiders, so some of the versions available in print and presented as authentic should be used with caution. The following is a version told at Acoma Pueblo and written down by C. Daryll Forde, a Euro-American man, in 1930.[1]

In contrast to the Judeo-Christian story of creation told in *Genesis,* Pueblo stories begin in a place that already exists, called Cipapu, an underground world. Two female beings were born. They grew slowly in the dark, but when they became adults, Tsitctinako spoke to them. Tsitctinako taught them language and gave each a basket from their father, Utc'tsiti, containing the seeds and fetishes of all the plants and animals in the world. The sisters planted four seeds of four different types of trees and waited for a long time until the trees grew tall. Finally a pine tree grew so tall it pushed a hole through the earth. The hole was too small for the sisters to fit through, so they used the badger fetish in their baskets to call up Badger and ask for help. Badger made the hole large enough for them to fit through, and they climbed up and into the light.

The first thing that Tsitctinako taught the sisters was how to face the east and pray to the sun with pollen and sacred cornmeal, to thank it for the light. Tsitctinako taught them prayers and songs and told them much about the world. When they asked about their father, Tsitctinako said that he lived "four skies above." Utc'tsiti created the world by throwing a clot of his own blood into space. This became the earth, and in it, he planted the two female beings so that they might grow. Tsitctinako told the sisters that they were created to bring life to everything in their baskets so that the world would be complete.

Up to this time, the sisters had no names of their own. Now one of the girls moved her hand and Tsitctinako named her Ia'tik, which means "Bringing to Life." Tsitctinako told her to name her sister. After much thought, Ia'tik noticed that her sister's basket was slightly more full than her own. So she named her Nao'tsiti, or "More of everything in the basket." Ia'tik became the mother of the Red Corn clan. Nao'tsiti became the mother of the Sun clan.

The whole story of Ia'tik and Nao'tsiti is long and full of many details, such as how they learned to plant, harvest, and cook corn; how they brought the animals to life and each had their own special characteristics; how they created the mountains and clothed them in growing things; and how they learned which fish, birds, or animals were good to eat and which were not. Many of these details are remembered and reenacted in Pueblo daily prayers and other ceremonies. Eventually, Ia'tik and Nao'tsiti became competitive with each other, as sisters sometimes do. Each tried to outwit the other. They began to have selfish thoughts.

One day Nao'tsiti met a snake who told her that she would be happier if she had a child. Tsitctinako had told the sisters that their father did not want them to think about having children, but Nao'tsiti followed the snake's instructions anyway. She sat down on a rock near a rainbow. Drops of water from the rainbow entered her and she became pregnant. After a time, Nao'tsiti bore two children, twin boys. Tsitctinako was angry and told the sisters that because they had disobeyed their father, she would have to leave them.

Again, there are many stories to be told about these boys. Nao'tsiti and Ia'tik found that they were indeed happier with children, although they still did not get along. Nao'tsiti disliked one of the twins, so Ia'tik raised him. When the children were almost grown, the sisters decided to go their separate ways, each taking one of the boys. They divided everything that remained in their baskets. Nao'tsiti took sheep, cows, seeds for wheat and vegetables, and many vegetables—all things that would help her to live, but all of which required a good deal of work. Ia'tik refused these things, saying that they would be too difficult to care for. Nao'tsiti took her son and went away to the east but predicted that some day they would meet again and Ia'tik would desire her possessions.

Ia'tik and the boy, Tia'muni, continued to live where they were placed by Utc'tsiti. Years passed, and Tia'muni became her husband. When their daughter was born, Ia'tik entered her into the Sun clan, the clan of her sister Nao'tsiti. On the fourth day after the child's birth, Ia'tik put pollen and sacred cornmeal into its hands and took it outside to pray to the sun. She did this with each of her children, teaching them the same ritual that she had learned when she came up from underground and into the light.

Ia'tik ruled over her growing family but eventually wanted the company of others who could rule with her. She took some earth from her basket and made spirits of the seasons. She sent Winter to live in the mountains to the north; Spring to the mountains in the west; Summer to the mountains in the south; and Autumn to the mountains in the east. She taught her children to pray to these spirits for the seasonal blessings of moisture, warmth, ripening, and frost. This is the origin of the four seasons. Then Ia'tik created other beings who would have the power to call the rain. To set them apart from human beings, she made them masks from buffalo skin, colored with different kinds of earth and decorated with feathers. Ia'tik gave them rules for their initiation ceremonies and instructed them to dance before her people to call the rain. At other times, the katsinas, or ancestral spirits, were to live in sacred chambers in the four mountains. This is the origin of the katsinas, who still come when called to dance and bring rain. Ia'tik taught the men to make similar chambers, called *kivas*, for their own ceremonies. The prayers and rituals detailed in the story of Ia'tik and Nao'tsiti became part of the fabric of daily life for their descendants.

This story is classified as an "emergence story," that is, it starts with a world under the surface of the earth from which the people emerge into the light. Emergence stories are found among other people in the Southwest, notably the Navajo. Laguna Pueblo scholar Leslie Marmon Silko reminds us that Native peoples can believe in the truth of these stories, or myths, without necessarily believing that every detail is literally "true." The Emergence is a movement from darkness to light, and a record of how her ancestors came to "a precise cultural identity."[2]

When the Spanish explorers and colonists arrived in the
Pueblo   sixteenth century, they found indigenous peoples who lived
Dwellings   in towns and villages that ranged in size from a few hundred
to a few thousand inhabitants. Pueblo communities were
often built on top of mesas, but some, especially in times of peace, were
built at the bottoms of valleys and canyons. Towns and villages were generally laid out around a plaza that could be used for ceremonial purposes.
The houses were built from clay, stone, and mud. A Spanish colonist who
admired the Pueblo towns wrote that

[t]he houses in this pueblo are built like military barracks, back to back . . . and
they are four or five stories high. There are no doors opening into the streets on
the ground floors; the houses are entered from above by means of portable hand
ladders and trap doors. Each floor of every house has three or four rooms so that
each house, as a whole counting from top to bottom has fifteen or sixteen rooms,
very neat and well whitewashed. Every house is equipped with facilities for
grinding corn, including three or four grinding stones mounted in small troughs
and provided with pestles; all is whitewashed.[3]

Spanish observers also described Pueblo houses as being well-stocked
with corn supplies, firewood, lumber, farming implements, and pottery.[4]

   The construction, upkeep, and maintenance of Pueblo houses was a
labor-intensive process. It was accompanied by a series of ceremonials and rituals that indicate the importance of the houses in their daily
life and cosmology. Puebloan peoples who lived in the desert generally
made their houses out of sandstone. Men used wooden tools to turn
rocks into worked blocks of stone that were then used to construct the
walls of the buildings. In the Rio Grande River Valley, where stones were
in short supply, the Pueblos used adobe (a sandy clay that can be turned
into building blocks when wet, and which forms a solid mass when dry)
to build their walls. Timber beams were used to support the roof. These
had to be carried in, sometimes from a great distance, from wooded areas
and forests in the mountains. The roof itself was built with four layers
because it had to support a substantial amount of weight. People spent
a good deal of time on the roofs of their houses, socializing, eating, or
pursuing other activities of daily life. The main beams, which functioned
as the structural base for the roof, were crossed with smaller poles that
were placed close together, except for the small opening needed to create a doorway from the house to the roof. This layer in turn was tightly
covered with small reeds or branches, which were then covered with
another layer of weeds, grass, brush, and twigs. Finally the entire house,
including walls and roof, was covered with plaster. This task was often
performed by women. To prevent erosion, the Pueblo built drains on
their roofs to minimize the impact of the short but torrential rainfalls that
could occur during the rainy season. When a family needed more room,

they simply started a new building, either adjacent to or on top of the earlier structure.[5]

The Pueblo peoples were farmers who planted corn, beans, squash, and melons. Communities along the Rio **Subsistence** Grande in New Mexico used the river to irrigate their fields. However, not everyone lived near a major river. Other people established their towns and villages on oases, where they built dams and small reservoirs to make maximum use the available water for farming. They planted fields at the bottoms of hills, mountains, and mesas, where they systematically directed the runoff from rainfalls as well as local spring water through small earthen dams to nourish their crops. At times, the harshness of the climate required people to travel a considerable distance to reach a suitable site for a field. This meant that some members of the community either had to stay in a previously abandoned settlement or build a makeshift shelter to live in while they tended their crops.

The Pueblos cultivated a variety of corn that had long roots and tough leaves, and which was reasonably resistant to drought and wind. The plant also had a short growing season. It was thus perfectly adapted to the harshness of the southwestern climate. Pueblo farmers planted their corn seeds deep in the ground to give the plants extra protection and moisture.

They also planted gardens with other types of plants. These were generally in close vicinity to the towns and to a reliable source of water. Here the Pueblo people grew plants such as beans, cotton, tobacco, chilies, peppers, and onions. The gardens were regularly cared for and during dry periods were watered by hand. To avoid wasting water, the Pueblo made smaller earth ridges around each plant. Furthermore, the gardens were surrounded by a small wall built of adobe and mud to protect their crop against hungry animals.[6]

People in the eastern pueblos enjoyed a year-round supply of water and fish, good grazing for livestock, and plenty of game animals, both large and small, for the hunters. Seasonal rains helped the women farmers, and there was often a surplus at harvest time that could be used for trade. However, the eastern pueblos were built in areas that had fewer natural defenses than their western kin. The combination of factors made them more desirable, and more vulnerable, to Spanish colonizers. The western pueblos in a region that spans the border of New Mexico and Arizona lived in a harsher environment but had better defenses. The people of Acoma, Zuni and Hopi pueblos built atop high mesas, which were difficult to attack, and had worked more intensively to raise crops and find enough grass for their livestock. While they also experienced the vicissitudes of colonization, their location and lifestyle proved to be ultimately beneficial for maintaining cultural and political autonomy.

Community played an important part in Pueblo daily
Social and   life. Pueblo society made few class and social distinc-
Religious Life   tions. Housing, food, access to material goods, and clothing were pretty much the same for everyone. In the harsh
lands of little rain of the Southwest, a town or village's survival strongly
depended on everyone contributing to the survival of the community
through their labor. Men, women, and children were all expected to work.
Not surprisingly, the Pueblos valued cooperation and communal cohesion over the accomplishments of an individual.

Early Spanish observers noted with surprise that Pueblo towns in the
sixteenth century were much more egalitarian than European societies at
the time. Elders and religious figures were highly respected and played
an influential leadership role in the community, in part because people
sought them out for advice. One Spanish visitor tried to describe Pueblo
society:

They have no rulers as in New Spain, but are governed by the counsel of their
oldest men. They have their priests, whom they call papas who preach to them.
These priests are the old men, who mount the high terrace of the pueblo in
the morning as the sun rises, and from there, like town criers, preach to the
people, who all listen in silence, seated along the corridors. The priests tell the
people how they should live. I believe they give them some commandments to
observe, because there is no drunkenness, sodomy, or human sacrifice among
them, nor do they eat human flesh, or steal.[7]

Another colonist commented on what seemed to him to be a surprising
degree of order in the communal life of the Pueblos. He wrote:

Their houses are always open and have no doors or other protection, because
the practice among them is never to take anything from each other.... When
one of the soldiers lost a Jewel and an Indian found it and learned whose it was,
he returned it of his own accord without compulsion. This is the common practice
among all of these Indians.[8]

Much of the ceremonial life in the pueblos literally took place away
from prying eyes in the ritual spaces known as *kivas*, from a Hopi word
that means "ceremonial chamber." Rituals and ceremonies that centered
around the chamber played an important role in Native daily life. The
Pueblos celebrated festivals to respect and celebrate the sun and corn, or
to bring rain. They believed that these ceremonies and rituals had to be
performed to guarantee the continuation of their way of life and to reinforce cooperation and cohesion in their communities.

Among the Hopi, the kivas were often large rooms that were built
underground. In contrast, Pueblo communities on the Rio Grande
more frequently built their circular kivas above ground. At Acoma
and Zuni Pueblos, the kiva was built into the house block as another

room. During much of the sixteenth century, when Spanish colonizers forbade the Pueblos to use their ceremonial chambers, other Native groups moved their kivas into their living quarters, to hide them from Euro-American view.

Although many religious ceremonies such as dances were conducted out on the plazas, the ceremonial chambers were still the place where the private parts of the ceremonials and rituals occurred, or where religious leaders and participants prepared for the public aspects of the ceremony that involved the entire community on the plaza. For instance, katsinas sometimes emerged from the kiva to perform their sacred dances for the community. These were masked male dancers in elaborate costume who appeared on certain occasions as the ancestral spirit beings who had the power to influence agricultural production, rain, and the general fortunes of the community, for better or worse.[9] Today, kachina dolls that represent the katsinas are a popular souvenir item for tourists (note that kachina and katsina are two different spellings of the same word).

DAILY LIFE AMONG THE APACHE AND THE NAVAJO

The Navajos and the Apache were relative late-comers to the Southwest, arriving sometime before the fifteenth century. They are closely related, as evidenced by the fact that both Navajo and Apachean languages are classified as southern Athabaskan languages of the Na-Dene language family. Thus, their language invokes a distant kinship with indigenous peoples in western Canada and the Pacific Northwest, as well as with each other. Yet their histories diverged long ago, as indicated by the differences between them. Today, Navajo and Apache are two distinct languages, each with multiple dialects.

Before their migration to the Southwest, these groups subsisted mainly by hunting and gathering. Afterward, many began to raise corn, beans, and squash—a skill adopted from their Pueblo neighbors. The groups and bands that were most influenced by Puebloan and later Spanish culture are today known as the Navajo and the Western Apache. The latter are divided into four groups: White Mountain, Cibecue, San Carlos, and Tonto Apache. The Eastern Apache Nations, including the Chiricahua, Jicarilla, Mescalero, Lipan and Kiowa Apaches, lived as hunter-gatherers and raiders on the southern part of the Great Plains. They hunted bison, deer, and antelope during communal hunts and used dogs to pull their household possessions from one place to another when they moved to a new camp. Like other people of the Great Plains, they quickly incorporated horses and guns into their daily lives after these were introduced by the Spanish in 1698.[10]

The circumstances of Eastern and Western Apache life demonstrate the limitations of the Euro-American practice of classifying Native North Americans by "culture area." By language and by historical memory, the

Eastern and Western Apache consider themselves to be closely related to each other. By outward appearances and early contact period lifestyle, it seems logical to classify them in different groups. The Eastern Apache look like other Plains Indians (without the war bonnets), especially in their adaptation to horses, which allowed their young men to build their reputations on daring raids and battle exploits. The Western Apache lived more like the Navajo, settling in one place and practicing intensive cultivation of their crops. The differences that grew up between them did not stop them from recognizing each other as Apache, or from acknowledging the distant kinship with the Navajo. They continued to assert their rights as a sovereign people and, whenever possible, responded to new circumstances in creative ways. The story of indigenous peoples in the period after European contact is often told in terms of loss, but it is also a story of tremendous cultural creativity and revitalization.

Life in the Fourth World Many Native American creation stories describe a world in which people are created in one place, where they live from "time immemorial." Navajo stories describe a long history of wandering. Their ancestors moved from one world to the next before finding their homeland. As in the Pueblo story of Ia'tik and Nao'tsiti, the Navajo story of creation falls into the category of emergence stories, where people move upward to emerge from one world to the next. Navajo stories are very specific that the movement from one world to another takes place because someone behaves badly and they are forced to leave.

Symbols, colors, metaphors, and practical advice from Navajo sacred stories are woven through the fabric of both daily and ritual life. For example, each of the worlds through which the ancestral Navajos passed is associated with a particular color. There is some variation in how the stories are told but in most versions the first world was black, the second world was blue-green, the third world was yellow, and the fourth world, the Southwest of today, is characterized as bright or glittering. With a literal reading of Navajo stories, the First World may be associated with the tundra of the far north. Details about the blue-green Second World share similarities with the landscape and animals found in western and central Canada. The yellow Third World has much in common with the eastern slope of the Rocky Mountains and parts of the Southwest. The glittering Fourth World brings the Navajo to the place that they call Dinétah, the Navajo homeland today.[11] Telling the same story in different terms, archaeologists and linguists agree that Athabascan speakers moved into the southwest six or seven centuries ago after a long migration from the north.

Apache oral traditions are different in that their memory of migration only goes as far north as northern Arizona. Apache sacred stories, religious ceremonies, and cultural geography are grounded in specific features of the landscape. A Jicarilla Apache version of the emergence story says that after the people came up from underground through a hole, they found a world bounded with ocean on four sides and a great lake in the middle. They traveled east, then south, then west, then north, with each tribe stopping where they wanted to. The Jicarillas, however, stayed close to the place where they came up from underground. They circled around it three times in their travels. Finally the Creator asked them where they wanted to stop, and they said, "In the middle of the earth." So they were led to a place near Taos Pueblo, which became their home.[12]

Living in the Southwest, the Navajos adopted agriculture, weaving, pottery, and basket making—all women's activities—into their daily lives. They already had some knowledge of planting from their generations of wandering, but the environment of the Southwest both allowed and demanded new ways of cultivating crops. The Navajos learned much from the Pueblo people who were already there, then transformed these new ways into unique forms that today are characteristic of Navajo culture. It is said that Navajo men initially tried to take what they needed through war. This history of immigration, adaptation, and early warfare is written in the very names by which the Navajo and Apache are known today in U.S. history books. "Navajo" comes from an Tewa Pueblo word for cultivated fields. "Apache" comes from the Zuni Pueblo word for "enemy." Early Spanish documents distinguish the Navajos from the Apaches by calling the former "apaches de navajo," or "strangers of the cultivated fields." Both groups refer to themselves as the Diné, meaning "The People."

Cornfield on the Navajo reservation, about 1880. Rituals related to planting, harvesting and giving thanks for corn are an important part of Navajo daily life. From Denver Public Library, Western History Collection.

Raids and Trade Both the Apache and the Navajo raided their neighbors as a means of subsistence when necessary. Raiding gave young men a chance to demonstrate bravery and establish their reputations. They took foods such as corn, material goods such as clothing and weapons, and in the post-contact years, livestock (which the Spanish had introduced to the region). Sometimes they also took children, who were then adopted. The raiding way of life caused tensions and animosity between raiders and nonraiders. One Spanish observer wrote on this matter:

The Spaniards and the Christian and peaceful natives of New Mexico are frequently harassed by attacks of the Apache Indians, who destroy and burn their pueblos, waylay and kill their people by treachery, steal . . . and cause other damages.[13]

With the coming of horses, raiders, who had until this point traveled by foot, became even more effective and swift in their incursions.

Despite the recurrent conflicts that took place between the raiding Navajo and Apache as well as the Pueblo and later the Spanish, there were also peaceful connections and accommodation among the various ethnic groups that inhabited the Southwest. In fact, trade and other cultural interactions shaped daily life in significant ways. Trade fairs, for example, often organized in the late summer or early fall, brought different groups together for nonviolent exchanges. One Spanish bishop described such an intercultural meeting in the mid-eighteenth century:

They come every year to the trading, or fairs. The governor comes to those fairs, which they call *rescates* (barter, trade), every year with the majority of his garrison and people from all over the kingdom. They bring captives to sell, pieces of chamois, many buffalo skins, and, out of the plunder they have obtained elsewhere, horses, muskets, shotguns, munitions, knives, meat, and various other things. Money is not current at these fairs, but exchange of one thing for another, and so those people get provisions.[14]

In the multicultural world that emerged in the Southwest during the decades and centuries after Spanish contact, the Navajo and many of the Apache also voluntarily adopted Pueblo and Spanish ways of living.

Hogans and Wickiups Housing among the Navajo and Apache was simple, but perfectly adapted to the natural environment of the Southwest and each group's way of life. The Navajo, for example, built small one-room houses called *hogans*, made of earth. These were bolstered by a pole in the center. The earth structure was supported by a dome-shaped frame made out of logs and strips of bark, which were covered by mud. The entrance of these buildings always faced east, reflecting the respect that the Navajos held for the sun. Moreover, the Navajos did not traditionally live in villages. Still, one could often see several hogans standing in close vicinity to one another. These were generally inhabited by kin. Navajo buildings were relatively small, perhaps 20 to 30 feet in diameter, since the Native peoples in the region spent most of their time outside. In poor weather, an entire extended family might be confined to the small living space. The everyday emphasis on protocol and mutual respect was heightened under such circumstances. Everyone was expected to be clean, organized, and respectful of their peers.[15]

The Western Apache lived in *wickiups.* These were oval-shaped huts made out of brush. When the weather turned colder, wickiups were winterized with leafy branches on the outside and insulated with animal hides. For warmth, the Apache also burned fires in their dwellings. Apache homes and settlements were quickly built, generally in easily defensible places; they were nonpermanent and suited the Apache way of life, which required a community to be mobile.[16]

Among both the Navajo and the Apache, the extended family and clans stood at the center of social organization. Every member of the family was expected to contribute to the subsistence of the community. **Family and Social Organization** Women gathered food and, in some areas, cultivated crops. Men primarily contributed meat. During times of hardship and stress men and women helped each other with their specific tasks. Children and elderly persons contributed to their families' subsistence to the best of their ability. Navajo and Apache people also belonged to a clan, a community of people who believed that they descended from the same forebear, and no marriage was to occur between men and women of the same clan.[17]

Chiefs or community leaders also played an important role in the Athabascan-speaking communities of the Southwest. A description of the qualities of a good chief provides a glimpse at the values and the communal ideals that members of this Indian nation cherished:

The leader is supposed to talk to his people. He is supposed to be sympathetic and tell them how to live, sympathetic in the sense of giving out horses and valuables to those who need them. The leader is supposed to give something to eat to everyone who comes around [in need]. He has control in time of war. You can't disobey him. The leader advises the people to help the unfortunate, to give to those whose luck is bad. He advises against fights in the camps; he doesn't want any quarrels within the group. He advises the people to be on the lookout all the time.[18]

Although Apache leaders often inherited their position from their fathers, a leader still had to be effective in order to get the support of his people.

While both men and women are honored in Navajo and Apache society, which are both matrilineal clan-based societies, women have a special place. This does not mean that women were put on a pedestal or treated as delicate **The Sunrise Ceremony** beings. During the first summer after a girl's first menstrual flow, she became the focus of her family and community during a ceremony called *kinaalda* in Navajo, *na'ii'es* in Apache, and in English, the Sunrise Ceremony. The exact form of the ceremony may differ from one community to the next but the general outlines are similar.

Each morning began at dawn when the young woman demonstrated her endurance with a long run to the east, the direction of the rising sun. Over the course of several days, she had to sing, pray, fast, and participate in specific rituals. On the last night, the young woman and her family stayed up all night with relatives and friends as a local medicine person sang and prayed for her. In the morning, when she returned from her run, everyone broke their fast with a special corn cake that had been baking underground through the night. In this ceremony, a young woman tests and demonstrates her strength, to herself and to the larger community. The community, in turn, accepts and embraces her as one who will become the mother of future generations of the People. Again, there is both responsibility and privilege as she gives and receives food, gifts, and blessings.

YUMA

The Yuma, or Quechan as many prefer to be called today, lived and live in the lower Colorado River valley, in what is today the border region between the states of Arizona and California. Before the construction of dams and the massive land irrigation that occurred in the West in the late nineteenth and twentieth centuries, which diverts much of the river's water, the Colorado was much more majestic and rich in sediment. The Yuma trace their origins to a sacred mountain, Avikwamé, in present-day California. The Yuma are a patrilineal people, that is, they trace their descent through the male line.

Subsistence The barren landscape of the Yuma homeland changed dramatically each spring, when the Colorado River became swollen with water from the melting snow in the nearby mountains. Soon the river burst its banks, temporarily flooding the land before receding. This created fertile flood plains in the region. Each spring, the Yuma cleared the land of bushes and brush before the flooding, then waited for the water to recede. They planted their crops on the now-fertile bottomlands.

Men and women worked together to grow food, performing complementary tasks. Men dug the planting holes, and women distributed the seeds. The Yuma planted crops such as corn, beans, and squash, and by the sixteenth century they also incorporated European plants such as wheat and melons. On less-productive land, the Yuma grew wild grasses, using the seed to make cakes. Although the fields generally required little work during the growing season, other than a bit of weeding, on occasion the dry climate required the Yuma to help their crops with water hauled up from the river. Generally, however, the silt-rich and fertile topsoil, renewed every year during the spring flood, retained enough moisture to sustain the year's crops.

Harvest time, like the planting season, was a labor-intensive period that involved the entire community. Men were generally in charge of bringing in the crops while women prepared the food for storage. Provisions were either collected in large earth pits dug on higher ground, or in food baskets measuring four to six feet in width, which were stored in elevated places such as on the top of a ramada (a flat-roofed shed). These measures protected the community's food supplies from additional flooding.[19]

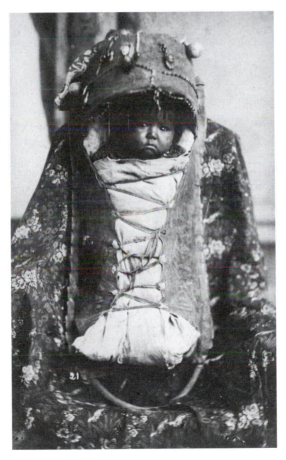

Yuma baby in a cradleboard, about 1880. By the late nineteenth century, photographs of Indian children such as this Yuma baby in a traditional cradleboard were made into post cards and sold to tourists. From Denver Public Library, Western History Collection.

During times of scarcity, especially in the winter and the spring, the Yuma lived by gathering, fishing, and hunting. Women and children gathered mesquite pods and screwbeans. The pods were used not only to make cakes, but when fermented in water, they could be used to make an intoxicating beverage. Though there were only a few animals in the Yuma's desert environment, men hunted for birds and rabbits. Fishing was a more substantial source of protein. Yuma men fished in the Colorado with nets and with hooks and lines. To improve their efficiency in fishing, they also blocked off a segment of the river so that fish could be caught more easily.[20]

Creation   The Yuma creation of the world begins with water. There was no land at all, and no sky until a mist rose out of the water to become the sky. Deep under the water lived a being who had no body, no breath, and no name. This was the Creator. Then the waters stirred and the being rose to the surface with his eyes closed. There, he stood upon the water and looked around, and named himself "Kokomaht," the All-Father. Then another being rose from beneath the waters, part of himself and yet other, that is, a twin. The twin asked whether Kokomaht came out of the water with his eyes open or closed. Kokomaht knew that his brother wanted to do him harm and so he lied, saying that he had opened his eyes while still under water. The twin opened his eyes and as he rose to the surface he was blind. Kokomaht named him "Bakotahl," the Blind One.

Kokomaht made the four directions, then he made the earth. Bakotahl tried to make something that resembled a human being but it had no hands or feet. Then Kokomaht made a human being, and it was perfect. He made a man, and then he made a woman. These were the first Yuma people. Then Kokomaht made other peoples, two of each, and 24 kinds in all. He made the Cocopahs, the Dieguieños, and the Mojaves. Together with the Yuma, these were the first four tribes. He made the Apache, Maricopa, Pima and Coahuila tribes, and so on. The very last ones that he made were the white people.

Eventually Kokomaht decided that the people needed to understand death as well as life. The people burned his body on a pyre, and cut their hair, and mourned. They learned to tear down the home of the deceased and destroy all of his or her belongings and cease to mention the name of the dead. This helped the deceased to start their new life in the spirit world with familiar things, and helped the living to make a clean break with the past.

Komashtam'ho, the son of Kokomaht, lived after him. Komashtam'ho is the one who brought the giant flood, that almost drowned all the animals. One man, Marhokuvek, begged him to stop. Komashtam'ho agreed and made a big fire to dry up the water. It burned so hot that it scorched the earth, creating the desert. Komashtam'ho destroyed the house where Kokomaht had lived and in the process struck the ground with a large pole. From this place, water welled up, which became the Colorado River. In this river swam the beings without hands or feet made by Bakotahl. These are fish and other water creatures.

Kahk, the Crow, brought corn and seeds of all kinds from the four corners of the earth. As he did this, he stopped four times, and each time he cried, "Kahk! Kahk!" This caused a great mountain to grow up. The Yuma stayed near this mountain with Komashtam'ho when all the other people made by Kokomaht spread out over the land, because they were special to him.

One day Komashtam'ho told the Yuma that he would have to leave them. He turned himself into four eagles: the black eagle of the west, the brown eagle of the south, the white eagle of the east, and the mysterious eagle of the north that no one has ever seen. He keeps watch over the Yuma to this day and helps them to receive advice from his father, Kokomaht, in their dreams. Bakotahl, the Blind One, lives under the earth. When he is restless, the earth trembles, thunder peals, and sometimes the mountains crack open to spit out fire and smoke.[21]

The Yuma lived in several villages that consisted of hundreds of people. The major unit of communal life was the household, made up of a network **Social Organization** of extended families and relations. Households were fluid networks. For instance, members of one unit could join another if relatives in a neighboring household needed extra labor, or if their home was getting so crowded that it became difficult to feed everyone. Single-family or individual households did not exist among the Yuma. This has largely to do with the fact that the bottomland agriculture practiced by the tribe required communal labor. The economic and subsistence needs of the community were reflected in the social organization of the tribe. Every affiliate of the household was expected to perform his or her responsibilities for the collective good. Duties such as farming, hunting, fishing, gathering, child care, and education were divided up in the community according to age, gender, and skill.

Yuma settlements also had leaders. Although the job was supposedly a hereditary office, passed from father to son, the role was usually fulfilled by the most able person in the community regardless of family background. A good leader had to exemplify Yuma communal ideals. He had to lead by example, encourage his people, give to the poor, and represent and look out for the interests of the community.

The floods of the Colorado River influenced Yuma settlement patterns along with subsistence and social organization. During the time when the Yuma worked their fields, from mid-spring to early fall, they lived on the Colorado River bottomlands, close to their fields. They resided in small huts, made out of arrowweed, and also built ramadas, flat-roofed structures used as sun shades but also for storage. After the harvest in the fall, Yuma households moved to higher grounds, where they were better protected from the spring floods. These settlements were called *ranche-rias*. Here, as in the valley, most Yuma lived in arrowweed huts and used ramadas. The rancherias also had one or two spacious earthen houses with flat roofs, which were occupied by the leaders and their households. Furthermore, the houses were utilized as meeting places and, in rough or cold weather, were used as a shelter for the community.[22]

Ceremonies

Ceremonies played an important role in the daily life of the Yuma. The tribe performed rituals and ceremonials to celebrate marriages, as well as to bury and to commemorate the dead. Initiation ceremonies for Yuma boys and girls, to help them in transition to their adult roles, also featured prominently in a community's culture.

Boys between the ages of 8 and 10 endured a four-day ritual to test their strength as well as their physical and mental endurance. Although the boys would not be considered adult for a few more years to come (until their mid-teens), the tribulations that they experienced in this ceremony prepared them for the lifeways of the warrior. The difficulty and challenge of their experience also created a special relationship among the boys of an age group, which often proved to be instrumental in battle, where friendship, loyalty, and close personal knowledge could give a war party an advantage over their enemies.

The boys' initiation ceremony began with the piercing of both of their nostrils. Pierced noses were the traditional mark of Yuma men, and they often adorned them with decorative jewelry. To keep the wound open, the adults who oversaw the ceremony would pulled a thread through the holes. Then, under supervision, the boys ran for 10 to 15 miles through blazing heat each day for the next four days. During this time, they were given very little nourishment. The boys moved north on the first day, west on the second, south on the third, and east on the fourth. At night, the adults who accompanied them gave the boys little chance for rest. The ceremony ended when the nose strings were replaced with a wooden stick.

For Yuma girls the initiation ceremony was a more private affair. It was celebrated among the women of the household and with invited guests. It occurred when a girl menstruated for the first time. The ceremony aimed to initiate and prepare the girls for their adult life. Every day, during the entire four-day ceremonial, the girl was to lie on her stomach in a shallow hole in the ground, surrounded by warm stones. Then all but her head was covered by warm sand, songs were sung, and she received advice on how a Yuma women should behave. At the end of the day, she was pulled out of the pit and cleaned. Furthermore, for the entire duration of the four-day ceremony the girls were not allowed to touch themselves. They could only scratch their bodies with a special stick. Girls were given little food, and especially no salt and meat. These were the same rules that applied to adult women of the tribe. The Yuma practiced menstrual seclusion, that is, menstruating women were expected to live in isolated huts away from the community and especially away from the men. During this period, they had to avoid salt and meat and were only allowed to touch their bodies with a stick.

After the four-day ceremony, young Yuma woman were now eligible for marriage. Marriages were generally arranged by the woman's parents and by the blood relations of her prospective spouse. Marriage helped to create strong bonds between different households, but a bad marriage could lead to trouble for everyone. For this reason, older relatives played a role in arranging marriages. Young women had little choice in the matter, although most parents took their daughters' wishes into account if it seemed reasonable to them. In the patrilineal Yuma society, husbands were generally a bit older than their wives. They were also allowed to marry more than one wife and in some cases were expected to do so. For instance, after the death of a man's brother, he was expected to offer to marry the brother's widow. This helped to maintain the connections between the different households even after a husband's death. However, the widow was free to decline the offer.[23]

DAILY LIFE AMONG THE PIMA

The Pima live in the Gila and Salt River region of Arizona. They call themselves the Akimel O'odham, or River People. The have lived in this area since long before the arrival of Europeans. Indeed, their creation stories say that they are the inheritors of the ancient Hohokam culture. "Hohokam" comes from a Pima word that loosely translates as "those who have gone before." They were and are farmers, using a system of irrigation to farm in the harsh desert climate. Extended families worked the fields in common, and community members also spent a good amount of time maintaining and constructing irrigation canals and wells. The Akimel O'odham predominantly farmed corn, beans, and pumpkins.

The Akimel O'odham are related to the Papago, who call themselves the Tohono O'odham, which means Desert People. Their homeland spans southern Arizona and the northern part of Sonora in Mexico. Tohono O'odham oral tradition says that they were led to this area by I'itoi, or Elder Brother, from a world under the surface of the earth. In contrast to the sedentary villages and irrigation farming of the Akimel O'odham, the Tohono O'odham structured their lives around two different ecosystems. They spent the winter in the mountains near a spring and moved to summer villages on the flood plains to plant and tend their crops.

The rancherias of the Pima, the homesteads in which extended families lived, were spread out around their irrigated farm lands. For much of the time that the Pima interacted with Europeans, their rancherias consisted of pole and thatch dwellings as well as brush-roofed shelters

Houses and Change over Time

without walls, which provided protection from the desert sun. Pima houses were generally round or oval shaped structures, with walls made out of woven brush that were covered with adobe.[24]

Yet in earlier times, roughly 700 A.D. to the twelfth century, the Akimel O'odham and their ancestors built and inhabited multistory structures, which they used not only as places to live, but also as defensive structures and as food warehouses. The builders often had to carry the mud for miles from the riverbank to their construction sites. Then they used wooden forms to shape the mud into bricks of dried clay, which in turn were used to construct buildings that were, according to one Spanish observer, "as large as castles." These structures could be four to five stories high. Casa Grande Ruin National Monument in Arizona, which can be visited today, is one surviving example of their ancient architecture. In 1624, a Spanish missionary wrote, "Their houses are better and stronger than those of other nations, with walls of great *adobes*, which they make of clay, and roof with earth-covered terraces." The multistory buildings were also useful for defensive purposes. For one, they provided a lot of room to store food for emergency situations. Furthermore, the occupants of the large dwellings could easily fire arrows at attackers either from the terraces of the building, or from openings in the protective outer walls.[25]

We do not know why the Pima abandoned these large multistory structures in the seventeenth century. Some scholars believe that the decline of the old ways was connected to climate changes similar to those that led to the disappearance of the Anasazi. Other scholars argue that the dramatic population decline caused by massive outbreaks of epidemics and diseases brought to the Southwest by the Spanish might be a factor. Among the Pima, for example, an outbreak of scarlet fever in 1637 was followed by smallpox in 1639. The epidemics killed an unbearable number of people. In the mid-nineteenth century, an American officer, Lieutenant Emory, rode through the area and noted many signs of devastation. He wrote, "[A]long the whole days march were remains of zequias [irrigation ditches], pottery, and other evidences of a once densely populated country." Emory saw "the remains of a three-story mud house, 60 feet square, pierced for doors and windows. The walls were four feet thick."

Archaeological evidence at places such as Casa Grande suggests that by the seventeenth century the Pima had began to burn houses in which people had died, perhaps adopted from the Spanish who burned the houses of people who died from disease in an effort to stop the spread of epidemics. It may be that River People abandoned their brick dwellings because pole and thatch burned more easily than the thick earthen-walled structures of older times.[26]

Social Organization   The rancherias played a significant role in the political, religious, and social life of the Akimel O'odham. The homestead was the abode of an extended family. It generally consisted of an older couple with their unmarried children. As a patrilocal people, married daughters went to live with the families of their husbands while married sons and their families lived in the households of his parents. A number of closely associated homesteads were loosely united into a political and military alliance. One of the male household heads functioned as the unofficial political leader of the community. These rancherias came together for collective celebrations of rituals and ceremonials. Similar to other Native nations in the Southwest, Pima cosmology and religion celebrated and hoped for social harmony and rain. Both were essential for survival in a harsh desert environment.[27]

THE WEAVERS AND ARTISANS OF THE SOUTHWEST

Native peoples of the Southwest grew cotton and wove blankets long before the Spanish came to the region in the sixteenth century. Archaeological evidence suggests that weaving and cloth production were already practiced by the Anasazi and Hohokam, the ancient civilizations of the Southwest whose way of life influenced groups such as the Pueblo and Pima peoples. The earliest Spanish travel accounts report the existence of cotton fields cultivated by indigenous peoples. In fact, the Spanish conquistadors demanded woven blankets as part of the tribute system that they imposed on many of the Native communities they encountered. The introduction of Churro sheep to the Southwest by the Spanish had a major impact on textile production in the region by introducing a new material from which to make traditional crafts, just as glass beads and trade cloth inspired new forms of creativity in the Northeast. By the seventeenth century, Native weavers began to spin yarn out of sheep's wool and used it to make blankets, dresses, cloth, and horse blankets.

Cotton production occupied an important place in the daily life of the people who cultivated it. For example, the Akimel O'odham planted cotton in early March and harvested it in late summer. After being cleaned and processed, they spun the fiber into thread. The Akimel O'odham had two kinds of loom for making cloth. Women generally worked in pairs on a ground loom, a large device built around four stakes driven into the ground in the shape of a rectangle. The ground pegs on the two shorter sides were then connected by two beams, which in turn were wrapped up and connected with thread. The hundreds of strings of thread between the two beams functioned as the foundation of the cloth. The women used a stick to separate the threads and a shuttle, that is, a wooden device wrapped around with a piece of cotton thread, to pass the thread back and forth, weaving over and under the supporting strands. After each crossing of the shuttle, the weavers used the stick to push the new thread tightly against the earlier woven strings. Older Akimel O'odham men also wove. They worked on smaller looms, one end of which was attached to a stake in the ground, the other wrapped around a rod tightened to the weaver's waist. On this belt loom, one person could make narrow pieces of cloth.[28]

The Navajo, arguably the most recognized and esteemed weavers of the Southwest, also wove blankets and garments out of sheep wool and cotton. This was a skill they probably adopted from their Pueblo neighbors sometime in the seventeenth century. During the period of colonial contact with the Spanish, the Navajo incorporated Churro sheep into their daily life. The sheep were used as a source for meat and for the production of wool. Navajo women used vertical looms to weave yarn made from sheep's wool and cotton to produce cloth.[29]

Native Americans in the Southwest also wove baskets of many shapes and sizes from local fibers such as cattail-reed stems, willow twigs, and the black fibers stripped from the seedpods of the devil's claw. Devil's claw grows wild in the desert, but Akimal O'odham women cultivated and bred it to produce longer seedpods, which were better for weaving. They used black strips of devil's claw to decorate their baskets with beautiful patterns of alternating light and dark.

Like other aspects of cultural adaptation and change, the baskets made by Native women in the Southwest changed over time. Before large-scale European settlement commenced in the mid-nineteenth century, most baskets were used as *kihau*, a basket carried on the back, or as food-storage containers. By the mid-nineteenth century, Pima women began to produce smaller baskets to trade with Euro-American women, who used them to store food and other household objects.[30] By the late nineteenth century baskets provided a source of income due to the increasing tourist trade.

Native Americans in the Southwest practiced other forms of arts and crafts for personal use, for trade, and to generate cash. Native artisans in the region produced, and still produce today, beautiful jewelry and pottery. The Navajo are especially noted as silversmiths, producing fine plates, decorations, belts, necklaces, bracelets, earrings, wrist guards, and other items that are often inlaid with locally found turquoise stones. Native peoples made exquisite pottery, in various forms and shapes, out of clay and used it for various purposes such as food and water storage, for ceremonies, and for decoration.

DAILY LIFE AND COLONIZATION

The Spanish and later the American presence in the Southwest, like the coming of European colonizers in other parts of the Western Hemisphere, dramatically altered Native American daily life. European colonization brought diseases never experienced by the Native Americans in the region, which killed a substantial part of the indigenous population. It also introduced new material culture and modes of economic production and led to an increase in warfare, rivalry, and starvation that changed Native patterns of trade and subsistence.

The Pueblo were one of the first Native communities in the region to experience the impact of European power. Spanish explorers had entered the Southwest several times in the sixteenth century, but it was only in the late 1500s that they set out to establish a permanent settlement. The Spanish hoped to use their colony in the region as a buffer zone to protect their wealthier colonies to the south, in present day Mexico. But King Philip II of Spain also wanted to colonize the region "to induce" the Native population "to hear and accept the holy gospel." He wanted the Spanish to "explain our holy Catholic faith" to the Indians "so that we may have communication with them in various languages and seek their conversion."[31]

The Spanish Conquest of the Pueblos

Spanish writers frequently commented on the "docility" and "obedience" of the Pueblo, who ran away at the sight of the Spanish conquistadors. The Pueblo had, however, experienced much violence at the hand of the Spanish ever since the first contact in the 1540s. These experiences taught them to be cautious. Despite or perhaps because of these early encounters, the Pueblo behaved very differently when the Spanish tried to settle the region in earnest. However, Pueblo resistance came at a high price.

In the early 1590s, the inhabitants of Acoma Pueblo resisted Spanish efforts to create a permanent colony on their land. They probably felt secure in this action because their village was in fact a formidable fortress, built on top of a sandstone mesa about 360 feet above the surrounding desert. Some time in December of 1598, the people of Acoma Pueblo refused to pay the corn flour and other goods demanded by the Spanish as tribute. The believed the payment demanded by the Spanish to be too high and unfair, so they resisted a Spanish patrol that came to collect the colonial levy. They resisted so fiercely that most of the Spanish solders were killed.

Spanish officials retaliated immediately. From their point of view, they could not afford to ignore such a challenge to their authority and prestige. They believed that continued Acoma resistance would threaten the future of their colonial project, so they sent a punitive expedition to Acoma Pueblo. The Spanish demanded that the "rebels" (rebelling against Spanish authority, perhaps, but asserting their own), must surrender immediately. The Acoma, thinking themselves secure in their village fortress, refused. Spanish forces attacked the pueblo and eventually managed to scale the mesa with powerful guns and two cannons that wrought unimaginable devastation to this community. Historians estimate that over 800 people were killed in one day, while only a few Spanish soldiers were wounded. The survivors, about 500 Pueblo men, women, and children, were put on trial and condemned to slavery. Pueblo men over the age of 25 had one foot cut off as punishment. Through such acts of intimidation, Spanish officials hoped to establish control over the Pueblo communities.[32]

The Spanish presence burdened Pueblo communities even when they were not at war. Spanish soldiers needed provisions, which they took from the indigenous population without compensation. Gines de Herrera Horta described this process in July of 1601:

Every month the Spaniards go out by order of the governor to all the pueblos to procure maize. The soldiers go in groups of two or three and come back with the maize for their own sustenance. The Indians part with it with much feeling and weeping and give it up of necessity rather than of their own accord, as the soldiers themselves told this witness.[33]

That same year, another Spanish observer accused Governor Onate himself of going

in person to another pueblo to seize their maize, and as the Indians had concealed it in some small rooms, he ordered the walls torn down. When an Indian reproved the act by a word in his native tongue, the governor gave him a thrust and pushed him down the terrace. He fell on his back and was killed instantly, never moving hand or foot.[34]

Raids like this depleted the food stores set aside by the Pueblos as a prudent measure designed to carry them through periods of drought. They typically had enough supplies to feed the village for three or four years, if necessary. The massive procurement of provisions by the Spanish could mean that a Pueblo community lost several years worth of supplies in one day. The impact was less dramatic but no less destructive over time when the Spanish claimed smaller amounts. Stored food was essential for a community's survival, and the Pueblo people suffered greatly from their loss.

Encomiendas and Missions In the seventeenth century, the Spanish introduced two new factors that had a particular impact on daily life in the Southwest: the *encomienda* system and Franciscan missions. Encomiendas were land grants given by the Spanish government to soldiers who had served in the army for five years. Worse, the ecomienda system gave legal permission for the new landowners to exploit indigenous labor for their own benefits, and implicit permission to use violence if needed to ensure compliance. Native peoples such as the Pueblos, living in their own homelands, were now forced to work the Spanish landlords' fields, herd their livestock, or work as servants in their houses. Although landholders and officials were technically obliged to compensate Native Americans for their labor, their reimbursement was often inadequate or nonexistent. Furthermore, there were rampant reports of labor abuse, such as the excessive exploitation of workers, whippings, and beatings. Native women and some men bore the added burden of rape and sexual abuse by the invaders.

The Spanish government at times reacted to these reports and tried to alleviate the suffering of Native workers. But most of these interventions were fruitless. Both colonists and colonial officials in the Southwest were interested in making a profit, and the central authorities were far away. Thus, the Native peoples in the Southwest could expect little protection from the colonial administration in New Spain.

Native labor in the Southwest was also exploited outside of the enco-mienda and the mission system. Officials and settlers, for example, forced Native women to work in colonial sweatshops, where they wove textiles. Native Americans were also forced to participate in the colonial economy in ways that mocked their formerly autonomous life: hunting, tanning hides, gathering pine nuts, and raising crops such as cotton and corn on their own fields. Instead of keeping these things for their own families, they were forced to sell most of their goods to the Spanish at a price much below their market value. Such economic interactions functioned as a thinly disguised system of tribute.[35]

Like the colonists, the Franciscan friars who accompanied the Spanish conquistadors exploited indigenous labor on their missions. Native villagers who either lived on the station or close by were forced to build churches and chapels, living quarters, stables, workshops, storage rooms, and sometimes schools. Amerindian men did carpentry and blacksmith work, and women wove textiles. The goods they produced were then sold or exchanged to benefit the mission. Native Americans had to work the extensive fields and took care of massive herds of livestock for the friars. They also looked after the horses, cleaned and maintained mission facilities and gardens, cooked, helped to run the church and services, and worked as interpreters. Some Spanish critics alleged that the Franciscans neglected their spiritual duties to the Natives because they were too busy taking advantage of indigenous labor. One Spanish official sardonically noted that the Amerindians in the region would perhaps be more familiar with the Christian religion, if they did not have "to guard and herd an infinite number of livestock, to serve as slaves, and to fill barns with grain, cultivated and harvested with their blood, not for their humble homes, but for those of the friars."[36]

The missionaries, who had little tolerance for Native culture, challenged the established way of life and the traditional culture of indigenous peoples in the Southwest. Those who lived near or in a mission were instructed to attend church regularly. There, among other things, they learned to pray, to sing church music, and to recite the catechism. The Franciscans objected to the established gendered division of labor that existed among the Pueblos. They urged men, for example, to become more involved in agriculture. They condemned traditional Native religion, rituals, and ceremonies. Instead of recognizing that the Pueblos and others had their own code of moral and sexual behavior, the missionaries labeled them as "promiscuous." The Franciscans castigated Amerindians for what they perceived as "immoral conduct," or acts of "idolatry." They made a special effort to root out the katsina rituals and built churches on top of kivas. Native people who violated the new rules imposed at the missions experienced a range of punishments that included shaving the head, whippings, and beatings.

In the seventeenth century, Franciscan missionaries tried to present an optimistic view of the number of Pueblos who embraced Christianity. Fray Alonso de Benavides, for instance, claimed that there existed thousands of loyal converts. He wrote that

[the Indians] are so well doctrinated and [such good] Christians that when wearing the bell for Mass and the [teaching of the] Doctrine, they all come with the greatest cleanliness and neatness . . . and enter the church to pray, as if they were Christians of very long standing . . . and the choristers in the chapels . . . sing every day in the church, at their hours, the Morning Mass, High Mass, and Vespers, with great punctuality. And all make confession in their tongue, and prepare themselves for the confession, studying out their sins and bringing them marked on knotted threads. And they are always of notable submission and affection toward the Religious who minister to them . . . and . . . have a notable affection for . . . the things of the Church, which they attend with notable love and devotion.[37]

Such accounts, however, did not necessarily reflect reality. Rather, they were often written by the missionaries to garner support for their enterprise in the Spanish empire.

There certainly was frequent resistance to Christianity among the Pueblos. The Franciscan missionary Benavides wrote, for example, of an encounter with a Pueblo religious leader and medicine man at the town of Jumanas.

I was in the middle of the plaza, preaching to numerous persons assembled there, and this old sorcerer . . . descended from a corridor with an infuriated and wicked disposition, and said to me: "You Christians are crazy; you desire and pretend that this pueblo shall also be crazy." I asked him in what respect we were crazy. He had been, no doubt, in some Christian pueblo during Holy Week when they were flagellating themselves in procession, and thus he answered me: "How are you crazy? You go through the streets in groups, flagellating yourselves, and it is not well that the people of this pueblo should commit such madness as spilling their own blood by scourging themselves."[38]

While it is true that some Pueblo people accepted Christianity, even these did not embrace Spanish religion and practices blindly. In fact, many remained skeptical about the Spanish influence on their society. Some of those who embraced Christianity continued their traditions, practices, and ceremonies hidden from the view of the missionaries.

In 1680, the continued efforts by the Franciscans and by Spanish government officials to repress Pueblo religious practices and culture led to a massive resistance movement. The Pueblo Revolt of 1680 was so successful that it forced the Spanish colonists, missionaries, and soldiers to retreat from the region. It took over a decade for the Spanish to return and reestablish control, which they did in 1692.

In the aftermath of Amerindian defiance, and to gain a permanent foothold in the Southwest, the Spanish adopted a less aggressive stance toward the Pueblos. They abolished the encomienda system, forced labor, and tribute payments. Trade became highly regulated, with fixed prices established by colonial officials to avoid the exploitation of Native Americans. Although far from perfect, as abuses directed against Native people still occurred on occasion, government officials were cautious about antagonizing the Pueblos, and they now more readily examined and attempted to ameliorate incidents of abuse. Furthermore, in the decades that followed the Pueblo Revolt, the Catholic Church lost some of the grip that it had held over the Pueblos.[39]

Beyond the presence of the encomienda and the mission system, the coming of Euro-Americans to the Southwest caused significant change in Native societies. Even the Navajo, who mostly avoided contact with Spanish missionaries and with Christianity, adopted certain elements of Euro-American culture into their way of life, especially sheep. Horses and cattle also came to play an important role in their daily life. Furthermore, the Navajos adopted new crops brought to the Southwest by Europeans such as wheat, peaches, and potatoes.[40]

Colonization and Changes in Daily Life

Pueblo villagers incorporated herding, the raising of livestock, blacksmithing, and the raising of European crops into their daily life. They raised peaches and apricots alongside their traditional crops. These were skills that they had learned as servants on missions or on encomiendas, or in later years as laborers on colonial farms. This description by a Franciscan missionary of Pueblo dwellings provides a glimpse at how parts of Spanish material culture had become incorporated into the Pueblos way of life.

The interior decoration of these houses varies according to the owner, but they usually have two or three prints, a wooden cross, some kind of chest, either plain or painted. The arms of the men and the harnesses of the horses are hung from stakes, and there are some *matlacahuitl* (a pole and net or rope used to hang skins/clothing out of reach of vermin) on which, like the secondhand dealers of Mexico, they hang their skins of buffalo, lion, wolf, sheep and other animals, and also their cloaks if they have any, and the rest of the clothing belonging to both men and women. Outside are the . . . henhouses. Around the pueblo, but not very near to it, there are corrals to confine livestock of various kinds, and small corrals for fattening pigs.[41]

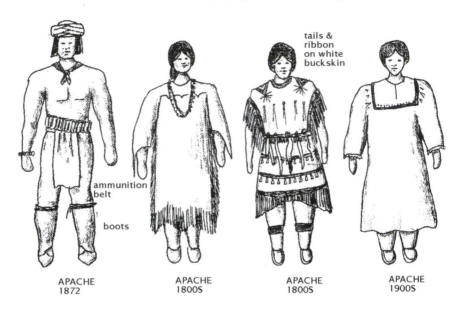

Apache clothing styles, nineteenth century. The modern adaptation of the Apache dress from the 1900s is clearly patterned on earlier fashions cut from large pieces of hide with a minimum number of seams. From Tara Prindle/nativetech.org.

The Pueblo, like the Apache and other Native peoples in the Southwest, selectively adopted elements of European society that they saw as beneficial to them.

These changes are apparent in clothing styles as people adapted new materials in traditional ways. Indigenous peoples in the Southwest continued to wear clothing made from tanned hides when they needed it to be especially durable, or waterproof, as with footwear. The advent of horse culture allowed male hunters to kill larger animals, providing skins that when tanned allowed women to make dresses in almost one piece. Euro-American trade goods allowed for new forms of creative expression, and buckskin clothing might be decorated with a colorful array of ribbons, trade beads, or small pieces of shiny metal in addition to older materials such as animal tails, fringe, or shell beads. By the late nineteenth century, in the era of reservation life when there was little opportunity to hunt large game animals, and less money to buy leather hides, women made their dresses on a similar pattern out of cloth.

American Colonization The coming of the Americans by the mid-nineteenth century brought new challenges to the Native peoples of the Southwest. Initially, most Americans who came into the area were just passing through on their way to California or the Oregon Territory. Many Amerindian nations, such as the Pueblo and the Pima, provided the American travelers with food, assistance, and help, despite the fact that some set-tlers took advantage of Native hospitality by stealing their livestock or by mistreating them. Increasingly, Americans became interested in coloniz-ing the lands of the Southwest. As on the Great Plains, as discussed in the next chapter, American colonization led to increasing pressure on Indian lands even as disease and warfare disrupted the social order and hunt-ing territories were depleted. In the face of such challenges, the Native Americans of the Southwest once again adapted their patterns of daily life to new circumstances to ensure their survival as a people.

NOTES

1. Richard Erdoes and Alfonso Ortiz, eds., *American Indian Myths and Legends* (New York: Pantheon Books,1984), 97–105.

2. Leslie Marmon Silko, *Yellow Woman and a Beauty of the Spirit: Essays on Native American Life Today* (New York: Simon and Schuster, 1996), 30–31.

3. Quoted in Alfonso Ortiz, *The Pueblo* (New York: Chelsea House, 1994), 33–34.

4. Ortiz, 33.

5. Charlotte and David Yue, *The Pueblo* (Boston: Houghton Mifflin, 1986), 21–45.

6. Yue, 89–94, Alice B. Kehoe, *North American Indians: A Comprehensive Account* (Upper Saddle River, NJ: Prentice Hall, 1992), 126–27.

7. Quoted in Ortiz, 23.

8. Quoted in Andrew L. Knaut, *The Pueblo Revolt of 1680: Conquest and Resistance in Seventeenth Century New Mexico* (Norman: University of Oklahoma Press, 1995), 34.

9. Yue, 75–77.

10. Kehoe, 142–43.

11. Frederick E. Hoxie, ed., *Encyclopedia of North American Indians* (Boston and New York: Houghton Mifflin, 1996), 422.

12. Erdoes and Ortiz, 83–85.

13. Quoted in Knaut, 69.

14. Quoted in Ortiz, 64.

15. Peter Iverson, *The Navajos* (New York: Chelsea House, 1990), 28.

16. Michael E. Melody, *The Apache* (New York: Chelsea House, 1989), 20–21.

17. Iverson, 28–30; Melody, 24–28.

18. Quoted in Melody, 28.

19. Robert L. Bee, *The Yuma* (New York: Chelsea House, 1989), 20–21.

20. Bee, 22.

21. Erdoes and Ortiz, 77–82.

22. Bee, 23–25, 29–30.

23. Bee, 27–29.

24. Kehoe, 117.

25. Henry F. Dobyns, *The Pima-Maricopa* (New York: Chelsea House, 1989), 25–26.

26. Dobyns, 25–27.

27. Kehoe, 117.

28. Dobyns, 20–22.

29. David W. Penney, *North American Indian Art* (New York: Thames Hudson, 2004), 97–98.

30. Dobyns, 22–23, 65–69.

31. Quoted in Knaut, 20.

32. Knaut, 36–47.

33. Quoted in Knaut, 62–63.

34. Quoted in Knaut, 63.

35. Our discussion of the encomienda system benefited from Ortiz, 43–45.

36. Ortiz, 46–47.

37. Quoted in Ortiz, 49.

38. Quoted in Knaut, 73–74.

39. Ortiz, 57–58.

40. Iverson, 24.

41. Quoted in Ortiz, 58–59.

7

DAILY LIFE IN CALIFORNIA AND THE GREAT BASIN

The two culture areas examined here—California and the Great Basin—comprise a vast section of the present-day United States, including the modern states of California, Nevada, and parts of Oregon, Utah, Wyoming, Idaho, and Arizona. This is a region of tremendous ecological diversity. It includes coastal areas, temperate rain forests, forests of fir and evergreens, snow-covered mountain chains, and thousand of square miles of flat valleys, lava plains, and deserts. In these various surroundings, Native American peoples established extremely dissimilar and complex ways of life.

Long ago, this extended region was a place of water and shade, rich in game, waterfowl, and fish, with plenty of nuts and vegetables to gather. Human beings living there 10,000 years ago lived in valleys or in high places overlooking the lakes where food was always available within a relatively short distance and surpluses were common enough that trade developed between valleys. The world changed about 6,000 years ago when a warmer climate led to the disappearance of many lakes and streams in the region today known as the Plateau, and even in California, people had to choose from fewer good places. The archaeological record shows an increase in the use of nets for fishing, which suggests that people needed to catch greater quantities of smaller fish than before, when large fish could be taken with spears. There are more implements connected with grinding and processing wild grains and nuts, such as grinding stones. This type of work, typically associated with women, is labor-intensive. Although there was still plenty of food, people had to work longer and harder for it. In the eastern parts of the Great Basin, mountain sheep became an important source of protein. Starting about 4,000 years ago, the archaeological record shows distinct culture patterns emerging that differentiated the peoples of California from those of the Great Basin culture area.[1]

INDIGENOUS PEOPLES OF CALIFORNIA

Prior to the arrival of Europeans, over 100 distinct languages were spoken in thousands of villages by hundreds of thousands of people within the borders of present-day California. Each of these languages had one or more dialects. As a region, California is bounded by ocean, mountains, and desert areas that give the region as a whole a character that is quite separate from the rest of North America. A. L. Kroeber, the famous early twentieth-century anthropologist and student of California Indians, identified three major culture areas within the boundaries of the modern state. Northwestern California, the land of the Yurok, Hupa, and Wintu, among others, is a rugged region shaped by dense forests and rocky coasts. Central California, inhabited by Pomo, Miwok, Patwin, Costanoan, and Salinan peoples, is characterized by coastal ranges and valleys, including the foothills of the Sierra Nevada Mountains. Southern California is a mixed region of lagoons, marshes, mountains, and semiarid landscape, the homeland of Chumash, Gabrieleño, Cahuilla, and Luiseño peoples. Yet, despite the geographic variety and the complicated mix of languages, Native Americans in the region shared many similarities in their material culture and their lifeways.[2]

Subsistence   Nuts—most commonly acorns and buckeyes—were a staple of daily life for Native Californians. After the nuts were gathered, they had to be processed to make them edible. This was a tedious and labor-intensive process. Acorns and buckeyes contain acids that are harmful to human beings. To be edible, the nuts had to be soaked, drained, and dried, with the process repeated several times to leach out all the poison. Then women ground them into flour that could be boiled to make mush or baked into bread.

Some Californians planted tobacco for ritual and ceremonial purposes. Only a few groups, mostly those living in close vicinity to the Southwest, grew maize, or Indian corn, a plant indigenous to the Americas and widely grown among Indian farmers in other parts of the continent. Summer rainfalls are limited in California, which might have slowed the introduction of maize agriculture, but this is not a sufficient explanation, since people could have used irrigation methods to enable the farming of corn, like the people of the Southwest. The more likely explanation is that corn had no particular attraction since they already had a reliable food supply from acorns and other nuts, enough to support a high population density. Further, the work of gathering and processing was part of the rhythm of ritual and seasonal life.

Native people supplemented their diet with gathering and hunting. They gathered seeds and fruits and hunted for small game, birds, and deer. Coastal peoples such as the Pomo and Miwok enjoyed great variety with both salt- and freshwater fish and clams. Clams had the added benefit of shells that could be turned into disc beads that were valued as currency in the region. Further inland, people also fished in such rivers as the Sacramento, where the annual runs of king salmon provided an opportunity for feasting and gathering as well provender. Abundant food, easy to get and easy to preserve, made it possible for indigenous peoples in California to live in small groups, in stable locations, over a long period of time. This in turn contributed to the great diversity of languages and lifeways across the region.

In southern and central California, Native people used fire to shape the environment. By burning off the woods, undergrowth, and brush in valleys and on foothills, Native Americans in the region were able to sow grasses, from which they could gather seeds, and to spur the growth of clover, which they ate as part of their diet in the spring. The newly created clearings also provided good forage for deer, attracting them, and making it easier for hunters to kill them.[3]

Most Amerindian groups in California lived in sedentary villages that varied in size and location. On a seasonal basis, all or part of the village might move to temporary hunting and gathering camps. The site of a village was determined by its nearness to resources of vital importance to subsistence, such as water, animal and plant life, fuel, and building resources. Native Californians generally located their villages on knolls or hills, if the natural landscape enabled them to do so. Such sites stood above the danger from floods and provided strategic advantages in case of enemy attacks.

Settlement Patterns and Dwellings

Villages were more than clusters of houses. They encompassed defined areas for spiritual and ritual practices such as ceremonial halls, dance grounds, burial grounds, sweat lodges, and retreats for menstruating women, whose company was seen as harmful to men. There were also playing fields for games and spaces for communal food storage.

As might be expected in a region of such geographic and cultural diversity, houses came in various shapes and forms and were built from different materials. The Chumash of southern California lived in large, domed dwellings that stood 5 to 15 feet tall and measured from 15 to 50 feet in diameter. They constructed their houses around a framework of willow poles, and the larger residences had an extra pole in the center for support. This structure was then interwoven with smaller poles, which were fastened together with strips of bark. This frame was covered with mats made of bulrushes or tule that were tied to the frame.[4]

Houses in northwestern California were rectangular structures made with planks, very similar to those found in the Pacific Northwest culture area. Other groups, such as the Patwin in the Central Valley, lived in large, round or oval earth houses that were partly below ground. The Patwin dug two to three feet into the earth and used the soil they removed to build a bulwark around the house. Then, they set up posts and beams as a framework, covering the scaffolding with earth. When the Patwin left their settlements for hunting and gathering excursions, they lived in wickiups, which were round or conical-shaped frame structures made out of poles and covered with bark. Other groups, such as the Pomo, who lived on the central Californian coast, lived in wickiups year around.[5]

Social and Religious Organization   Many of the larger Californian societies, such as the Patwin, were socially stratified. At the top of this class system was the chiefly lineage. This group was followed by ranked specialists, including craftspeople such as the artisans who made shell discs, or ritual specialists, who today would be called shamans. These individuals mastered skills of special value to their peers, which explains their elevated social standing. Next followed the commoners, who contributed much to a village's subsistence. War captives were at the bottom of the social ladder and remained there until they either escaped or were released by their captors after some years of service.

Chiefs were the political leaders of a community. They were generally chosen from a noble lineage and were typically close relatives such as sons or brothers of the previous leader, from whom they had inherited the office. A capable daughter could also become chief, especially when there were no suitable male candidates available from the nobility. Chiefs played important roles in the daily life of indigenous societies in California. They oversaw trade, diplomatic relations, food production and distribution, and ceremonies and celebrations. They took care of the needy as well as guests of the village. An incompetent leader could be deposed if a consensus emerged within the community that his or her leadership was unsatisfactory.

Healers also played an important role in villages. As with the position of chief, this was generally a hereditary office passed on within a family to a person who demonstrated great aptitude in the skills required for this profession. Healers spent years studying the skills and techniques of Native American medicine from a parent, grandparent, or other healer before they set out to diagnose and cure diseases on their own. Healers learned what herbs and songs to use for specific diseases as well as practical skills such as how to mend bone fractures by tying a piece of wood to an injured arm or leg to keep it in a stable position while it healed.[6]

There was and is an extreme diversity in the ceremonial and ritual life of the California Indians. For example, Patwin men dressed in feathers and blackened their faces to personify spirits, much like the katsinas of the Southwest. In a ceremony accompanied by music from drums, the specially-selected spirit dancers brought blessings and health to a community. This ritual was followed by social dances that included everyone in the village, which served to unify the entire community.

In contrast, Pomo communities had very different ceremonies and rituals. For instance, at puberty, the boys and girls of the upper lineages were brought into the communal dance house. There, as part of an initiation rite, they were lectured by masked spirits about the Pomo past, as well as on the moral and spiritual knowledge and values of their people. The children's ears and noses were then pierced, and from this point on they began to wear jewelry and ornaments—a sign that distinguished the upper class from the commoners. In the following years, they were expected to learn skills such as healing or specialized crafts such as the production of shell money. These specialties were not taught to the children of commoners.

The Hupa of northwestern California had at least one sweat house in every village. These multipurpose male spaces were used for sweating, that is, a ritual that used steam and extreme heat to cleanse both the body and the spirit. Women did not need to sweat as their bodies cleansed themselves every month. Sweat houses were also gathering places for teaching, storytelling, singing, and camaraderie among men. Some of the men and older boys also slept there. Family houses were mainly

white deer
dance regalia

HUPA
1800S
(CALIFORNIA)

abalone
shells

Hupa man and woman, nineteenth-century dress. The first settlers who went to California in search of gold encountered diverse cultures with a highly developed ritual life. One ritual performed only by men was the White Deerskin Dance, where men invoked the spirit of the deer. Women adorned themselves with elaborate jewelry and clothing decorations made from shells beads. From Tara Prindle/nativetech.org.

women's space. Each village also had a communal building used for healing and ceremonies. The two most important ceremonies were both held
in September. The White Deerskin Dance was danced only by men, who
wore tanned white deerskin skirts and capes as well as special necklaces
made from shells and elks' teeth. The dance was accompanied with singing and perhaps a whistle, but never drums. The purpose of the dance
was to revitalize the world for another year. The Jump Dance aimed to
bring prevent sickness, famine, and other natural disasters.[7]

In southern California, Native peoples engaged in elaborate mourning rituals to commemorate their dead. The celebrations were usually
staged by a village, but neighboring communities were invited to join
in. In fact, the visitors helped the bereaved members of the village, who
organized the ceremony to ritually cleanse themselves after the mourners
had undergone a service of crying and weeping to commemorate their
lost ones. The visitors also presented the hosts with beautiful baskets
and new clothing so that the mourners could don them in place of their
mourning rags. Guests were expected to give their hosts money, generally
in the form of shell beads, to pay for the healers. In exchange, the visitors
received food and highly desirable goods such as baskets and ornaments.
The cycle of mourning and gift-giving was reciprocated sooner or later
when the visitors became hosts for their own mourning rites. In fact, alliances existed between families in different communities whose members
had been ceremonial partners for a long time. Mourners also made gifts
to the dead, who were burned on pyres. Finally, once the official mourning rituals were completed, everyone sat down to feast, trade, dance, and
gamble. These highly structured mourning ceremonials strengthened the
bond between the living and the dead. At the same time, they renewed
diplomatic and reciprocal ties within a community as well as between
neighboring groups.[8]

Baskets   Baskets and basket making played an integral part in the
daily life of indigenous peoples in California. Women wove
them from materials collected from their surroundings. Baskets
were used to collect, mill, store, and cook food. They were used to carry
things ranging from collected food items to young children. Tightly
woven baskets were used as sieves for leaching acorns. Woven nets were
used to fish and to catch birds.[9]

Beyond their utilitarian value, baskets played a key role in mourning
rituals and other aspects of social and ceremonial life. For example, Pomo
parents gave their young children baskets to play with. They presented a
child with a specially made and decorated basket when they reached an
important stage in their life, such as when a girl had her first menstrual
flow. The family of a bride-to-be gave baskets to the groom's family. This
offering demonstrated that the daughter, who would move in with her
new husband's family, was a skilled worker who came from a family
of means. A special type of basket decorated with bird feathers or shell

beads symbolized affluence. These were displayed to show an individual's, a family's, or a community's wealth.

Spanish explorers sailed north from Mexico and to the southern parts of California in 1539 but did not establish a **Mission Life** significant presence until almost two centuries had elapsed. The establishment of Franciscan missions was part of the larger tactics of the Spanish empire to secure the region, as officials feared competition from the British, who were moving in from the east, and the Russians moving down from the north. As in other parts of the continent, Christian missions had a significant impact on Native peoples. They altered, challenged, and threatened almost every aspect of daily life. Native people resisted the earliest attempts to convert them, in some cases with violence. After that missionaries and soldiers worked together to enforce order at the missions.

Recent Amerindian converts, or neophytes, provided most of the labor on the missions. Similar to the Franciscan missions in the Southwest, the priests and soldiers on the missions delegated or managed Amerindian workers, or served as instructors to teach skilled trades such as iron work, woodworking, or masonry, which would benefit the operation of the mission stations. Native people built and maintained the buildings, worked the fields, and herded and took care of the missionaries' livestock. They also made pottery, worked as blacksmiths, and wove clothes.

Friars imposed strict regulations and routines on Native peoples who lived on or close to the missions. Native men, women, and children learned Catholic doctrine, religious hymns, and prayers. One church official described the routine of daily life at the missions:

Half an hour after sunrise, having taken their breakfast of atole [a cereal], the neophytes assemble in the church to hear holy Mass, during which they recite the catechism . . . in their language. From the church they go to their homes, take up their implements and work until half past eleven. Then they take their meal which consists of boiled wheat, corn, peas, beans. Then they rest until two o'clock, in winter until three, at which time they go to work at their tasks until an hour before sunset. They then take their supper . . . as in the morning, return to church to recite the . . . catechism, and sing. Having finished the function of the church, they return to their homes.[10]

This rigid organization of daily life was quite different from what Native Californians were accustomed to in precolonial times, when they only spent a few hours a day on subsistence activities and the remaining time was spent on leisure activities or in preparation for ceremonies and celebrations.

Friars also enforced a new set of social codes, deriding indigenous moral codes and beliefs as sinful. For instance, missionaries kept unmarried Indian males and females separate from one another by having them sleep in separate dormitories. This was done to prevent premarital sexual relations. Furthermore, and with varying success, the missionaries pushed Amerindian peoples to give up their precontact religious rituals and beliefs.

Mission life brought many challenges to the Native peoples of California. Neophytes worked under harsh conditions that paralleled slavery in all but the name. People who ran away from the missions, if caught, faced cruel punishment. They were chained in irons and dragged back to the mission to be publicly flogged. Flogging was also a general punishment meted out to those who were deemed by the friars to be unruly.

In contrast to the varied diet previously enjoyed across the region, mission workers lived on a stable but unsatisfying regimen of a wheat dish called atole. Poor nourishment, along with the close living quarters and harsh working conditions, strengthened the dramatic impact of epidemic diseases. These diseases spread when people from the missions went to visit their relatives in other places. Further, when high mortality rates depleted the Native population at the missions, new recruits were brought in by force, if they could not be persuaded. Thus, Spanish missions and colonization had a horrific impact on native societies. Scholars estimate that the Indian population of California dropped from about 300,000 people in precolonial times to 30,000 in the mid-nineteenth century, when the California Gold Rush began.[11]

Native American Labor and the California Gold Rush

California's Native population contributed to Spanish, Mexican, and colonial economies. As in other Hispanic borderland societies, aboriginal labor played a central role in California, not only on the missions, but also on the large farms of colonists. Here Amerindians worked the fields and tended the herds of Spanish landowners. Despite the devastating impact of epidemic disease, Native Americans were the largest demographic group in California through the mid-nineteenth century. The United States annexed lands in the Southwest after its victory in the Mexican-American War in the mid-1840s. The California Gold Rush of 1848 and 1849 led to a massive influx of American immigration to the region. These Euro-American settlers were keen to make a fortune, even if it meant dispossessing the indigenous population. In 1850, just a few years after the gold rush began, California became the thirty-first state of the Union.

Life under the Americans was no better than it had been under the Spanish or Mexican colonial governments. Native Californians continued to do much of the most tedious, dangerous, or labor-intensive work in agriculture and mining, although some of these jobs were soon taken by Chinese workers who came to America during these years in search of a better life. Native peoples worked these jobs because they had to. With little independent access to the means of subsistence, they needed cash as much as anyone else. The increasing use of machines in place of manual labor in the late nineteenth century allowed farming to become a major business in the state, but it became harder than ever to earn a living through farm work.

Native workers also played an important role during the early gold rush. In the central mining district in 1848, for example, more than half of the 4,000 miners were Amerindians who worked for white mine owners. Richard Mason, the territorial governor of California, observed that the native miners used "pans or willow baskets, [to] gradually wash out the earth and separate the gravel by hand, leaving nothing but gold mixed with sand," from which they removed the precious metal. They produced gold "in sufficient quantities to satisfy" their white employers, who made significant profits. According to Mason, two investors once hired four white miners and "about a hundred Indians," and in one week made a $10,000 profit for themselves. Yet, by 1849, Euro-American workers already resented the competition from Indians who worked for lower wages, and they began to push Native workers out of the mining industry.[12] Horrific incidents of extralegal violence took place. Both agricultural and mine workers faced abuse from white employers who tried to enforce "discipline" under harsh conditions. There were frequent accounts of employers who refused to pay Amerindian workers for their services, as well as reports of whippings and beatings of laborers—some to the point of death.

The large-scale colonization of California by Euro-American settlers had a devastating impact on the area's native population. It led to an increase in the spread of disease, alcoholism, labor abuse, and the sexual exploitation of Amerindian women. Colonization utterly disrupted Native American daily life in California.

American Colonization and the Disruption of Daily Life

As in so many other parts of the Americas, Euro-Americans introduced a vast array of diseases to which California Indians had little immunity. An article published in a Sacramento newspaper in 1851, for instance, pointed out that on the Upper Sacramento "sickness prevails to a considerable extent among the tribes of Indians in the vicinity of the river." An eyewitness "noticed on the road a number of unburied bodies, and in the huts and woods many who were lying prostrate with disease. The ranks of the aborigines are rapidly wasting away."[13] Such outbreaks disrupted indigenous lifeways all over the region.

Alcoholism was another force that disrupted the patterns of daily life. Newspapers frequently wrote of incidents that involved drunken individuals and groups of Amerindians. This became part of the negative image of Amerindian peoples that portrayed alcoholism out of context, with no consideration for how much trauma aboriginal peoples in California had endured or the degree to which colonization had undermined traditional modes of authority and social control. Alcohol contributed to violent crimes, including murder, and there were reports of alcohol abuse even among Native children. Thus, alcohol undermined social cohesion among Native communities in California.

Colonization hit Native California women especially hard. During times when they were unable to get food by traditional means or could not find paid work with white settlers, some women resorted to prostitution to get the cash needed to feed their children and their families. There were widespread reports of sexual abuse, exploitation, forced concubinage, and rape by Euro-American men. One woman was sexually assaulted by four soldiers and tried to resist, giving one of her assailants a stab wound that proved to be fatal.[14] These assaults, and the underlying attitudes that allowed Euro-Americans to treat indigenous women this way, had a significant impact on the daily life of all Native Americans. "It is difficult to imagine," writes historian Albert Hurtado, that California Indian women

were not fearful, angry, and resentful because of rape and the necessity of prostitution and concubinage. We can only guess about the effects of Indian-white sexual relations on Indian family life. Did Indian husbands give sympathy and support to their raped spouses, or did sexual assaults create strain on Indian marriage and family life that could not be eased? The answer to this question no doubt varies from case to case and culture to culture, but rape and other forms of sexual exploitation almost certainly inflicted damage on individual Indians and their society that transcended the immediate harm inherent in the acts themselves.[15]

Military Campaigns and Massacres

Military campaigns against Native peoples were a common occurrence in the history of white-Indian relations in California. Whether they were Spanish, Mexican, or Americans, each in turn contributed to the aboriginal bloodshed on California soil. However, much of the violence was extralegal, in the sense that it was not officially condoned. Current scholarship has begun to analyze acts committed by vigilantes or militias as part of a total system that aimed to discipline and control aboriginal people through the threat, or fact, of violence.

An especially vicious campaign was launched by the Second Infantry of the U.S. army in May of 1850 against a Pomo village accused of harboring those who had killed two American men. It is not clear whether or not the murders came from this particular village, but there was a strong feeling among the Amerindians that these killings were justified. The two men were accused of abusing their Native workers and then refusing to pay them. Worse, it was believed that they had raped Pomo women. U.S. forces struck decisively and harshly against the Indians. Captain Lyon, who commanded the military operation, described the assault:

Early on the morning of [May] 15th, the two shores being guarded, the landing of the island was effected, under a strong opposition from the Indians, who, perceiving us once upon their island took flight directly, plunging into the water, among the heavy growth of tula which surrounds the islands, and which on the eastern and northern sides extends to the shores. Having rapidly cleared the island, I saw no alternative but to pursue them into the tula . . . and pursue and destroy as far as possible. The tula was thus thoroughly searched, with severe protracted efforts, and with most gratifying results. The number killed I confidently report at no less than sixty, and doubt little that it extended to a hundred and upwards. The Indians were supposed to be in number about 400 . . . The rancheria extending about half way around the island, was burnt, together with a large amount of stores collected in it.

The military unit moved on to another Native village that Lyon believed to be connected to the death of the two American men. The village was abandoned by the time they arrived. The soldiers turned a third village, whose inhabitants, according to their Captain, had been "the most active participants in the atrocious murders." He wrote,

Their position being entirely surrounded, they were attacked under most embar-rassing circumstances; but as they could not escape, the island soon became a perfect slaughter pen. . . . Their numbers killed I confidently report at not less than 75, and have little doubt it extended to nearly double that number.[16]

An estimated 135 to 250 Amerindian people—including women and children—were killed during an operation launched in retaliation for the death of two American men.

Across California, hundreds of massacres led to thousands of fatalities among the Native population. Newspapers, local histories, and native oral traditions widely chronicle this sad history. Not everyone approved, and eastern newspapers in particular condemned these actions. An article printed in a San Francisco newspaper in 1860, for instance, described the following incident.

Between three and four o'clock on Sunday morning last, (26 February), an attack was made by a party of white men, upon Indians at several villages around Humboldt Bay. At Indian Island, opposite of the town of Eureka, and distant but a few hundred yards, more than 40 Indians were killed, three fourths of the number being women and children. On the beach, south of the entrance of the bay, forty or fifty Indians were also killed. It is also reported, and is no doubt true, that a simul-taneous attack was made upon the villages on Eel river. From what was known in Eureka not less than two hundred Indians—men, women and children—were killed on this Sabbath morning.[17]

Massacres and murders were further encouraged by the practice of U.S. and state officials who paid rewards to bounty hunters for killing Amerindians. Such a source of income encouraged some vigilantes to make a living by killing Native Americans and cutting off their scalps for reimbursement. Military campaigns, massacres and racial killings along with disease, missions, pressures on land, and other socially disruptive forces introduced by colonization, severely interrupted, threatened, and undermined the established patterns of daily life among the Native Americans of California.

DAILY LIFE IN THE GREAT BASIN

The Great Basin, a culture area consisting of Nevada and parts of California, Utah, Oregon, Montana, Wyoming, and Idaho, is often referred to as the great American desert. It is a region of geographical and natural diversity, and an environment that shaped its aboriginal inhabitants' way of life. It is an astonishing landscape with deserts, deep-cut canyons where agave and cacti grow, open basins with creosote bushes and mesquite trees, some river valley areas with fertile floodplains, and oases with springs and streams, as well as mountain ranges wooded with pinion pine trees or ponderosa pines and in higher elevations with aspen, fir, and spruce.

This region was and is inhabited by the Shoshone, the Utes, and the Paiutes, who probably moved into the Great Basin from Death Valley, California, about a thousand years ago.[18] All three groups speak related languages from the Uto-Aztecan family, although the Shoshone language is classified as Numic, a distinct branch. These groups took on distinctive characteristics after 1700, when some adopted the horse culture of the Great Plains while others did not.

The Shoshone, also known as the Snake People, are related to the Comanches of the southern plains by language and through intermarriage. They adopted horse culture after 1700 and expanded their hunting territories as far as the Bighorn Mountains on the east, north to the Yellowstone River and the plains of Montana, west to the place where the Snake River flows into the Columbia River in Washington state; and south to the Uinta Mountains of Utah and parts of northwestern Colorado. This period was short-lived, however, and by 1750 they were pushed back by the Blackfeet, Bloods, Piegans and Crows to the north and limited by the expansion of Sioux, Cheyenne, and Arapaho peoples on their eastern borders. By 1840, most Shoshone people lived west of the Rocky Mountains, although Shoshone hunters continued to visit their familiar hunting grounds.

The Northern and Southern Paiute called themselves "Numu," or "The People." They are thought to have entered the Great Basin from Death Valley, California, over a thousand years ago. They developed a flexible system of seasonal movements and subsistence activities that took advantage of every possible resource. Their diet included over 150 types of seed, including pine nuts and camas bulbs, which were gathered and processed by women.

The Bannock are Northern Paiutes who moved from western Oregon onto Snake River plains of Idaho. They lived near the Northern Shoshones.

However, they are distinct from the Northern Shoshone and from other Paiutes because they adopted key elements of Plains culture in the late seventeenth century, including horses, the practice of counting coup and taking scalps in war, the Scalp Dance, which celebrated these exploits, and later, the Sun Dance, a ritual in which young men endured great depriva-tion and physical pain in the belief that their sacrifice would benefit the people for the year to come. The identification and classification of indig-enous peoples in the Great Basin is complicated by the different historical choices made by individual groups, so, for example, while the Bannock lived close to the Northern Shoshone and today share a reservation with them, the latter did not adopt horse culture.

The Utes also adopted horses. By the late eighteenth century, they ranged over a wide territory on horseback, hunting and gathering in ways that expanded their former modes of subsistence but also raiding neighboring tribes. This in turn contributed to a new emphasis on mate-rial goods. Women continued to practice their seasonal rounds of com-munal gathering. During the summer, they gathered in large bands of 200 or more family camps.

Subsistence

Prior to 1700, people of the Great Basin lived in small communities, consisting of one to several extended fami-lies. Multiple communities, generally from the same band, came together to collect and process foods such as pine nuts. These were also occasions for social gatherings and ceremonies. Independent groups could also come together in times of war.

White travelers to the region looked at the indigenous patterns of daily life with disdain and described the Paiutes in particular as if they were animals. Thomas Farnham, for example, wrote in an ill-informed account in 1839:

Here live the "Paiutes" . . . the most degraded and least intellectual Indians known to the trappers. They wear no clothing of any description—build no shelters. They eat roots, lizards, and snails. . . . They provide nothing for future wants. And when the lizards and snails and wild roots are buried in the snows of winter, they are said to retire to the vicinity of timber, dig holes . . . deposit themselves in them, and sleep fast until the weather permits them to go abroad again.[19]

Farnham's account reveals a deeply held bias against gathering, which he viewed as women's work, and "degraded" foods such as roots, lizards, and snails, which were far less glamorous—and less manly—than the mighty buffalo of the Plains. However, survival in this culture area required inge-nuity, adaptation, and exploitation of the natural environment.

Great Basin subsistence patterns were skillfully adapted to the harsh natural environment they lived in. Many Indian communities in the region cultivated the lands around rivers and springs. They grew such crops as maize, squash, melons, herbs, pumpkins, beans, sunflowers, and a variety of grasses for the seeds. In many instances, agriculture was made possible through the use of irrigation ditches made by using digging sticks. Indians in the region worked their fields in common. After planting they weeded the crop from time to time until harvest time.

Like some of the Indians in the Southwest, native groups in the Great Basin such as the Paiute also grew devil's claw, the seedpods of which they used to weave designs into their baskets. Among the Indians in the region, baskets came in various shapes and forms. They were used in rituals and for decoration but also had utilitarian purposes since natives used baskets for cooking, storing, and carrying food and other goods.

Native Americans in the Great Basin region supplemented their diet through hunting and gathering, and local groups even left their fields for days and sometimes weeks to pursue these strategies of subsistence. The men hunted for large animals such as antelopes, mountain sheep, and deer, and smaller animals such as rabbits, ducks, porcupines, tortoises, gophers, squirrels, quail, and chuckwalla lizards. Native women were in charge of gathering foods, although men often went along on such excursions to help. They collected a wide variety of plants such as leafy greens, several varieties of seeds, pinion nuts, bulrush, agave, barrel cacti, roots, mesquite pods, and flowers.[20]

Leadership   Chiefs were the leaders in Great Basin Indian communities. Traditionally they were males and descendants of a chiefly lineage. They had specific ceremonial, social, and diplomatic duties, such as serving as their community's spokesperson with the outside world. They kept things running smoothly within a settlement by encouraging people to be productive and by advocating peace within the group. But it was the council and its members that made key decisions that impacted the community. Although the chief could offer his opinions, he had to comply with their decisions. Thus, the political powers of chiefs were quite limited, and communities were generally guided through consensus. If a leader overreached his authority, members of the community could replace him with a new chief.

Courtship and Marriage   Courtship and marriage were an important component of daily life in the Great Basin. Both were regulated by a strict set of social and moral expectations that young people and their families were expected to adhere to. For instance, young women among the Paiute were not allowed to talk to young men who were not part of their extended family except during social dances. These dances gave youngsters an opportunity to meet potential mates. These were occasions for young people to put on "their best clothes, adorned with beads, feathers or shells" and to socialize with people.[21]

When it was time to find a spouse, young men often traveled for some distance from one band to another in search of a compatible partner. Once it was known that there was a "marriageable woman" living in a community, young men who were not her relatives could come forward to pursue her. Sarah Winnemucca, a Paiute woman, wrote that this "courting is very

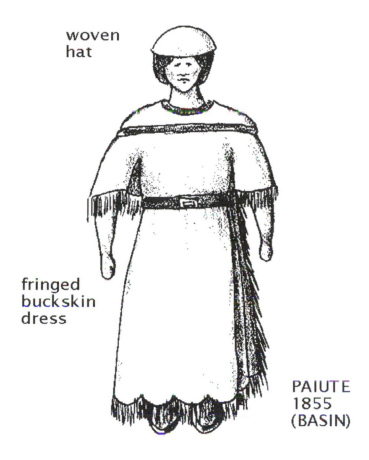

woven
hat

fringed
buckskin
dress

PAIUTE
1855
(BASIN)

Paiute women's clothing, nineteenth century. This buckskin dress is cut with simple lines but decorated with fringe and a metal buckle acquired through trade. The woven hat offers shade from the hot sun. From Tara Prindle/nativetech.org.

different from the courting of white people. He never speaks to her, or visits the family, but endeavors to attract her attention" by showing off his skills. According to Winnemucca, a young man who wanted to pursue a serious courtship had only one good option for spending time with his chosen one with propriety. He had to dress himself in his best clothing and visit her family dwelling after everyone had gone to bed for the night. Marriageable young women slept next to their grandmothers or another older woman charged with taking special care of them. Once inside, he sat down at her feet. Winnemucca continued:

He does not speak to either young woman or grandmother, but when the young woman wishes him to go away, she rises and goes and lies down by the side of her mother. He then leaves as silently as he came in. This goes on sometimes for a year or longer, if the young woman has not made up her mind. She is never forced by her parents to marry against her wishes. When she knows her own mind, she makes a confidant of her grandmother, and then the young man is summoned by the father of the girl, who asks him in her presence, if he really loves his daughter, and reminds him, if he says he does, of all the duties of a husband. He then asks his daughter the same question, and sets before her minutely all her duties. And these duties are not slight. She is to dress the game, prepare the food, clean the buckskins, make the moccasins, dress his hair, bring all the wood. . . . Then he is invited to a feast and all his relatives with him.[22]

After the wedding celebration the groom typically lived with the family into which he had married. The couple soon moved into their own home.

Birth, Puberty, and Death   The birth of a child, just as courtship and marriage, was also regulated by ceremonial taboos, and restrictions. Sarah Winnemucca wrote that after the birth of the first child

[b]oth father and mother fast from all flesh, and the father goes through the labor of piling the wood for twenty-five days, and assumes all his wife's household work during that time. If he does not do his part in the care of the child, he is considered an outcast. Every five days his child's basket is changed for a new one, and the five are all carefully put away at the end of the days, the last one containing the navel-string, carefully wrapped up, and all are put into a tree, and the child put into a new and ornamented basket.

Through these elaborate interactions the father helped his wife in practical ways and also demonstrated his respect toward the mother and child. These customs and rituals served to strengthen the bond between parents and child, and demonstrated that both mother and father were responsible for their offspring.[23]

Puberty was another rite of passage that played a central role for the Indian people who lived in the Great Basin culture area. Sarah Winnemucca observed that among the Paiute,

boys are introduced to manhood by their hunting of deer and mountain-sheep. Before they are fifteen or sixteen, they hunt only small game, like rabbits, hares, fowls, etc. They never eat what they kill themselves, but only what their father or elder brothers kill. When a boy becomes strong enough to use larger bows made of sinew, and arrows that are ornamented with eagle-feathers ... he kills game that is large . . . Then he brings home the hide and his father cuts it into a long coil which is wound into a loop, and the boy takes his quiver and throws it on his back as if he was going on a hunt, and takes his bow and arrows in his hand. Then his father throws the lop over him, and he jumps through it. This he does five times. Now for the first time he eats the flesh of the animal he has killed, and from that time he eats whatever he kills.[24]

Like young Indian women among several Southwestern societies, the Paiute girls of the Great Basin underwent a special initiation ceremony when they had their first menstruation. For the remainder of their cycle, the girls lived in seclusion, away from the main settlement. They were not allowed to eat meat or salt and had to avoid touching themselves, to the extent that they were given a special stick to use when scratching themselves. The adherence by boys and girls to such taboos and rites, the Paiute believed, would guarantee them health and a long life, but it would impress on the teenagers that they had now transitioned into adulthood.[25]

Death was another major milestone in the cycle of life that Great Basin Indians honored with ceremonials. Among the Paiute Indians, deceased members of a community were either cremated or buried, and a dead person's possessions were also burned or put in the ground. Most often the dead were buried in the house in which they had died. On occasion, the ritual burial took place away from the settlement, or the deceased were cremated by burning the dwelling in which they had died. In any case, the Paiute would abandon any home in which a death had happened A dead person's animals, such as a horse or a dog, were also killed, and mourners would abstain from eating meat and salt for several days. As in many other Indian societies in North America, relatives would cut their hair as sign of mourning. Moreover, the Paiute, like their neighbors in the California culture area, celebrated festivals to honor the dead of their communities.[26]

The Gold Rush brought thousands of Euro-Americans to California after 1848. To get there, they had to travel through the region on the Oregon or California Trails. These

American Colonization in the Great Basin

migrants knowingly or unknowingly used up many of the resources vital to native survival. Their livestock and horses ate the grasses and plants. The increased traffic disturbed the game habitats so central to Great Basin subsistence. Some Euro-American travelers fired their weapons at Native Americans out of fear or for sport.

Mormon families in search of a safe haven for themselves began to move into the Salt Lake Valley in 1847. Within a decade, there were 40,000 Mormon settlers in the area. Ute chief Wakara fought back in what is known as the Walker War, which lasted from the late 1840s to the mid-1850s. Another chief, Black Hawk, led what has become known as the Black Hawk War in the 1860s.[27] It seems ironic to name U.S. military technology after a warrior who fought desperately to preserve his homeland from U.S. encroachment.

Sarah Winnemucca was born around 1844 and remembered those days. In her later life she wrote, "I was a very small child when the first white people came to our country. They came like a lion, yes, like a roaring lion, and have continued so ever since, and I have never forgotten their first coming."[28] Her grandfather, who became known as Captain Truckee, believed that these events fulfilled an ancient prophecy and that the Paiutes must make every effort to get along with the newcomers. However, not everyone believed him. Winnemucca recalled a frightening day when rumors spread through the camp that "some white people were coming." Her mother had heard stories and feared that they would all be killed and eaten up but could not run fast or far with two small children to carry. Instead she buried them up to their necks, planting sage bushes to protect them from the hot sun, and warned them to be perfectly quiet. Imagine the fear that the little girls felt, and the fear that could drive a mother to do such a thing.[29]

Initially the Shoshone, Ute, and Paiute peoples of the Great Basin tried to accommodate the Americans. They signed "Treaties of Peace and Friendship" that allowed Americans to travel through their lands, with seemingly minor concessions to allow the U.S. army to build a fort or two and use natural resources that were not particularly valued by the Native peoples. Then gold was discovered in the Wind River Mountains, and the rush of immigrants began, with the U.S. army there to protect them. Before Sarah Winnemucca reached her fourth decade, many of her people were living on reservations and the number of people who died from warfare or disease reduced some groups by as much as 80 percent of their former strength.[30]

Euro-American settlers took over the best farmland. They cut off or destroyed Native access to water and to food resource areas. They cut down the pinion trees. Settler livestock destroyed many of the grasslands used by Native peoples to collect seeds. There were also reports of violence and massacres committed by Euro-American miners and settlers. White migrants, settlers, and miners also brought epidemics such as measles, whooping cough, mumps, cholera, malaria, tuberculosis, and scarlet fever.

During these difficult years, a prophet arose among the Paiutes in Nevada. About 1870 a minor chief named Tävibo, which means "white man," had a vision that a great upheaval or earthquake would come in a few months. All of the material possessions of the white people would be swallowed up but their material goods would survive. The Indians would be left to enjoy everything. Later he had a second vision that clarified his prophecy. He said that both whites and Indians would be destroyed, but that the Indians would be resurrected and then live forever. In a third and final vision, he saw that only those Indians who believed would live again. Tävibo's visions mark the beginning of a major revitalization movement that would become known as the Ghost Dance, but his role is less remembered than that of his son, Wovoka, who was also known as Jack Wilson.[31]

Wovoka was about 14 years old when his father died. He grew up working for a white couple named David and Abigail Wilson, and he took his English name from this family. On January 1, 1889, during a solar eclipse and suffering from a fever, Wovoka was chopping wood for the Wilsons when he had a great revelation. In this vision, he went to heaven and saw God. He also saw his ancestors, alive and well. God told Wovoka that he must go back and tell his people to be good and love one another, and not to fight, or steal, or tell lies. He gave Wovoka a dance to teach to his people, based on the traditional Paiute Round Dance. They were not to work for the white man, but for themselves. If they did all of these things, they would see their loved ones again.

Wovoka never called his vision the Ghost Dance; that name was given to it by the Lakota, who sent a delegation to learn more about this prophecy. He never advocated that people should dance themselves into a trance or wear the painted shirts that later Ghost Dancers believed would make them invulnerable to bullets. Neither did he preach the destruction of Euro-Americans. All of these elements were added by others. He did gain a reputation among his own people for his ability to predict the weather, and for performing unusual acts such as causing ice to form on the river in summer. He sometimes fell into trances in public and claimed that during these times, he was visiting heaven. Apparently he did believe that his new power made him invulnerable to bullets. However, he stopped proselytyzing after the U.S. army massacred a group of Ghost Dancers at Wounded Knee in 1890. Anthropologist James Mooney of the Bureau of American Ethnography interviewed Wovoka in 1891 and described him as a "tall, well-proportioned man with piercing eyes, regular features, a deep voice and a calm and dignified mien. He stood straight as a ramrod, spoke slowly, and by sheer projection of personality commanded the attention of any listener."[32] Wovoka died in 1932 at the age of 74.

In later life Sarah Winnemucca followed her grandfather's path and tried to work with the U.S. army as an interpreter and guide. Later she turned to public lectures in which she sought to educate white Americans about the "wrongs and claims" of her people. The wrongs and claims were many. Yet the Paiutes, and their neighbors and kin throughout the Great Basin and California, were a people who were well-adapted to survive harsh conditions in a changing world. By the end of the nineteenth century many had died and the survivors were mostly living on reservations that they sometimes share with people who had been their enemies, such as the Arapaho who were sent to live on the Wind River Reservation in 1878. Some people held to the old beliefs. Others, like Sarah Winnemucca and Jack Wilson, found new ways to lead their people. The struggle for survival in modern America had begun.

NOTES

1. Alice B. Kehoe, *North American Indians: A Comprehensive Account,* 2nd ed. (Upper Saddle River, NJ: Prentice Hall, 1992), 332–36.

2. Kehoe, 402.

3. Kehoe, 402–4.

4. Robert O. Gibson, *The Chumash* (New York: Chelsea House, 1991), 44, 22.

5. Kehoe, 404.

6. Kehoe, 404–5.

7. Frederick E. Hoxie, ed., *Encyclopedia of North American Indians* (Boston and New York: Houghton Mifflin, 1996), 262–63; Reginald and Gladys Laubin, *Indian Dances of North America: Their Importance to Indian Life*, Civilization of the American Indian Series (Norman: University of Oklahoma Press, 1989 [1977]), 411–12.

8. Kehoe, 406–9.

9. David W. Penney, *North American Indian Art* (New York: Thames & Hudson, 2004), 131–34.

10. Quoted in Gibson, 75.

11. On mission life see Gibson, 74–79; Kehoe, 409–11.

12. Albert L. Hurtado, *Indian Survival on the California Frontier* (New Haven, CT: Yale University Press, 1988), 104.

13. Newspaper article, Sacramento, 1851 in Robert F. Heizer, ed., *The Destruction of California Indians* (Lincoln: University of Nebraska Press, 1993), 274–75.

14. Newspaper article, San Francisco, 1859 in Heizer, 281.

15. Hurtado, quote, 191. For a general discussion of these issues see chapter 9.

16. N. Lyon to Major E.R.S. Canby, May 22, 1850, in Heizer, 244–45.

17. Newspaper article, San Francisco, 1860, in Heizer, 255–56.

18. The following discussion is drawn from Hoxie, 457–57, 586–87, 655.

19. Robert J. Franklin and Pamela A. Bunte, *The Paiute* (New York: Chelsea House, 1990), 21.

20. On subsistence see Franklin and Bunte, 27–32.

21. Sarah Winnemucca Hopkins, *Life among the Piutes: Their Wrongs and Claims* (Bishop, CA: Chalfant Press, 1969), 45.

22. Hopkins, 48–49.

23. Hopkins, 49–50.

24. Hopkins, 50–51.

25. Franklin and Bunte, 40.

26. Franklin and Bunte, 41.

27. Hoxie, 655.

28. Hopkins, 4.

29. Hopkins, 11.

30. Hoxie, 656.

31. For a brief introduction to Wovoka, see the biographical essay by Michael Hittman in Hoxie, 700–702. For further research, the two best sources are James Mooney, *The Ghost-Dance Religion and Wounded Knee* (New York: Dover Publications, 1973) and Michael Hittman, *Wovoka and the Ghost Dance: A Sourcebook* (Carson City, NV: Grace Dangberg, 1990). Mooney interviewed Wovoka; Hittman interviewed people from Wovoka's family and community.

32. James Mooney quoted in Hoxie, 702.

8

DAILY LIFE IN THE PACIFIC NORTHWEST

The Pacific Northwest encompasses two contiguous culture areas: the Northwest Coast and the Plateau. The Northwest Coast stretches 1,500 miles, from Alaska down through British Columbia and western Washington to the southern border of Oregon, in a long but narrow strip of land that averages 100 miles in width, bounded on the east by the Cascade Mountains. The Plateau region lies between the Cascades and the Rocky Mountains, lower than the mountains but higher than the Columbia and Frasier River basins that define its particular character. This includes the inland parts of British Columbia, most of Washington state, and portions of Oregon and Idaho.

The indigenous peoples of both of these regions depended heavily on fish, and especially salmon, for protein. Both supplemented their diet with hunting, gathering, and berry-picking, with little or no need for agriculture in this land of plentiful resources. Riverine highways formed by the Columbia and Frasier Rivers and their tributaries made it possible for people to trade. People met each other at places such as the Dalles, an important fishing area on the lower Columbia River. Following the Columbia, one could travel inland almost due east from the Pacific Ocean before turning north, into the Plateau.

In the early eighteenth century a new influence entered the Plateau from the Great Plains to the east. The Kutenai, Flatheads, Nez Percé, and Yakimas, among others, adapted the use of horses and expanded their hunting into Montana and Wyoming for buffalo. When the Lewis and Clark expedition came to the area in 1805, the easternmost people of the Plateau looked like people from the Great Plains, with buckskin clothing, hide-covered tipis, and feathered headdresses. The connection between the riders of the eastern Plateau and the salmon-and-canoe people to the west was not readily apparent to the members of the expedition.[1] This is a classic example of the changes in daily life that took place in Native North America from the early period of European and American contact to 1900.

THE NORTHWEST COAST

The Northwest Coast encompasses radically different ecosystems, from ice and snow to deep forest to broad grasslands and stark volcanic foothills. Modern maps divide this culture area into geopolitical entities that make little sense from an indigenous perspective. The region begins with the Tlingit people in Alaska, which is part of the United States. It continues south through the homeland of the Haida, Tsimshians, Kwakiutl, and Nootka in British Columbia. The Puget Sound spans the U.S.-Canadian border. On its shores, small but distinct Lushootseed groups, also known as Coast Salish, enjoyed the bounty of fish and shellfish from its sheltered waters. The Lushootseed include Klallam, Lummi, Puyallup, Shohomish, and Tulalip peoples. Further south, the Washington-Oregon coast supported the Makah, Quinault, Chinook, Tillamook, Coos, and others.

The peoples of the Pacific Northwest are, and were, as diverse as one might expect. Aboriginal people spoke at least 45 different languages representing nine language families, including Athabaskan (Na-Dene), Tsimshian, Wakashan, Chimakuan, Salishan, and Penutian. The Tlingit and Haida languages are isolates, meaning that there are no related languages in another part of the world.[2] In the 1950s William Shelton, a Snohomish chief, related the following oral tradition about how this diversity came to be, and how people worked together despite the language barriers. The Snohomish and other people in the Puget Sound area say that the world was made by a male Creator, sometimes called the Changer or Transformer.

Together We Can Lift the Sky

When Changer made the world, he started in the east. Slowly, he moved west, creating the land and its people. He gave each group of people a different language. When he reached the Puget Sound, he liked it so much that he decided to stop there. He still had many languages left, so he scattered them up and down the coast.

The people could not talk to each other, with so many languages, but among themselves they complained about how Changer made the world. Their biggest complaint was that the sky was too low. Some people bumped their heads on it. Others crossed into the Sky World by climbing tall trees, even though it was forbidden for them to go there. Finally, the wisest men of all the tribes met to discuss the problem. They thought that if they all worked together, they could push the sky higher, but they were unsure of how to go about it. One man said it could be done if all the people and birds and animals worked together and pushed at the same time. Another man objected. He pointed out that they all lived in different places and their people spoke different languages. How would they be able to coordinate their efforts and push at the same time? They talked and talked, looking for a solution. Finally one man suggested that they use a signal. At the right time, someone would shout "Ya-hoh!" This meant "Lift together!" in all of their languages.

The wise men sent messages to tell everyone to get ready. They prepared poles made from the giant fir tree that they could use to push up the sky. On the appointed day, they were ready—people, animals, and birds. The wise men shouted, "Ya-hoh!" Everyone pushed at the same time, and the sky rose up a few inches. They did it again, and again, until the sky was as high as it is today. That is how they worked together to lift the sky.[3]

The oldest signs of human occupation in the Northwest Coast date back eight to ten thousand years. The archae- **Ancient History** ological record is not as helpful as it might be because the people of this region did not make pottery. Pottery is one of the most important artifacts for archaeologists because it does not decay. The main artifact from this period is flaked stone, that is, stone shaped by a labor-intensive process of striking one stone with another to cause pieces to flake off. It took great skills to shape stones in this way.[4]

By about 3,000 years ago, people on the Northwest Coast lived in a seasonal round of fishing, hunting, and gathering that has similarities to how their descendants lived at the time of European contact. In the northern parts of the territory, new features preserved in the archaeo-logical record include bark mats, poles, increasingly complex tools, and evidence of seasonal site occupation. People ate fish but also hunted land mammals. The inhabitants of present-day British Columbia left behind large shell middens, which indicates that they visited the same place each year over a long period of time. This contradicts the common assumption that nomadic people wander at random. Larger villages based on a fishing economy appeared in the lower Columbia River Valley, near Portland, Oregon, at a slightly later date. The distinct ethnic groups documented by early European accounts date to about 700 years ago.[5]

The distinctive material culture of the Northwest Coast developed in a land of temper- **Daily Life in the Early** ate climate and abundant food resources that **Contact Era** gave people an unusual amount of leisure time in their daily lives. All along the coast, people enjoyed salmon, halibut, cod, shellfish, and sometimes whale meat. They gathered berries in season and hunted to add meat to their diet. It is estimated that about 200,000 people lived here before the arrival of Europeans. It is unusual for the population density to be so high in a culture that does not practice agriculture.[6] Each unique ecosystem in the Pacific Northwest offered particular types of food. These differences were evened out by social networks that shared and traded food in ritual ways. These exchanges took place between kin-based houses and clans, sometimes in more formal exchanges between communities.

Totem Poles

Just as the people of the Northeastern Woodlands made many things from birch bark and wood, the people of the Northwest Coast built their lives around giant red cedar trees. The most emblematic feature of Northwest Coast material life is the carved wooden logs that are commonly known as totem poles, although this word comes from a practice known among the Ojibwe people who lived far to the east, near the Great Lakes. Tlingit leaders commissioned skilled carvers to create these highly stylized works that used crests and other symbols to mark important deeds or events. They might be used to frame the doorway of a house, so that anyone going in or out would have to pass by it. They might also be used in burials, or erected in public places for all to see. New poles were raised with much feasting and gift-giving, and people told stories about the events depicted on them. Totem poles became increasingly elaborate after the introduction of metal tools from the European fur trade.

Weaving and Basketry

Women used a variety of plant fibers for weaving, from spruce roots to the inner bark of the cedar tree, to cat-tails, wool obtained from dogs and mountain goats, and even bird down. Using a method called twining, which involves twisting the fibers, women made baskets so tight that they could hold water, along with capes, hats, robes, and mats. Coast Salish women to the south extended their weaving activities to include full-sized looms, for which they spun wool.

Salmon

Salmon fishing took place from late spring and through the summer. There were five species of salmon to be caught: pink salmon, coho salmon, chum or dog salmon, chinook, and sockeye. Each had a different spawning season. In contrast to Atlantic salmon, which return to the same place year after year to spawn, the Pacific salmon only does it once, after which it dies. There are many rituals related to catching, eating, and preserving salmon. The first catch of the year was shared by everyone in the community, with each person taking just a small bite, as they thanked the salmon for returning. Large parties gathered for salmon fishing. Men used nets, traps, baskets, and spears to catch the salmon. Women and children processed the catch, slicing and cleaning the fish, then hanging it so that it could be preserved by smoking. This gendered division of labor gave both women and men an important role to play in feeding the family and community.

Whaling

The Makah developed a remarkable system of navigation that allowed them to travel far out to sea in giant cedar canoes. They began to hunt whales on the open ocean over 2,000 years ago, although they stopped about 1920 because there were too few whales left. Whale meat provided food, and the fat, or blubber, could be turned into oil that was an important part of the Makah diet. They also hunted other sea mammals such as seals, which provided food, oil, and waterproof skins, and sea otters, which were valued for their skin and teeth. Whales and other sea mammals were valued beyond food as part of Makah ritual and ceremonial life.

Ranked Society and Houses

Daily life in most Northwest Coast communities was shaped by a person's sex, social class, and family. Each person belonged to a "House," that is, an extended household. Membership was defined more by social bonds and obligations than biological kinship. Each House included people from three or four different social classes: nobles, commoners (ranked into an upper and lower group in some groups), and slaves, who were people captured in raids or acquired through trade. Given the extensive trading that took place along the length of the Northwest Coast, war captives from one place could end up as slaves far away.

Like the Iroquois longhouse, the House is a metaphor for both political and family organization. The physical arrangement of space reflects the social order and also reproduces it, as people were reminded of their place in life every time they entered. Among the Tlingit, for example, the physical house is a large rectangle built of cedar or spruce planks. The peaked roof is held up by four carved and decorated corner posts and a strong ridge beam. At its highest point, the house stood 14 feet tall, tapering down to 6 feet at the eaves. Inside, the space was larger than one might imagine from just looking at the outside. The sunken floors were dug out to create a lower-level platform, where people might sit and conduct the business of everyday life, and an upper level with sleeping compartments. Up to six families lived in each house, an average of 40 to 50 people in all. Ordinary goods and food were stored in the main part of the house, but items deemed to be sacred or House treasure were kept in a special storeroom to the rear, away from the main flow of traffic.

Each house had a separate area in the rear for the nobility. The commoners lived along the sides in the main part of the house. Each family had their own fire for heat and for cooking. Some claimed their place via kinship, and others earned a place through work. Their status, however, was markedly different from that of the slaves, mostly captives taken in war or the children of such captives, who slept near the door. The communal center space of the House had a large public hearth where meals were cooked for the nobles and for guests.

Among the Tlingit and other northern groups, each House also had its own crest. These crests functioned somewhat like a corporate logo, except that they included more than just a visual symbol. The House crest included its distinctive stories, names, songs, dances, carvings, masks, and regalia. It also included specific places, including graves; sites associated with specific resources such as fish, shellfish, berries, or game; and the House itself. Known crests include Raven, Owl, Whale, Sea Lion, Salmon, Frog, Sun, Moon, Wolf, Eagle, Bear, Orca, Shark, Halibut, and Thundercloud. Crests are often associated with stories about how they came to the House, which usually involves someone sacrificing themselves for the good of others.[7]

Settlement Patterns

Permanent villages were most heavily occupied during the winter months, when there might be over 500 inhabitants. Villages were laid out with rows of houses facing the water of a bay that sheltered the people from storms. The house extended beyond the building where people lived to encompass the surrounding area. It included work areas for drying and smoking fish and stretches of beach where House canoes were launched and stored. In warmer weather, people moved to smaller camps for seasonal fishing, hunting, and gathering. During that time, people relied on the dried salmon, berries, and other provisions that they had stored during the other months of the year, although they continued to eat fresh fish and meat when available.

Stories

Certain things made a House more than just a collection of people in a particular type of dwelling. Each House had its own unique stories. These stories include the full range of folklore and oral tradition, including sacred stories, historical events, and lessons about the land and its resources. They belonged to a House like other forms of property. Some stories could only be whispered to very near kin, and each house had its own stories that others were not supposed to tell. This is very different from the Euro-American belief that an anthropologist or other outsider can come into a community, "collect" stories, and publish them.

Religion and Ceremonial Life

Daily life on the Northwest Coast was shaped by the belief that human beings shared the world with spirit beings who could offer help and protection if asked properly, but who could also make trouble if offended. Religion and ceremony infused daily life in ways large and small, not just during the major ceremonial events. Shamans were people who acquired a reputation for supernatural power, which they often used to play tricks or to humiliate their rivals. (The generic word "shaman" fails to convey the diversity and specificity of ritual practitioners found across Native North America, but we use it here for lack of a better word.)[8]

Both boys and girls went through special rituals at puberty to find out if they had any special powers or guides. Some families believed that the power could be handed down to the youngest son. People could be born with power, or acquire it at puberty or through family rituals. On the Northwest Coast, power was a public affair. People with the same type of power were expected to join the appropriate cult, or secret society. On acquiring a special power, each person also learned a spirit song, most often given to them in their dream or vision. Novices danced while trained singers sang their spirit song. The dance was different for each person as they tried to convey what they had learned without naming their new powers directly, which was taboo. The medicine person had to guess it from their dancing. Spirit dancers were supposed to dress like the spirit they had seen in their visions. Typically, both men and woman wore a kind of crown on their heads made from shredded cedar bark, decorated with long streamers and sometimes also with small shells. Some wore small hemlock branches tied around their heads, necks, waists, arms, and legs. Others painted their bodies with red or black, or both, and glittering mica dust could be added for extra effect.

Spirit dances took place only during the winter, from November to March. They were held in large community buildings. They generally began in the evening and lasted until morning, with as many as 45 spirit dances taking place in a single night. The singers accompanied themselves by beating on boards with sticks, with elaborately carved wooden rattles, or with large wooden box drums, about five feet square by two feet deep, that hung from the ceiling. Spirit dances ended with a giveaway, that is, a dance in which goods were redistributed within the community.[9]

Potlatch

The potlatch is a public feast held to mark the life-cycle events such as naming, puberty (for girls), marriage, death, the building of a new house or clan totem pole, and the installation of new chiefs. A key characteristic of the potlatch is the ritual giving of gifts. These were also occasions to make amends or demonstrate one's own status. Headmen and people from the noble class invited others to come for a feast that lasted several days. Part of the ceremony included the ritual recitation of the host's genealogy and family stories. The gifts were given in a way that affirmed but also created social ranking. High-status guests received more and better gifts. To accept a gift was to accept the giver's estimation of your own rank in the society. Potlatches were most elaborate in the north among groups such as the Tlingit, Kwakiutl, and Tsimshian; however the basic practice is found throughout the Northwest Coast.

Raids and Warfare

Goods were also distributed by raiding other groups. Prior to European contact, warriors wore wooden helmets and armor. They fought with clubs, bows and arrows, daggers, and spears. The point of warfare was to gain glory, goods, and slaves, who were treated as trade goods in many cases. In some villages, up to a third of the people were slaves. Large-scale wars where many people died were rare. A Tlingit oral tradition says that one time, the fighting between two villages continued for so long that neither was able to store food for the winter. It soon became clear that this would be a problem. One of the leaders decided that they must make peace at any price. He walked into the open and offered to give himself up as a sacrifice if they would make peace so that everyone could gather food. The other side agreed. They killed him, then made peace, and both sides had food for the winter.[10]

Commerce

Intertribal trade was a characteristic of Northwest Coast societies. In the north, people traded with the interior Athabaskan Subarctic tribes. The Tlingit, for example, traveled upriver in wooden canoes, then traveled on foot over the Chilkat and Chilcoot mountain passes. Male slaves were expected to carry heavy pack baskets on their backs, supported with straps over the shoulders and across the forehead to ease the weight. Pack baskets could weigh over a hundred pounds per man. Women were expected to carry up to 65 pounds on their backs in similar fashion. Even the dogs were called into service, wearing saddlebags that weighed up to 25 pounds. Older women were valued on such expeditions because they were known to be good at bargaining and at keeping track of exchanges. The Tlingit bartered goods such as cedar baskets, fish oil, smoked fish, and dentalia shells, a special kind of shell found on Vancouver Island, for goods such as moose and caribou hides, snowshoes, and copper ore.[11]

In the south, which had less wealth in relation to the north, an extended trade network developed inland with the people of the Plateau. The Chinook developed a notable position as middlemen. Indeed, a special trade jargon developed called Chinook jargon, which is mixture of Chinookan, Salishan, and European words and expressions. Inland traders followed the Columbia River. One notable place for trade was near the Dalles, located at the point where the Columbia River halts its north-south journey on the central Plateau and takes a sharp turn to the west and the Pacific Ocean. This was a logical place for trading because it was also well-known as a place to catch fish. During the spawning runs, people gathered there from many different places. Indeed, archaeological evidence shows that a nearby site known as the Five Mile Rapids has been occupied continuously for at least 9,500 years.[12]

The first extended contact between Europeans and the Northwest Coast began in 1778, when Captain James Cook and his crew made a huge profit from selling sea otter pelts in China.[13] British, Russian, and Spanish fur traders soon became frequent visitors to these coasts. Russian fur traders established a fort at Sitka, Alaska, in 1799 that became the base of the Russian-America Fur Company. The British-owned Hudson's Bay Company established a fort on the Fraser River, in British Columbia. By the mid-nineteenth century, sea otters in the region had been overhunted and their population declined.

Encounters with Europeans and Americans

In the familiar story that accompanied the arrival of Europeans all across the continent, epidemic diseases swept along the coast and killed up to 80 percent of the people in some Northwest Coast villages. A different type of sickness appeared with the introduction of alcohol and venereal disease brought by the traders. A few chiefs became rich because they were able to monopolize the trade. However, they and their people tended to live close to the trading posts and forts where fur trade exchanges took place. Other people stayed away, and these early contacts had relatively little impact on their daily lives.

The trading societies of the Northwest Coast readily absorbed new items: iron and copper goods, trade cloth, blankets, and ready-made clothing, guns, and ornaments such as jewelry and glass beads. They traded in alcohol, especially rum. In exchange, they provided the Europeans with otter and beaver furs. They also developed a business supplying traders with meat and fish. Indeed, the European traders were more dependent on their Tlingit suppliers than vice-versa. A Russian report from 1860 makes this clear:

the Kolosh [Tlingit] cannot in any respect be regarded as dependent on the Company[,] rather it may be said that the Company's colonies on the American coast depend on them; for the Kolosh have only to begin to make a little noise to deprive the port and its entire population of all fresh food and even of the opportunity to show their faces a few yards outside the fortification.[14]

In other words, the Tlingit had the ability to starve the traders by refusing to deliver fresh food as well as the power to frighten them into staying inside the fort.

Groups such as the Tlingit and Kwakiutl, who lived nearest to European trading posts, became middlemen in the fur trade. In the Puget Sound region to the south, the Chinook dominated the trade. European traders soon learned that they were sharp traders who would walk away rather than accept an unsatisfactory deal.

Fur traders did not have the incentive to impose changes on indigenous peoples in the manner of missionaries and settlers in other places. They relied on Native people for food and other supplies that would only be forthcoming as long as their Native allies continued their traditional rounds of subsistence and production. However, there were unintended long-term effects from this period of contact. Previously, Native peoples produced only what they needed for themselves and for a stable amount of trade. Now there was more emphasis on producing what the traders needed. Male leaders became more visible when Europeans refused to treat women leaders as equals. In the wake of the epidemics, leaders sometimes died without leaving any clear successors. Commoners who previously had little chance of rising into the noble class sometimes took advantage of these circumstances to elevate themselves by using wealth accumulated from the new trade with Europeans. In some cases the potlatch was seen more as an opportunity to bribe one's way into power than as a demonstration of wealth, as in the older tradition.

By the late nineteenth century, a new aspect of trade emerged as artisans began to craft traditional goods for a new market. Euro-American tourists in search of authentic artifacts that could be displayed in their parlors at home eagerly purchased miniature totem poles, textiles decorated with shell beads, and other objects. The tourist trade brought a much-needed infusion of cash into an economy that was increasingly losing its independent basis for subsistence.

Other changes took place as European and American goods were adapted in ways that speak to the creativity and vitality of Native American cultures. A report from the Puget Sound area about 1878 describes a group of Klallam men and women performing a War Dance that they had borrowed from the Makah:

There were nearly twenty-five dancers, mostly men, who were dressed in American style except that they had no shoes and wore parti-colored shawls and blankets thrown around them. One man carried an open umbrella. Their heads were bound with head-bands of cedar bark or kerchiefs, in which were long white or gray feathers generally topped with red. Much feathery down was sprinkled over them. They had hollow wooden rattles and tails and wings of hawks or eagles in their hands. Their faces were blacked in various ways. With the music of the drum and singing they jumped around in a space twenty feet in diameter, throwing their arms wildly about, now up, now nearly to the ground, with movements quick as those of a cat in the midst of hot fire.[15]

Stereotyped views of Native American culture assume that all changes associated with Euro-American colonization involve culture loss. This example shows the transformations and creative borrowings that took

Display of Coast Salish arts and crafts, about 1880. The Coast Salish, like other indigenous peoples of the Northwest Pacific, developed rich forms of material culture and ritual life. By the late nineteenth century, the loss of much of their own land base made it necessary for them to use traditional skills to make "arts and crafts" for sale to tourists. From Denver Public Library, Western History Collection.

place as people kept their ceremonies and customs relevant to a changing world.

THE PLATEAU

The Plateau area includes mountain forests, streams, valleys, and canyons, which provide abundant resources for human life, as well as volcanic wastelands. The region takes its shape from three rivers: the Fraser River, which comes down through British Columbia, the Columbia River, which connects the inland parts of the Plateau to the Pacific coast, and the Snake River, which branches off from the Columbia in the center of the Plateau and curves its way south and east toward the Continental Divide and the Great Plains. The Plateau includes the eastern parts of Washington and Oregon, a small section of northeastern California, northern Idaho, western Montana, and, to the north, part of British Columbia.

The northern Plateau is an area of forests and moderate rainfall. The southern Plateau, sometimes called the Columbia Plateau, is semi-arid and reaches high temperatures in summer. The winters are harsh and extremely cold.

The two main language families represented in the Plateau are Salishan and Sahaptian. Salishan-speaking peoples include the Shuswap in the north and the Kalispel, Coeur d'Alene, Flathead, Colville, Okanogan, and Spokane peoples of the upper Columbia River basin. Sahaptian languages are spoken by the Yakima, Klickitat, Umatilla, Wallawalla, and Nez Percé people of the middle Columbia River basin and the lower Snake River. Sahaptian is a branch of the Penutian language family. It is related to the language spoken by the Klamath and Modoc of south-central Oregon, as well as to the Maidu and Wintu language of northern California. The Kutenai in the north speak a language isolate, a unique but distinctly Algonkian language. On the lower Columbia River, inland from the Puget Sound, the Cowlitz speak a Chinookan language.[16]

Ancient History Human beings have lived in parts of the Plateau region for over 11,000 years. It is believed that people traveled south from Alaska who spoke Macro-Penutian, that is, a language ancestral to Penutian and Uto-aztecan. This period is identified as the Old Cordilleran culture. People lived by hunting, fishing, and gathering. Old Cordilleran culture is characterized by a particular type of spear point that is double-pointed and leaf-shaped. Spear points of this type and other objects that resemble Old Cordilleran material culture have been found in the Great Basin, southern California, Mexico, and parts of South America. Old Cordilleran objects have also been found in the inland parts of the Northwest culture area that date back 7,500 to 9,500 years. Archaeologists trace the movement of these early people east across the Plateau and into present-day Idaho.

Approximately 7,000 to 8,000 years ago, after the glaciers receded, elements of Desert culture became dominant in the southern part of the plateau region. Desert culture is typified by the use of milling stones to grind grain and the use of baskets. Another important climate shift took place about 4,500 years ago, creating the conditions in which the regional differences we know today appeared.

Newcomers identified as the Northern Forest culture spread out across the central plateau about 3,000 years ago. This culture is characterized by more fishing and less hunting, and more settlement along the major rivers. The people are likely ancestral to the Salishan people of today. They introduced new technology such as techniques for grinding and polishing stone, which enabled them to make beautiful stone pipes and effigies, as well as techniques for working copper. Over time they intermarried and merged with other groups to form the beginnings of Plateau culture. With better tools and techniques, they were able to make better use of food resources, including fish, roots, and small game hunting, and their numbers increased. With more settled communities, local variations in culture and language emerged.

In the fifth century A.D., some 1,500 years ago, new culture influences entered the Plateau region as trade increased with the peoples of the Northwest Coast. By about 1000 A.D. the social organization of Plateau societies had become increasingly sophisticated. Other new influences came from the Great Plains, especially in the eastern parts of the Plateau.

Coyote is a trickster, a powerful being who cannot resist a good joke. Many stories are told about him in the Plateau. In the early days of the world, there were not too many human beings yet. One of the few man-like beings was Coyote. When people tell stories about Coyote, they are mostly stories about what not to do. Coyote was greedy, stupid, and proud. He was also wise. He got into trouble because he would hear about something new and go dashing off without taking time to think or plan. One day he heard about five sisters who lived at the mouth of a big river. They had a fish trap full of wonderful fish, called salmon. In those days, these were the only salmon in the world. Every day, they ate a salmon, then threw its bones back into the water and the salmon came back to life. To add variety, they went out every morning along the shore like shore birds, plucking fresh greens, digging up roots, and picking berries. To Coyote, the combination of beautiful women and food was irresistible. People warned him that the sisters were selfish and would not share with anyone, but he went anyway to see for himself.

Coyote Releases the Salmon

As he neared the place where the sisters lived, he could feel that strangers were unwelcome. He decided to turn himself into a baby and appeal to the maternal instincts of the sisters. Coyote turned himself into a baby in a cradleboard. The cradleboard was made of wood, and it floated on the river while protecting the baby. When one of the sisters went to the trap to get a salmon, he cried until he was red in the face. The woman heard him and brought him home. The other sisters fussed over him. Only the youngest sister was suspicious. She pointed out that the baby's eyes were the eyes of someone devious . . . like Coyote. The others ignored her. They were having too much fun cuddling the baby.

One of the women noticed that the baby had teeth, which surprised them. The baby must be older than it looked. Instead of feeding it broth, they fed it bits of cooked salmon. Coyote enjoyed it thoroughly. His eyes got big and he gurgled with delight. The women were enchanted. The next morning, they took care of the baby again and went out to gather food as usual. Coyote thought about starting his work right away but he was lazy and decided to take a nap. The sisters came home for lunch and went out again. Then Coyote got busy.

For the next 10 days, Coyote worked at making the tools he would need to dismantle the trap: five stone bowls and five picks, or pry bars. Every day when the sisters came home, they played with the baby and took care of it, feeding it salmon and changing its diapers. The youngest sister continued to be suspicious. She noticed that the baby was developing muscles. The next day, she lingered while her sisters went off as usual. She saw a man who looked like Coyote trying to destroy their trap and free the salmon. She yelled, and her sisters returned. They took turns attacking Coyote with their digging sticks while he worked frantically to pry open the trap. Coyote protected his head with one of the stone bowls he had made earlier, but each time the bowl eventually shattered before their fury. He used the picks he had made earlier to pry open the trap, but each time the pick shattered before he succeeded. It was a race. Finally he managed to pry open the trap just as the youngest sister shattered the last of the five bowls. The trap fell apart and the salmon swam away. Coyote left, and told the salmon to follow him upstream.[17]

After that, the salmon came every year. In recent times concrete dams on the Columbia River prevent the salmon from going upstream as it used to. Some people hope that Coyote will return to break up those dams. His curiosity gets him in to trouble, but he also does good in the world.

Daily Life in the Early Contact Era

The people of the Plateau lived in small semi-permanent fishing villages on major streams. Each village was autonomous with its own leaders, although sometimes multiple villages formed a band. Leadership was based on ability rather than heredity and chiefs could be either male or female. Both war chiefs and peace chiefs led by example and persuasion rather than force of authority. With little competition for resources, warfare consisted mainly of raiding parties launched to avenge a grievance or against outsiders. Western Plateau culture shows the influence of contact with the Northwest Coast. People on the eastern Plateau incorporated elements of Plains culture, especially after the introduction of horses after 1700.

Dwellings

During the winter, people lived in so-called winter villages located in warm valleys along the inland waterways, although these villages were sometimes occupied year-round. The circular houses with earthen roofs known as pit houses were dug about five feet deep into the ground, measuring 10 to 16 feet in diameter. The roofs could be either flat or domed. People entered the house through the roof. Sometimes larger houses were built in a rectangular shape measuring up to 100 feet in length and large enough to accommodate two to eight families. Food was stored in pits or placed on wooden platforms. Sleeping quarters were placed along the outer walls with the fire pit or family hearth in the center. In warmer weather, families lived in tipis, mobile dwellings framed with poles and covered with mats woven from rushes or bark. When it came time to move, the poles were left behind and only the outer coverings were taken to the new location.

Subsistence

The yearly cycle of seasonal subsistence was dominated by the annual salmon runs, when people gathered at the falls of the major rivers and their tributaries. Indeed, the central place of salmon in Plateau life is one of the characteristics that link it to the people of the Northwest Coast and make them distinct from the peoples of the Great Basin, with whom they otherwise have much in common. Five kinds of salmon came up the river from the Pacific Ocean and into the interior of the Plateau from late spring through the summer months. Salmon was eaten fresh in season. It was stored for later consumption by slicing it up and drying it on specially made racks, or dried and pounded into meal. Other fish included sturgeon and eels. The diet of salmon was supplemented with deer, elk, antelope, mountain sheep, and bear, as well as small game such as rabbits and squirrels. Women gathered roots such as camas and bitterroot that could be cooked in earth ovens and pounded into a flour that stored well. Berries and other greens added important variety both in terms of nutrition and taste.

Women of the Plateau were skilled at weaving. They used grass, twined Indian hemp, sagebrush, and willow   **Material Life** bark to make ropes, baskets, hats, bedding, fishing nets, and nets used for hunting rabbits. Tule, a type of rush, was woven into mats that were used to cover floors and the outside of houses. Tule mats were also used as shrouds for the dead. Some basket were woven so tightly that they could be used as cups or as containers for carrying water. They were even used as cooking vessels. Heated stones were dropped into a basket full of water or stew ingredients until the water boiled. More stones would be added until the stew was done.

Men hunted mainly with the bow and arrow, although they also used spears. In combat, they struck their enemies with war clubs and protected themselves with wooden armor. The most important tool for women was the digging stick, sometimes tipped with hard material from antlers. Digging sticks were especially useful in digging up camas and other roots. For grinding, they used pestles made from basalt or granite, and other tools from bone.

The western parts of the Plateau show the influence of extended contact with the peoples of the Northwest Coast. This includes the practice of flattening the forehead of infants. People who practiced this custom viewed the resulting pointed head as an attractive trait. Ironically, the inland Salish, the one group that did not practice this custom, were called "Flatheads" by their neighbors. This term was most likely meant in a derogatory way because their heads were flat and not pointed. Other characteristic traits of the people of the western Plateau include pierced noses, dressing in clothing made from shredded bark, and the use of wooden armor in warfare, as well as the style and shape of their large canoes. The people of the eastern Plateau show the influence of Plains culture, especially after about 1700 when they adopted the use of horses. This influence began first with the Flatheads (Salish) and Kutenai, then spread to the Cayuse, Nez Percé, and Yakima.

A huge regional network connected the peoples of the Plateau and the Northwest Coast. The largest intertribal trading center   **Trade** was at the head of the Columbia Gorge near the Dalles, where the ready availability of fresh salmon allowed thousands of people to gather for trading fairs. Plateau people traded salmon that had been dried, pounded into meal, and stored in bags made from salmon skin and cattails. They acquired dentalium and other shells from the Pacific coast, obsidian, baskets, meat, clothing, slaves, and later horses. Trade fairs were key arenas of culture exchange.

Social and Political Life   In contrast to the emphasis on rank on the Northwest Coast, Plateau society was relatively egalitarian with a strong ethic of sharing and reciprocal obligation.

Important ties were defined by kinship. Trade established social relations, as did intermarriage. Since people rarely married within their own villages, the people of the Plateau were widely interconnected through marriage ties. These networks lasted even after the death of a spouse because the survivor was encouraged to marry his or her deceased partner's sibling. Leaders could have more than one wife, giving them two important assets: extended kin ties, and greater access to the products of women's labor such as preserved food and clothing, which were essential for upholding the chiefly obligation to show hospitality to others. In the gendered division of labor on the Plateau, women gathered plants, processed and prepared food, and had the primary responsibility for young children. Men provided meat and fish and played a greater role than women in politics, diplomacy, and warfare.

Religion and Ceremonies   Human beings shared their world on the Plateau with other, nonhuman beings, including animals, plants, stars, the wind, and physical objects such as stones or mountains. Men and women had personal relationships with their guardian spirit helpers. These nonhuman beings were not gods, nor did people "serve" them. Rather, people said prayers to establish good relations with guardian spirits, following established protocol that dictated the form for polite relationships, to ask for help and guidance in times of need.

At puberty, boys and girls made a vision quest to seek their guardian spirit, which might be an animal or a natural force such as the thunder. Their guardian spirits taught them a song and shared some of their power. Men or women with unusually powerful spirit guardians became noted healers. People showed respect to their guardian spirits during the Winter Spirit Dance, a great feast that lasted for several days.

Horses on the Plateau   Horses were introduced through contact with Shoshone people to the south about 1730. The Plateau had rich natural grasses that could support large herds of horses, and the easternmost peoples quickly incorporated horses into their daily lives. These groups had hunted buffalo on the plains prior to this, but the arrival of horses allowed an unprecedented expansion of these activities. Now larger groups could travel to Montana and Wyoming on a regular basis, where they sometimes stayed for up to two years. They adopted elements of Plains culture that include leggings (which protected the legs on horseback), tipis covered in hide, parfleches, and feathered headdresses. The Cayuse became so wealthy from their herds of horses during this period that they stopped fishing altogether. Instead, they traded buffalo for fish. During this period the autonomous village was patterned into a more centralized political organization that the Euro-American newcomer called tribes, although the term and concept are not indigenous to North America. Warfare and raiding became increasingly important to gain material goods and slaves but also as a way for men to demonstrate bravery and gain honor.

The earliest written records for the inland peoples of the Plateau begin in 1805 with the arrival of the Lewis and Clark expedition, sent to map the new American West by President Thomas Jefferson. The people they met on the eastern Plateau were not the timeless, unchanging Indians of popular stereotype. Instead, the distinctiveness and power of their way of life are a remarkable

Lewis and Clark and a New Era on the Plateau

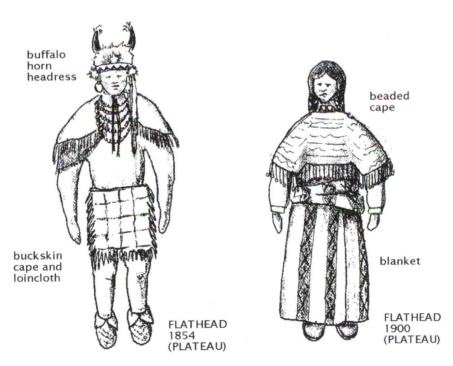

buffalo horn headress

beaded cape

buckskin cape and loincloth

blanket

FLATHEAD 1854 (PLATEAU)

FLATHEAD 1900 (PLATEAU)

The Interior Salish or Flatheads of the eastern Plateau region made extensive use of deer and buffalo hides in their material life and rode horses like their neighbors on the Great Plains to the east. From Tara Prindle / nativetech.org.

testament to the resiliency of indigenous lifeways, considering that in recent generations they had experienced epidemic diseases that killed up to 90 percent of the population, as well as the introduction of horses, which transformed daily life.

On September 4, 1805, William Clark described a meeting with the Flatheads, whom he referred to as the Tushepau nation. There were

33 Lodges with about 80 men, 400 Total, and at least 500 Horses, these people rec[ei]ved us friendly, threw white robes over our Sholders & Smoked in the pipes of peace, we Encamped with them & found them friendly.[18]

As happened elsewhere across North America, trade goods arrived in Native communities long before Euro-American peoples. Clark noted that the Flathead warriors used guns as well as bows and arrows.[19]

The Lewis and Clark expedition opened the way for the United States to assert its claim to what was then called the Oregon Territory, which stretched from the Rocky Mountains to the Pacific and included present-day British Columbia. In their wake, a wave of Euro-American invasion spread across the Plateau. First came the fur traders: American, but also British and Canadian. The fur trade period lasted only to the 1840s, barely a generation, but "progress" was on their heels in the shape of Euro-American settlers in search of a better life than they had in the East.[20] Missionaries also arrived, in some cases at the request of Native leaders, who wanted to learn more about the white man's religion.

STRATEGIES FOR SURVIVAL

In 1843 the first American emigrants began to follow the Oregon Trail. As more and more non-Native people moved into the region, the indigenous people began to suffer new ills, including race-based prejudice, outright violence, and the well-meaning efforts of reformers to promote assimilation. It became extremely difficult to pursue seasonal modes of subsistence in this new world. Along the Pacific coast, some people turned to working in canneries and commercial fisheries that had been built on their lands, because they needed money to support their families.[21]

The United States signed a series of treaties with the people of the Northwest Coast and the Plateau in the 1850s. In these treaties, the United States agreed to provide a monetary payment to be held in trust for the benefit of the tribes, since as Indians they were viewed as being unable to manage their own money. The United States agreed to provide education and health care. Certain lands were set aside or reserved for the original inhabitants. Certain rights were also reserved, such as the right to fish for salmon and whales and other aboriginal subsistence activities. Each treaty pushed the people onto smaller and smaller pieces of land. It also brought the federal government into their daily lives, since Indian agents were appointed to oversee life on the reservations. Some of the agents were fair and honest men, but too many were corrupt. One thing that the people kept was the right to fish for salmon and whales to feed themselves and their families. However, these treaties were not always respected. The Nez Percé homeland once constituted 13 million acres of land. Today, thanks to broken treaties and legal maneuvers, they hold 80 thousand acres, a mere fraction of their original lands.

About 1860, a Wanapum man named Smoholla had a vision that the end of the world was coming, and that at that time, all of their ancestors would be resurrected. **Smoholla: Revitalizing Ancient Traditions** Like other prophets of revitalization, Smoholla urged his followers to abandon the ways of the white man, especially farming and reservation life. The way to salvation, he preached, was to return to traditional beliefs and practices, including the spirit songs and dances that honored their guardian spirits. His message was a direct response to the destruction of indigenous lifeways. Smoholla wanted his people to survive not just in body but in spirit, as Indian people. Although he preached a return to tradition, his message, like that of Handsome Lake, Neolin, Wovoka, and other prophets, incorporated elements of Christian belief. The *Wáashat* religion, also known as the Dreamer, Seven Drums, or Longhouse religion, is founded on Smoholla's vision. It spread rapidly across the Plateau and continues to this day.[22]

Officials in the United States and Canada prohibited the potlatch in the late nineteenth century. In part, they argued that it was a bar- **Suppressing the Potlatch** baric practice that prevented the Tlingit and other Northwest Coastal groups from assimilating into the modern world, by which they meant a society based on the economic system of capitalism. It made no sense to them that people would save up all their lives to accumulate wealth and then give it away or destroy it to enhance their own social prestige. The Tlingit and others found ways to continue some of this tradition, but due to the public nature of the potlatch, it was hard to conduct this ceremony in secret. The suppression of potlatches affected the broad network of community and intertribal bonds that it had supported.

The story of Chief Seattle, for whom the city of Seattle, Washington, was named, is a compelling narrative of a **Chief Seattle** brave and resourceful leader who envisioned a world in which his people, the Lushootseed of the Puget Sound region, would partner with the American newcomers in creating a new world. Seattle was born around 1786 on an island in Puget Sound to parents from two different Lushootseed groups. His father, Schewable, was Suquamish. His mother, Sholitza, was Duwamish. Later in life, Seattle said that he was present as a young child when British Captain George Vancouver anchored the *H.M.S. Discovery* off Bainbridge Island in 1792. He never forgot the excitement of that event, and the sense that these newcomers brought new power and abilities with them.

As a young man, Seattle participated in numerous raids against neighboring groups such as the Cowichans of Vancouver Island, the S'Klallam on the north shore of the Olympic Peninsula, and others on the upper Snoqualimie River. This was a time of turmoil and prophecy for his people as they struggled to adapt into a world where epidemics had greatly reduced their numbers, and as everyone scrambled for a piece of the new fur trade. Seattle was a big man with a commanding presence. By the 1830s, he was known as a wise leader and a formidable enemy.

Seattle's life took a major turn in the 1840s after the death of one of his sons, which affected him deeply. He became a Catholic and received baptism in 1848, probably from the Oblates of St. Mary Immaculate in Olympia. His children were also baptized and raised as Catholics. From this point forward, Seattle gave up war and worked to build better relations with the American settlers who were coming into the region in great numbers. He encouraged them to settle among his people with the expectation that they would develop good trade relations. He worked with American businessmen to establish fisheries in 1851 and 1852. The Americans who settled nearby named their community Seattle in his honor.

In 1855, Seattle was the first to sign his name to a treaty in which the United States purchased 2.5 million acres of land. The terms of the treaty were uneven, protecting some interests but not others, and in its wake the Americans spread out with an energy that many Lushootseed perceived as arrogance. When the signers sold part of their land, reserving everything else for themselves, they probably did not imagine that these lands would come to be "reservations." The difference is that the United States insisted that Native peoples had to remain within the boundaries of these lands. If they left in groups, they were considered to be hostile or in rebellion and U.S. soldiers were sent out to bring them back. When individuals left in search of a better life, they were viewed by the United States as having forfeited their status as Indians, joining the mainstream of American life.

The treaty was so controversial among the Lushootseed that they repudiated both the treaty and Seattle's leadership. This led to the conflict known as the Yakima War, which lasted from 1855 to 1857. Seattle continued to believe that the best hope for the future lay with the Americans as allies, and he apparently gave them intelligence that contributed to their eventual victory. His strategy worked to some extent. While Seattle's influence was insufficient to gain clemency for Leschi, a key leader in the Yakima War, he established good relations with Indian agents and businessmen that led among other things to the establishment of a sawmill town where Amerindians could work for fair wages in an environment where whiskey sellers and other predatory entrepreneurs were not allowed in.

Sadly, Seattle's vision of two peoples working together was never fulfilled. By 1865 the newly incorporated town of Seattle passed an ordinance that made it illegal for any Indians to live permanently within the city limits. Chief Seattle was forced to leave the place where he once invited the Americans to settle. He died in 1866.[23]

The great Nez Percé chief known as Chief Joseph was born in 1840 near the Grand Ronde River in northeastern   **Chief Joseph** Oregon. His birth name was Hin-mah-too-yah-lat-kekht, which means "Thunder Rolling in the Mountains." His parents were early converts to Christianity and his father took the name Joseph when he was baptized in 1839. Later, probably in the 1860s, Hin-mah-too-yah-lat-kekht received the same name. The two men were known as Old Joseph and Young Joseph to the American settlers who moved into the region.

The Nez Percé had maintained friendly relations with the Americans since their first meetings with the Lewis and Clark expedition in 1805. They even fought on the American side during the Yakima War of 1855–1857. Old Joseph signed the Treaty of Walla Walla with the United States in 1855 but expressed many reservations about the sincerity of the U.S. promises. By the 1860s, both Josephs had lost faith in Christianity and the prospect of good relations with the newcomers. They began to follow the Dreamer religion taught by the prophet Smohalla, who urged people to reject Euro-American ways and return to their own beliefs. Their worst fears bore fruit after gold was discovered on Nez Percé lands in 1860 and thousands of miners invaded their land, without any objection from U.S. officials. Instead, government commissioners forced a new treaty in 1863 that reduced the Nez Percé lands from 5,000 square miles to less than 600. This treaty split the Nez Percé into two factions. Those who supported the Lapwai Treaty were mostly Christians. Those who rejected the document that they called the "thief treaty," including Old Joseph, espoused the need to follow traditional beliefs. Old Joseph tore up his copy of the treaty as well as the Bible he had received in his youth. When Old Joseph died in 1871, he begged his son to remember that the land held his body. To sell the land would be to sell the bones of his mother and father.

In 1877 the U.S. army ordered that all of the nontreaty Nez Percé must confine themselves to the new reservation at Lapwai. Following an outbreak of violent resistance, the Nez Percé decided that if they had to leave their homes in the Wallowa Valley, they would choose their own destination. Over a thousand men, women and children took as many of their belongings as they could carry and set out to walk over 1,700 miles to what they hoped would be a safe haven in Canada. Outlaws in their own land, they fled before the U.S. army, fighting several battles although only about one quarter of their party were fighting men. They were forced to surrender just 40 miles short of the border crossing to freedom. Chief Joseph became famous in eastern newspaper accounts as the leader and mastermind of this heroic, tragic journey. Recent scholarship shows that the primary strategist was a man named Looking Glass. Joseph played an important role, however. He was the one appointed to guard the women and children, the Nez Percé's hope for the future.

Chief Joseph never stopped working to help his people. In the aftermath of these events, the Nez Percé were forced to walk on another horrific journey, this time to prison at Fort Leavenworth in Oklahoma. Joseph launched a new type of campaign to win sympathy and clemency for his people, appealing to military officials, President Rutherford B. Hayes, and even giving an interview that appeared in the influential journal, the *North American Review.* Eventually 300 survivors were allowed to move back to the Northwest. Half went to Lapwai Reservation and Chief Joseph led the other half to the Colville Reservation in eastern Washington. In 1900, he had an opportunity to visit his father's grave in the Wallowa Valley. He found that it had been desecrated by robbers, and that a local white dentist was exhibiting Old Joseph's skull as a curiosity. Chief Joseph died in 1904.[24]

Christine Quintasket (Mourning Dove) The history of the people of the Plateau region, viewed from the perspective of the legal and geographic limits placed upon them by the United States, is a sad litany of loss. This is only part of the story. The losses and hardships were real, but as with all human beings living under terrible conditions, people still found ways to laugh, to reassure their children, and to make daily life seem as normal as possible under the circumstances. This quality is captured in Christine Quintasket's autobiography when she writes about her childhood. Quintasket was born on the Colville Reservation in eastern Washington state in the 1880s, a time when her people "were well into the cycle of history involving their readjustment in living conditions," yet "long enough ago to have known people how lived in the ancient way before everything started to change." Her father was Okanogan and her mother was Colville, both Salishan-speaking peoples. Under her pen name, Mourning Dove, she published two important works in her lifetime. *Cogwea* (1927) is a novel that counters prevailing stereotypes about "stoic Indians" with characters that experience a range of human emotion. *Coyote Stories,* published in 1933, is a collection of traditional Salishan Coyote stories that she modified for a non-Native audience by removing the elements that might be offensive or misunderstood.[25]

Quintasket describes the summer fishing at Kettle Falls, a prime fishing spot on the upper Columbia River, where five species of salmon came each year on their spawning runs up the river.

The Indians gathered at the falls every year to spear salmon and dry it for the winter. All the surrounding tribes were welcome at this summer resort of my Colville people. It was a beautiful place to camp, with cliffs overhanging the falls on the west side and trails leading to the water between the high grayish-white rock formations that so often glistened in the sunlight. On the east side were flat rock slabs much closer to the whirling pools, where campers could most easily get water. The falls passed on either side of a large central rock that created a smooth backwater behind it. The area near the falls was filled with mist, ribboned with many colors creating a faint rainbow on a summer evening. . . .

Tribes generally camped in specific areas, and Colville hospitality saw to it that no visitor ever left without a full load of dried salmon. The Colville camped on both sides of the falls to oversee the fishing. The east side encampment included Kalispel, Spokan, Coeur d'Alene, and Flathead, while the west side were the Okanogan, Sanpoil, Squant, and Wenatchi.[26]

Quintasket describes what it was like to see the men and women go about their work. The men built large scaffolds out of logs that extended over the falls, making it easier to spear or net the salmon. They also placed large baskets woven from red willow in strategic locations to catch any salmon that fell back as it failed to leap over the falls. The women worked steadily along the banks of the river, cutting up salmon and laying it out to dry. Reflecting the communal nature of this endeavor, the catch was distributed by a man known as the Salmon Tyee, or divider, who allocated fish according to the size and needs of each family. Quintasket notes, "It was equally divided among all, both workers and visitors, regardless of how much labor they had put in, every day at noon and dusk. Everyone got an equal share so that that fish would not think humans were being stingy or selfish and so refuse to return."[27]

In the evening, Quintasket and her mother went visiting among the other camps. In one, she smelled "a terrible odor" that she later learned was an herb used to ward off the sickness or death caused by a shaman. The evenings were a time for bonfires, games, and lively singing. People gambled for stakes that included piles of robes, blankets, and other goods, including cash. These games helped to redistribute wealth. There were athletic competitions that involved running, jumping, and archery. On Sundays, however, they rested, and many people went to church at the Goodwin mission, about ten miles away. Reflecting the intertribal nature of the gathering at Kettle Falls, people prayed and sang hymns in different languages. After the service, women and men left by separate doors and gathered at the front of the church, where the chiefs present spoke a few words from the steps to reinforce the priest's words.[28]

Although her life presented many hardships and challenges, Christine Quintasket's parents raised her to value the old ways and yet look to the future. She wrote, "I was always a dreamer about my future and that of my people. . . . Whatever I dreamed or imagined, I always bore in mind the teachings of my parents that truthfulness and honesty must be the objective in future life. This was the measure of a successful person. It was the foundation of all my teachings as a child."[29]

NOTES

1. Alvin M. Josephy Jr., *The Indian Heritage of America* (Boston: Houghton Mifflin, 1968, 1991), 73–74, 131–37.

2. Nancy Bonvillain, *Native Nations: Cultures and Histories of Native North America* (Upper Saddle River, NJ: Prentice Hall, 2001), 445.

3. This story is adapted from Richard Erdoes and Alfonso Ortiz, eds., *American Indian Myths and Legends* (New York: Pantheon Books, 1984), 95–97.

4. Barry A. Pritzker, *Native American Encyclopedia: History, Culture and Peoples* (New York: Oxford University Press, 2000), 162–63.

5. Pritzker, 162–63.

6. Bonvillain, 445.

7. Jay Miller, "Alaskan Tlingit and Tsimshian," page 2, essay included in *Native Americans of the Pacific Northwest*, http://lcweb2.loc.gov/ammem/award98/wauhtml/aipnhome.html. *Native Americans of the Pacific Northwest* is a Web-based resource developed by the University of Washington that includes photographs, documents, and scholarly essays. It is now part of the Library of Congress American Memory Web site.

8. Josephy, 77.

9. Reginald Laubin and Gladys Laubin, *Indian Dances of North America: Their Importance to Indian Life*, Civilization of the American Indian Series (Norman: University of Oklahoma Press, 1989 [1977]), 397–400.

10. Josephy, 76–77.

11. Miller, "Alaskan Tlingit and Tsimshian."

12. Josephy, 79, 133.

13. Pritzker, 164.

14. Quoted in Bonvillain, 455.

15. Quoted in Laubin and Laubin, 404.

16. Josephy, 131–32.

17. Jay Miller, "Salmon, the Lifegiving Gift," *Native Americans of the Pacific Northwest*, 4.

18. Bernard DeVoto, ed., *The Journals of Lewis and Clark* (Boston: Houghton Mifflin/Marine, 1953, 1997), 233.

19. DeVoto, 236.

20. Josephy, 136–37.

21. Pritzker, 165.

22. Pritzker, 251.

23. David M. Buerge, "Chief Seattle and Chief Joseph: From Indians to Icons," *Native Americans of the Pacific Northwest*, 1–2.

24. Buerge, 3.

25. Jay Miller, "Introduction," in *Mourning Dove: A Salishan Autobiography*, ed. Jay Miller (Lincoln: University of Nebraska Press, 1990), xix–xvi. Quotations from page 3.

26. Miller, ed., *Mourning Dove*, 99–100.

27. Quotation from Miller, ed., *Mourning Dove*, 101.

28. Miller, ed., *Mourning Dove*, 105–7.

29. Miller, ed., *Mourning Dove*, 32–33.

9

DAILY LIFE ON THE GREAT PLAINS

Although colonization of Native peoples and white settlement of indigenous lands had occurred in many different parts of the country, the story of the taking of the Great Plains has come to occupy a special place in American history, popular imagination, and myth. Conventional histories of the region that describe the story of how white Americans "won the West" mark the travels and feats of white explorers, fur traders, and settler pioneers in their wagon trains. They also commemorate the cattle drives, the cowboys, and the building of the transcontinental railroads. These developments were and are often celebrated as part of fulfilling America's Manifest Destiny—a concept that originated in the 1840s and implied that it was the providence of Anglo-Americans to conquer the North American landmass and to spread their institutions and civilization. Yet, the Native peoples of the Great Plains still too often play a marginal role in these conventional histories popularized by Wild West series and Hollywood films. In these stories, Native Americans are time and again portrayed as either victims or as the "savage" opponents of national expansion. Yet, often little attention is given to how historic developments influenced the daily lives of Native Americans, and how, ultimately, the region's indigenous peoples lost the West they once had known.

At the same time, it is the Great Plains Indian that has come to represent the popular image of the Native American for many non-Indians in the United States and all around the world. The often stereotypical representation of a Native American with a feathered headdress, on the back of a painted pony, holding a bow and arrow or a rifle, has become a common picture that prevails in the minds of many. Still, it is important to remember that the Native world of the Great Plains, as that of other regions, was one of many Amerindian nations. As in other areas, Native American peoples of the Plains were connected with some of their neighbors through various kin connections. With others they engaged in long-standing rivalries. The Plains was a region of diverse cultures, ways of subsistence, and social organization that shaped Native American daily life.

GREAT PLAINS CULTURE BEFORE AMERICAN EXPANSION

The Great Plains, the arid grasslands of North America that stretch eastward from the Rocky Mountains to the Missouri River and southward from Saskatchewan to Texas, were in flux long before Americans colonized the region. The landscape of the Plains is one of vast distances, large skies, few trees, little rain, and often strong winds. In the fifteenth and sixteenth centuries, many of the Native peoples that inhabited or eventually migrated to the region subsisted on farming. Groups like the Mandans, the Pawnees, the Omahas, the Hidatsas, and the Arikaras lived as semisedentary farmers in the fertile river valleys of the Great Plains, especially in the more agriculturally productive eastern parts. With the arrival of horses on the Great Plains, introduced to the region as a result of Spanish colonization in the Southwest, a dramatic transformation happened in the daily life of many Native Americans. Especially by the seventeenth and eighteenth centuries, a growing number of Native American groups came to embrace the horse as a tool to aid in the hunt for buffalo. This led some Great Plains Indians, like the Crows, to abandon agriculture, to switch to a less sedentary way of life, and to embrace the bison (buffalo) hunt as the main staple of their economic subsistence. Other buffalo hunters, like the Kiowas, the Blackfeet, the Lakotas, the Cheyenne, the Arapahos, and the Comanches were relatively recent arrivals on the Plains. They are believed to have moved to the region from outlying areas. Thus, the emergence of the Native nomadic buffalo hunter of the Great Plains, an image so engrained in the popular perceptions of Indians of North America, is a relatively recent historical development.

Great Plains Farmers Many Native American farmers of the Plains lived in villages of round and rectangular houses. On the southern Plains, some groups like the Wichita or the Hasinai lived in villages that consisted of beehive-shaped grass houses. To the north, Native farmers framed their homes with posts and for insulation covered them with earth. Their houses had a fireplace near the entrance, which was generally a short passageway, built somewhat higher than the interior living space. This maximized the circulation of air, while minimizing the loss of heat. Yet, this architectural makeup also gave the houses a dark and smoky character. Native earth-lodge farming settlements on the Great Plains were often fortified with stockades and ditches, and they were generally constructed on bluffs or terraces overlooking the fertile floodplains of the river. Here, farmers grew corn (maize), squash, beans, sunflowers, and a few other plants, which, once they were harvested, were stored in deep pits in the house floors. The farmers also supplemented their diets with bison meat (buffalo), which they obtained in often extensive hunts. During such hunting excursions for meat and skins, Great Plains farmers built smaller portable versions of their pole houses or hide tipis as accommodation. Archaeological evidence also suggests that the farming communities in the region were tied into long-distance trade networks with other parts of North America. Furthermore, they practiced elaborate rituals and ceremonies similar to the Sun Dance practiced by the buffalo hunters and discussed in more detail later in this chapter, which the farmers believed would aid in a favorable outcome in their agricultural as well as their hunting pursuits.[1]

Before the coming of horses, the farming peoples of the Plains were surrounded by smaller bands who hunted bison and other game on foot and gathered food as their main means of subsistence. Prior to, but also with the arrival of the horse, which led to a significant increase of buffalo hunting groups on the Plains, hunter-gatherers could on occasion raid their farming neighbors for resources. Such competition certainly led to rivalries. Yet, at the same time, nomadic hunters and semisedentary farmers also traded for skins, corn, and other resources and goods.

Horses led to a revolutionary transformation in the daily life of Native Americans on the Great **The Arrival of Horses** Plains. It is likely that Native groups on the southern Plains gradually obtained horses from the Spanish in the sixteenth or seventeenth centuries. Over the next decades and centuries, horses gradually spread from the southwestern Plains northward, as Native tribes carried out an active horse trade. Along with the horse, Great Plains Indians also diffused the knowledge of horsemanship, harnessing, the breaking in of wild horses, and proper care and handling of the animals. Thus, and especially by the eighteenth and nineteenth centuries, Native life in hunter-gatherer societies on the Great Plains came to be dominated by the horse.

The horse provided a high degree of mobility and an increased standard of living to hunter-gatherer societies. It enabled communities to travel for long distances. It also allowed them to change campsites more frequently and provided hunter-gatherers with better access to water and fuel. The horse could be used to transport young children and elderly persons. Horses could also pull Plains hunters' food rations, material goods, and poles, furs, and skins used for the tents or tipis, which, since the arrival of the horse, had increased in size and had become more comfortable. Thus, Native hunting communities accumulated more material goods than in the pre-horse days, and even horses themselves came to be seen as a sign of a community's, a family's, or an individual's wealth and status.

Plains People and the Buffalo

The coming of the horse also enabled Native hunters to become much more efficient in their pursuit of the buffalo. A skilled individual or a team of mounted hunters could pursue a band or herd of bison, focus in on the slower and weaker animals, and kill their prey either by bow and arrow, with a lance, or with a rifle. This provided a community with much needed food supplies. The pursuit of buffalo could also be more dramatic at times. Captain Benjamin Louis Eulalie de Bonneville, a European traveler observing a hunting party, wrote about one hunter:

One of the Indians attached to the party, finding himself on horseback in the midst of the buffaloes, without either rifle or bow and arrows, dashed after a fine cow that was passing close by him, and plunged his knife into her side with such luck and aim as to bring her to the ground.[2]

In such encounters, a hunter could prove his masculinity and his talent as a fighter and a provider for his community, skills that were highly valued and played a central role in Plains hunting societies.

Yet it was the speed and endurance of the horse that made a successful hunt possible. After the hunt was over, horses would often carry the meat

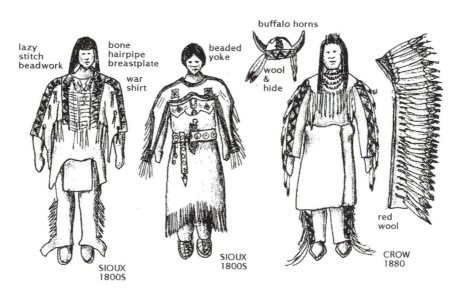

Plains clothing, nineteenth century. The long war bonnet made from eagle feathers, a staple of Hollywood westerns, looks good when a warrior is on horseback but would have dragged on the ground in traditional warfare, prior to the introduction of horses in the late sixteenth century. From Tara Prindle/nativetech.org.

to camp, a task also performed by women, especially at times of a successful chase, when horses were quickly loaded up. According to many scholars, the hunter-gatherer way of life, improved by the use of the horse, and
based on the subsistence on buffalo, led to a substantial increase in the
food supply and resulted in growing population numbers.

An old Assiniboine saying demonstrates the central role that the buffalo
played in subsistence.

The buffalo gives food from his flesh and clothing from his hide. The marrow,
sinew, bones, and the horns can be used by the people, so that a skilled woman
can make many different kinds of food and the family does not eat the same thing
each day. It is also with the man, who can make many things from the buffalo for
use in war, hunting, and pleasure. All these things the buffalo offers to the ones
who heed the talks of the old men and the old women who know that the lives of
the people and the growth of children depend on the buffalo.[3]

Whether it was the meat of the buffalo or the hide used to make tipis,
clothing, or decorations, most parts of the buffalo were utilized by the
Plains Indians. As the quote above suggests, women played a key role in
putting the buffalo to good use. They made a variety of soups and dishes
out of buffalo meat.

Even for everyday meals, women had to be prepared to feed visitors
and guests due to Plains Indians' commitment to sharing and hospitality.
Luther Standing Bear wrote for example that

[t]he good wife always kept plenty of food stored and cooked so that it could be
served at any moment. The thought was not only to meet the food requirements
of the family, but to be able to serve any one who came to the tipi, strangers or
relatives, children who came in from other tipis, or any old people whom children
might bring in.[4]

Women also used the buffalo skins not only to make tipis, but also to decorate and to improve the insulation of their homes. They also used the hide
to make garments, bags, robes, soles, blankets, moccasins, gloves, caps, and
scarves. Plains Indians turned buffalo bones into war clubs, shovels, knives,
and dice, and horns into spoons, ladles, and cups. Their pillows, ornaments,
medicine balls, and ropes were often made out of buffalo hair. Buffalo
stomachs made good water containers, and their contents were used as skin
ointments. Men also helped with the processing of the buffalo and other
domestic chores. They "cut down trees for the ponies and for wood, made
and repaired saddles, cut up meat conveniently for drying, and when there
was nothing else to be done, gladly amused the baby of the family."[5]

The Trade in Guns

Guns were another major factor in transform-
ing Native American daily life on the Great Plains.
The same trade networks used to distribute horses
were employed to exchange guns although generally in the opposite

direction. Whereas the horse trade originated from the Southwest, the gun trade originated in the Northeast. Whereas the Spanish are believed to have been the source of horses, European fur traders with contacts to the Atlantic seaboard colonies, and an interest to purchase buffalo and other animal skins and furs were the source of guns. But it is important to emphasize that much of the exchange in guns, horses, and other trade goods in the seventeenth, eighteenth and nineteenth centuries was run by Native American middlemen.

Competition on the Great Plains   Buffalo, a wealth of other resources, and later horses and guns made the Great Plains an increasingly attractive place for Native American communities. Thus, the Great Plains were a region in flux. In fact, groups like the Kiowas, the Blackfeet, the Lakotas, the Cheyenne, the Arapahos, the Comanches, and others are believed to have moved to the plains from outlying areas in the centuries before American colonization. These developments led to increasing competition among rival groups over the rich hunting territories and other resources, and spurred the emergence of what scholars have described as warrior cultures, which played a central role in the daily life of Great Plains hunting societies.

Thus, Plains Indian societies valued young men and warriors who occupied a special role in a community. "[W]hen they" were at home, they "were shown a good deal of attention by the women." The Lakota Indian Luther Standing Bear wrote that this "was but natural, as it was the hunters, scouts and warriors who bore the greatest dangers, and consequently were the recipients of much care and consideration. Young warriors bearing for the first time the hardship of life were specially considered by the women."[6] Warriors who returned from campaigns against enemies were also shown respect by their communities. Plenty-Coups, a Crow Indian, described his war party's reception after a successful horse raid against an Arapahoe settlement. "[W]e rode into our village singing of victory, and our chiefs . . . came out to meet us, singing Praise Songs. My heart rejoiced when I heard them speak my own name."[7]

Plains Indian societies had clear structures and rules about who was a warrior and what tasks he had to perform. A Cheyenne Indian named Wooden Leg wrote:

The warrior days of a Cheyenne man began at the age of about sixteen or seventeen, or sometimes a little earlier for such activities as were not very difficult or risky. They ended somewhere between thirty-five and forty, according to particular circumstances. The regular rule was, every man was classed as a warrior and expected to serve as such until he had a son old enough to take his place. Then the father retired from aggressive fighting and the son took up the weapons for that family. If a man came into early middle age without any son, he adopted one. If he had more than one son, he might allow the additional one or more to be adopted by another man who had none. By following this system, all of the offensive fighting was done by young men, mostly the unmarried young men.[8]

Great Plains Indian social codes also inhibited elder male members of society from partaking in unnecessary combat, as their experience, council, and advice was seen as an asset to a community. Wooden Leg wrote that if

a warrior's father or some other old person put himself unnecessarily forward in a battle he was likely to be criticised for his needless risk, and also the young warriors felt aggrieved at his taking from them whatever honors might be gained in the combat. In general, the young men were supposed to be more valuable as fighters and less valuable as wise counselors, while the older men were estimated in the opposite way. It was considered as being not right for an important older man to place himself as a target for the missiles for the enemy, if he could avoid such exposure. Even in a surprise attack upon us, it was expected the seniors should run away, if they could get away, while the more lively and supposedly more ambitious young men met the attack.[9]

In a world of rivalry and contest over natural resources, masculinity, fighting skills, and the devotion to the survival and prospering of one's community played a central role in Plains Indian daily life.

The habits of the buffalo and ecological cycles also influenced the religious life of the Native hunters of the **The Sun Dance** Great Plains. The Sun Dance, a ceremonial that drew hundreds and thousands of people together in large encampments, who all had to be fed, occurred in the summer at a time when the grasslands of the plains were lush, and when large bison herds gathered before the rut. Scheduling the Plains Indians' Sun Dance in the summer made the procurement of extensive stocks of meat easier, and enabled buffalo-hunting communities to feed large gatherings of people. Thus, and unlike the farming people in the region who had their stores of agricultural products and performed religious festivals and rituals year round, the ceremonial calendar of Plains Indian hunters depended on ecological cycles and the seasonal behaviors and patterns of the bison.

For Plains societies, summertime gatherings like the Sun Dance provided a highpoint in the year's social calendar, but the ceremonial also functioned as a means to unify and integrate members from various bands and groups who all desired to receive spiritual regeneration through their participation. During the ceremonial occurred much socializing, trading, visiting, games, and athletic competition, courting of potential spouses, diplomatic and political negotiating between allied groups, and adjudicating of disputes. Yet, the Sun Dance, and the spiritual renewal and unity it created among its participants remained at the center of the gathering. The Sun Dance had to be a large event because its spiritual leaders and participants were spread among a number of groups and bands that typically met at the ceremonial.

The Plains Indians believed that the purpose of the Sun Dance ceremonial was to foster the relationship between their community, their God, and the spiritual world. One anonymous Blackfoot Indian observed: "It has been our custom, during many years, to assemble once every summer for this festival, in honour of the Sun God. We fast and pray, that we may be able to lead good lives and to act more kindly towards each other." The staging of a Sun Dance demonstrated a community's gratitude and appreciation for the continuity of the cycle of life so important to the Plains Indians way of living. "We believe that the Sun God is all powerful, for every spring he makes the trees to bud and the grass to grow. We see these things with our own eyes, and, therefore, know that all life comes from him." Furthermore, the Sun Dance was seen as a universal ceremony in which people could participate without discrimination based on age, sex, and ethnic background.[10]

Sun Dance participants often underwent intense preparations to get ready for the ceremony, including for example in many cases meditation, vision quests, and instruction by religious leaders in their community. The ranks of Sun Dance participants were made up of people who took part in the ceremonial in fulfillment of a promise they had given in time of desperation or need such as in battle or during the sickness of a child, to obtain spiritual aid from the supreme power either for themselves or for another person, or who were seeking to prepare themselves for a higher spiritual position in their community. It was the contributions and donations of the participants and families that in large part supported the huge gatherings.

The Sun Dance itself was (and is) an intricate four-day ritual, although the social gatherings accompanying the ceremony often lasted for several more days. In final preparation, the community and its spiritual leaders gathered building materials for the ceremonial lodge such as leafy boughs to screen it, they made the required symbolic items, and they prepared and rehearsed for the ceremonial. The Sun Dance began with the felling of a selected tree and the dragging of its trunk to the encampment, which then, after the community gathered, was raised by dozens of men with ropes as the center pole of the lodge, an act accompanied by the prayers of a religious leader. Now, around this framework of smaller poles and ropes, assistants built the ceremonial lodge. Washakie, a Shoshone, observed that "[t]he sun dance hall … is constructed in a large circular corral perhaps some hundred feet in diameter, the circumference of which is lined on the outside with branches of trees." After the completed construction, dancing commenced. Washakie described the ceremonial importance and meaning of the Sun Dance.

Each dancer has a certain place in the dance hall which he must keep throughout the duration of the dance when he enters it. Two small poles or young saplings of pine or cottonwood are placed on each side of the dancer. The bark of these saplings may be peeled off or not, whichever the dancer may wish. If the dancer is a medicine man or has been wounded in battle sometime he should show this on the poles or saplings by painting them red, which signified his blood was lost in battle. The center pole which should always be a cottonwood was chosen by the originators of the dance because of its superiority over all other trees as a dry land tree growing with little or no water. This tree represents God. The twelve long poles that are placed from the top of the center pole down to the circumference of the dance hall represent, according to our indian beliefs the twelve apostles of God, our Father.

The eagle feathers at the top of the poles above the center pole also represent the twelve apostles of our Father, or God, and also being sacred bird of our race, we indians naturally regard the eagle with the highest esteem. The buffalo head in the crotch in the center pole represents a gift from God, our Father above, to his indian children for food and clothing.[11]

After the Sun Dance ended, the ceremonial hall, along with the sacrifices given by the community, was left standing for it to be reclaimed by the Supreme Being through natural decay.[12]

In the Native spiritual life on the Great Plains, both among hunters and farmers, medicine pouches played a central role. These were and are collections of sacred symbols of special meaning to their owners. They can consist of animal skins, bones, feathers, seeds, sage or sweetgrass, stones, and shells. These protective charms are associated with their bearers' guardian spirit, or in case of the plants symbolized the ecological cycle of life, and were to give its owner special spiritual powers or blessings.[13]

Medicine Pouches

Pictographs, paintings, and drawings played a central role in Plains Indian arts and life. Already in ancient times, Native American artists left images on rocks throughout the northwestern plains. Such pictographic art depicts for example hunting scenes or warriors with large shields. Whether on stone, hide, or paper, the Native peoples of the Great Plains used images to tell their life stories and their people's histories. Such pictographs provide a unique source for understanding the historical events that Native Americans of the Great Plains emphasized as influencing their daily life.

Native Histories: Winter Counts and Other Images

Many Great Plains Indians had a unique way of writing their history through winter counts. These were pictographic images painted in a spiral on a buffalo robe. Each picture symbolized a memorable event of the year and would allow its maker to recall important experiences from the past. Sometimes a winter count was produced by an individual to record his life history. At other times it was the work of members of two or three generations, or the work of a single person who tried with the help of elders to retrace events from the past. Winter counts recorded the outbreak of epidemics, enemy raids, skirmishes, and warfare with Anglo-American as well as Amerindian enemies, natural phenomena like meteor showers or eclipses, treaties, peace negotiations, and events of importance to the life of the robe's creator.[14]

Buffalo hides were worn as garments, such as shirts and robes, and by the mid-nineteenth century were also used to depict historic episodes. At times, they combined several different events. These "histories on hide and paper" were often filled with biographical detail. A buffalo robe in the Musée de l'Homme collection in Paris from probably the eighteenth century, for example, illustrates either a single fight or several fights between Native warriors on horseback and their enemies on foot. Men also used paper, pens, and pencils to show their war exploits and important events in their daily life. Such pictures could show the killing of an enemy, important battles, trade interactions with different groups, the death of an esteemed horse in battle, scenes of a buffalo hunt, or other events of importance in the life of a warrior. Sometimes tipis and other lodgings were also painted with visionary experiences, or more infrequently with battle scenes.[15]

As the world of Great Plains Indians changed in the late nineteenth century, the drawings and paintings of Indian men began to reflect their new and unfamiliar experiences. For instance, Zotom, a Kiowa who was one of 71 southern Plains warriors who was arrested and sent to Fort Marion in St. Augustine, Florida, in 1875, incorporated this prison experience into his art. One of his drawing shows the newly arrived warriors standing on the walls of Fort Marion overlooking a bay with ships and lighthouses, a topographical landscape very alien to the Great Plains Indians. By anyone's imagination this must have been a terrifying picture and experience for the Indians who were thousands of miles away from home and had never seen the ocean before—a feeling captured by the drawing. Other pictures by Zotom depict, for example, the long journey to Fort Marion by train, the preaching by ministers to the Indian inmates, and the pursuit and the killing of a Cheyenne chief named Grey Beard who had tried to escape during the train ride to Florida. Zotom was also one of several Indian prisoners who made drawings for sale to white visitors. Thus, a majority of these images evade references to combat, and show hunting, dancing, and ceremonial scenes.[16]

AMERICA'S CONQUEST OF THE PLAINS AND THE TRANSFORMATION OF INDIAN LIFE

By the second half of the nineteenth century the Plains Indian way of life that relied on the buffalo was increasingly challenged. The encroachments by the American military, settlers, and railroads in the region, developments accompanied by the deliberate mass killings of bison herds by white hunters, led to dramatic changes in the daily life of Native communities in the region.

The Impact of Disease on the Great Plains   As in other parts of the Americas, disease had a significant impact on the daily lives of the indigenous peoples of the Great Plains. It hit Plains Indians hard, and often preceded the encroachments by American settlers.

A Kiowa legend of the encounter between the Kiowa trickster hero Saynday and Smallpox provides a glimpse at how Plains Indians perceived, reacted to and explained alien disease as forces that impacted their daily life.

"I come from far away, across the Eastern Ocean," Smallpox answered. "I am one with the white men—they are my people as the Kiowas are yours. Sometimes I travel ahead of them, and sometimes I lurk behind. But I am always their companion and you will find me in their camps and in their houses."

"What do you do?" Saynday repeated.

" I bring death ," Smallpox replied. "My breath causes children to wither like young plants in spring snow. I bring destruction. No matter how beautiful a woman is, once she has looked at me she becomes as ugly as death. And to men I bring not death alone, but the destruction of their children and the blighting of their wives. The strongest warriors go down before me. No people who have looked on me will ever be the same." And he chuckled low and hideously. With his raised forearm, Smallpox pushed the dust of his face and Saynday saw the scars that disfigured it.[17]

As this quote alludes to, epidemics had a scary and devastating impact on communities, families, and Native daily life. Although the overall impact of disease is difficult to assess, it is not hard to imagine what the loss of a father, mother, child, sibling, grandparent, and on many occasions even several relatives and close community members meant in the life of an individual, and what its implications were for the survival of a society.

Although the overall numbers for disease losses are hard to quantify, the impact of epidemics was dramatic. Scholars argue that as many as half of the Amerindian population of the plains died in the smallpox pandemic of 1779–1781. Another major smallpox epidemic occurred in 1801–1802. Researchers also argue that Plains Indian farming populations were generally more severely afflicted by disease than the horse cultures that surrounded them. The disease factor shifted the power advantage even further to the nomadic horse peoples. The 2,000 Mandans, farmers who lived in villages along the Missouri River in North Dakota, for example, suffered a devastating smallpox outbreak in 1837. Largely due to disease, the Mandan population in the region had already declined from an original estimated populace of 15,000 people in the first half of the eighteenth century. By October 1837 there were only 138 Mandans still alive. Nearby Hidatsa and Arikara settlements also suffered, losing an estimated half of their population. Horse people suffered from the pressures of epidemics as well. In 1816, more than 4,000 Comanches died of a smallpox epidemic. The Sioux were also hit hard by the disease in 1819.[18] Thus, epidemics turned the Native world of the Great Plains upside-down.

A Challenge to Native Daily Life on the Plains: Miners, Settlers, and U.S. Policy

Epidemics were barely the only challenge that Plains Indians faced. By the mid-nineteenth century the gold rush in the West, and the increasing demand for more land for agriculture, spurred by a belief in "Manifest Destiny," a conviction that in the views of Anglo-Americans entitled them to occupy the continent from the Atlantic to the Pacific, brought many white intruders to the West. These newcomers would challenge Great Plains Indians' daily lives in many ways.

The discovery of gold in California in 1848 and 1849 led a growing number of white settlers, in search of a new life and wealth in the West, to travel across the plains. These immigrants brought more diseases such as scarlet fever, cholera, and measles, which added to the deaths in Indian communities in the region. The wagon trails' encroachment into Indian country also led to conflict. Yet, "contrary to Hollywood's obsession with Indian raids on wagon trains," writes historian Colin Calloway, "emigrants crossing the plains to Oregon and California experienced relatively little hostility from Indians. Of 250,000 emigrants who crossed the Plains between 1840 and 1860, only 362 died in all the recorded conflicts with Indians." Instead Native Americans often acted as guides and assisted white travelers, and traded for food, horses, guns, and cloth with them. Still, many Plains Indians, according to Thomas Harvey, the superintendent of Indian Affairs at St. Louis in 1845, saw white immigrants as intruders who "have no right to be in their country without their consent." They "complain that the buffalo are wantonly killed and scared off, which renders their only means of subsistence every year more precarious."[19]

Plains Indians faced, however, more than just travelers passing through, since white settlers increasingly also claimed land on the Great Plains that the Natives considered theirs. The conquest of the Great Plains began in the South. The settlement of Texas by white Americans who won independence from Mexico in 1836 was also accompanied by the defeat and dispossession of the Native American inhabitants of the region. The local Amerindian populations were either driven north or into Mexico, however not without resistance. The Comanches, for example, fought against the Texas Rangers and settlers until the end of the southern Plains War in 1875.[20] Between the 1860s and 1890s, millions of American settlers, urged on by offers of free government land and railroad publicity campaigns, also increasingly moved onto Native American lands in Colorado, Kansas, Nebraska, and the Dakotas. The intrusions by white migrants and processes of U.S. colonization on the Great Plains would increasingly challenge Native daily life in the region.

Anglo-American views of the Native American peoples of the Great Plains in the mid-nineteenth century certainly varied widely. General George Crook, who had frequently fought against Indians, told an audience that "with all his faults . . . the American Indian is not half as black as he has been painted. He is cruel in war, treacherous at times, and not over cleanly. But so were our forefathers." Thus, in this for nineteenth-century America sympathetic view of Native Americans, the Indian had only one chance of survival, and that was to change his way of life to confirm to white norms. Other white observers disagreed with this view. They saw the Plains Indians as a race of people to be exterminated. In the words attributed to General Philip Sheridan they believed that "the only good Indian I ever saw was a dead Indian." In the end, most whites saw Plains Indians as in the way of progress, and no matter what attitudes Anglo-Americans had toward them, American policy, the coming of miners, white farmers, land speculators, and the railroad, proved extremely harmful to the Native Americans' way of life.[21]

As in other regions, massacres committed by white militia and vigilantes disrupted the patterns of daily life of Great Plains Indians and sent terror through numerous Indian

Scars of Violence: The Sand Creek Massacre of 1864

communities. The Sand Creek Massacre of 1864 was one of the most infamous bloodbaths in the history of the American West. It was committed against the band of the prominent Cheyenne chief Black Kettle.

In September of 1864, a period of considerable tensions in Colorado, Black Kettle had negotiated for peace with the territory's governor John Evans. Black Kettle and his people initially agreed to settle next to Fort Lyons. The fort's commander, however, ordered the band to resettle a good 40 miles away from the military post at Sand Creek. There on November 29, 1864, a Colorado militia unit of 700 men under the command of Methodist clergyman Colonel John Chivington attacked the Cheyenne settlement. Black Kettle's band of about 500 people—a village that consisted of over 300 women and children—were shot at without warning, even though the Cheyenne raised an American flag and a white flag of surrender. The soldiers killed everyone unable to flee, scalped and mutilated dead bodies, killed women who pleaded for their lives, and even used a toddler for target practice. Little Bear, a survivor of the Sand Creek massacre, described the gruesome incident:

I passed many women and children, dead and dying, lying in the creek bed. The soldiers had not scalped them yet, as they were busy chasing those that were yet alive. After the fight I came back down the creek and saw these dead bodies all cut up and even the wounded scalped and slashed. I saw one old woman wandering about; her whole scalp had been taken off and the blood was running down into her eyes so that she could not see where to go.[22]

Black Kettle, who survived the carnage at Sand Creek and despite his experience continued to pursue peace with the United States, died along with over 100 of his people in another massacre against a Southern Cheyenne village on the Washita River in 1868.

Little Bear's above-quoted account provides a glimpse not only of the harrowing sight at the Sand Creek or any other of the many massacres committed against Native Americans, but it also alludes to the scars that such an event left with the survivors. A description by Bear Head, a Blackfoot Indian survivor of the massacre on the Marias of 1870, committed by the U.S. military against his village, which had stayed at peace with the Americans, and which was largely occupied by women and children, seconds Little Bear's experiences and provides further insight into the pains felt by those who survived such horrific acts of violence. Bear Head described his reactions in the aftermath of the slaughter.

I sat before the ruin of my lodge and felt sick. I wished that the seizers [Blackfeet name for soldiers] had killed me, too. In the center of the fallen lodge, where the poles had fallen upon the fire, it had burned a little, then died out. I could not pull up the lodge-skin and look under it. I could not bear to see my mother, my almost-mothers, my almost-sisters lying there, shot or smothered to death. When I went for my horses, I had not carried my many-shots gun. It was there in the ruin of the lodge. Well, there it would remain.[23]

American soldiers murdered over 173 Blackfeet that day. The majority of them were old men, women, and children. They also killed 300 horses. Such violent experiences stayed with the survivors and scarred them for life. They also have become an important part of the collective memory and thus not only shaped the daily life of many Native American communities in the West in the second half of the nineteenth century, but continue to do so to this day.

Native Americans and the Railroad

The railroad played a crucial role in the colonization of the American West and in undermining the Plains Indians' way of life. The first transcontinental railroad was completed in 1869 and was followed by other lines that sprang up in the region in the following years. For Native Americans, however, the railroad became an "engine of destruction" for the world that they had known.

The railroad, and the white hunters, soldiers, and settlers that accompanied it, aided significantly in the almost extinction of the buffalo, on which many of the Plains Indians' way of life depended. The bison herds of the Great Plains were systematically slaughtered starting in the 1860s and were especially targeted in the 1870s and 1880s. By 1900 the number of buffalo had shrunk from an estimated 40 million or more prior to white colonization to about 1,000.

White hunters played a key part in the mass extermination of the buffalo. Initially they killed the animals to sell the meat to the railroad companies, which used it to feed their construction crews who were building the new railroad lines. By the early 1870s, however, a New York tannery invented a process that turned buffalo skins into leather. This development spurred the mass slaughter of the buffalo on the Great Plains by white hunters, for whom the killing of these creatures became a very lucrative business. Furthermore, the railroads not only attracted a growing number of white farmers to the Great Plains who could sell their agricultural product to the market more easily, but it also enabled leather producers to relatively cheaply transport bison skins from the Great Plains to the east coast. From 1872–1873 alone, trains carried around 1,250,000 buffalo hides that had been slaughtered by white hunters on the plains. In 1873, a group of 16 American hunters was rumored to have killed 28,000 bison over the period of only a few months. The animals' meat was generally not used and was left to rot. An English traveler on the Arkansas River in 1873 observed for example that "for some thirty or forty miles along the north bank . . . there was a continual line of putrescent carcasses, so that the air was rendered pestilential and offensive to the last degree."[24] In addition, many of the buffalo skins were wasted, either because white hunters killed more buffalo than they could process, or because they were inexperienced in skinning the animals and thereby destroyed or damaged the buffalo hide. Sources indicate that in 1872 for each hide sold on the market, three to five animals were killed. Thus, the efforts by white hunters aided dramatically in the mass extermination of the buffalo. The coming of the railroads and the killing of the buffalo were also welcomed by military and political officials, who increasingly advocated the mass extermination of the animals as an effective way to starve the Plains Indians into submission.[25]

The mass extermination of the buffalo impacted Native American daily life on the Great Plains tremendously. Excerpts of a Kiowa tradition provide a glimpse at what a tough blow the killing of their major means of subsistence was for the hunter-gatherers among the Plains Indians.

The buffalo were the life of the Kiowas. . . . [W]hen the white man wanted to build railroads, or when they wanted to farm and raise cattle, the buffalo still protected the Kiowas. . . . [Then] there was war between the buffalo and the white men. . . . The white men built forts. . . . [and] hired hunters to do nothing but kill the buffalo.[26]

The mass killing conducted by white hunters, and enabled by the railroad, had destroyed what the Native peoples saw as the natural balance of their world in the Great Plains.

Accounts of massacres, the coming of the railroad, and the encroachments by whites on their lands spurred a massive outcry among many Native Americans in the West. It led a growing number of Plains Indians

Resistance, Accommodation, and the Terror of American Expansion

to believe that peaceful interaction with the Americans was impossible. Resistance to U.S. expansion, as well as adapting to the rapid changes brought forth by the white colonization of the Great Plains, became an increasingly central feature in Native American daily life in the second half of the nineteenth century. Confrontations occurred all over the Plains in which Native Americans resisted the loss of their land and attempted to defend their way of life throughout the 1850s, 1860s, 1870s, and 1880s.

In their punitive expeditions against the Plains Indians, the United States also took advantage of a well-known feature of their daily life. The military often assaulted Native settlements during the winter months, a time of the year in which Plains Indians were ill-prepared for war and vulnerable to attacks. During this season, Indians were largely immobile in their camps. Here they endured shortages of forage, fuel, and meat and, because of the weather conditions, did not expect attacks from outsiders.

Setting up camp for a Buffalo Bill show, about 1901. Even as Americans sought to confine Native peoples to reservations, they paid good money to "real Indians" to demonstrate "authentic" lifeways. This created an opportunity for Native people to earn money off the reservation without having to work in factories. Here a group of Plains Indians set up a tipi as part of a demonstration for Buffalo Bill's Wild West Show. From Denver Public Library, Western History Collection.

But with the aid of the railroad, better equipment, and a sophisticated infrastructure that supported the soldiers with supplies, the U.S. military was able to rage a "winter war of terror" against the Plains Indians.[27] From the 1850s to the 1870s the constant fear of experiencing military attacks on one's encampment or village was an ever-present feature in the daily life of many Native children, women, and men on the Great Plains.

Encouraged by ancient rivalries with enemy groups, and enticed by monetary and material benefits, some Native American fighters also chose to assist the U.S. military as scouts and interpreters. These men had often grown tired of fighting against the military, wanted to get even with ancient Indian rivals, and/or believed that resistance against the United States was futile. Even though they supported the military, scouts and interpreters were in many cases considered to be civilians. They were permitted to wear the clothes they wanted and carried their own weapons. The military also used scouts and interpreters to obtain stolen horses, to translate, to explore, and to lead troops that pursued enemy Native groups.[28] At other times, Native American fighters contributed more actively to the American military agenda. Uniformed Apache scouts were, for example, used when General Crook was in pursuit of Geronimo and the Jicarilla Apache, and they attempted to get them to surrender. The Apaches who assisted Crook believed that the Jicarilla's resistance had been harmful to the Apaches.[29]

CONCLUSION

Disease, the destruction of buffalo herds, alcohol, U.S. military conquest, and the coming of white hunters, miners, and farmers forever changed the daily life of the Indians of the Great Plains. Yet, this was hardly the last challenge to their way of life. For the remainder of the nineteenth century the U.S. government would fight a different war against the Native peoples of the West. Government officials and social reformers wanted the Indians to live like white Americans. This battle turned into a conflict over the souls and minds of the Indians. To this struggle in Native American daily life, we will turn our attention in the next chapter.

NOTES

1. Alice B. Kehoe, *North American Indians: A Comprehensive Account*, 2nd ed. (Upper Saddle River, NJ: Prentice Hall, 1992), 293–94.

2. Quoted in Francis Haines, *The Plains Indians* (New York: Crowell, 1976), 67.

3. James Larpenteur Long (Assiniboine), "Buffalo Staff of Life For the Indians," in *Great Documents in American Indian History*, ed. Wayne Moquin and Charles Van Doren (New York: DaCapo Press, 1995), 62.

4. Luther Standing Bear, "Indian Family Life," in Moquin and Van Doren, 41.

5. Standing Bear, 44.

6. Standing Bear, 43.

7. Plenty Coups, "Stealing Horses from the Arapahoe," in Moquin and Van Doren, 69.

8. Wooden Leg, "The Years of a Warrior," in Moquin and Van Doren, 60.

9. Wooden Leg, 60.

10. Quotes from Anonymous, "What Harm is our Sun-Dance?," in *Native American Testimony,* ed. Peter Nabokov, rev. ed. (New York: Penguin Books, 1999, 1978), 224–25.

11. Washakie, "The Sun Dance," in Moquin and Van Doren, 75.

12. For more information on the Sun Dance see for example Royal B. Hassrick, *The Sioux* (Norman: Oklahoma University Press, 1964), 279–88; Kehoe, 315–18.

13. Kehoe, 318–19.

14. See for example Lone Dog, "Lone Dog's Winter Count," in *Our Hearts Fell to the Ground: Plains Indian Views of How the West Was Lost,* ed. Colin G. Calloway (Boston: Bedford/St. Martins, 1996), 31–36. See also Melburn D. Thurman, "Plains Indian Winter Counts and the New Ethnohistory," *Plains Anthropologist* 27 (1982), 173–75.

15. David W. Penney, *North American Indian Art* (New York: Thames and Hudson, 2004), 113–16.

16. See for example Penney, 116–17.

17. "I bring Death," in Calloway, 52.

18. Colin G. Calloway, *First Peoples: A Documentary Survey of American Indian History,* 2nd ed. (Boston: Bedford, 2004), 265–66.

19. Calloway, *First Peoples,* 267.

20. Calloway, *First Peoples,* 266.

21. Edward Barnard, ed., *Story of the Great American West* (New York: Reader's Digest, 1977), 269.

22. "The Sand Creek Massacre," in Calloway, ed., *Our Hearts Fell to the Ground,* 105. On the Sand Creek Massacre see also Barnard, 225.

23. "Account of the Massacre on the Marias," in Calloway, ed., *Our Hearts Fell to the Ground,* 109.

24. Quoted in Richard White, *"It's Your Misfortune and None of My Own": A New History of the American West* (Norman: University of Oklahoma Press, 1991), 219; Mary Ellen Jones, *Daily Life on the Nineteenth Century Frontier* (Westport, CT: Greenwood Press, 1998), 162.

25. Our discussion of the railroad, the Indians, and the buffalo benefited from Barnard, 268–69; Jones, 160–64; White, 219.

26. Quoted in Jones, 164.

27. Barnard, 229.

28. Barnard, 231.

29. Barnard, 240–41.

10

THE SURVIVAL OF THE "DISAPPEARING INDIAN"

In the American West, the late nineteenth century provided many challenges to Native American daily life. Military resistance to American colonization had ceased to be an option. Many Amerindian people struggled to survive. Resources had become scarce. Hunting became restricted or impossible as the U.S. military stepped up its campaign to confine Native American groups onto reservations. Yet reservations were not the only challenge. Native people encountered religious, social, and legal repression, a cultural assault on their children in boarding schools, and efforts by the federal government to privatize the lands they once held in common. East of the Mississippi, some Native people continued to live on their original homelands, sometimes identifying themselves as Indians, other times passing as white or "colored," especially for those who intermarried with people of African descent. The few protections available to western peoples, such as the federal regulation that Indian lands could only be taken with the approval of Congress, were not applied to Native communities in the east because "everyone knew" that they had died out or moved away. All across the continent, Native Americans endured federal, state, and institutional efforts to undermine their political and economic sovereignty. But they also continued their struggle to survive in a world of increasingly narrowing options.

REFORMERS AND RESERVATIONS

At the same time as the American military was fighting wars against the Native peoples of the West, other white Americans who described themselves as the "friends of the Indians" were working to change Native American lives in more peaceful, although no less destructive, ways. They were white eastern humanitarians who were frequently members of church- and religious-based philanthropic organizations. These self-proclaimed "friends of the Indians" imagined reservations as the key instrument to save Amerindians from what they saw as false ways. This approach underscored Anglo-American beliefs in the superiority of their society, and it dismissed the value of Native American cultures and ways of life. In the minds of most whites in the late nineteenth century, as in earlier years, it was the Indians who had to change "their ways, and learn how to be like white men." Sharing these views, one general on duty in the West reported to the capitol in Washington, D.C. that the reform efforts were a "grand experiment to make civilized human beings out of savages." He believed that this could be accomplished by gathering Indians together "little by little into a reservation away from the haunts and hills and hiding places of their country." There, the high-ranking officer believed, white Americans could "teach the children how to read and write; teach them the art of peace; teach them the truths of Christianity. Soon they will acquire new habits, new ideas, new modes of life."[1]

Reservations had long played a central role in the lives of Native Americans east of the Mississippi. English colonizers first created them in the seventeenth century in their Atlantic seaboard colonies to remove Amerindians from their lands and to open the lands up for white settlement. Reservations also became places where missionaries attempted to introduce Christianity, European-style farming, and their cultural and social values. The United States also adopted this system, often using military pressures and questionable treaties to create numerous Native American reservations, and by the mid-nineteenth century the United States introduced Native reserves in the West.

As in colonial times, mainstream society in nineteenth-century America came to look at reservations as places where one could change the Indians, so that they would conform to Anglo-American stereotypes about how Native Americans should live. Their priorities included:

1. to put Indians to work as farmers or herders, thereby weaning them from their "savage life" and making them self-supporting
2. to educate young people of both sexes in order to "introduce to the growing generation civilized ideas, wants and aspirations"
3. to allot parcels of land to individual Indians, not to the tribe, in order to foster individual pride of ownership rather than tribal loyalty
4. to dispose of surplus reservation lands remaining after the individual titles had been obtained, with the money from sales to be used to provide for Indians expenses
5. to treat Indians like all other inhabitants of the United States under the laws of the land[2]

The movement to reform the Indian was influenced by the moral and social reform movements that played a significant role in nineteenth-century America. Activists in these groups confronted issues such as slavery, women's rights, temperance, poverty, and prostitution. Reformers also became active among families who had recently immigrated to the United States. As with Native Americans, they tried to change these newcomers to conform to Anglo-American norms.

Reformers had a strong ally in President Ulysses S. Grant. The president, in his efforts to change Native American societies, advocated the implementation of what came to be known as "Grant's Peace Policy." The main purpose of this policy was to dismantle Native communities. Its advocates argued that this approach would lead to acculturation and eventually to the full assimilation of Native Americans into American mainstream society. Like the reformers, Grant believed that such a dramatic transformation was to be achieved through the creation of reservations, annuity payments in forms of rations and supplies to be given to Indians, the setting up of schools and missions in reservation communities, and the eventual privatization of Native American reservation lands through a policy called allotment.

The president turned to white reformers to aid him in his policy to transform Native communities and to change the Indian. In 1869, Congress endorsed the creation of a Board of Indian Commissioners, which was largely staffed with white Christian reformers. It was to supervise the appropriations of funds for Indians, and to provide a report on programs and policies that dealt with Native Americans. The board especially encouraged and favored the creation of reservations, which was seen as the core element in a successful "peace policy." Many members of the board also pushed for the end of community ownership of tribal lands and favored their privatization. Another big blow to Native sovereignty was the abandonment of the treaty system in 1871, which was favored by white reformers and federal officials. Historian of U.S.-Indian relations and Catholic priest Francis Paul Prucha writes on the abolition of the treaty system and the role that white reformers played in it that it was not a

simple story of honest and faithful men and women fighting against the forces of selfishness and evil, for many righteous Christian reformers came to see in the treaties a hindrance and a block to the advancement of the Indians distinct from the rest of American citizens, and the chief obstacle was tribalism in all its manifestations. Unless tribalism and its remnants were destroyed, they believed, there was little chance that the Indians as individuals could be completely absorbed into mainstream America.[3]

In a sense, white reformers and federal officials had an vested interest in undermining sovereignty. Both wanted Native Americans to become the wards of the government. Federal law forbade Native spiritual and ritual practices as well as the creation of tribal police forces. These developments provided a major challenge to the daily life of many Native Americans in the West.

Obviously, the plans of nineteenth-century American reformers and officials did not materialize quite in the way they imagined. Native Americans on reservations did not all blend into the general population. Many were simply not willing to give up their community values, their beliefs, and their group identity as a people. They also did not want to be like white people. Through initiative, accommodation to changed circumstances, and resistance, they attempted to redirect the course of American policies to fit with their own goals and aspirations as best as they could.

UNITED STATES AGENTS, TRIBAL POLICE, AND RESERVATION LIFE

Although white reformers and government officials used a lot of rhetoric about the "peace policy" and changing the Amerindians living on reservations, the implementation of this agenda was anything but smooth and efficient. Their efforts were often disorganized, damaged by corrupt U.S. agents, and undermined by the poor quality of land given to Native Americans. This factor, along with Native American resistance to efforts of assimilation, thwarted federal plans to transform reservation Indians into Christians, farmers, and ranchers.

It is important to underscore, though, that federal and white reform efforts on reservations attempted to undermine traditional Native cultures and tribal authority structures. Agents, the official representatives of the U.S. government, were the key figures in implementing federal policies that influenced Native daily life. Agents, alongside missionaries, teachers, farmers, and clerks intruded on Native societies, attempting to turn buffalo hunters into farming families, in which men farmed while women fulfilled domestic chores, and children went to school. Agents were supposed to provide food and protection. Thus, they took on many of the traditional roles performed by Native chiefs, thereby undermining the chiefs' authority. At times, Amerindians complained that agents were autocratic and even dictatorial rulers who enriched themselves at the expense of the people they were supposed to serve. Sarah Winnemucca, a Paiute Indian from Nevada and an outspoken critic of the reservation policy in the late nineteenth century, wrote a long list of complaints about the corruption of federal agents. For instance, she reported an incident in which one "agent sold an Indian man some powder," a violation of the law. After the Native traveled away from the agency,

he was met by one of the agent's men, who shot him dead on the spot, because he had the powder. My brother and I did not know what to do. All our people were wild with excitement. Brother and I thought he [the agent] did wrong to sell the powder to one of our men, knowing it was against the law . . . this is the way all the Indian agents get rich.

Another agent threatened to make Winnemucca and her brother leave their reservation. After they refused, the agent had her brother arrested by soldiers and had him put into prison on Alcatraz Island off San Francisco Bay.[1]

Traditional leadership in Great Plains societies was also undermined by policies that fostered division within Indian societies. For instance, the U.S. government supported tribal police forces set up in the 1870s, which were manned by Indian police officers under the command of white agents. In a sense, the use of tribal police forces was an extension of the use of Native American scouts in the U.S. military. Agents also recruited Native American tribal judges. The work was appealing to some Native Americans because it provided steady employment and income. It was also a symbol of status. But just like the recruitment of Indian military scouts divided Native communities in earlier years, the use of Native police officers and judges had a similar effect. Indian police officers and judges gained at least a limited interest in supporting the official agenda of cultural transformation and suppressing Native customs. This often went against the majority interests in their communities. Native police officers, for instance, suppressed traditional dances and religious practices such as the Sun Dance. At times they also participated in acts of violence to undermine potential political threats. For example, Indian police officers killed the influential Lakota leader Sitting Bull at a time of political tensions on the Pine Ridge reservation. Thus, the recruitment of Native police officers and judges undermined the ability of Amerindian communities to put up unified positions and resistance to U.S. demands.

Native police officers and tribal judges also were responsible to enforce the prohibition of polygamy. Many Great Plains Indians saw this as nothing less than an assault on their social order. The policies caused tremendous tensions and heartbreak in many families. A Lakota named Old White Bull responded to the demand that he had to separate from one of his two wives:

What! . . . these two women are sisters, both of whom have been my wives for over half a century. I know the ways of the white man; he takes women unknown to each other and to his law. These two have been faithful to me and I have been faithful to them. Their children are my children and the grandchildren are mine. We are now living together as brother and sisters. All the people know that we are happy together, and nothing but death can separate us.[5]

The use of Native Americans in law enforcement as police officers and judges also ensured that animosities about assaults, changes, and reforms were often directed against the indigenous representatives of the state rather than white agents.

Apache policeman. This Apache policeman wearing a badge, ammunition belt and handgun seems to have assimilated to "modern" American lifeways. Men who might have been warriors before the reservation period sometimes turned to work as scouts or tribal police as a way to serve their people. From Denver Public Library, Western History Collection.

CROW DOG'S CASE AND THE MAJOR CRIMES ACT OF 1885

Native American sovereignty and legal systems suffered another blow with the Major Crimes Act of 1885. Following the murder of an Amerindian leader called Spotted Tail by a man named Crow Dog on a Lakota reservation, the federal government wanted to bring Crow Dog to trial. The crime had been settled in a traditional Lakota manner by an exchange of horses between Crow Dog's and Spotted Tail's family—a custom referred to by the Lakota as the "covering of the dead." Still, U.S. authorities had Crow Dog arrested, despite treaty rights that guaranteed judicial jurisprudence to the Lakota. Crow Dog was tried and sentenced to be executed. Eventually, in the appeal process, the Supreme Court overturned the federal courts decision, arguing that the government had no jurisdiction over Indian laws on reservations.

Federal lawmakers responded quickly to this decision. Only two years after the Supreme Court's ruling in the case known as *Ex Parte Crow Dog*, Congress passed the Major Crimes Act of 1885. This law granted the federal government jurisdiction over reservations in such crimes as burglary, rape, manslaughter, and murder. Thus the Major Crimes Act brought U.S. legal interference and control into Native American daily life, as Native communities were stripped of their rights to penalize criminals in their societies according to their customs . It challenged Native sovereignty and led to a dramatic change in federal–tribal relations. It symbolized a complete federal interference with Native political structures and reinforced the difficulties that Native communities already experienced through other government and privately sponsored attempts to "reform" their societies.

NATIVE AMERICANS AND RESERVATIONS: "FROM PRISON TO HOMELAND"

For some Native Americans life on the reservation literally started out with a real or quasi-prison experience. The federal government, for example, transported some Great Plains Indians to the east were they were detained in military forts. Thousands of Navajo were marched from their homelands and held near Fort Sumner in eastern New Mexico. Here the dire situation caused rampant disease, prostitution, and depression. Herrero, a Navajo headman who lost several of his children during his people's banishment, told an investigator that his people were "dying as though they were shooting them with a rifle." He also complained of the poor quality of the land on which his people could not raise sheep and on which "the crops do not come out . . . well." The federal government forced the Navajo to stay in eastern New Mexico in semi-confinement for four years, before allowing them the arduous return to a reservation near their homelands in Arizona in 1868. Nearly a quarter of the Navajo perished during their exile.[6]

The plans of the federal government and white reformers to change the Amerindians were also impeded by the often poor quality of reservation lands given to Native Americans. As white settlers claimed the best land for themselves, most reservation lands were simply too arid to support agriculture. Irrigation was not available to Native Americans.

Furthermore, many Native Americans on the Great Plains had to learn some of the skills they needed to become farmers and to live like white Americans. The Arapaho artist Carl Sweezy observed for example in his memoirs:

We knew of nothing about how to harness a work horse or turn a furrow in a field or cut and store hay, and today I suppose there are men living in cities who know no more about these things than we did. Our women did not know how to build a fire in a cook-stove or wash clothes in a tub of water. It was a long time before we knew what the figures on the face of a clock meant, or why people looked at them before they ate their meals or started off to church. We had to learn that clocks had something to do with the hours and minutes that the white people mentioned so often. Hours, minutes, and seconds were such small divisions of time that we had never thought of them. When the sun rose, when it was high in the sky, and when it set where all the divisions of the day that we had ever found necessary when we followed the old Arapaho road. When we went on a hunting trip or to a sun dance, we counted time by sleeps.[7]

As this quote shows, life on the reservation meant a significant transformation in daily life.

Furthermore, and although federal policies encouraged acculturation, assimilation, and even cultural repression on Native American reservations, indigenous communities had different plans for their future. Amerindian culture and societies were more resilient than U.S. officials and white reformers expected. Instead of becoming part of or blending into American mainstream society, as reformers imagined, Native Americans instead attempted to retain their group identities and cultural values and tried to preserve their communities as well as possible. Native Americans, in the words of one historian, transformed reservations "from prisons into homelands."[8]

Gradually, reservations became places where Native Americans tried to maintain their sovereignty and recreate and maintain the communities that had so long shaped their daily lives. They tried to make the best out of their new homes. Carl Sweezy wrote:

My people had everything to learn about the white man's road, but they had a good time learning it. How they laughed when a war pony, not understanding what it was supposed to do when it was hitched to a plough or wagon, lunged and jumped away and threw them flat on the ground, with the plough or the wagon riding high in the air.[9]

Native Americans on reservations altered many of their cultural, social, and economic practices. On the Great Plains, many Native Americans now built wooden houses and barns and worked the soil with plows. Increasingly Native Americans would be seen wearing blue jeans and cotton dresses. They also used government supplies and foods and shopped in stores, many owned by Indians.

LAND: ALLOTMENT AND DISPOSSESSION

Realizing that American Indians turned reservations into homelands, white officials and reformers who had initially favored the system now came to oppose it. Increasingly, they viewed reservations as places that interfered with their plans to have Native Americans assimilate into mainstream society. They were now keen on finding ways to break up reservations. This would, reformers believed, undermine Indian communities and lead to the dispersal of Amerindians into American society. In the minds of white people, this would help Indians to become "civilized " and lift them out of their "poverty." The Allotment Act of 1887, also known as the Dawes Act, named for the Massachusetts senator who sponsored it, became the federal policy to achieve this goal. It was a major effort by American officials to restructure Native societies socially, economically, and politically.

Senator Henry Dawes described what he saw as the shortcomings in Native American societies after visiting the so-called "Five Civilized Tribes" in Indian territory, which had been removed in earlier decades during the period of removal discussed in chapter 5.

> The head chief told us that there was not a family in that whole Nation that had not a home of its own. There was not a pauper in that Nation and that the Nation did not owe a dollar. It built its own capitol . . . and it built its schools and its hospitals. Yet the defect of the system was apparent. They have got as far as they can go, because they own their land in common. . . . [T]here is no enterprise to make your home any better than that of your neighbors. There is no selfishness, which is at the bottom of civilization. Till this people consent to give up their lands, and divide them among their citizens so that each can own the land he cultivates, they will not make much more progress.[10]

Although white reformers like Dawes were willing to acknowledge that American Indians lived in functioning communities, they abhorred the communal social organization in Native societies. Reformers instead advocated that Native Americans should accumulate private property and live in small families and rely less on the extended family networks who played a central role among many groups. By doing this, white reformers believed, Native Americans would not only change to plow agriculture, move into cabins, and wear the same clothes as members of mainstream society, but they would ultimately cease to be Indians. Allotment policy, in the words of Theodore Roosevelt, was "a vast pulverizing engine to break up the tribal mass."[11]

The Dawes Act included five main provisions, which provided a significant challenge to the way of life and subsistence of many Native American communities and individuals. First, the Dawes Act authorized the president to allocate allotments of 160 acres to the heads of Indian households. Younger persons and orphans were provided with less land. Second, after reservations were surveyed and tribal membership rolls prepared, Indians were to select their lands. If they failed to do so, the government agent would select and distribute their land. Third, the government held title to the allotted land in trust for 25 years. In this period, according to federal officials, Native Americans should be protected from being taken advantage of by land speculators and were to acquaint themselves with private landownership. Fourth, Native Americans whose land was allotted became "civilized" and were to obtain citizenship. Five, "surplus" reservation land could be sold.

The Dawes Act was essentially a policy of dispossession. The selling off of the so-called "surplus" lands dramatically hit the territorial base of Native communities. From the beginning to the end of the allotment policy, lasting from 1887 to 1937, tribal land holdings in the United States fell from 138 to 48 million acres.

Land allotment failed to satisfy the economic needs of Native Americans. In the American West, most reservation lands were poor. Thus, 160 acres was often too small of a land basis for people to become agricultural or pastoralist producers. Since the government and not American Indians held title to allotted lands, they were also unable to obtain loans to invest in machinery, equipment, or livestock to start up farming or herding businesses. Many impoverished Amerindians leased their lands to whites. When later legislative changes relaxed the 25-year restriction on land sales, many Natives had few options but to sell their land. Thus, in the following decades allotted reservations became checkerboards of Native and non-Native properties.

In addition, land allotment challenged the fundamental social and community values, which had shaped the daily lives of Native peoples for centuries. For the hunter-gathering horse cultures of the Great Plains, for example, the demands by American mainstream society to become farmers challenged their cultural values and worldviews, which advocated a different connection to the land than that required by farming. Many Great Plains Indians considered plowing a destruction of the land and the planting of crops a violation of the will of the Great Spirit. "Buffalo came first, in our minds," wrote the Arapaho artist Carl Sweezy, "as long as any were left; we "went buffalo" when buffalo were plenty, not when crops were laid by or schools dismissed. And since the promised Government issues of food and calico and lodge cloth were often delayed, so that we went cold and hungry while we waited, it is small wonder that among the older people especially, the buffalo road seemed the one to follow."[12]

Efforts by white reformers to get Indians in the West to adopt Anglo-American ways of agriculture also challenged long-established gender roles in Native communities that provided social balance between men and women. In the farming societies of the Great Plains, where women were the main agricultural producers, the reformers' insistence that men became the farmers and that Native women pursue domestic activities deprived females of part of their economic power and social value. For men, whose social standing and identity was based on their value as hunters and warriors, options that had been increasingly limited, it was a difficult choice to embrace an activity that in their social norms was considered "women's work." This assault on gender relations and other social values and norms was not an easy transition in the daily lives of many Native Americans.

Many Native communities criticized and resisted the policy of allotment and saw it as a threat to their subsistence and survival. The Red Lake Indians in northern Minnesota, for example, protested the plan to parcel up their land. Having already given up three million acres to whites, they wanted to lose no more land. "We have seen the White Earth Reservation despoiled, the Indians cheated and defrauded of their lands, and both the old and young men, and even women, debased and degraded by the use of whiskey." Their loss of land, the Red Lake Indian community believed, would have the same result for them. "Our land is sacred to us," they said; "we want to keep it till we die for our children and their children."[13]

The federal government also supported other policies that undermined Native American control of their land and sovereignty. At a time when the oil and mining industries were expanding at a rapid pace in much of the West, several Native American reservations that had at first appeared of little value due to the poor quality of the land now gained in value. These reservations were located on a wealth of mineral resources. To counteract this development, Senator Charles Curtis introduced a bill to Congress that gave control of mineral leasing rights on Native American lands in the Indian Territory (later Oklahoma) to the Secretary of the Interior. Although the so-called Curtis Act initially only targeted the allotment of Chickasaw and Creek lands, it set a precedent for undermining the collective mineral and land rights of other Native American communities in the future.

There was also Native American resistance to the Curtis Act. The Cherokee, for example, attempted to lobby in Congress against it. They obtained, however, little access to federal politicians, while they saw oil company representatives walking in and out of the congressional committee deliberating on the legislation. A discouraged Cherokee leader, D.W.C. Duncan, observed:

I am in a fix, . . . you will not forget that when I use the word "I" I mean the whole Cherokee people. I am in a fix. What am I to do? I have a piece of property that doesn't support me, and is not worth a cent to me, under the same inexorable, cruel provisions of the Curtis law that swept away our treaties, our system of nationality, our very existence, and wrested out of our possession our vast territory.[14]

Yet, federal policies in the late nineteenth-century had little understanding and concern for the social, economic, and geographic realities which shaped Native American daily lives and cultural traditions. Federal policies that targeted indigenous land bases and sovereignty in the late nineteenth and early twentieth-century, challenged Native American communities at their core. These developments worried many Native Americans, who wondered about how they would survive as a culture and individuals in the future.

BOARDING SCHOOLS

The education of Indian youths also came to play an important role in American officials' and reformers' plans to "assimilate" the Indian into mainstream society. They argued that the education of young Native Americans in Anglo-American culture and values would speed up the processes of "assimilation." White reformers argued that through education they wanted "to kill the Indian to save the man." Initially young Native Americans attended schools on reservations. In the late nineteenth and early twentieth centuries, however, boarding schools, such as Carlisle Indian Industrial School in Pennsylvania, became the main instrument for federal officials and reformers to change Native American societies. In boarding schools, reformers believed, Native children would be removed from Indian influences that would disturb educators' efforts to assimilate their students.[15]

For Native American children and teenagers, however, the boarding school experience led to dramatic changes in their daily life. They were pulled out of their familiar surroundings, their community, and their culture. Native families were often pressured to let their children go off to school by agents who threatened to cut the government supplies on which many Great Plains Indian had come to depend for survival. At other times, Indian children were forcefully removed by police or military. They were separated from their families, often living hundreds and thousands of miles from their homes. Amerindian boarding-school students also had few if any opportunities to go home since school administrators were reluctant to let students leave to see their families. They were afraid that the children would "go back to the blanket," meaning that they would reclaim their Indian identity and not return to school. In many instances, Native students spent their summers with white families, where they were often used as laborers around the house and to work in businesses. At boarding schools and during home stays with white families in the summer months, young Native Americans encountered staff, families, and environments unsympathetic to their cultures. In fact, these people believed that to remove or "kill the Indian" in the young Natives would be the best for their future. They wanted to completely transform the Indian students.

For many young Native Americans, the boarding-school experience was devastating. Conditions at schools were quite deficient. Boarding schools were poorly supplied, and students were often inadequately fed on a monotonous diet. The students were treated with harsh discipline and beaten for violating school regulations. In an effort to undermine young Native Americans' sense of identity and cultural pride, they often were told that the ways of their peoples were "savage" and "barbaric," and that they had to "be like the white man." Furthermore, the cemeteries of boarding schools were filled with students who had died of various diseases or of the tremendous psychological pressures, or who had committed suicide.

The boarding school experiment was set up to completely change Native American students. They were forced to give up their traditional dress and to change to school uniforms. The cutting of hair was another dramatic experience for Amerindian students. In many Great Plains societies the cutting of hair was a sign of mourning. A young boarding-school student named Luther Standing Bear later wrote about his experience:

One day . . . [w]e were all called together by the interpreter and told that we were to have our hair cut off. . . . Finally I was called out of the schoolroom, and when I went into the next room, the barber was waiting for me. He motioned for me to sit down, and then he commenced work. But when my hair was cut short, it hurt my feelings to such an extent that the tears came into my eyes. I do not recall whether the barber noticed my agitation nor did I care. All I was thinking about was that hair that he had taken away from me. . . . Now after having had my hair cut, a new thought came into my head. I felt that I was no more Indian, but would be an imitation of a white man. . . .[16]

In an effort to undermine the Indian identities of the students, the schools also forced them to accept Anglo-American names.

There was also a consolidated assault on Native languages in the boarding schools. Teachers regularly reprimanded American Indian students

Carlisle Indian Industrial School, before and after. Students at the Carlisle Indian Industrial School were photographed on their arrival at the school and again after they were "civilized." The young Pueblo men in this series were given uniforms and haircuts, literally cutting them off from the sustenance of their families and religious beliefs. From *New England Magazine*, April 1895.

who spoke their language. For instance, Elsie Allen, a Pomo girl at a boarding school in California, was punished and beaten with a strap. She wrote:

[E]very night I cried and then I'd lay awake and think and think and think. I'd think to myself, "If I ever get married and have children I'll *never* teach my children the language or all the Indian things that I know. I'll *never* teach them that, I don't want my children to be treated like they treated me." That's the way I raised my children.[17]

Like this former student, many boarding-school graduates, having their language beaten out them, refused to instruct their children in their native language for fear that they would be reprimanded in the future.

Many Native Americans students tried to make the best of their often unsuitable training and attempted to face the challenges as well as they could. Luther Standing Bear wrote:

I now began to realize that I would have to learn the ways of the white man. With that idea in mind, the thought also came to me that I must please my father as well. So my little brain began to work hard. I thought that some day I might be able to become an interpreter for my father, as he could not speak English. Or I thought I might be able to keep books for him if he again started a store. So I worked very hard.[18]

Yet at boarding schools the educational focus was largely on vocational training and not on academics. Young males were trained in agriculture and to become manual laborers. Females received "domestic training," preparing them for lives as domestic servants or housewives. Despite the rhetoric of using education as a means to "uplift the Indian," the schools were primarily educating their students to assume a place at the bottom of America's socioeconomic ladder. Luther Standing Bear, for example, complained that he spent hours of his school day working in the tin shop making "hundreds of tin cups, coffee pots, and buckets." Yet, he realized that "[a]fter I had left the school and returned home, this trade did not benefit me any, as the Indians had plenty of tinware that I had made at school."[19]

Nevertheless, the boarding-school experience also brought together young Native Americans from different Indian communities. As they met in the schools, they discovered that they shared many similarities. From this realization grew a pan-Indian perspective that forged links between tribes and created a stronger sense of ethnic identity.

Education also provided opportunities to some Native Americans. A young Dakota boarding-school graduate named Charles Eastman, also known as Ohiyesa, would later go on to college. He graduated from Dartmouth and earned an M.D. from Boston University. He became a doctor on the Pine Ridge reservation, and a prominent spokesman on Native American issues. The schools also trained numerous other articulate Indian leaders and spokespeople who applied the skills learned in class. Some spoke out against racism, injustice, corruption, and unjust laws and advocated for the equality and rights of Indians. Others used their writing skills to write letters to officials and to newspapers to publicize injustices committed against their people.

GHOST DANCE RELIGION AND THE WOUNDED KNEE MASSACRE OF 1890

The challenges in the late nineteenth century led some Native Americans in the West to choose traditional ways to cope with the dramatic changes to their daily lives. By the 1880s, as hunger, disease, and despondency plagued the reservations, religious traditions that promised a better future or the reinstatement of a better past gained in appeal in many Indian communities. It is important to underscore, though, that federal government officials were resolute in their attempts to eliminate Native American religious practices and leaders. American officials instead wanted Amerindian peoples to adopt Christianity.

In Native American communities hope was a tool of survival, and it found expression in the late nineteenth-century messianic movements that accompanied the military defeats and the surrender to reservation life. At that point for many Indians in the West, it surely seemed that their world was lost, their future was extremely uncertain, and their existence was on the verge of annihilation by white efforts that attempted to undermine their traditions and beliefs. Yet, as among Eastern Woodland Indians in earlier years, religious prophets came to the aid of their people and provided leadership for a spiritual resistance to the processes of colonization.

Among the Paiute Indians in Nevada, for instance, several prophets gained in popularity. These religious leaders played a central role in founding the Ghost Dance religion—a name that Plains Indians gave to a new religious movement that spread among many indigenous communities in the West. On the Walker River Reservations in Nevada, the teachings of a prophet called Wodziwob, also known as Fish Lake Joe, were influential on the Ghost Dance movement. He predicted the destruction of white Americans, the resurrection of Indian dead, and the return to the traditional Indian way of life. This message appealed to many Indians in the American West. Wovoka, another Paiute from Nevada, and founder of the 1890 Ghost Dance movement, received his revelation early in 1889. In his vision, Wovoka had crossed over into heaven seeing his ancestors alive and well. There he learned that he was to abstain from fighting and working for white people, and to dance the Ghost Dance, or Round Dance as the Paiute call it.

The Ghost Dance religion inspired many Native American followers in the West. It became popular, for example, among many of the Sioux reservations on the northern plains. Here in 1890 the situation was desperate. Just the year before, the Sioux had lost more of their land under false government promises that they would receive more supplies.

On the contrary, officials decreased their rations, and the Sioux found themselves on the brink of starvation.

In such desperate times the millenarian Ghost Dance religion provided an alternative and a new vision in the daily lives of many Sioux (Lakota). It brought hope to its followers. People gathered for rituals that lasted for several days and nights, dancing themselves into trances. Many dancers shared similar visions with Wodziwob and Wovoka. They spoke of seeing dead friends and family members, who told them that if the Indians kept dancing, all the dead would return along with the buffalo, and their old way of life would be restored. Some also believed that the Ghost Shirts they wore would protect them from white bullets.

American officials and settlers were frightened by the Ghost Dance movement in the Badlands of the Dakotas. Rampant rumors spurred these fears. As with other Native American religious movements in the nineteenth and early twentieth centuries, the federal government attempted to suppress it. The U.S. army also significantly increased the presence of its troops in the region.

Such developments worried many Natives in the area, and the situation escalated late in 1890. On December 15, 1890, tribal police shot the respected Hunkpapa Lakota leader Sitting Bull. A band from the Cheyenne River Reservation under the leadership of Big Foot, among whom the Ghost Dance had become popular, and who were traveling to the Indian agency of their reservation to obtain their supplies, felt threatened when they heard of Sitting Bull's murder as well as the increased presence of American troops. Thus Big Foot and his people moved south, over the frozen and wind-swept prairie, hoping that the situation on the Pine Ridge Reservation would be safer. After traveling about 200 miles, on December 28, the Seventh Cavalry tracked down the band, forced the Indians to set up camp at the Wounded Knee Creek, and several hundred soldiers surrounded the camp.

On the morning of December 29, the soldiers began to disarm and mistreat the Amerindians. This included the harassment and searches of the women by American soldiers. What occurred afterward is not clear. Apparently, one of Big Foot's men did not want to surrender his weapon, and in an ensuing struggle a shot went off. Rampant firing followed, and Indians were cut down by military bullets and shrapnel.

The Oglala Sioux holy man Black Elk, a young man of about 27 at the time of the massacre, later wrote that on the morning of December 29 he awoke to the sound of distant gunfire. In response, he rode toward Wounded Knee Creek, where he had heard the shots coming from. He reflected on the pain and suffering of what he saw on that day.

By now many other Lakotas, who had heard the shooting were coming up from Pine Ridge. . . . We followed down along the dry gulch, and what we saw was terrible. Dead and wounded women and children and little babies were scattered all along there where they had been trying to run away. The soldiers had followed along the gulch, as they ran, and murdered them in there. Sometimes they were in heaps because they had huddled together, and some were scattered all along. Sometimes bunches of them had been killed and torn to pieces where the wagon guns hit them. I saw a little baby trying to suck its mother, but she was bloody and dead. . . .

Men and children were heaped and scattered all over the flat at the bottom of the little hill where the soldiers had their wagon-guns, and westward up the dry gulch all the way to the high ridge, the dead women and children and babies were scattered.[20]

Ohiyesa, Charles Eastman, the young Dakota physician who had just come to work on the Pine Ridge reservation in 1890 after completing his studies in New England, arrived at the Wounded Knee site two days after the massacre had occurred, to treat the mutilated and wounded people. A major blizzard had inhibited his earlier arrival. Moving around the site he described the following scene.

Fully three miles from the scene of the massacre, we found the body of a woman completely covered with a blanket of snow, and from this point on we found them scattered along as they had been relentlessly hunted down and slaughtered while fleeing for their lives. Some of our people discovered relatives or friends among the dead, and there was much wailing and mourning. When we reached the spot where the Indian camp had stood, among the fragments of burned tents and other belongings we saw the frozen bodies lying close together or piled upon one another. I counted eighty bodies of men who had been in the council and who were almost as helpless as the women and babies when the deadly fire began, for nearly all their guns had been taken from them.[21]

Eventually 146 Indians were buried on the massacre site in a mass grave. Forty-four were women and 18 were children. Twenty-five soldiers also died at Wounded Knee. Yet many more would succumb to their injuries in the following days and weeks. Several historians estimate the actual number casualties as high as 300 to 350 people.

"I STILL LIVE": LOOKING TOWARD THE FUTURE

For the Lakota, the mass grave at Wounded Knee became a shrine to the injustice of white society. The Wounded Knee massacre of 1890 came to symbolize a low point in American history. In 1900, the population figures of indigenous people in the United States reached a mere 250,000, down from several millions in 1492. Yet, despite the predictions of many Euro-Americans in the late nineteenth and early twentieth centuries, Indians never disappeared.

Even as the United States worked to eradicate Native sovereignty through force or assimilation, Indians and Indian-made goods became a marketable commodity for Americans who associated them with a romantic fantasy of a preindustrial past. Men like Geronimo, who had been hunted by U.S. soldiers only a few years before, found that one way to ameliorate the misery of their lives in army prisons or on reservations was to have their photograph taken for sale to tourists. Others, like Luther Standing Bear, joined wild west shows and later became "Hollywood Indians" to support themselves and their families. One woman from the

Navajo woman weaving, about 1904. The Navajo practiced weaving and textile production long before the Spanish came to their homeland. The introduction of a new breed of sheep, new equipment for weaving and a new demand by the Spanish for horse blankets encouraged creative adaptation of the older practice. By the end of the nineteenth century, Navajo weavers were known across the continent for their beautiful rugs and textiles, and these products were much in demand by tourists. From Denver Public Library, Western History Collection.

Great Plains joined up with Buffalo Bill so that she could travel east. This was the only way she could afford to visit the grave of her child who had died at Carlisle.

Euro-Americans also found it pleasurable to "play Indian."[22] An illustrative photo is humorously entitled, "Anachronism." It was taken by sisters Frances and Mary Allen, photographers who worked in Deerfield, Massachusetts, in the early twentieth century. The town of Deerfield turned a faltering rural economy into a tourist mecca by building memorials to their ancestors who died in the 1704 "French and Indian" raid on Deerfield. Each year, the town lovingly reenacted the raid complete with "Indians" in dark stockings and bad wigs. Few Native people would recognize themselves in this caricatured portrayal. Conversely, Euro-Americans often failed to recognize "real" Indians. In 1856 the missionary at the Abenaki village of Odanak, in Quebec, noticed that visitors hoping

"Anachronism," about 1910–1916. The Old Deerfield Pageants of the early twentieth century attracted tourists with their promise of an authentic recreation of the past. This photograph playfully poses "an Indian" with a camera, photographing two other pageant participants. Ironically, real Native people living in the area were virtually invisible because they did not dress like "Indians." From "Anachronism," Frances and Mary Allen, Photographers (1910–1916), #1996.14.0579. Memorial Hall Museum, Pocumtuck Valley Memorial Association, Deerfield, Massachusetts.

to see Indians were disappointed to find people who dressed and acted like French Canadians.[23]

Ironically, the best economic option for Native people in many cases was to exploit this interest by donning feathers and beads to sell crafts to Euro-American tourists. The alternative was going to work in a factory, on a whaling ship, in domestic service, or in some other occupation that would take them away from home and expose them to racism. Across the

Joseph Laurent and his family, Abenakis from Odanak, about 1884. Tourists in Quebec, looking for the legendary "St. Francis Abenaki," were often disappointed when they encountered real Abenakis dressed in the height of Victorian fashion. The village of St. Francis is today known as Odanak, which means "at the village." From A. Irving Hallowell Collection; American Philosophical Society, Philadelphia.

continent, Native American women and men found ways to turn traditional activities into businesses that brought in much-needed cash. In the
Southwest, tourists discovered crafts made by Navajo silversmiths and
weavers. In the Northeast, Native economies were energized by a new
demand for basketry in the Victorian home as well as a new market for
souvenir miniatures, that is, doll-sized versions of traditional objects such
as wigwams and birchbark canoes. Tourists at places such as Niagara
Falls, New York and Old Orchard Beach in Maine bought these objects to
display on their mantels back home, a safe and pleasant reminder of their
encounter with an exotic other.[24]

The Abenakis at Odanak, in Quebec, saw a new influx of cash into their
village in the period. They spent the winters at Odanak, making baskets and other craft items. In the summers they dispersed through New
England and other summer vacation spots to sell their wares. Each family
had its own particular spot. This pattern echoes the seasonal subsistence
of their ancestors. Joseph Laurent, who was a chief at Odanak at the time,
had a talent for entrepreneurial activities. He purchased baskets from
people at Odanak and sold them at a trading post that he established in
Intervale, New Hampshire, in the White Mountains, a popular tourist destination. Laurent and his family spent the summer working so hard that
they hired local Euro-American women as domestic help, because their
time was better spent making baskets.[25] The Abenaki Trading Post sold
baskets, miniatures, and innovative goods such as Victorian tea cozies
and napkin holders woven from ash splints and sweetgrass. Apparently
Joseph Laurent took the ignorant or racist comments of his clientele in
good humor. Many years later his son, Stephen Laurent, described how
his father handled particularly credulous customers. Joseph Laurent
explained to one man, who must have been asking too many questions,
that he was bowlegged because his mother had tied a log between his
legs when he was a child. The purpose of this, allegedly, was to enhance
his snowshoeing ability and to fool his enemies by leaving only one track.
The man went away marveling at the strange customs of the Indian, and
Laurent commented, "The white man will swallow everything, arrow,
bow and quiver, just so long as it's an Indian that tells it!"[26]

Laurent and his contemporaries to the west fought with different
weapons but their battle for dignity was no less heroic. The formal studio portrait of Laurent and his family exemplifies the material success
that Laurent gained from selling baskets. About the same time, Laurent
published a volume of Abenaki grammar that was written in Abenaki
and English. Most Abenakis at time spoke Abenaki and French, although
many people were trilingual. In the preface to *New Familiar Abenakis and
English Dialogues*, he wrote, "The primary intention [of this book] is to aid
the young generation of the Abenaki tribe in learning English. It is also
intended to preserve the *uncultivated* Abenaki language from the gradual
alterations which are continually occurring. . . ." Yet Laurent's dialogues

include Abenaki equivalents for phrases such as, "Let us inquire when the steamboat starts," and "Yes, we can go direct to London by the steamer, or else cross to Dover, and thence to London by the railway."[27] Clearly, Laurent envisioned a future in which Abenaki people would claim the best of both worlds.

At the turn of the twentieth century, Native Americans prepared themselves to wage a different kind of war. There were many opinions about what the goals should be, and how to achieve them, but the desire to move into the future as Indian peoples brought them together to work for political goals, including citizenship, which was granted with the Citizenship Act of 1924. The task of organizing as Indians was complicated by the fact that non-Natives seldom recognized them for who they were and Native people sometimes refused to recognize each other. This dynamic was especially complex in regions with triracial communities, such as southern New England. When an active group of civic-minded Native leaders formed the Indian Council of New England in Providence, Rhode Island, in 1924, they adopted the motto: "I still live." Native peoples had experienced extraordinary changes and challenges since 1492, but they still understood themselves to be sovereign Indian peoples. The challenge for the next century would be to explain that to everyone else.

NOTES

1. Quoted in Alvin M. Josephy Jr., *500 Nations: An Illustrated History of North American Indians* (New York: Alfred A. Knopf, 1994), 355.

2. Francis Paul Prucha, *The Great Father: The United States Government and the American Indians,* abridged ed. (Lincoln: University of Nebraska Press, 1986), 194–95; also quoted in Mary Ellen Jones, *Daily Life on the Nineteenth-Century American Frontier* (Westport, CT: Greenwood Press, 1998), 241–42.

3. Francis Paul Prucha, *American Indian Treaties: The History of a Political Anomaly* (Berkeley: University of California Press, 1994), 334.

4. Sarah Winnemucca, "The Way Agents Get Rich," in *Native American Testimony: A Chronicle of Indian-White Relations from Prophecy to the Present, 1492–1992,* ed. Peter Nabokov, rev. ed. (New York: Penguin, 1992) 198–202.

5. Quoted in Colin G. Calloway, ed., *Our Hearts Fell to the Ground: Plains Indian Views of How the West Was Lost* (Boston: Bedford, 1996), 157.

6. Herrero, "We Lost Everything," in Nabokov, 196–98.

7. Carl Sweezy, "We had Everything to Learn," in Nabokov, 210.

8. Frederick E. Hoxie, "From Prison to Homeland: The Cheyenne River Reservation before World War I," in *The Plains Indians of the Twentieth Century,* ed. Peter Iverson (Norman: University of Oklahoma Press, 1985), 55–75.

9. Sweezy, 210.

10. Quoted in D.S. Otis, *The Dawes Act and the Allotment of Indian Lands,* ed. Francis P. Prucha (Norman: University of Oklahoma Press, 1973).

11. Quoted in Colin G. Calloway, ed., *First Peoples: A Documentary Survey of American Indian History,* 2nd ed. (Boston: Bedford, 2004), 341.

12. Carl Sweezy, "On Taking 'the New Road'," in Calloway, ed., *Our Hearts Fell to the Ground*, 127–28.

13. Janet A. McDonnell, *The Dispossession of the American Indian, 1887–1934* (Bloomington: Indiana University Press, 1991), 21–22.

14. Quoted in James Olson and Raymond Wilson, *Native Americans in the Twentieth Century* (Provo, UT: Brigham Young University Press, 1984), 72–73.

15. For a good overview of boarding school history, see David Wallace Adams, *Education for Extinction: American Indians and the Boarding School Experience, 1857–1928* (Lawrence: University Press of Kansas, 1995).

16. Luther Standing Bear, "Life at Boarding School, 1879," in Calloway, ed., *Our Hearts Fell to the Ground*, 174–75.

17. Quoted in Calloway, *First Peoples*, 351.

18. Standing Bear, 176.

19. Standing Bear, 176.

20. John G. Neihardt, *Black Elk Speaks: Being the Life Story of a Holy Man of the Oglala Sioux* (Lincoln: University of Nebraska Press, 1979), 259–60.

21. Quoted in Peter Iverson, *"We Are Still Here:" American Indians in the Twentieth Century* (Wheeling, IL: Harlan Davidson, 1998), 10.

22. See Philip J. Deloria, *Playing Indian* (New Haven, CT: Yale University Press, 1998).

23. Thomas M. Charland, *Les Abénakis d'Odanak: Histoire des Abénakis d'Odanak, 1675–1937* (Montréal: Editions du Levrier, 1964), 333, citing Joseph Maurault's 1856 report on Indian Affairs. Maurault saw this as a sign of progress, and in the same report he described those Abenakis who haunted the shores of lakes and rivers as miserable specimens, unfortunates, idiots, and degraded people.

24. Ruth B. Phillips, *Trading Identities: The Souvenir in Native North American Art from the Northeast, 1700–1900* (Seattle: University of Washington Press/Montreal: McGill-Queen's University Press, 1998).

25. Gary W. Hume, "Joseph Laurent's Intervale Camp: Post-Colonial Abenaki Adaptation and Revitalization in New Hampshire," in *Algonkians of New England: Past and Present*, Proceedings of the Dublin Seminar for New England Folklife, 1989, ed. Peter Benes, 101–13 (Boston: Boston University Press, 1991).

26. Stephen Laurent, "The Abenakis: Aborigines of Vermont—Part II," *Vermont History* 24 (January 1956): 5–6.

27. Joseph Laurent, *New Familiar Abenakis and English Dialogues* (Quebec: L. Brousseau, 1884), 5, 111.

BIBLIOGRAPHY

Adams, David Wallace. *Education for Extinction: American Indians and the Boarding School Experience, 1857–1928*. Lawrence: University Press of Kansas, 1995.

Archer, Gabriel. "The Relation of Captaine Gosnols Voyage to the North part of Virginia, begunne the sixe and twentieth of March [1602]." In *The English New England Voyages, 1602–1608*. Ed. David B. Quinn and Alison M. Quinn. Hakluyt Society Publications, 2nd ser., no. 161. London: The Hakluyt Society, 1983.

Axtell, James. *The European and the Indian: Essays in the Ethnohistory of Colonial America*. New York: Oxford University Press, 1981.

Axtell, James. *The Indian Peoples of Eastern America: A Documentary History of the Sexes*. New York: Oxford University Press, 1981.

Baker, Emerson W. and John G. Reid. *The New England Knight: Sir William Phips, 1651–1695*. Toronto: University of Toronto Press, 1998.

Barnard, Edward, ed. *Story of the Great American West*. New York: Reader's Digest, 1977.

Baxter, James Phinney, ed. *Christopher Levett, of York: The Pioneer Colonist in Casco Bay*. Portland, ME: The Gorges Society, 1893.

Bee, Robert L. *The Yuma*. New York: Chelsea House, 1989.

Berkhofer, Robert Jr. *Salvation and the Savage: An Analysis of Protestant Missions and American Indian Response*. Lexington: University of Kentucky Press, 1965.

Biggar, H. P., ed. *The Works of Samuel de Champlain*. 6 vols. Toronto: The Champlain Society, 1936.

Bonvillain, Nancy. *Native Nations: Cultures and Histories of Native North America*. Upper Saddle River, N.J.: Prentice Hall, 2001.

Bowden, Henry Warner. *American Indians and Christian Missions: Studies in Cultural Conflict*. Chicago: University of Chicago Press, 1981.

Bragdon, Kathleen J. *Native People of Southern New England, 1500–1650*. Norman: University of Oklahoma Press, 1996.

Bridenbaugh, Carl and Juliette Tomlinson, eds. *The Pynchon Papers*, vol. 2. *Selections from the Account Book of John Pynchon, 1651–1697*. Boston: The Colonial Society of Massachusetts, 1985.

Bruchac, Marge. "Reclaiming the Word 'Squaw' in the Name of the Ancestors," 1999. Available at www.nativeweb.org/pages/legal/squaw.html.

Buerge, David M. "Chief Seattle and Chief Joseph: From Indians to Icons." In *Native Americans of the Pacific Northwest*. Available at http://lcweb2.loc.gov/ammem/award98/wauhtml/aipnhome.html.

Calloway, Colin G. *The American Revolution in Indian Country: Crisis and Diversity in Native American Communities*. New York: Cambridge University Press, 1995.

———., ed. *After King Philip's War: Presence and Persistence in Indian New England*. Hanover, NH: University Press of New England, 1997.

———. *First Peoples: A Documentary Survey of American Indian History*. 2nd ed. Boston: Bedford, 2004.

———. *Our Hearts Fell to the Ground: Plains Indian Views of How the West Was Lost*. Boston: Bedford, 1996.

———. *The World Turned Upside Down: Indian Voices from Early America*. Boston: Bedford, 1994.

Campbell, Lyle and Marianne Mithun, eds. *The Languages of Native America*. Austin: University of Texas Press, 1979.

Cayton, Andrew R.L. *Frontier Indiana*. Bloomington: Indiana University Press, 1996.

Charland, Thomas M. *Les Abénakis d'Odanak: Histoire des Abénakis d'Odanak, 1675–1937*. Montréal: Editions du Levrier, 1964.

Colden, Cadwallader. *The History of the Five Indian Nations, depending on the Province of New-York in America*. Ithaca, NY: Cornell University Press, 1986.

Conkey, Laura E., Ethel Boissevain, and Ives Goddard. "Indians of Southern New England and Long Island: The Late Period." In *Northeast*. Ed. Bruce Trigger. Vol. 15. *Handbook of Northamerican Indians*. 20 vols. Gen. ed. William C. Sturtevant. Washington, DC: Smithsonian Institution, 1978. pp. 177–89.

Cook, Ramsay, ed. *The Voyages of Jacques Cartier*. Trans. H.P. Biggar. Toronto: University of Toronto Press, 1993.

Cornelius, Carol. *Iroquois Corn in a Culture-Based Curriculum: A Framework for Respectfully Teaching About Cultures*. Albany: State University of New York Press, 1999.

Cronon, William. *Changes in the Land: Indians, Colonists, and the Ecology of New England*. New York: Hill and Wang, 1983.

Crosby, Alfred W. *The Columbian Exchange: Biological and Cultural Consequences of 1492*. Westport, CT: Greenwood Press, 1972.

Day, Gordon M. "The Western Abenaki Transformer." *Journal of the Folklore Institute* 13 (1976): 77–84.

———. "Western Abenaki." In *Northeast*. ed. Bruce Trigger. Vol. 15 of *Handbook of North American Indians*. 20 vols. Gen. ed. William C. Sturtevant. Washington, DC: Smithsonian Institution Press, 1978. pp. 148–59.

Deloria, Philip. *Playing Indian*. New Haven: Yale University Press, 1998.

DeVoto, Bernard, ed. *The Journals of Lewis and Clark*. New York: Houghton Mifflin/Marine, 1997 [1953].

Dobyns, Henry F. "Indians in the Colonial Spanish Borderlands." *In Indians in American History*. 2nd ed. Ed. Frederick E. Hoxie and Peter Iverson. Wheeling Ill.: Harlan Davidson, 1998.

———. *The Pima-Maricopa*. New York: Chelsea House Publishers, 1989.

———. *Their Numbers Become Thinned*. Knoxville: University of Tennessee Press, 1983.

Dorris, Michael. "Indians on the Shelf." In *American Indians and the Problem of History*. Ed. Calvin Martin. New York: Oxford University Press, 1987.

Dowd, Gregory E. *War Under Heaven: Pontiac, the Indian Nations, and the British Empire*. Baltimore: Johns Hopkins University Press, 2002.

Durham, Jimmie. "Geronimo!" In *Partial Recall: With Essays on Photographs of Native North Americans*. Ed. Lucy R. Lippard. New York: The New Press, 1992.

Eckstorm, Fannie Hardy. *Old John Neptune and Other Maine Indian Shamans*. Portland, ME: The Southworth-Anthoensen Press, 1945.

Eliade, Mircea. *Shamanism: Archaic Techniques of Ecstasy*. Trans. Willard R. Trask. Princeton, NJ: Princeton University Press, 1964.

Erdoes, Richard and Alfonso Ortiz. *American Indian Myths and Legends*. New York: Pantheon Books, 1984.

Feest, Christian F. *The Powhatan Tribes*. New York: Chelsea House Publishers, 1990.

Fenton, William. "Northern Iroquoian Culture Patterns." In *Northeast*. Ed. Bruce Trigger. Vol. 15. *Handbook of Northamerican Indians*. 20 vols. Gen. ed. William C. Sturtevant. Washington, DC: Smithsonian Institution, 1978. pp. 296–321.

Franklin, Robert J. and Pamela Bunte. *The Paiute*. New York: Chelsea House Publishers, 1990.

Gibson, Robert O. *The Chumash*. New York: Chelsea House Publishers, 1991.

Gipson, Lawrence Henry, ed. *The Moravian Indian Mission on White River*. Indianapolis: Indiana Historical Bureau, 1938.

Goddard, Ives and Kathleen J. Bragdon. *Native Writings in Massachusett*. 2 vols. Philadelphia: American Philosophical Society, 1988.

Gookin, Daniel. "Historical Collections of the Indians in New England (1674)." *Massachusetts Historical Society Collections* 1st ser., 1 (1792): 141–227.

Graymont, Barbara, *The Iroquois*. New York: Chelsea House Publishers, 1988.

Green, Michael D. *The Creeks*. New York: Chelsea House Publishers, 1990.

Haefeli, Evan and Kevin Sweeney. *Captors and Captives: The 1704 French and Indian Raid on Deerfield*. Amherst: University of Massachusetts Press, 2003.

Haines, Francis. *The Plains Indians*. New York: Crowell, 1976.

Hamell, George R. "Strawberries, Floating Islands, and Rabbit Captains: Mythical Realities and European Contact in the Northeast During the Sixteenth and Seventeenth Centuries." *Revue d'études canadiennes/Journal of Canadian Studies* 21, no. 4 (Winter 1986–1987): 72–94.

Hassrick, Royal B. *The Sioux*. Norman: Oklahoma University Press, 1964.

Havard, Gilles. *The Great Peace of Montreal of 1701: French-Native Diplomacy in the Seventeenth Century*. Trans. Phyllis Aronoff and Howard Scott. Montreal: McGill-Queen's University Press, 2001.

Heckewelder, John. *History, Manners, and Customs of the Indian Nations*. Philadelphia: Historical Society of Philadelphia, 1881.

Heizer, Robert F., ed. *The Destruction of California Indians*. Lincoln: University of Nebraska Press, 1993.

Herndon, Ruth Wallis and Ella Wilcox Sekatau. "Colonizing the Children: Indian Youngsters in Servitude in Early Rhode Island." In *Reinterpreting New England Indians and the Colonial Experience*. Ed. Colin G. Calloway and Neal Salisbury. Boston: Colonial Society of Massachusetts, 2003.

Hinderaker, Eric. *Elusive Empires: Constructing Colonialism in the Ohio Valley, 1673–1800*. New York: Cambridge University, 1997.

Hittman, Michael. *Wovoka and the Ghost Dance: A Sourcebook*. Carson City, NV: Grace Dangberg, 1990.

Hopkins, Sarah Winnemucca. *Life Among the Piutes: Their Wrongs and Claims*. Bishop, CA: Chalfant Press, 1969.

Howard, James. *Shawnee!: The Ceremonialism of Native American Indian Tribe and its Cultural Background*. Athens: Ohio University Press, 1981.

Hoxie, Frederick E., ed. *Encyclopedia of North American Indians: Native American History, Culture, and Life from Paleo-Indians to the Present*. New York: Houghton Mifflin, 1996.

———. "From Prison to Homeland: The Cheyenne River Reservation Before World War I." In *The Plains Indians of the Twentieth Century*. Ed. Peter Iverson. Norman: University of Oklahoma Press, 1985. pp. 55–75.

Hudson, Charles. *The Southeastern Indians*. Knoxville: The University of Tennessee Press, 1976.

Hume, Gary W. "Joseph Laurent's Intervale Camp: Post-Colonial Abenaki Adaptation and Revitalization in New Hampshire." In *Algonkians of New England: Past and Present*. Ed. Peter Benes. *Proceedings of the Dublin Seminar for New England Folklife, 1989*. Boston: Boston University Press, 1991.

Hurtado, Albert L. *Indian Survival on the California Frontier*. New Haven: Yale University Press, 1988.

Iverson, Peter. *"We Are Still Here": American Indians in the Twentieth Century*. Wheeling, IL: Harlan Davidson, 1998.

———. *The Navajos*. Chelsea House Publishers, 1990.

Jameson, J. Franklin, ed., *Johnson's Wonder-Working Providence, 1628–1651*. New York: Barnes and Noble, 1967.

Jones, Mary Ellen. *Daily Life on the 19th Century Frontier*. Westport, CT: Greenwood Press, 1998.

Josephy, Alvin M. *500 Nations: An Illustrated History of North American Indians*. New York: Alfred Knopf, 1994.

———. *The Indian Heritage of America*. Boston: Houghton Mifflin Company, 1991 [1968].

Kehoe, Alice B. *North American Indians: A Comprehensive Account*. 3rd ed. Upper Saddle River, NJ: Prentice Hall, 2006.

Knaut, Andrew L. *The Pueblo Revolt of 1680: Conquest and Resistance in Seventeenth-Century New Mexico*. Norman: University of Oklahoma Press, 1995.

Kraft, Herbert. *The Lenape: Archaeology, History and Ethnography*. Newark: New Jersey Historical Society, 1986.

Laubin, Reginald and Gladys Laubin. *Indian Dances of North America: Their Importance to Indian Life*. Norman: University of Oklahoma Press, 1977.

Laurent, Joseph. *New Familiar Abenakis and English Dialogues*. Quebec: L. Brousseau, 1884.

Laurent, Stephen. "The Abenakis: Aborigines of Vermont—Part II." *Vermont History* 24 (January 1956): 3–11.

Leacock, Eleanor Burke. "Introduction." *The Origin of the Family, Private Property and the State in Light of the Researches of Lewis H. Morgan* by Frederick Engels. New York: International Publishers, 1972.

Lindholdt, Paul J., ed. *John Josselyn, Colonial Traveler: A Critical Edition of "Two Voyages to New-England."* Hanover, NH: University Press of New England, 1988.

Mann, Barbara Alice. *Iroquoian Women: The Gantowisas.* New York: Peter Lang, 2000.

McBride, Bunny and Harald Prins. "Walking the Medicine Line: Molly Ockett, a Pigwacket Doctor." In *Northeastern Indian Lives, 1632–1816.* Ed. Robert S. Grumet. Amherst: University of Massachusetts Press, 1996. pp. 321–47.

McConnell, Michael. *A Country Between: The Upper Ohio Valley and Its Peoples, 1724–1774.* Lincoln: University of Nebraska Press, 1992.

McDonnell, Janet A. *The Dispossession of the American Indian, 1887–1934.* Bloomington: Indiana University Press, 1991.

McKee, Jesse O. *The Choctaw.* New York: Chelsea House, 1989.

Melody, Michael E. *The Apache.* New York: Chelsea House, 1989.

Merrell, James H. *The Catawbas.* New York: Chelsea House Publishers, 1989.

———. *The Indians' New World: Catawbas and their Neighbors from European Contact through the Era of Removal.* Chapel Hill: University of North Carolina Press, 1989.

Miller, Jay, ed. *Mourning Dove.* Lincoln: University of Nebraska Press, 1990.

———. "Alaskan Tlingit and Tsimshian." In *Native Americans of the Pacific Northwest.* Available at http://lcweb2.loc.gov/ammem/award98/wauhtml/aipnhome.html.

———. "Salmon, the Lifegiving Gift." In *Native Americans of the Pacific Northwest.* Available at http://lcweb2.loc.gov/ammem/award98/wauhtml/aipnhome.html.

Milner, George. *The Moundbuilders: Ancient Peoples of Eastern North America.* New York: Thames & Hudson, 2004.

Mooney, James. *The Ghost-Dance Religion and Wounded Knee.* New York: Dover Publications, 1973.

Moquin, Wayne and Charles Van Doren, eds. *Great Documents in American Indian History.* New York: DaCapo Press, 1995.

Nabokov, Peter, ed. *Native American Testimony: A Chronicle of Indian-White Relations from Prophecy to the Present, 1492–1992.* Rev. ed. New York: Penguin, 1992.

Nash, Alice. *Spirit, Power and Protocol.* Amherst: University of Massachusetts Press, in press.

Neihardt, John G. *Black Elk Speaks: Being the Life Story of a Holy Many of the Oglala Sioux.* Introduction. Vine Deloria, Jr. Lincoln: University of Nebraska Press, 1979.

Nicolar, Joseph. *The Life and Traditions of the Red Man.* Bangor, ME: C.H. Glass & Co., 1893.

O'Brien, Jean M. *Dispossession by Degrees: Indian Land and Identity in Natick, Massachusetts, 1650–1790.* Cambridge: Cambridge University Press, 1997.

O'Donnell, James H. III. *Ohio's First Peoples.* Athens: Ohio University Press, 2004.

Olson, James and Raymond Wilson. *Native Americans in the Twentieth Century.* Provo, UT: Brigham Young University Press, 1984.

Ortiz, Alfonso. *The Pueblo*. New York: Chelsea House Publishers, 1994.

Otis, D. S. *The Dawes Act and the Allotment of Indian Lands*. Ed. Francis Paul Prucha. Norman, OK: University of Oklahoma Press, 1973.

Penney David. *North American Indian Art*. New York: Thames & Hudson, 2004.

Perdue, Theda and Michael D. Green, eds. *The Cherokee Removal: A Brief History with Documents*. Boston: Bedford Books, 1995.

Perdue, Theda. *Slavery and the Evolution of Cherokee Society, 1540–1866*. Knoxville: University of Tennessee Press, 1979.

———. *The Cherokee*. New York: Chelsea House Publishers, 1989.

Philips, Ruth B. *Trading Identities: The Souvenir in Native North American Art from the Northeast, 1700–1900*. Seattle: University of Washington Press/Montreal: McGill-Queen's University Press, 1998.

Plane, Ann Marie. "Putting a Face on Colonization: Factionalism and Gender Politics in the Life History of Awashunkes, the 'Squaw Sachem' of Saconet." In *Northeastern Indian Lives, 1632–1816*. Ed. Robert S. Grumet. Amherst: University of Massachusetts Press, 1996. pp. 140–65.

———. *Colonial Intimacies: Indian Marriage in Early New England*. Ithaca, NY: Cornell University Press, 2000.

Pocumtuck Valley Memorial Association. *Raid on Deerfield: The Many Stories of 1704*. Available at www.1704.deerfield.history.museum.

Pritzker, Barry A. *Native American Encyclopedia: History, Culture and Peoples*. New York: Oxford University Press, 2000.

Prucha, Francis P. *American Indian Treaties: The History of a Political Anomaly*. Berkeley: University of California Press, 1994.

———. *The Great Father: The United States Government and the American Indian*. Abridged. Lincoln: University of Nebraska Press, 1986.

Quinn, David B. and Alison M. Quinn, eds. *The English New England Voyages, 1602–1608*. Hakluyt Society Publications. 2nd ser., no. 161. London: The Hakluyt Society, 1983.

Rand, Silas Tertius. *Legends of the Micmacs*. New York: Longmans, Green, and Co., 1894.

Richter, Daniel K. *Facing East from Indian Country: A Native History of Early America*. Cambridge, MA: Harvard University Press, 2001.

———. *The Ordeal of the Longhouse: The Peoples of the Iroquois League in the Era of European Colonization*. Chapel Hill: University of North Carolina Press, 1992.

Riding In, James. "Geronimo (Goyathlay)." In *Encyclopedia of North Americacn Indians: Native American History*. Ed. Frederick E. Hoxie. New York: Houghton Mifflin, 1996. pp. 220–23.

Salisbury, Neal. "The Indians' Old World: Native Americans and the Coming of Europeans." *William and Mary Quarterly* 53, no. 3 (July 1996): 435–58.

Seaver, James E. *A Narrative of the Life of Mrs. Mary Jemison*. Ed. June Namias. Norman: University Press of Oklahoma, 1992.

Shaffer, Lynda Norene. *Native Americans before 1492: The Moundbuilding Centers of the Eastern Woodlands*. Armonk, NY: M.E. Sharpe, 1992.

Siebert, Frank T. "The First Maine Indian War: Incident at Machias. 1676." *Proceedings of the 14th Algonquian Conference* (1976): 137–56.

Silko, Leslie Marmon. *Yellow Woman and a Beauty of the Spirit: Essays on Native American Life Today*. New York: Simon and Schuster, 1996.

Simmons, William S. *Spirit of the New England Tribes: Indian History and Folklore, 1620–1984*. Hanover, NH: University Press of New England, 1986.

Sleeper-Smith, Susan. *Indian Women and French Men: Rethinking Cultural Encounter in the Western Great Lakes*. Amherst: University of Massachusetts Press, 2001.

Smith, John. "A Description of New England (1616)." *Collections of the Massachusetts Historical Society*. 3rd ser., 5 (1836): 95–140.

Smith, William, ed. *The St. Clair Papers*. Freeport, NY: Books for Libraries, 1970.

Smits, David D. "The 'Squaw Drudge': A Prime Index of Savagism." *Ethnohistory* 29 (1982): 281–306.

Standing Bear, Luther. *My People the Sioux*. Boston: Houghton Mifflin, 1928.

Starna, William A. and José António Brandão. "From the Mohawk-Mahican War to the Beaver Wars: Questioning the Pattern." *Ethnohistory* 51, no. 4 (Fall 2004): 725–50.

Strachey, William. "The historie of trauaile into Virginia Britania (1607)." In *The English New England Voyages, 1602–1608*. Ed. David B. Quinn and Alison M. Quinn. London: The Hakluyt Society, 1983. pp. 397–415.

Strobel, Christoph. *Contested Grounds: The Transformation of the American Upper Ohio Valley and the South African Eastern Cape, 1770–1850* (Ph.D. Dissertation: University of Massachusetts Amherst, 2005).

Sturtevant, William C., ed. *Handbook of North American Indians*. 20 vols. Washington, DC: Smithsonian Institution, 1978–2004.

Sugden, John. *Blue Jacket: The Warrior of the Shawnees*. Lincoln: University of Nebraska Press, 2000.

Tanner, Helen Hornbeck, ed. *Atlas of Great Lakes Indian History*. Norman: University of Oklahoma Press, 1987.

Thomas, Peter A. *In the Maelstrom of Change: The Indian Trade and Cultural Process in the Middle Connecticut River Valley, 1635–1665*. New York: Garland, 1990.

Thurman, Melburn D. "Plains Indian Winter Counts and the New Ethnohistory." *Plains Anthropologist* 27 (1982): 173–75.

Thwaites, Reuben Gold. *The Jesuit Relations and Allied Documents: Travels and Explorations of the Jesuit Missionaries in New France, 1610–1791*. 71 vols. Cleveland, OH: Burrows Brothers, 1896–1901.

Tinker, George E. *Missonary Conquest: The Gospel and Native American Cultural Genocide*. Minneapolis: Fortress Press, 1993.

Tooker, Elisabeth, ed. *Native North American Spirituality of the Eastern Woodlands: Sacred Myths, Dreams, Visions, Speeches, Healing Formulas, Rituals and Ceremonies*. New York: Paulist Press, 1979.

———. "Women in Iroquois Society." In *Extending the Rafters: Interdisciplinary Approaches to Iroquoian Studies*. Ed. Michael K. Foster, Jack Campisi, and Marianne Mithum. Albany: SUNY Press, 1984. pp. 109–23.

Turgeon, Laurier. "The Tale of the Kettle: Odyssey of an Intercultural Object." *Ethnohistory* 44, no. 1 (1997): 1–29.

Underhill, John. *News from America; or, A New and Experimentall Discoverie of New England; Containing, A True Relation of Their Warlike Proceedings These Two Years Last Past, with a Figure of the Indian Fort, or Palozado ...* London: Printed by J.D. for Peter Cole, 1638; repr. New York: Da Capo Press, 1971.

Van Lonkhuyzen, Harold W. "A Reappraisal of the Praying Indians: Acculturation, Conversion and Identity at Natick, Massachusetts, 1646–1730." *The New England Quarterly* 63, no. 3 (1990): 396–428.

Vaughan, Alden T., ed. *The Puritan Tradition in America, 1620–1730*. Rev. ed. Hanover, NH: University Press of New England, 1997 [1972].

Versteeg, Dingman. Longhand notes and translations of a manuscript account book kept by Evert Wendell, "Trade with Indians, Albany 1695–1726." New York Historical Society.

Wallace, Anthony F. C. *Jefferson and the Indians: The Tragic Fate of the First Americans*. Cambridge, MA: Harvard University Press, 1999.

Wallace, Paul A. W. *The White Roots of Peace*. Philadelphia: University of Pennsylvania Press, 1946.

Wallis, Wilson D. and Ruth Sawtell Wallis. *The Micmac Indians of Eastern Canada*. Minneapolis: University of Minnesota Press, 1955.

White, Richard. *"It's Your Misfortune and None of My Own": A New History of the American West*. Norman: University of Oklahoma Press, 1991.

———. *The Middle Ground: Indians, Empires, and Republics in the Great Lakes Region, 1650–1815*. New York: Cambridge University Press, 1991.

Whitehead, Ruth Holmes. *Stories from the Six Worlds: Micmac Legends*. Halifax, NS: Nimbus Publishing Ltd., 1988.

Williams, John. *The Redeemed Captive Returning to Zion* (1707). Boston: Applewood Books, 1987.

Williams, Roger. *A Key into the Language of America* (1643). Ed. John J. Teunissen and Evelyn J. Hinz. Detroit, MI: Wayne State University Press, 1973.

Winslow, Edward. *Good News from New England* (1624). In *The Story of the Pilgrim Fathers, 1606–1623 a.d.; as told by themselves, their friends, and their enemies*. Ed. Edward Arber. Boston: Houghton, Mifflin & Co., 1897. pp. 583–86.

Wright, Harry Andrew, ed. *Indian Deeds of Hampden County*. Springfield, MA: [n.p.], 1905.

Yue, Charlotte and David Yue. *The Pueblo*. Boston: Houghton Mifflin Company, 1986.

Zeisberger, David. "History of Northern American Indians." Ed. Archer Butler and William Nathaniel Schwarze. *Ohio Archaeological and Historical Publications*. Vol. 19. Columbus OH: F. J. Heer, 1910.

INDEX

Abenaki, 5, 63, 67, 249, 251–52

Acoma (Pueblo village), 141, 145, 146, 161–62

Adornment, 21, 40, 182; jewelery, 23, 24, 50, 156, 160, 173, 197; tattoos, 49. *See also* Beads; Feathers

Agriculture. *See* Farming

Akimel O'odham (Pima), 157–59, 160, 166–67

Alcohol, 73–74, 91–92, 102, 115, 177, 197

American Revolution, 71–72, 76, 81, 96–97

Anasazi, 141, 159

Apache, 147–52, 229

Art, on clothing, 13, 22, 24, 50–51, 166; embroidery, 22, 51, 60; ledger books, 222; paint, 40, 187; winter counts, 221

Baskets, 7–8, 40, 63, 109, 142–43, 149, 160, 174–75, 177, 182, 192, 196, 200, 203–4, 211, 251

Beads, 21–24, 171, 174, 197. *See also* Wampum

Beaver, 3–4, 20, 27–28, 46, 66

Blackfeet, 220, 226

Black Kettle (Cheyenne), 225–26

Brant, Joseph (Mohawk), 76

Brothertown Indians, 75–76

Buffalo, 114, 143, 189, 204–5, 215–17, 219, 221–22, 224, 226–27

Cahokia (Mound Builder city), 84

Canoes, 19, 22, 39, 71, 90–91, 109, 193, 196, 203

Captives and captive-taking, 70–72, 94, 115, 172, 193–94

Cartier, Jacques, 19, 46

Cash economies, adaptation to, 60, 133–34, 160, 176–77, 211; from tourism, 198, 251; prostitution, 178, 233, 237; wampum as currency, 49

Caughnawaga. *See* Kahnawake

Ceremonies, 7, 18–20, 35, 38, 40–42, 108, 110–12, 141, 146–47, 172–74, 194–96, 204, 207, 215; Condolence, 32, 42–43, 45–46, 65; Green Corn, 40–41, 112; initiations, 143, 156–57, 173, 185; potlatch, 195–96, 198; requickening, 70; sun dance, 181, 219–21; sunrise dance, 181, 219–21;

suppression of, 207. *See also* Ghost Dance

Champlain, Samuel de, 4, 19, 46

Cherokee, 107, 110–11, 117–23, 125–30, 241; Eastern Band of, 130–34. *See also* Trail of Tears

Chickasaw, 107, 115–16, 123, 241

Childhood, 10–12, 14, 64, 94, 109, 118, 127, 143, 173–74, 184–86, 210–11, 242–44

Choctaw, 107, 111–12, 123–24, 130

Chumash, 171

Clan mothers, 44–45, 71, 76

Clans, 31–32, 35–37, 40, 48, 142–43, 151, 192, 195

Clothing, 24, 40, 60, 71, 141, 174, 203, 217; coats, 24, 27, 49, 51, 56; footwear, 8, 9, 40, 56, 118, 124; moccasins, 22, 40, 71, 184, 217; post-contact changes in, 24, 56, 60, 71, 166, 51; snowshoes, 9, 22, 39, 251

Comanche, 223–24

Confederacies, 12–13, 18, 57, 107; Iroquois, 64–65, 69–70, 72, 76–77; Ohio, 87, 97, 99–101; origins and structure, 36–37, 42–46; Powhatan, 107–9, 113

Corn, 33–34, 37–39, 40, 63, 112, 143–45, 147, 152, 175; cultivation of, 7–8, 13, 27, 85, 141, 152, 157, 170, 215; and English, 25, 27, 113–14, 129; intertribal trade in, 9, 150; origins of, 34–35, 142, 155; and Spanish, 161, 163; women and, 13, 38, 89, 100, 109

Corn husk dolls, 14

Creation, 127, 157; Algonkian, 5–6; Apache, 148–49; Iroquois, 32–35; Navajo, 148; Pueblo, 142–43; Snohomish, 190–91; Yuma, 154–55

Creek. *See* Muskogee

Crops. *See* Farming

Crow Dog (Lakota), 236–37

Culture heroes: Changer, 190–91; Coyote, 201–2; Gluskabe, 5; Moshup, 5; Odziozo and Tabaldak, 5; Sky Woman, 32–35

Curtis Act (1898), 130, 241

Dalles, the, 189, 196, 203

Dance, 18–20, 41, 111, 143, 147, 172–74, 181–82, 186, 195, 198, 204, 207, 219–21, 235

Dawes Act. *See* General Allotment Act

De Soto, Hernando, 106–7

Deganawidah (Iroquois), 32, 43–45

Delaware, 76, 86, 89, 92–95, 99–100

Diplomacy, 45, 108; calumet (peace pipe), 64–65; Covenant Chain, 65; Great Peace of 1701, 69–70. *See also* Leadership; Treaties

Disease. *See* Epidemics; Sickness

Dreams, 33–34, 40, 155, 195, 209

Eastman, Charles, M.D. (Dakota), 244, 247

Education, 14, 60, 68, 75, 101–2, 117–19, 133, 155, 164, 173, 173, 206, 232; boarding schools, 241–45; Carlisle Indian Industrial School, 243, 248–49; Cherokee Female Seminary, 129; through storytelling, 5, 10, 35, 141–43, 173. *See also* Literacy

Encomiendas, 162–63, 165

Epidemics, 4, 20, 42, 46, 51, 55, 57–58, 85, 107, 113, 158, 176–77, 186, 222–24

Families. *See* Social organization

Farming, 7–9, 28, 37–38, 81, 85, 89, 93, 109, 112, 139, 145, 147, 149, 155, 157, 170, 181, 214–15; colonial context of, 91, 100–102, 117–18, 121–22, 129, 163, 177, 232, 234, 237, 239–40. *See also* Corn

Feathers, 21, 143, 174, 198; eagle, 24, 184, 216, 221; ostrich, 24; used in clothing and textiles, 114, 172

Fish, 154–55, 190, 196–97, 203, 211; cod, 3, 9. *See also* Salmon

Fishing, 8–9, 17, 38, 56, 109–10, 154, 169, 171, 194, 202, 205–7, 210–11; nets, 8, 109, 154, 169, 174, 203; spears, 8, 38, 109, 169, 192, 210–11; weirs, 8, 38; whaling, 193

Five Civilized Tribes, 127–30, 239. *See also individual tribes*

Five Nations. *See* Haudenosaunee

Flathead. *See* Salishan

Food storage and preservation, 3–4, 8–9, 39, 85, 153, 160, 171, 192–93

Fur trade, 3–4, 16, 20–24, 27–28, 38, 46–48, 56, 69, 206; beaver, 3, 9, 20, 35, 46, 90, 197–98; deerskins, 90, 115; impact on subsistence, 3, 90, 93, 114–15; indigenous trade networks, 47–48, 56–57, 82–84, 196–97, 203–4, 215, 217–19

Games, 35, 171, 211; gambling, 74, 211; ishtaboli, 111–12; lacrosse, 41

Gendered division of labor, 13–15; defined, 7; examples of, 10, 89, 192–93, 204; impact of colonization on, 115, 118, 163, 240; implications of, 15; women's work, 12.

General Allotment Act (1887), 130, 233, 238–41

Ghost Dance, 186–87, 245–47

Gold Rush, 176–77, 185–86, 224

Government. *See* Political life

Handsome Lake, 72–73; Code of, 73–74

Haudenosaunee (Iroquois), 31–53, 55, 66–67, 70–72; Cayuga, 36, 45; Mingos, 86; Mohawk, 37, 40, 44, 46, 49, 51–52, 66–67, 69–70, 72, 76–77; Oneida, 72, 75–76; Onondaga, 33, 37, 42, 48, 52, 77; Seneca, 37, 52, 70–74, 86; Tuscarora, 32–33, 72, 76, 107. *See also* Ceremonies, Condolence; Confederacies; Handsome Lake

Hohokam, 157

Hopi, 141, 146–47

Horse culture, 150, 166, 180–81, 189–90, 204–6, 216–19, 240

Horses, 65, 226, 236; introduction of, 115, 147–48, 202, 214–15; use as farm animals, 72, 118, 126, 129, 237

Horticulture. *See* Farming

Houses, 12, 20, 85, 108, 165, 171–74, 185, 193–94, 214–15; adobe, 140–41, 144–45, 158; earth, 156; hogans, 150–51, 172; longhouses, 12, 37, 39, 50 (*see also* Confederacies, Iroquois); pit, 202; post-contact changes, 59, 63, 72, 94, 117, 129–30, 157–58, 238; wickiups, 151; wigwams, 10, 12–13, 59, 61, 94, 251; witus, 12–13, 59

Hunting. *See* Subsistence

Hupa, 170, 173–74

Huron. *See* Wendat

Indian Removal Act (1830), 105–6, 121–27

Iroquois. *See* Haudenosaunee

Irrigation, 145, 152, 157–58, 182

Jemison, Mary (adopted Seneca), 170–72

Joseph (Nez Percé), 209–10

Kachina dolls, 147

Kahnawake (Mohawk village), 52, 66–68, 70, 76

Katsinas, 143, 147, 164

King Philip (Wampanoag). *See* Metacomet

Kivas, 143, 146–47, 164

Kutenai, 189, 200

Kwakiutl, 196–98

Land: hunting territories, 26, 48, 115, 180, 218; Indian deeds, 24–28; indigenous understandings of, 26–28; role of debt in land loss, 28, 64, 132. *See also* General Allotment Act; Indian Removal Act; Treaties

Laurent, Joseph (Abenaki), 251–52

Leadership, 13, 16–18, 61–63, 87–88, 108, 146, 151, 155, 159, 172, 182, 202, 235; impact of colonization on, 17; land loss and, 27–28; women, 63–63, 198

Lewis and Clark Expedition, 189, 205–6

Lineage, 13, 172–73, 182; matrilineal, 31–32, 36, 48, 111, 121, 151; patrilineal, 152–53. *See also* Clans

Literacy, 60–61, 119
Little Turtle (Miami), 88, 101–2
Livestock, 28, 74, 102, 115, 126, 129, 131, 145, 150, 162–63, 165, 167; cattle, 61, 72, 130; pigs, 28, 165; sheep, 159–60, 170, 237
Longhouse. *See* Confederacies, Iroquois; Houses

Mahicans, 42, 76
Major Crimes Act (1885), 236–37
Makah, 193, 198
Marriage, 14–15, 16, 45, 111, 120, 151, 157; courtship, 18, 182–84; divorce, 61; polygamy, 12, 16–17, 235
Massacres, 98–99, 178–80, 187, 225–26, 245–47; Wounded Knee Massacre (1890), 187, 245–47
Material culture, 39–40, 93, 191–94, 203; adobe, 140, 144, 158; bark, 12–13, 20, 21, 39, 60, 90–91, 108, 150, 171–72, 191–92, 195, 198, 202–3, 251; bone, 7, 20, 22, 40, 203, 217, 221; cotton, 141, 159–60; mica, 23, 84, 195; post-contact changes in, 24, 49–51, 93–94, 165–66; wool, 159–60. *See also* Art; Trade Goods; Weapons
Medicine and healing, 19–20, 41–43, 56, 58, 108, 172, 174, 195
Menominee, 76, 91, 93
Mesa Verde, 141
Metacomet (Wampanoag), also known as King Philip, 24, 62–64
Miami, 86, 88, 90, 102
Mi'kmaq, 4, 9–10, 17–19, 27, 42, 46, 56
Mingo, 86
Missionaries, 20, 112–13, 206, 249–50; Franciscan, 163–65, 175–76; Jesuit, 9, 51–52, 63, 67–68; Moravian, 92–94, 96, 99; Protestant, 60, 72, 75, 117–18, 126; Quaker, 102
Missions, 51–52, 63, 65–68, 77, 98, 162, 175–76, 211; "praying towns," 61–63
Mohegan, 75
Mound Builders, 82–85, 106–7, 114
Mourning Dove. *See* Quintasket, Christine

Music, 18–19, 41, 68, 74, 111, 163, 172, 174, 195, 198, 218
Muskogee, 106–7, 110–11, 123–25, 241

Narragansett, 7, 13, 19, 24, 48, 57, 59, 64
Natchez, 114
Navajo, 141, 147–52, 160, 165, 237, 251
Neolin (Delware), 95–96

Occum, Samson (Mohegan, Brothertown), 75–76
Oconaluftee (Cherokee village), 130–31
Odanak (Abenaki village), 67, 68, 249–50
Oral tradition, 32–33, 55–57

Paiute, 180–87, 234–35, 245. *See also* Ghost Dance; Wovoka
Papago. *See* Tohono O'odham
Patuxet (Wampanoag village), 4, 20
Patwin, 172
Peace pipe. *See* Diplomacy; Tobacco
Pima. *See* Akimel O'odham
Plenty-Coups (Crow), 218
Political life: factionalism, 52–53, 62–63, 70, 72, 87, 97, 114, 128, 132, 209–10; government by consensus, 87, 108, 110, 172, 182. *See also* Confederacies; Leadership; Sovereignty
Pomo, 170–74, 178, 244
Pontiac (Ottawa), 87, 95
Potlatch. *See* Ceremonies
Powwow, origins of the word, 19
Pratt, Richard, 133
Prophets: Handsome Lake (Seneca), 72–74; Neolin (Delaware), 95–96; Smoholla (Wanapum), 207, 209; Tävibo (Paiute), 186; Tenskwatawa (Shawnee), 100–101; Wovoka (Paiute), also known as Jack Wilson, 186–87, 245
Prostitution, 178, 233, 237
Protocol, importance of, 11, 16
Pueblo (people), 140–47, 149, 161–66

Quechan (Yuma), 139, 152–57
Quintasket, Christine (Okanogan), also known as Mourning Dove, 210–11

Rancherias, 156–59, 179
Rape and sexual abuse of women, 163, 177–78, 237
Reece, Sally (Cherokee), 118
Reformers, 231–34, 238–45
Removal. *See* Indian Removal Act (1830)
Reservations, 76–77, 130, 133, 181, 186–87, 206–10, 231–41, 245
Revitalization movements, 74, 87, 96, 100, 116, 207. *See also* Ghost Dance; Prophets
Ridge, John (Cherokee), 120, 125–26, 128
Ross, John (Cherokee), 126

Salishan, 189–90, 200, 203, 205–6, 210–11; origins of the name "Flathead," 203
Salmon, 171, 189, 192–93, 201–4, 207, 210–11. *See also* Fish; Fishing
Seattle (Lutshootseed), 207–9
Seminole, 113, 125, 128
Sequoyah (Cherokee), 119
Shawnee, 86–88, 90, 92, 97–102
Shoshone, 180–81, 186, 204, 220
Sickness, 19–20, 41, 60, 88, 127, 172, 174, 211, 220, 237
Slavery: Amerindians enslaved by Euro-Americans, 59, 64, 106, 113, 116, 161; Cherokee slaveholders, 121, 128–29, 132; indentured servitude as, 64; indigenous practices, 114–15; intertribal, 193, 196, 204–5; runaway slaves, 113, 125
Sovereignty, 37, 82, 96, 120–26, 131–33, 231, 233–34, 236–38, 241, 251–52
Squaw: origins of the word, 18; "squaw drudge," 8, 14; squaw sachems, 18
Standing Bear, Luther (Lakota), 217, 243–44, 248
St. Francis (Abenaki village). *See* Odanak
Stories, 5–6, 14, 16. *See also* Creation

Storytelling, 10, 14–15, 141, 173; oral tradition, 32–33, 55–57
Stung Serpent (Natchez), 114
Subsistence, 6–10, 60, 69, 85, 130–31, 180–82, 202–3, 206, 215, 217, 227; berries, 9, 39, 191; game birds, 8, 9; maple sugar, 21, 38; seals, 9, 193; seasonal patterns of, 3–4, 6–10, 37, 41, 75, 109–10, 139, 145, 152–54, 170–71, 180–81, 191–93, 228, 250; Three Sisters, 74. *See also* Cash economies; Wage labor
Sweat lodge, 173

Tarrantines. *See* Mi'kmaq
Tecumseh (Shawnee), 88, 96, 100–101
Tenskwatawa (Shawnee), 96, 100–101
Tlingit, 190, 192–94, 196–97, 207
Tobacco, 7, 11, 33, 35, 39, 65, 85, 109, 145, 170
Tohono O'odham (Papago), 157–59
Tools, 4, 20–21, 86, 144, 200; awls, 50; crooked knives, 20; digging sticks, 203; mortar and pestle, 34, 144, 203; post-contact changes, 20–21, 23, 40, 50–51, 102, 192; scrapers, 20
Totem poles, 20–24, 49–51, 166, 196; and status, 27–29
Tourist trade, 147, 160, 198, 248–51
Trade goods, 20–24, 49–51, 166, 196; and Native middlemen, 46, 56, 206, 218. *See also* Wampum
Trail of Tears, 124, 127
Transportation: canoes, 90–91; horses, 150, 189–90, 204–5, 215; railroads, 227
Treaties, 64–65, 76, 97–98, 123–26, 131, 186, 206–7, 208–9, 236, 241; broken promises, 102, 207; Great Peace of 1701, 69–70; Treaty of Fort Stanwix (1784), 70; Treaty of Greenville (1795), 99–100, 102; Treaty of New Echota (1835), 125–26, 128; Treaty of Walla Walla (1855), 209; end of treaty-making (1871), 233
Turtle Island, 34–35

Ute, 180, 181, 185–86

Wage labor, 176–77, 206, 208, 242, 244

Wampanoag, 4–6, 18, 20, 24, 57, 60–63

Wampum, 23–24, 27, 43, 48–49, 65

Wars: Beaver Wars, 48, 57; Civil War (U.S.), 128, 132; intercolonial, 70; intertribal, 5, 42–49, 57, 69–70, 149, 160–61, 196, 202, 203, 205; King Philip's War (1675–1678), 62–64; Iroquoian mourning wars, 41–42, 70; Ohio Valley, 95–101; Pequot War (1637), 58–59; Pueblo Revolt (1680), 161–65; War of 1812, 37, 82, 101; Yakima War (1855–1857), 208–9

Weapons, 196; bow and arrow, 22, 158, 206; guns, 22, 38, 95, 116, 150, 161, 206, 217–18, 246–47; war clubs, 22, 196, 203, 217

Weaving, 91, 159–60, 163, 192, 203; mats, 12–13, 37, 60, 108–9, 171, 191, 202–3

Wendat (Huron), 39, 47–48, 51–52, 66–67; relation to Wyandots, 52, 86

Winnemucca, Sarah (Paiute), 82–87, 234–35

Wooden Leg (Cheyenne), 218–19

Wovoka (Paiute), also known as Jack Wilson, 186–87, 245

Wyandot, 97, 101. *See also* Wendat

Yakima, 189, 200, 203, 208

Yonaguska (Cherokee), 131

Yuma. *See* Quechan

About the Authors

ALICE NASH is Associate Professor of Native American and Early American History at the University of Massachusetts-Amherst. Her research interests center on the impact of colonization on the indigenous peoples of northeastern North America with a particular focus in family and gender relations. She is the author of *Spirit, Power and Protocol: Wabanaki Histories to 1800*, (forthcoming).

CHRISTOPH STROBEL is an Assistant Professor of History at the University of Massachusetts Lowell. He teaches courses in world, Native American, African, and Middle Eastern history. Much of his research and writing deals with issues of race and colonization.